Embroidery

Embroidery

Traditional designs,
techniques and patterns
from all over the world

Mary Gostelow

MARSHALL
CAVENDISH
EDITIONS

Editor:
Susannah Read

Art Editors:
Mike Blore
Jane Willis

Assistant Editors:
Eve Barwell
Penny David
Lindsay Vernon

Editorial Assistant:
Janet Mundy

Designers:
Rick Fawcett
Bill Mason
Ingrid Mason
Madeline Serre

Picture Research:
Annette Brown
Barbara Fraser
Kay MacQueen

Production:
Mike Emery

Publisher:
Frances Lincoln

Art Director:
John Strange

Embroiderers:
Elizabeth Ashurst: pages 16, 20, 44, 56, 183, 196, 230
Carolyn Cannon: pages 30, 72, 94, 160, 170, 184, 258
Kirsten Cooke: page 238
Poula Hamilton Fairley: page 68
Margaret Humphrey: pages 78, 98, 154, 224
Heather Pooley: page 126
Margaret Rivers: pages 107, 146, 270
Kathleen Smith: pages 114, 188, 202, 244
Tania Smith: page 213
Angela Swann: page 53
Elizabeth Upton: pages 132, 140, 261

Artists:
Clare Brooks
Mary Curd
Graham Corbett
Richard Corfield
Richard Phipps
Michael Ricketts
Elsa Wilson

Published by
Marshall Cavendish Editions
a division of
Marshall Cavendish Books Limited
58 Old Compton Street
London W1V 5PA

First published in 1977

Reprinted 1978
© Marshall Cavendish Limited 1977

ISBN 0 85685 236 8

Colour reproduction by Sackville Press Billericay Ltd, Billericay, Essex.
Printed in Great Britain by Southernprint Ltd.

Contents

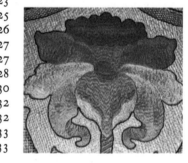

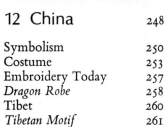

Introduction

The centuries-old tradition of decorating textiles with embroidery offers a wealth of information on design, costume and many aspects of social history as well as a rich source of inspiration both for embroiderers and for all designers. This book gathers together, in full colour, the history, designs and techniques of embroidery throughout the world, with over four hundred photographs of exquisite historical and traditional pieces as well as numerous drawings and diagrams.

Embroidery has served a number of different purposes. In some parts of the world girls still work particularly beautiful embroideries for their trousseaux while hill-tribe girls in northern Thailand decorate special costumes to wear in flirtation ceremonies. Clothes with religious or ceremonial significance have always been richly embroidered, often in sumptuous materials, and some of the earliest embroideries served funerary purposes in places as far apart as Peru and Siberia. On a more modest level, people have always devoted considerable time and care to working rugs, covers, hangings and other household items, in local styles.

The thirteen chapters of this book each deal with a region of the world. They examine characteristic local designs, styles and techniques as well as fabrics, yarns and dyes and the traditional ways of using them. A map of each region locates significant embroidery groups and centres, and shows the geographical features that influence their materials and styles.

The use of cotton, flax, wool and silk grounds and thread in embroidery is universal, and stitches such as satin stitch, chain stitch and cross stitch are found virtually throughout the world. Some designs and techniques clearly followed trade routes. Tambouring, long popular in China, came into vogue in 18th-century France, and blackwork was probably brought to Spain, and so to the rest of Europe, by the Moors. European techniques were disseminated throughout the world by settlers, and were in turn influenced by local factors. Other methods are

found in only one area, such as the intricate quillwork of the North American Indians or the colourful reverse-appliqué *molas* of Central America.

Some embroidery motifs have an almost universal significance: it is fascinating to find the tree of life, the earth mother and the eight-pointed star recurring in a variety of forms and materials in different parts of the world. Local customs and materials make other designs readily identifiable. The influence of religion and of particular cultural traditions has been considerable. Symbolism was particularly important in China, where embroidered birds denoted rank, and where innumerable abstract and stylized devices were worked on garments. Colour also plays a significant role in embroidery—as in India, where red is associated with contentment and consequently features prominently in hangings embroidered as marriage gifts. As well as the more conventional textiles, a great variety of grounds and objects have been incorporated in traditional embroidery, giving three-dimensional effects often echoed in modern designs: raffia and cowrie shells are found in African work; fish skin and suede in that of North America, and in India beetles' wings have been used as spangles.

For the embroiderer and the would-be embroiderer this book is packed with practical information. Stitches are illustrated, and listed in the index. Thirty-five embroidery patterns adapted from designs illustrated in the book show how to work traditional designs in up-to-date projects. They can be applied to existing garments, made into hangings, pictures or simple garments and accessories. Most are suitable for the complete beginner while offering inspiration to the experienced embroiderer. The many charts and designs throughout the book can be worked in various ways and the graphs used for needlepoint or any counted-thread technique. Many of the photographs can also be scaled up and used by the embroiderer as the basis for designs.

Latin America

The embroidery tradition in Latin America stretches back many thousands of years. The most important embroidery areas are concentrated in Middle America and on the west coast of South America, many of them having very strong links with early Indian cultures.

Some of the oldest embroideries in the world come from South America, produced by the Paracas, Nazca and Tiahuanaco peoples and dating back to the 5th century B.C. They take the form of mantles, shirts, loin cloths, capes and other clothing which has been preserved in funerary bundles.

Today it is still clothing that is decorated with embroidery, and also religious and other hangings, some of which take the form of stitched pictures.

Embroidery threads are spun from locally produced cotton and sometimes wool. Some imported silk is also used.

Most of the ground fabrics—that is, the fabrics on which the embroidery is worked—are produced locally. Cotton is the ground most commonly used and its cultivation in South America dates back to at least 2500 B.C. Today it is grown in many parts of Latin America and is particularly important in Peru, Brazil, Guatemala and Argentina. Smaller quantities are grown throughout Mexico and Middle America and most of the South American countries have some cotton production.

In the high Andes region to the west fibres are also obtained from three different animals, all of them members of the camel family. Both the llama, *Lama glama*, and the alpaca, *Lama pacos*, are domestic animals not known in the wild, leading scientists to believe that they have a very long history of domestication. Alpaca wool, once used for royal robes, is lightweight and much sought after and the thicker llama wool is considered somewhat inferior to it.

The vicuña, *Lama vicugna*, lives in the wild in small bands of females led by one male. It is now rare and has been made a protected animal in Peru. Cloth from its fine silky fleece was particularly prized by the Incas.

Although sheep were introduced by Europeans shortly after the discovery of America at the end of the 15th century, very little wool has been used in traditional embroidery.

Dyeing has long been a skilled art in Latin America. Some of the earliest grounds and threads were dyed in a bath of indigo, prepared from the leaves of the plant of that name.

Reds were obtained with cochineal dye made from the dried, pulverized bodies of the female *Dactylopius coccus*, a cactus-eating insect. The strength of the dye would be varied to give

Brightly coloured appliqué on tunics stitched by the Cuna Indian women of the San Blas atolls off mainland Panama.

Feathers often appeared in early Inca embroidery. This symbol of the sun god Pachacama is one of the few remaining examples.

a whole range of colours from orange and scarlet to crimson and black.

Another red was produced from the powdered wood of the brazilwood tree. Considerable quantities of brazilwood dye were exported, especially to North America, from the late 17th century until the advent of chemical dyes.

Other natural dyes were produced from a wide range of minerals, flora and fauna, including a yellow dye from the bark of the false pepper tree, *Chinus mollis*. Today, however, the use of natural dyes has virtually died out and most embroidery fabrics are chemically dyed.

Latin America may be divided into five ethnographic regions: (1) Mexico; (2) Middle America (Guatemala, Belize, Honduras, El Salvador, Nicaragua, Costa Rica and Panama); (3) Indo-America (Venezuela, Colombia, Ecuador, Peru, Bolivia and Paraguay); (4) Mestizo-America, a mixture of European and American people (northern part of Brazil); (5) Euro-America (southern Brazil, Uruguay, Argentina and Chile). These ethnographic regions are more important from an embroidery point of view than the countries, since many groups practising embroidery straddle national boundaries, whereas they rarely cross ethnographic frontiers.

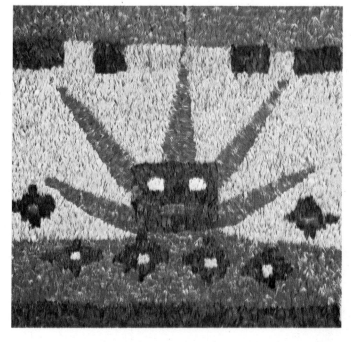

Mexico

Part of the Mexican coat of arms depicting the legendary snake-bearing eagle that showed where the capital was to be built.

Very few examples of Mexican embroidery survive from before the overthrow of the local Aztec rulers by the Spaniards in 1519, and embroidery since that date has shown marked Spanish influence.

Some reminders of the Aztec culture remain in modern embroidery design and one of them, the snake-bearing eagle, also forms part of the Mexican coat of arms. According to legend, the Aztecs were told by their god Huitzilopochtli that they would see an eagle with a snake in its mouth land on a prickly pear in the middle of an island. There they should build their capital city. In 1325 the prophecy came true and the Aztecs founded Tenochtitlan, now Mexico City, on a small island in the middle of Lake Texcoco.

This snake-bearing eagle is often depicted in peasant embroidery, generally with the design outline worked in back stitch and infilled with pattern darning. The design is frequently worked on rough cotton and used for the front panel of a shirt.

Much interesting costume embroidery is found throughout Mexico, but this is generally for personal use, and very

Oaxaca suit.

Mexican men's traditional costume includes a white cotton shirt, above, with richly embroidered bands on the shoulders and sleeves and round the hem.

The free-flowing floral design on the colourful shirt (right) is perhaps less typical than the traditional geometric bird and flower motifs, worked in repeating patterns (left).

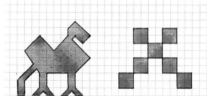

A shirt front decorated with a repeating geometric pattern worked in cross stitch, a favourite stitch with Mexican embroiderers.

little is offered for sale. A lady's outfit from Patzcuaro, west of Mexico City, consists of a shirt with yoke and short sleeves tucked into a full skirt of white cotton, which has its top turned over and out to form a waist ruff. Blue cross-stitch embroidery covers the yoke and runs down the centre of the sleeves. A band of embroidery is also worked on the hem of the waist ruff.

Mexican men sometimes wear heavy cotton shirts with embroidered bands forming a round yoke. Once again the embroidery is often worked in cross stitch, and there is also embroidery on the matching trousers.

Few Mexican Indians now wear traditional embroidered costume for everyday use. One exception are the Huichol Indians in the Tepic area of the west of the country.

Huichol women still embroider shirts, trousers, bags and belts for the men of their family. Embroidery is executed in running stitch and darning stitch, often with a bright red and blue colour scheme on a ground of white cotton. Design motifs are repeating and sometimes take the form of simple versions of a 'Greek key' pattern.

Elaborate regalia is worn by this musician in Mexico City for a street festival. A collar of appliqué shapes replaces the traditional shirt.

Dating from the early 16th century this rare example of Aztec embroidery is worked with feathers stitched to a net or canvas ground.

Middle America

The two main centres of embroidery in Middle America are found at its southern and northern extremes, namely in Panama and Guatemala. The people are mestizos, of mixed Spanish and Indian descent, and their embroidery shows very strong Spanish influence. It is usually worked with stranded silks on a ground of cotton. Textiles are no longer woven locally and the materials are imported. The stitching takes the form either of counted-thread work, with a predominance of cross stitch, or free-form designs executed mainly in satin stitch.

Traditional male dress includes the *montuno*, a long-sleeved, collared shirt with a fringe round the bottom. The front neck opening is slit to breastbone height, and the surrounding yoke panel is embroidered. Symmetrically placed devices are embroidered below the yoke and round the hem, and often a band of solid geometric patterning is added below them, immediately above the fringe.

The traditional costume of many of the Hispanic Indian women is the *pollera*, a full-length dress made of some 9 m (10 yd) of fine cotton. The skirt has flounces decorated with applied embroidery motifs of fine cross stitching worked in one colour. The designs are usually floral, often depicting vines or poinsettias, and all of them show Hispanic rather than Indian influence. It takes one woman working alone about a year to complete a *pollera*.

Cuna

The Cuna Indians live in the Archipelago de las Mulatas off the Caribbean shore of Panama and on the nearby mainland. There are four main groups of Cuna, and the San Blas are the most important from an embroidery point of view. They are famous for their *molas*, which are colourful reverse appliqués.

There are three main categories of appliqué: overlaid appliqué, in which a device cut from a contrasting piece of fabric is sewn on top of the basic ground fabric; inlaid appliqué, in which a piece of contrasting fabric is cut to fit exactly into a hole in the ground fabric; and reverse appliqué, in which a design is cut in the main ground and the contrasting fabric is sewn underneath so that it shows through. In the case of *mola* appliqué, the designs are cut through various layers of fabric in step fashion giving an effect rather like that of a contour map.

Molas are made of plain cotton fabric with bright scarlet usually the dominant colour. Generally three or more different coloured fabrics are used one on top of the other, but there are some striking two-colour examples. The raw edges of each step of a *mola* appliqué are turned under and hemmed to the next step.

Originally the Cuna dressed themselves simply in body paint but only one reminder of this custom remains today in the form of a vertical black line painted on the noses of some women. When French Huguenot settlers introduced

A panel of colourful *mola* reverse appliqué has been let into the front of this cotton shirt.

Cross stitch decorates this *montuno* round the bottom (motif A), at centre front (B) and as a border (detail, C).

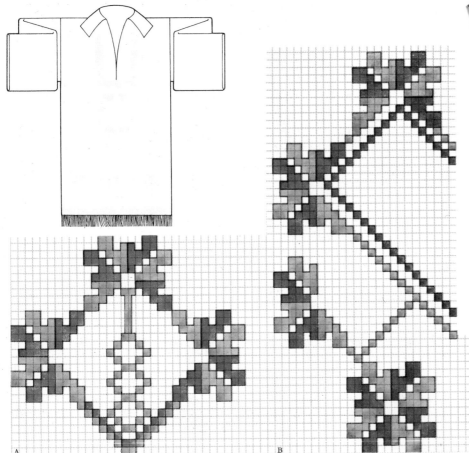

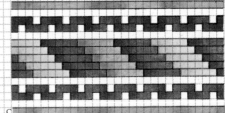

Three types of appliqué: *overlaid*, where a contrasting shape is hemmed to the ground fabric, *inlaid*, where the contrasting shape fits into a hole in the ground fabric, and *reverse*, where the contrasting fabric is sewn underneath a hole in the ground fabric.

Molas, colourful reverse appliqués, made up of several layers, are worked by Cuna Indian women. This design being offered for sale to visitors to Panama has been cut through two layers of cotton fabric so that the dark ground forms a bold outline to the animal and bird motifs.

Overlaid appliqué.

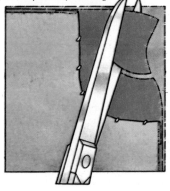

Inlaid appliqué.

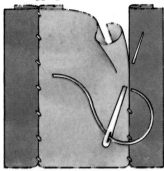

Mola (reverse) technique.

Molas, depicting a three-headed bird, above, and stylized monkey, used as unusual cushion covers.

Eagle *mola* in two colours.

clothing to the Cuna, the Indians simply transposed the body paintings of their ancestors onto cotton fabric. The art of stitched decoration is therefore probably mid-19th-century in origin.

Certainly few *molas* exist that are anything like a hundred years old. Since local climatic conditions make cotton susceptible to fungi and other diseases and to rotting through sunlight, most of the oldest remaining *molas* were stitched only a few decades ago. They are known as *mukan* or 'grandmother' *molas* and are recognizable by the narrow tread of each cut step. More recent examples often have wider treads.

Many of the designs on *molas* are derived from traditional and pre-Christian religious sources. They include the shapes of the coral reefs around the Cuna's island homes, and designs from the Pap Ikala religion, which believes in the omnipotence of the god Tiole. Other religious devices include devils, spirits and monsters like dragons and centaurs. A two-headed bird is often found on *molas*, as are representations of the *wekko* bird, which is reputed to live off snakes. Other designs show Christian influence and yet others are derived from birds, flowers and trees.

Cuna women make *molas* exclusively

for their own use, demonstrating a great sense of humour in their use of caricature in the designs. Men are often shown with downcast faces and with rather solid limbs as if they have the cares of the world on their shoulders. Motherhood is a frequent theme of Cuna designs, represented by birds and animals with foetal shapes inside the main mother body. Frequently youngsters of the same species are shown grouped around the parent. This aspect of *mola* design probably stems from the Cuna custom of telling children that babies are brought from heaven by birds, from the jungle by deer, or from the sea by dolphins.

Molas

You will need:
a piece of red cotton fabric
    28 x 20 cm (11 x 8 in)
a piece of green cotton fabric
    the same size
red sewing cotton
white sewing cotton or
    embroidery silk
small, sharp, pointed scissors
red and green felt-tipped
    pens or crayons (optional)

Fish Motif

Trace the motif and transfer it to the red fabric as described on page 274. If you wish, indicate the colour of each area with coloured pens or crayons on the tracing to make a working guide.

With the design uppermost, pin the red fabric on top of the green and baste round the edges. Add two or three more lines of basting stitches across the fabric.

Embroidery

Each drawn line represents a fold line.

Pick one of the places where the red fabric is to be folded back to reveal the green and insert the point of the scissors about 2-3 mm (⅛ in) outside the line. Make a short cut about 1 cm (⅜ in) long. Use the needle or the point of the scissors to turn the cut edge under as far as the fold line, first clipping to the line at corners and on curves so that the turning lies flat. Pin if necessary.

Using red cotton, and stitching through both layers of fabric, catch down the folded edge with fine slip-stitches.

Now make another short cut, turn the edge and stitch. Continue until the motif is finished. Do not be tempted to make long cuts, for the design will be less accurate and more difficult to work. Instead, try to build up a steady rhythm of cutting, folding and stitching just a few millimetres at a time.

Work the eyes in chain stitch using white cotton or a single strand of silk.

Remove the basting threads and press the motif on the wrong side using a damp cloth and a medium–hot iron.

This small fish motif, based on an original *mola* (above), may be used as a pocket, a decoration for a bag, or as an insert in the bodice of a child's dress. Using only two pieces of fabric, it is ideal for first attempts at reverse appliqué.

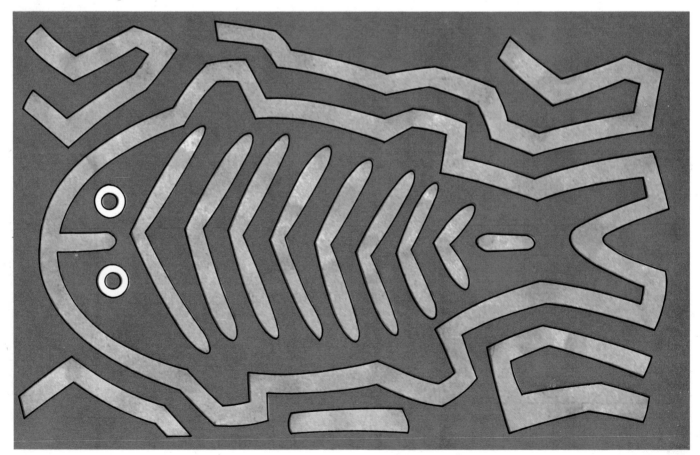

This larger *mola*, with its vibrant colours and bold design, makes a bright cushion cover or unusual wall hanging. It is worked in a mixture of reverse and overlaid appliqué.

You will need:
pieces of cotton fabric in
    assorted colours:
red 44 x 36 cm (16½ x 13½ in)
green 44 x 36 cm (16½ x 13½ in)
deep yellow 44 x 36 cm
    (16½ x 13½ in)

black 44 x 36 cm (16½ x 13½ in)
blue 23 x 23 cm (9 x 9 in)
mauve 23 x 23 cm (9 x 9 in)
black 46 x 23 cm (18 x 9 in)
white 13 x 13 cm (5 x 5 in)
olive 13 x 13 cm (5 x 5 in)
sewing cottons to match

pieces of cotton fabric in:
lemon yellow
orange
pea green
magenta
turquoise
scarlet

Rabbit Motif

Scale up the design as described on page 274, spacing the grid lines 2 cm (¾ in) apart. The finished *mola* will be 37 x 29 cm (14½ x 11½ in).

Transfer the design to the red fabric. Lay the large piece of black fabric on top of the green, and the red on top of that. Pin them together, inserting small pieces of olive, blue, turquoise, magenta, orange and black between the red and the green, where they will be revealed for the slit-like patterns round the edges.

Work several rows of basting stitches, both horizontally and vertically, through all layers of fabric. Space them 2-3 cm (¾-1 in) apart.

Make a separate tracing of the yellow outlines of the rabbits and transfer them to the yellow fabric. Cut them out, leaving narrow turnings, and set the pieces to one side.

Embroidery

Begin cutting, folding and stitching the reverse appliqué as for the fish motif. Work the design from the edges in towards the middle. Sew the slit shapes first and then the red and green outlines of the rabbits, stopping after you have stitched the green outline to the black bottom layer.

Remove the red rabbit shapes from the centre and trim around the edges, leaving narrow turnings.

Pin and baste the yellow rabbit shapes in position, inserting small pieces of white fabric underneath for teeth. Turning in the edges, sew the pieces in position with tiny stitches to form overlaid appliqué. Sew the red shapes on top.

Work the fox- and cat-like creatures in mauve and black and blue and black overlaid appliqué. Make extra tracings of the outlines if necessary.

Add the spots, eyes and stripes on the rabbits' ears using overlaid appliqué.

Finish the eyes of each of the two smaller animals with a large french knot worked in black.

Finishing

See page 272 for instructions for turning the embroidery into a wall hanging.

Middle American Mestizos

Most of the people of Nicaragua and El Salvador are also mestizos. Cotton is produced in western Nicaragua where, because of the heat, it is the fabric most favoured for making clothes. Garments are frequently embroidered.

Blouses are generally short-sleeved with decoration worked in satin stitch or pattern darning round the neck or across the front of the yoke. Colouring is either polychrome or restricted to two or more shades of one colour.

Stitched decoration is also found on some religious and secular hangings. One such hanging takes the form of a square of black cotton embroidered with a peacock design worked in running stitch. It may have been used as a household hanging or as a cover for food.

Maya

The Maya Indians have inhabited what is now southern Mexico, Guatemala, Belize and Honduras for about 5000 years. The great Mayan city-building period came between A.D. 100 and 900 in what is now Guatemala. These centres were gradually abandoned in the 9th and 10th centuries in favour of the drier climate of Yucatán, but by the time of the Spanish conquest in the 1520s these cities, too, had declined.

The Maya were skilful textile artists who grew, spun and wove their own cotton. Dyeing was done after spinning and before weaving. Black, the Mayan symbol of war, was obtained from soot. Yellow, symbol of ripe corn and hence of food, was extracted from hydrous iron oxide. Red, symbol of blood, came from iron oxide or brazilwood, and blue, symbol of sacrifice, came from a blue chromiferous clay. A deep purple was obtained from the *Purpura patula* mollusc, and other colours came from wild tomato, blackberry and avocado.

Maya women today wear clothes that are similar to those of their ancestors. They wear shirts known as *huipils* made from a single folded piece of fabric with a vertical slit cut for the neck. The sides are joined beneath the arms.

Both the front and the back of a *huipil* are sometimes embroidered either in a random spot motif design or in a more regular geometric arrangement.

Pattern darning from El Salvador, with parallel straight stitches giving a woven effect.

The *huipil*, a simple sleeveless shirt, is worn by Maya women.

Yucatán Maya

Maya continue to inhabit the Yucatán peninsula, a tropical forest area to the north of Guatemala. Like the Quiché, much of their finest embroidery is to be found on the *huipil*. The characteristic Yucatán version, however, is generally sleeveless and the cut-out neck hole tends to be horizontal or square rather than vertical.

Yucatán embroidery is generally worked in satin stitch and colouring can be strikingly simple. Petals of flower motifs, for instance, are executed in satin stitch in bold primary colours.

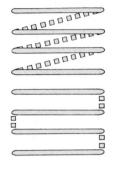

People of the Guatemalan village of Chichicastenango perform the Dance of the Conquest re-enacting the arrival of the Spanish conquerors.

Two-sided satin stitch, with the stitches crossing behind the fabric, uses more yarn than the 'ladder'-shaped surface variety.

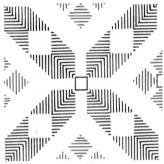

Geometric satin stitch motif with stitches worked at right angles.

Detail of multi-coloured geometric design on a *huipil*, worked in pattern darning.

Quiché

The Quiché, also known as the Chichi, are a sub-group of the Maya who today live in the mid-western highlands of Guatemala. Most are subsistence farmers, though some now are seasonal agricultural workers on the Pacific coast.

Considerable Spanish influence is apparent in Quiché religious and household embroidery. Many design themes, for instance, have been taken directly from embroideries brought to Central America by the Spanish settlers. To a more limited degree Spanish influence is also seen in embroidered decoration on clothing.

Traditionally a Quiché man wears a plain black suit of local wool with a printed cotton turban and waist sash. The tightly fitting jacket is embroidered by his own hand in many different colours of silk thread in a floral or spiral design. The trousers have two false pocket flaps which are sometimes embroidered. The embroidery is often in satin stitch of either the two-sided or the more economical surface variety, and some pattern darning and chain stitch are also used.

The Quiché lady wears a costume that is almost pure Maya. Her *huipil*, sometimes sleeveless, is tucked into a full dirndl skirt consisting of a single tube of local wool or cotton. Around the tube is a horizontal band of embroidery worked in pattern darning, chain stitch or satin stitch. The designs are of geometric birds, snowflakes or diamonds.

Huipil Blouse

You will need:
1.3 m (1½ yd) white or
  natural cotton fabric 90 cm
  (36 in) wide
0.5 m (¾ yd) natural linen
  crash or evenweave linen
  17-21 threads per 2.5 cm
  (1 in) 90 cm (36 in) wide
0.2 m (¼ yd) black cotton
  fabric 90 cm (36 in) wide
1 hot-water dye in wine
  colour
dusty pink sewing cotton
black sewing cotton
crewel or tapestry wool in
  six colours:
dark blue 4 skeins
scarlet 1 skein
white 2 skeins
wine 5 skeins
red 1 skein
dull pink 1 skein
12 cm (5 in) diameter
  embroidery frame

This is an ingeniously simple
garment, ideal for would-be
dressmakers who find traditional
paper patterns a chore to follow.
Only three straight strips of fabric
are required for the *huipil*.

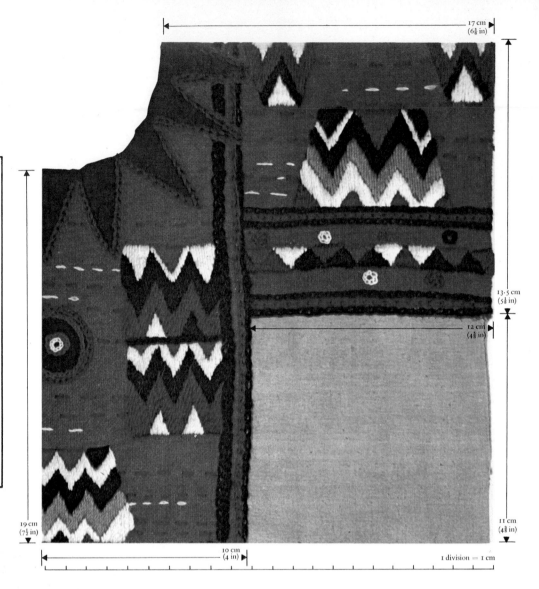

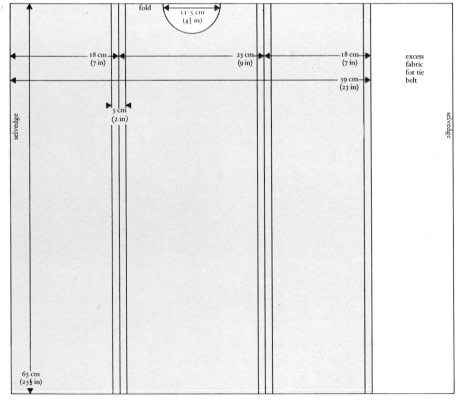

Size

The measurements given are for an 81 cm
(32 in) bust, but any size may be cut from
the same amount of fabric. As it is a
straight garment, the size may be calculated from the hip measurement. Halve it,
add 7.5 cm (3 in) for ease of movement
and 5 cm (2 in) for turnings. Divide the
result into three, allowing a proportion-
ally greater width for the centre panel.

Preparing the Fabric

Cut the cotton fabric into three strips
the sizes you have calculated, plus an
extra 2.5 cm (1 in) on all edges to allow
for shrinkage. Cut three strips of linen
the same widths, one 50 cm (20 in) long,
and the others 28 cm (11 in).

Dye the linen strips for ½–¾ hour and
dip the cotton strips in the same mixture
for one minute to obtain a dull pink tint.
(See page 272 for notes on dyeing.)

Trim the dyed strips to size and overcast all raw edges to prevent fraying.

Using a card template (see page 272)
cut out a piece of black cotton fabric for

the collar. To make the template, draw three circles on a common centre of 10 cm (4 in), 13 cm (5¼ in) and 20 cm (7⅞ in). Divide the circumference of the largest circle into 17 equal segments of 4 cm (1½ in) each. Mark the centre of each segment and draw a perpendicular line from it to the middle circle. Draw more lines from the end of the perpendicular line to the segment marks to form the sunray pattern.

Cut out the pattern along the sunray lines and along the smallest circle. Use the pattern to make a cardboard template.

Embroidery

The embroidery is worked on the linen strips which are applied to the cotton fabric before making up the garment.

Baste a circle of 12 cm (4¾ in) diameter on the centre of the centre panel for the neckline.

Trace and scale up the design (see page 272). Indicate the boundaries of the embroidery on the linen by withdrawing threads, leaving a 2.5 cm (1 in) border on all edges. (For sizes larger than the one illustrated, cut the tracing down the centre and slide the halves apart to fit.) Transfer the design to the fabric.

Work all the patterned panels in satin stitch, setting the stitches parallel to the long edges of the strips. Hold the work in a frame to avoid puckering.

Cut a circle of black cotton fabric 3 cm (1¼ in) in diameter and slipstitch it in position. Work two circles of chain stitch round the edge and two in the middle.

Baste the embroidered panels to the centres of the cotton strips. Neaten the bottom edges of the linen with herringbone stitch and cover the joins with two rows of chain stitch. Quilt the layers of fabric together with rows of running stitch in red and white. The rows should run parallel to each other across the strip.

Work bands and circles of chain stitch on the outer panels.

Cut out the neckline and make an opening of 12 cm (4¾ in) down the centre back. Pin the collar in position on the right side of the centre panel so that it overlaps the neckline evenly all round and one sunray is aligned with the centre front.

Overcast the neck opening and outer edge of the collar. Clip the inner edge of the collar and turn to the inside; sew down with herringbone stitch.

Making the Huipil

Press each section face down on a folded blanket using a damp cloth and a medium-hot iron.

Taking care to leave the sides of the centre linen panel free, pin, baste and stitch together the long edges of the three panels. Work a row of chain stitch over each seam.

Overlap the embroidered centre panel onto the side panels and work two rows of chain stitch over the join. Work two more rows of chain stitch round the edge of the collar.

Join the sides of the *huipil*, making the seams 36 cm (14 in) long, measuring from the bottom edge. Turn up the hem.

Bind the back opening with black cotton and finish with a button and loop. Turn in and bind the armholes.

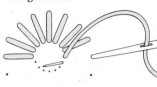

Chain stitch.   Stem stitch.   Straight stitch.

Indo-America

Early Paracas embroideries, worked in muted shades of maroon and brown pattern darning, looked very similar to weaving.

An embroidery of the Necropolis period, with human and anthropomorphic figures holding the shrunken heads of their captives.

One of the most important and most ancient embroidery areas lies in the Andes mountains around Cuzco in Peru and on the shores of Lake Titicaca on the border between Peru and Bolivia. This is where the Tiahuanaco once lived, the area now inhabited by the Quechua and Aymara.

A little further south, on the southern coast of Peru, lived the Paracas and the Nazca, many of whose artefacts have been preserved due to the extreme dryness of the climate.

The Paracas people flourished from about 900—400 B.C., forming one of a whole series of cultures that stretched back until as early as 4000 B.C. Their centre was a peninsula in the Ica region of Peru, a desert area where rain was virtually unknown.

An anthropomorphic figure with extra limbs and parasitical figures attached to its hands.

Loop stitch is worked from left to right. Loops in the first row are free at the top. They are caught down by a second row worked above them, and so on.

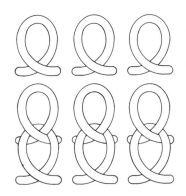

Pattern darning is sewn with long straight stitches parallel with the weave of the fabric.

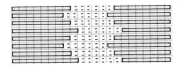

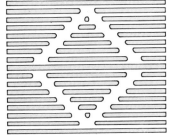

Paracas

The importance of Paracas embroidery cannot be overrated. The quality of the textiles was extremely high and the colouring and astringent wit of much of the design were outstanding. Most of the embroideries are funerary pieces, many of them from the Cerro Colorado tombs discovered in 1925 by the Peruvian archaeologist Julio C. Tello.

These deep shaft tombs contained more than four hundred mummy packs with spectacular fabrics inside them. The finely woven shrouds were embroidered with figures in harmonious colour. Sometimes only the border was embroidered, and sometimes embroidery covered almost the entire piece. Not surprisingly the designs appear to have had religious significance.

Paracas embroidery seems to have been a male art. Embroiderers used a basic ground fabric of cotton or wool from the alpaca, vicuña and llama. It was usually woven to the required size so that it did not have to be cut, which explains why Paracas embroideries are often found with four selvedges.

Stitchery yarn was cotton or wool and sometimes human hair was used for cording. The stitches in most common use were straight stitch, which is also known as flat stitch, chain stitch and loop stitch. This last stitch, which was found primarily in the south of the Paracas region, was worked in wool on a plain-weave cotton ground. Straight, stem and loop stitches were worked either in lines parallel with the weave of the fabric or in regular oblique lines.

Pattern darning was also popular. This was worked with long straight stitches sewn or woven exactly parallel with the threads of the ground fabric so that the effect was almost that of a woven design.

The history of the Paracas culture is

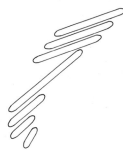

Enlarged detail showing how stem stitch was used by Paracas embroiderers to stitch the curved outlines of their motifs.

complicated. From an embroidery viewpoint it is necessary to concentrate on two eras, the Paracas Cavernas and the Paracas Necropolis, named after burial grounds excavated between 1925-30. The style of Cavernas designs, from the middle period of the Paracas culture

Anthropomorphic beings with extra limbs and parasitical faces attached to the hands and feet featured in Paracas designs.

These two regal figures with strange headdresses are worked in feathers on a poncho from Lambayeque in Peru.

Typical zoomorphic figure with the head of a cat and tail of a fish.

(about 500–200 B.C.), is almost caricature; the human and anthropomorphic beings displayed have extra limbs and parasitical faces attached to hands and feet, and cats, monkeys and other animals are also portrayed. Colours are frequently muted, with maroons and browns predominating.

During the later Necropolis period embroidery design became more free-flowing. Curvilinear outlines were achieved by altering the lengths and angles of stem stitches, and device outlining became more realistic.

One of the most common embroidery motifs was the anthropomorphic Oculate Being. Bodies were still often shown in contorted shapes, often with their heads thrown back, and people were embroidered with many surplus appendages. But the line of the designs was so much less geometric than that of Paracas Cavernas

that the humorous quality of many of the motifs gained considerably.

Another aid to identification of Necropolis embroidery is the preponderance of bright shades of blue, green, red and yellow. Overall colouring was much more forceful than the muted shades used earlier.

Many of the figures displayed on Necropolis embroideries hold trophied heads—that is, shrunken heads from the bodies of captives. Representations of bird and animal life also appeared in the designs, sometimes in the form of a double-headed eagle, which may also have been a condor, an Andean vulture that has wings 3 m (10 ft) or more across. Bird devices were often worked in striking colour combinations, with perhaps a pink and orange twin-bird worked in stem stitch and straight stitch on a ground of indigo cotton.

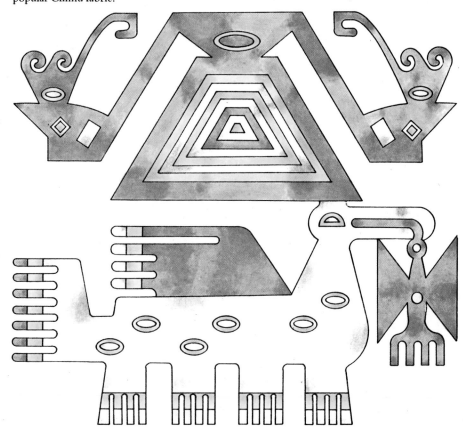

Bird motif originally worked in horizontal pattern darning on a ground of fine cotton gauze, a popular Chimú fabric.

Chimú

The Chimú Empire, also called the Kingdom of Chimor, flourished in the 14th and 15th centuries. The capital, Chan-Chan, covered more than fourteen square miles near where the Peruvian city of Trujillo stands today.

Chimú embroidery made much use of a ground of fine cotton gauze, decorated mainly with pattern darning or with outline embroidery worked in stem stitch. Designs were worked in fewer colours than the Nazca embroideries and included birds and fish, with emphasis on diagonal outlining.

Compared with the embroidery motifs of some of the other pre-Inca cultures, those of Chimú are relatively simple. The figures have fewer extra appendages, animals, and other addenda, which were common in Paracas and Nazca work.

Many other cultures existed at the same time as the Chimú, but their identity is blurred, and no evidence of embroidery exists for them. They, together with the Chimú, fell under the imperial sway of the Incas in the 15th century.

Fragment and detail of a 14th-century Chimú llama wool fabric.

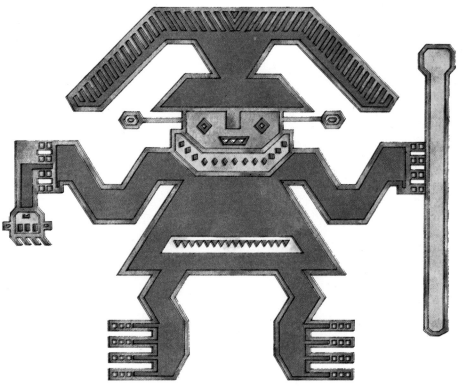

Detail of a Peruvian ceremonial featherwork bib showing two symbols of the sun god Pachacama.

Peruvian men from Cuzco, high in the Andes, wear traditional ponchos heavily embroidered with pattern darning.

Quechua

The Quechua, modern descendants of the Incas, are spread throughout the highlands of Ecuador, Peru and Bolivia. Their history goes back to the 13th century when the Incas were a small tribe living in the Cuzco area in the Middle American highlands. The Incas' rise to power did not begin until the reigns of Pachacute (1438-71) and his son Tupac (1471-93). In a period of 30 years they conquered their neighbouring tribes, including the Aymara and Chimú, and expanded as far as the Colombia-Ecuador border and northern Chile.

Most of the Inca population were farmers who not only produced all their own food and clothing but also a large enough surplus to support the nobility, the religious establishment and the craftsmen. Craftsmen were state employees selected for training from among the young peasant children.

Women were trained to weave on the backstrap loom and learned practically every technique known to modern textile manufacturers. The fabric they produced for the emperor and the priests remains unsurpassed in its fineness and beauty.

After the conquest of 1532, the Spaniards retained the local government structure, replacing the Inca nobles with Spaniards, who were also given ownership of large tracts of land. Much use was made of forced labour, especially in the newly opened silver and mercury mines. The nobility disappeared through death and intermarriage, and the crafts declined.

Today, in the more isolated farming communities, Quechua ways have not changed much from those of the Incas, and in language, diet and dress the people closely resemble the Indians the Spanish conquered.

Most traditional embroidery today takes the form of poncho or *liclla* decoration. The origin of the poncho is obscure. It consists either of one square piece of wool fabric or of two long pieces sewn together, as in the case of the earlier Nazca poncho. The neck opening is usually a vertical slit.

The warp of a modern Inca poncho generally runs horizontally across the garment, which means that the selvedges are to the bottom of both the front and the back. The side edges are either woven in or hemmed under.

The poncho is worn by both men and women but the *liclla* is exclusively a female garment. It is a long, rectangular shawl with two ends hanging down in front. The bulk of the shawl, to the back of the wearer, forms a pouch in which babies are carried.

Embroidery of a poncho or *liclla* is executed in pattern darning and chain stitch. Many of the patterns are geometric, with lines of stitching running parallel to the weft producing designs that run up and down the garment.

'Inca' motifs are strong and forceful. For instance, what seems to be an African lion stands squarely on four stout legs. His stylized mane is perfectly suited to the fine spiral lines of chain stitch, which are used throughout. Some areas of the design have been left unworked so that the ground fabric of thick red cotton shows through. The black outlining of the lion is typical of much modern 'Inca' embroidery. The separation of segments within the design leads to a stained-glass window effect.

Some of the more luxurious of today's 'Inca' embroideries are displayed at religious and other festivals, where the Indians sometimes re-enact the pageantry of their Inca forefathers. In remote Quechua villages it is not unusual to come across a snake dance, with men and boys forming a jovial procession through the streets. A herald leads the way for the actor playing the role of the Inca emperor. Both the herald and the emperor may wear cotton tunics lavishly embroidered with imported silks and gold threads. Designs include the sun, symbol of the Inca sun god Pachacama, and realistic human and bird shapes, worked in chain stitch.

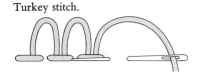

Turkey stitch.

One of the symbols of officialdom in Tiahuanaco, this stylized cat is often embroidered on hats.

Tiahuanaco

The name Tiahuanaco comes from the ruins of a great city in Bolivia near the southern end of Lake Titicaca. The culture seems to have been widespread and another centre, which has not been extensively excavated, has been found near Huari, in the central highlands of Peru. Little is known about the Tiahuanaco people, though some scholars postulate they were Aymara, a group who still inhabit the region. The dates for the Tiahuanaco period have been debated, but the period 500 to 1000 A.D. seems probable.

No Tiahuanaco embroidery has been preserved from the Lake Titicaca area, where the damp climate causes material to disintegrate rapidly. Various examples, however, have been recovered from the coastal desert, where the people had trade contact with the highlands.

Tiahuanaco designs are angular and strong: a stylized cat, one of the symbols of Tiahuanaco officialdom, appears frequently on the hats.

The Tiahuanaco were obviously attentive to their headwear, and some striking, individualistic hats are to be found in collections in many parts of the world. A Tiahuanaco hat consisted of a brim cut in one piece and joined to a tall four-sided crown, each corner of which was topped by a large knot about 5 cm (2 in) high. The crown was decorated with loop stitching, and the brim was sometimes worked with turkey stitch in bright colours.

Aymara

The Aymara Indians live on the Altiplano of Bolivia and in the central Andes of Peru. Their legends tell nothing about their past or where they came from.

Aymara culture is a combination of Indian and Hispanic. The Indian heritage includes a love of carnivals and other festivals. Dances such as the *palla-palla*, a satire of the European invaders of the 16th century, and *waka-tokoris*, a representation of bull-fighting, are popular. Festivals are a blend of pantheistic pre-Columbian religion and some Christian influences, and the Indians still revere Pachacama and his wife Pachamama, the Earth Goddess.

Aymara embroidery is particularly

A Peruvian woman wearing a heavily embroidered felt hat to a village festival.

Aymara Indians in Bolivia perform a satirical dance representing the Spanish invasion.

associated with festival regalia. Many festive costumes are accordingly decorated with embroidery, imitating the dress of the Aymaran pre-Columbian ancestors. Embroidery is done by the men, who generally work in satin stitch on ground fabrics of local cotton or of alpaca or llama wool.

Women wear a full-length dress of alpaca with a buckled belt round the waist and with it a short over-jacket decorated with appliqué and stitched braid. Men wear pantaloons and a short tight-fitting appliquéd alpaca jacket, rather like that of a bull-fighter. Their shirt is of cotton, decorated round the neck with satin stitch worked in floral or geometric motifs.

Running stitch.

Detail of a Nazca feathered cloak
showing a jaguar with bared
teeth. The angular outline is
caused by the rigid feathers.

Nazca

Nazca culture dates from 100 B.C.-
A.D. 700 and is named for the people who
lived in the Rio Grande de Nazca and the
other valleys near the present town of
Nazca on the southern coast of Peru.

As in the earlier Paracas cultures,
Nazca embroiderers used ground fabrics
of cotton or alpaca and other wools. The
main embroidery stitches were stem
stitch and loop stitch. Colouring was
bright and more complex than in some of
the Paracas embroideries, and more than
a hundred shades have been identified on
Nazca fabrics. Clear primary colours
predominated in the earlier Nazca
textiles but later artisans restricted themselves to various shades of one colour.

A Nazca poncho consisted of two 32
cm (12½ in) widths of woven cotton
fabric joined together, with a hole left
for the neck. In one example, the edges of
the cape were decorated with two rows
of ten blocks of design. Each block was
filled with a bird embroidered in various
two-colour combinations of stem stitch.

A red cotton belt has also been discovered with birds and flowers embroidered at random along the entire
length. Once again the motifs were
worked in stem stitch.

Later Nazca embroideries were even
more markedly geometric than the early
ones and sometimes highly abstract.
One cloth of dark brown double-weave
cotton, measuring 55 x 53 cm (21½ x 21
in), is decorated with several horizontal
bands each of which contains a different
motif. The bands are divided into eight
identical squares, forming fifty-six small
blocks in all. Each block is filled with
outline embroidery worked in running
stitch. It is possible that this cloth was a
Nazca almanac or calendar.

Nazca artists did not confine their
talents to the usual embroidery media.
Sometimes they worked with feathers,
which they stitched to net or canvas.
Working with bird feathers somewhat
hampered the usually uninhibited Nazca
artists, who must have been constrained
both by the length and rigidity of the
feathers and by the limited number of
colours. However, one superb example
remains in the form of a marvellous poncho covered with blue, green, yellow,
orange and black feathers. Each device in

the design shows a regal figure with legs
wide apart and arms stretched out.

One of the most famous embroideries
from this period is a ceremonial cloth
that was buried with a chieftain or priest.
The cloth consists of a plain-weave white
cotton frieze measuring 124 x 49 cm
(49 x 19½ in) and woven with various
anthropomorphic devices. Around this
centre panel is a border varying in width
from 5-7 cm (2-2¾ in), which is embroidered throughout in fine loop stitching
with twelve different colours of
fine single-ply wool. The outer border
shows ninety small figures accompanied
by llamas and jaguars. Many of the
human figures are repeated again and
again.

Much debate has taken place concern-
ing the meaning of the procession on the
border. The only unifying factor in the
design is the extreme exuberance of the
people and it has been suggested that the
border may depict a procession celebrat-
ing the arrival of spring.

Many of the figures carry batons or
staves, some of which have minute
parasitical persons or trophied heads
clinging to them. Other figures carry
throwing sticks similar to those portrayed
on Nazca pots. Also depicted in the

embroidery are Nazca weapons such as a
knife, sling and darts which are represented as simple rods since it is difficult to
embroider a fine point in loop stitch.
Thirty-nine of the figures carry plants,
some of which can be identified as sweet
potato, cactus and beans.

This ceremonial cloth also shows exact
details of the Nazca costume. Some of the
people in the procession are wearing a
breech cloth, a band of fabric passing
between the legs and fastening onto a
waist belt. Over the breech cloth is a
sleeveless tunic made of a single piece of
wool about 175 cm (70 in) long, doubled
over to form back and front, with a slit
for the neck opening. Sometimes the
tunic is decorated with a square woven
yoke of another colour and sometimes
with shrunken heads.

Others wear cloaks or furs round their
shoulders. They have one, two or three
earplugs in each lobe, and their black hair
is covered with a horizontal headband
known as a *llautu*, which is a woollen
cord about 2 cm (nearly 1 in) across,
which was wound tightly round the
head two or three times. Three of the
border figures wear beige wigs similar to
those made from llama hair found in
contemporary graves.

Angular animal motifs, some with two heads, were often worked in close parallel lines of stem stitch.

A section of one of the most detailed and well-preserved Nazca embroideries. The border contains ninety small loop-stitch figures.

Peruvian Eagle Bag

Preparing the Fabric

Cut out the four pieces of calico, leaving a margin around the embroidery area as shown. Transfer the design to the bag flap (see page 272).

Embroidery

Working with the fabric in a frame, outline all the motifs and sections of the stars in back stitch.

Fill in the motifs with blocks of satin stitch. Work the eyes with tiny rings of back stitch.

Fill in the background with satin stitch, again worked in blocks.

Making the Bag

Damp stretch the embroidery (see page 272). Trim the margin to a uniform 1 cm (⅜ in) all round. Place the flap face down on the end of the bag section and machine round the bottom and side edges.

Turn the work right side out. Turn in the top edges of the embroidery and slip-stitch them in place.

Taking a 1 cm (⅜ in) seam allowance, hem round the three remaining sides.

Join the two handles along one of the short edges to make one long strip. Fold it in half lengthwise, right sides together, and machine the long edge and one short edge. Turn it right side out and press. Turn in and slipstitch the remaining raw edge.

Fold up the bottom of the bag as far as the flap. Baste the ends of the handle between the back, bottom and front of the bag so that it forms a gusset, and then machine stitch.

Stitch the piping cord round the area of embroidery.

Finish with a hook and eye fastening.

Embroidered collar from a llama's ceremonial harness which inspired the design of the bag.

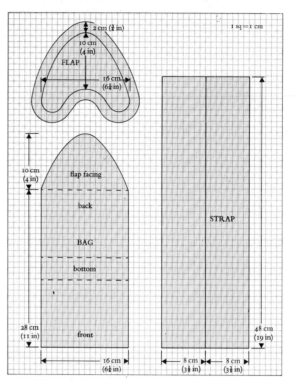

You will need:
0.4 m (½ yd) white calico
  90 cm (36 in) wide
soft embroidery cotton in
  six colours:
white 2 skeins
green 1 skein
blue 1 skein
red 1 skein
mauve 1 skein
pink 1 skein
0.6 m (¾ yd) pink piping cord
white sewing cotton
pink sewing cotton
hook and eye

This pretty little shoulder bag is quick and easy to make. Wear it as a gay accessory with summer dresses, selecting embroidery colours to suit your wardrobe.

Actual-size pattern for the bag flap. Use this to trace the outlines for the embroidery and as a key to the colours of the satin-stitch blocks.

European influence is seen in the cross stitch, satin stitch and buttonhole stitch of Riobamba.

Ecuador

The rest of northern Indo-America does not now produce much indigenous embroidery, although Ecuador produces a little. Ecuador's main embroidery centre is Riobamba, high in the Andes near the famous volcano Chimborazo. The women, who are both Indian and mestizo, embroider with silk and cotton thread on a cotton ground. Most of the embroidery is done in satin stitch. Designs are usually floral, with many-petalled flowers worked in solid blocks of bright colours. All work shows European inspiration.

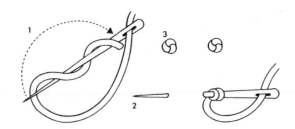

French knot.
Wind the thread twice round the needle and take a small stitch in the fabric, coaxing the threads down the needle as you do so.

Euro-America

The ethnographic zone of Euro-America, which comprises Chile, Argentina, Uruguay and the southern part of Brazil, does not possess much indigenous embroidery. The avalanche of European settlement has diluted the culture of the local peoples, and local crafts have suffered in consequence. Indians in these countries did some embroidery before the Europeans arrived, but not much is known about this work and virtually nothing has been preserved. What embroidery does exist, therefore, shows mainly European influences. Both for religious and secular usage, embroidery styles and designs follow those of the Spanish and Portuguese who settled in Euro-America from the 16th century.

Euro-American embroidery often includes pulled-thread work, satin stitch and other universal techniques introduced by immigrants.

Folk needle-painting from Ninhue, worked in chain stitch, romanian stitch and french knots.

Ninhue

Fortunately the non-indigenous nature of the embroidery does not entirely preclude the execution of local themes. In Chile in particular at least two newly established centres have been producing folk needle-painting that illustrates the heritage of the people themselves.

One such centre is at Ninhue, an agricultural village near Chillan, some 200 miles south of Santiago. The main Ninhue embroidery project was started in 1971 by Carmen Benavente de Orrego-Salas to stimulate the local women to be creative. She taught her first class in a small room lent by the village priest and, thereafter, women of all ages would gather once a week to work their needle-paintings. When they began, the women had no knowledge at all of embroidery stitches.

Colourful folk designs are embroidered in chain stitch, romanian stitch, and french knots using silk or cotton thread on a cotton ground. They depict scenes of people dancing and also scenes of general festivity.

Chilean needle-painting is also worked on Isla Negra, where women embroider colourful scenes of everyday life.

Design from a Mestizo-American beadwork belt (bottom). Beads are held to the ground by individual retaining stitches.

Isla Negra

Another modern embroidery centre is at Isla Negra, an island off the central coast of Chile. The patron was Señora Lenore Sobrino de Vera, who provided her students with embroidery wools and cotton fabric on which to work. In Isla Negra work, however, the stitches are sometimes haphazard in direction and length and are clearly of secondary importance to the overall design. Isla Negra embroidery can truly be said to be needle-*painting*.

Isla Negra embroideries record events in the lives of the artists and their families. The titles of the pictures ('The port', 'Oxcart bride') are sometimes misleading, since all the embroideries consist of many sub-plots, random in their arrangement. The figures differ greatly in size, most of them being out of proportion one to another and also out of perspective.

A typical needle-painting shows a white-haired lady, her hair in a bun, sitting knitting in her kitchen. Two children are playing ball and a man in a straw hat is carrying a basket of oranges. These, and similar everyday activities, appear again and again in Isla Negra pictures. A variety of domestic animals is also shown, although sometimes it is difficult to tell a sheep from a goat!

Both the Ninhue and the Isla Negra embroideries illustrate ways in which a piece of embroidery might become a family souvenir or a record of local life.

Brazil

Mestizo-America comprises most of Brazil, and the population is of mixed American Indian and European origins, although there are many of both African and Asiatic descent. Some African influence is to be found in many of the arts and this may also be true in stitchery design. Stitched bead designs from Mestizo-America, with each bead held to the ground fabric by a retaining stitch, contain a degree of symmetry similar to that found in African beadwork. Strangely, a Tukano Indian belt from the Rio Uaupes, a river in the Upper Amazon basin, has a step motif akin to much design from northern Africa and the Middle East. Whether any direct connection exists is unknown.

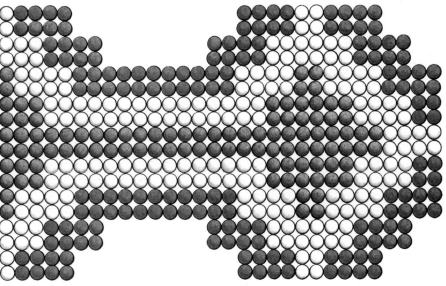

North America

Embroidery in porcupine quills on a ground of water-repellent birchbark is characteristic of North America. This box was made by the Micmac, an Algonquian-speaking tribe of the Eastern Woodlands Indians.

Beadwork is another form of decoration used by Indians. This detail of a vest is made from imported velvet, a favourite fabric with the Ojibwa until it became too expensive in the mid-19th century.

The popular North-American pastime of quilting often brought groups of people together to work communally in quilting bees, as shown in this painting by an unknown 19th-century artist.

The embroidery of North America falls into two categories, the work of Indian embroiderers and that which has been introduced and developed by settlers since the beginning of the 17th century.

At first Indian embroiderers worked on grounds made from the skins of bison, caribou, moose and seal. They made shirts and leggings for both men and women, often cutting the edges in fringes so that the rain would run off easily.

Birchbark was another water-repellent fabric. Thin slivers of bark from the trees of the *betula* family were used by some tribes to make shoes and moccasins.

The more conventional ground fabrics such as cotton, wool and linen were also used. One form of wild cotton is native to North America, and threads and fabrics made from it were used before the arrival of Europeans. Sheep were introduced by the

early settlers, who produced wool on a small scale. Today the main wool-growing region is in Texas, but sheep farming is also extensive in many other areas with the exception of the south-east and the most northerly parts of the continent.

Embroidery on birchbark was sometimes worked with thread made of porcupine quills, a form of work seldom found outside North America. The stiff white quills, tipped with black, were 3-5 cm (1-2 in) in length and taken from the back and tail. Indian men and women chewed the quills to make them pliable and then moulded one quill to another to form a long sinewy thread. Quill thread was laid on the surface of the ground fabric and couched in pleats, usually with cotton thread or hair. Later work was stitched right through the ground fabric with a steel needle.

Hair was also used as embroidery thread, much of it taken

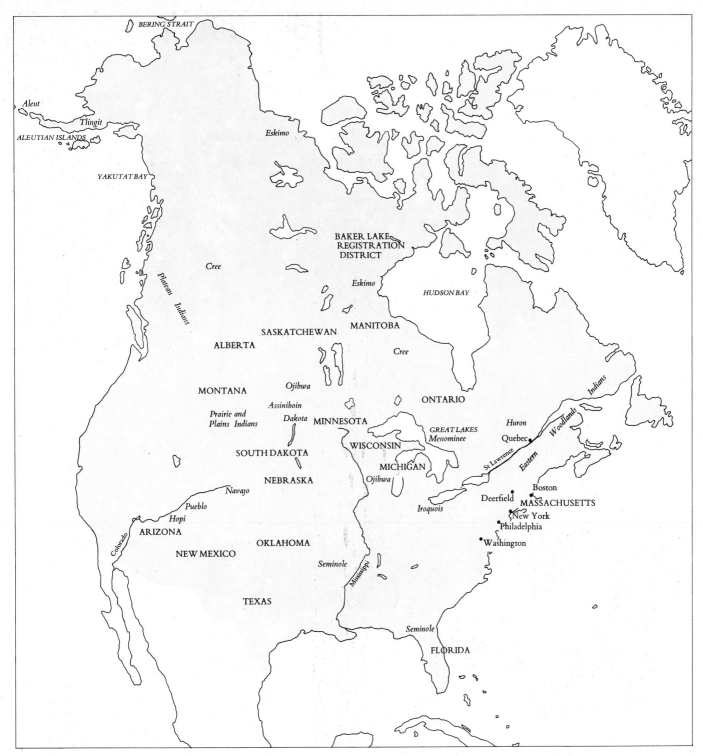

from the caribou, the American reindeer *Rangifer*. The hairs used for embroidery might be matt or slightly glossy and came from the dewlap of the animal.

The use of moosehair as embroidery thread was perfected by Ursuline nuns in Canada as a substitute for expensive silk thread in vestments and other church embroidery.

Moosehair was used in embroidery on birchbark and woollen broadcloth. Sometimes it was combined with appliqué. Bundles of hairs could also be laid together and couched, with either moosehair or cotton thread.

Fish-skin appliqué, with pieces of fish skin used both for ground fabric and applied motifs, was practised in Alaska and western Canada as well as in eastern Siberia. The pieces of fish skin were stitched together with thin strips of fish gut, generally by hemming.

Production of traditional Indian embroidery declined during the long period of confrontations with the settlers, who brought with them the styles and patterns of their homelands, as well as silks, cottons, linens and wools in both thread and fabric form.

Forms of stitchery most often associated with 17th-century North America include crewel, quilting, needlepoint or canvas work and patchwork or pieced work, which was largely an American invention. Because supplies of new fabrics were not readily available, inventive women joined together small pieces of leftover fabric.

A high percentage of the embroidery of today consists of needlepoint, crewel work, and all forms of counted-thread embroidery. It is mostly worked at home for personal use, but some commercial embroidery in the form of cushions and chair seats is sold either as kits or in completed form.

Pueblo back stitch.

Pueblo

Ceremonial dress of the Taos
Indian with heavily embroidered
apron, bracelets and headdress.

Hopi designs are usually simple
repeating blocks. This *manta* is
embroidered with pattern darning.

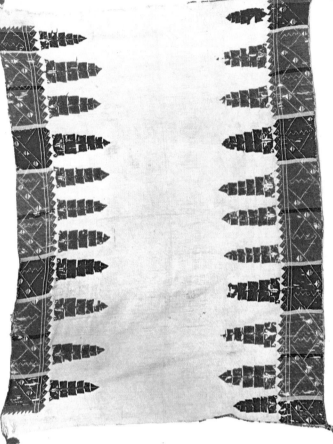

The Pueblo Indians live in north-eastern Arizona and north-western New Mexico. Their name comes from the Spanish word *pueblo*, meaning village or people.

The Pueblos produce some embroidered articles of clothing and banners. In general it is the men who embroider, although today a few women are joining them. The main items of traditional clothing are, for the man, a breechcloth, kilt and shirt, and for the woman, a loose below-the-knee dress worn over leggings. The dress may be a *manta*, a length of cloth which can be either wrapped around the body to form a dress or used as a free-flowing scarf. Embroidered bands are worked along the selvedges of the *manta* and vertically across one end of the length of cloth forming the man's kilt.

Unique to Pueblo embroidery is the pueblo back stitch. Two threads of embroidery yarn are worked at once and the two are twisted between back stitches made through the ground fabric. The finished appearance of this form of back stitch is of one continuous twisted cord with no visible means of support. Lines of pueblo back stitch are used for most of the infilling of embroidery devices. Outlines and some infillings are worked in buttonhole stitch, chain stitch and satin stitch.

Embroidery is generally worked with silk or wool yarn on a ground of cotton, which is often left undyed. Traditional embroidery yarn colours are the black and the green of baize ravellings, and some use is now made of shades of red and indigo, from chemical dyes.

Pueblo design is distinguished by its strict geometric uniformity. It is nearly always worked on borders and consists of carefully aligned repeating motifs. The effect is somewhat solid, the blocks of colour separated only by a narrow outline of ground fabric which is left unworked. These narrow dividing lines are found around each repeating motif. Sometimes dividers are left through individual motifs, running parallel, perpendicular or at an angle to the border.

A popular way of dividing a border is to leave two horizontal 'ground lines' running across the design, breaking it up into three sections. The widest section is always the lowest band and the narrowest section the central band. The repeat, or space taken by one complete cycle of design, need not be the same on each band.

The Hopi are the westernmost subgroup of Pueblos, living in north-eastern Arizona.

As with all Pueblo Indians, it is the men who are responsible for most of the embroidery, decorating costume items and a few ceremonial hangings. Embroidery is worked on a ground of cotton in pueblo back stitch, buttonhole stitch, satin stitch and pattern darning.

Hopi designs consist of simple repeating blocks used either alone or as a web on which a motif is worked representing a Hopi deity. Emblems of one of their gods are sometimes worked in radial blocks of satin stitch, thus incorporating figures into a geometric framework.

Simple buttonhole stitch, made by looping the thread under the needle after a vertical stitch.

Navajo beaded headdress. Much Indian beadwork is secured to the ground fabric by the 'lazy squaw' method of threading several beads between stitches.

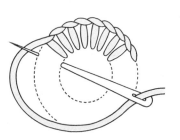

Hopi design for pattern darning might be worked in traditional black and green of baize ravellings with chemically dyed red.

Eastern Woodlands

Before the disruption of their existence by intensive European settlement, the Eastern Woodlands tribes lived in an area which stretched from north of the Great Lakes to South Carolina. The two main linguistic groups were Iroquoian- and Algonquian-speaking.

Eastern Woodlands women once decorated leggings, moccasins and aprons with porcupine-quill embroidery couched in pleats but now, with the tribes long since scattered, little Eastern Woodlands embroidery is worked.

The Iroquois today live mainly on

Dyed deerskin cloth embroidered by Iroquois with laid and couched quillwork in pleated formation.

Ojibwa coiled horsehair.

Huron petal.

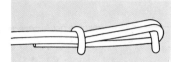

Border design taken from
Menominee woman's leggings.

Leggings are part of traditional
Indian dress for both men and
women. These, from the Chippewa,
are decorated with silk and beads.

The manufacture of moccasins
provided an important source of
income for the Huron. These are
embroidered with moosehair.

reservations in New York State and
Ontario. Traditionally they have been the
most matriarchal (and matrilineal) of the
Eastern Woodlands Indians and women
appear in many Iroquois myths. Supernatural power is particularly important
in Iroquois design. They have a word,
orenda, which refers to Iroquois belief in
the sun, moon, trees and other spirits
rendered in personal terms. Human
beings and animal and star shapes are
therefore still seen worked together in

many designs of Iroquois embroidery.

The Huron, a subdivision of the Iroquois, have a long history of commercial
embroidery. By the end of the 19th century they were producing some 140,000
pairs of suede moccasins a year. These
were sold through wholesale dealers in
many parts of North America, especially
in the Yukon goldfields.

The embroiderers used quillwork
stitched in pleated formation. They also
used bundles of horsehairs tied together

with cotton, laid on the moccasins and
couched to the ground fabric with long
straight stitches.

Distinguishing points of Huron horsehair embroidery are the petal and bud
formations. The petal is formed by a
bundle of hairs doubled back and under
and sometimes padded. The bud shape is
achieved by twisting the main 'stalk' of
the bundle of horsehairs. Both are found
on moccasins.

A few moccasins are still worked by
Huron women today. They are, however, mostly decorated with stitched
beadwork.

One of the main divisions of Algonquian-speaking Indians is the Ojibwa,
or Chippewa, who once lived along the
northern shores of Lake Huron. Today
the 80,000 remaining Ojibwa are scattered among reservations in Michigan,
Minnesota, Montana, North Dakota,
Wisconsin, Ontario, Manitoba and Saskatchewan.

The women still work some moosehair embroidery stitched on birchbark,
now primarily for sale outside the community. In the past they also made
extensive use of local horsehair as embroidery yarn but since about 1920 the
supply has been augmented by horsehair
bought from the Hudson's Bay Company.

Ojibwa horsehair embroidery is unusual in that, instead of using bundles of
hairs which are laid and couched to the
ground fabric, one hair at a time is tightly
coiled around a filler of a bird's quill.
After a certain number of coils the hair is
stitched through the ground fabric.

The Ojibwa have also practised more
usual forms of embroidery. Like many

Huron bud.

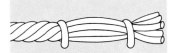

Flattened quills are laid in pleats and held with running stitches through the folds.

The modern baby-carrying sling is derived from those exquisitely embroidered by Indian women.

of the other Eastern Woodlands Indians they worked quill stitching on a ground of moose or caribou hide. Designs were simple, with geometric coloured bands and undulating lines. This kind of unsophisticated decoration is found on Ojibwa shirts, leggings and quivers.

Another group of Algonquian-speaking Eastern Woodlands Indians is the Menominee, great hunters and fur traders who came originally from the Menominee River area between Lake Superior and Lake Michigan. Some still live in Menominee County, the poorest county in Wisconsin.

The Menominee attributed personality to the sun, moon, rocks, trees and other inanimate objects and some of their beliefs are illustrated in embroidery on aprons and other costume items.

Menominee embroidery was worked by women on ground fabrics of imported cotton or black felt. The embroidery was mostly stitched with porcupine quills in pleated, laid and couched work. Some cotton thread embroidery was also worked, mainly in running stitch and stem stitch.

Menominee women also used to work cotton appliqué. Colourful repeating applied motifs formed bands of decoration on black felt leggings. Cut-out motifs of bright, plain-coloured, imported cotton would be hemmed round the bottom of each legging and up the outer side, parallel to the seam. The block of appliqué was about 12 cm (5 in) wide.

A popular Menominee repeating design in chain stitch with two bands of quillwork.

Prairie and Plains

Seminole dirndl skirt, decorated with patchwork made by stitching, cutting and re-stitching fabric strips. Bias and straight bindings add colour to the borders.

North American Indian patchwork is most often associated with the Seminole, who used to live both in Florida and around Seminole City, Oklahoma, part of the Great Plains. Today the Seminole live mainly in Florida. Their name, which was first given to them about 1775, is thought to mean runaway or pioneer and to come from the Spanish *cimarrón*, wild.

Seminole women still work colourful patchwork. They stitch strips of fabric together by machine, and then cut the fabric up again across the strips. These are then assembled to make patterns. The completed fabric is made up into shirts and anoraks for the men and full dirndl skirts for the women as well as borders for their Spanish-type shawls. The model for this decoration may indeed have been Iberian; the Indians possibly wanted to copy the colourful brocade clothing worn by some of the 18th-century Spanish settlers.

Seminole patchwork designs are geometric. Long narrow strips of applied cotton are attached as streamers forming a continuous horizontal band round the skirts. Other smaller pieces of fabric are applied, two together, to make diagonal crosses, a device that is repeated at equal intervals round the entire body of the skirt. Bias and straight bindings are also used to make the patterns more intricate.

The territory of the Prairie and Plains Indians of North America originally stretched from Alberta to Texas. Few of the Indian groups, however, are today in their original homelands.

Many of the tribes were more or less nomadic. Others were more settled, but both groups were keen hunters for food and skins to use in clothing. Aside from the Seminole of Oklahoma, the most important Prairie and Plains Indians from an embroiderer's viewpoint are the Dakota, the Cree and the Assiniboin.

Apart from the cotton used by the Seminole, most of the Prairie and Plains Indians' clothing was of animal skin (buffalo, elk, antelope or deer). Men wore skin shirts reaching almost to their knees. Sometimes the shirt was collarless, almost a T-shirt in design; in other instances it was more tailored, with a collar and buttoned front yoke and with inset sleeves and fitted cuffs. Embroidery would be worked on the front yoke with a floral design in stitched beadwork, the individual beads held in place with a long running stitch. The design would be repeated twice, vertically. Stitched beadwork also covered the long outer-leg

Detail of a motif used on the dress. The method of securing several beads on long stitches forms a pattern similar to satin stitch.

Plains-Indian woman's dress with shoulders and sleeves heavily decorated with stitched beadwork. The dress would be worn over leather leggings.

Quarter of a design once used on the suede arrow bag of a Plains Indian. The embroidery was in pleated porcupine quillwork.

Ornamental leather headdress from the Northern plains, with pleated quills and fringe of beads and quills.

Indian shoulder bag with long leather fringe and beadwork decoration. Many Assinboin designs transpose well to needlepoint.

seams of the leggings worn beneath the shirt. A repeating design of flowers and leaves, the whole design outlined with a fine stitched line of tiny white beads, would effectively hide the seam.

As in other North American Indian areas, leggings were made of tubes of skin held by strings to the waist belt. Women wore long dresses over their leggings. Both men and women wore moccasins. Heads were usually left uncovered.

Skin clothing was decorated with quillwork, beadwork or silk and cotton thread. Occasionally men's shirts were not embroidered at all, but were painted to depict war exploits of the wearer.

A Plains arrow bag consisted of one piece of soft suede about 50 x 25 cm (20 x 10 in), folded in half. Two smaller pieces of suede each about 17.8 x 25 cm (7 x 10 in), were sewn inside the fold, one at either end of the long piece. The smaller pieces were then attached round three sides to form pockets. A vertical slit was cut in the bag to form two handles, and the top and bottom of the bag were fringed. A symmetrical embroidery design was worked on one outer end of the bag in lines of pleated porcupine quillwork in red, blue, black and yellow.

The word 'Dakota' means allies and the Dakota Indians, sometimes known as Sioux, comprise three main groups

each subdivided many times. The Dakota today number about 40,000, living mainly on reservations in North and South Dakota, Montana and Nebraska.

Dakota women were in times gone by particularly skilled in porcupine-quill and bead embroidery. They worked geometric, floral and figurative patterns, and each design is said to have had symbolic meaning for the embroiderer. Figurative designs found in all forms of Dakota decorative art included the buffalo and the bear, both important in Dakota belief.

The women used to work embroidery mainly for home use, but until a few years ago some was also for sale.

The Assiniboin are a subdivision of the main Dakota, who split off from the parent tribe before the 17th century. The men were fine warriors and in more peaceful times were often noted for their prowess in horse stealing. Women looked after the crops and the home. They also made particularly beautiful geometric beadworks, with large blocks of design carefully aligned on men's shirts, leggings and belts and on their own dresses and moccasins.

Stitched-bead designs were symbolic, some of them conveying themes of Assiniboin belief. The two principal deities of the Assiniboin were Sun and Thunder, worshipped publicly on such occasions as the Horse Dance, the Sun

Sioux shirt made of animal skin.
On non-pliable leathers much of
the beadwork was done by taking
near-surface stitches which
did not pass right through to the
wrong side.

Cree man's outfit of shirt and leggings with fur trimming, hair fringe and braid binding the cuffs and hem. The strict symmetry of the geometric stitched beadwork is typical of Indian design.

Dance and the Medicine Lodge Dance, an annual three-day event.

The 5,000 Assiniboin today live in Southern Saskatchewan, Manitoba, Montana and North Dakota. They no longer work traditional embroidery but Assiniboin stitched-bead designs transpose well to needlepoint and other modern forms of embroidery.

The Cree groups at one time occupied an immense area from east of the Hudson Bay as far west as Alberta. Partly due to continual wars and intermittent epidemics of smallpox and other European diseases, only scattered groups remain today, numbering in all no more than 70,000.

The Cree were the traditional friends of the Assiniboin and, like them, were Algonquian-speaking. Most important of the various Cree groups were the Woodland (or Swampy) Cree, who lived mainly by hunting caribou, moose, bear, beaver and hare, and the Plains Cree, who hunted bison.

Cree religion centred on the search for animals, and one important ritual was the Shaking tent rite which was performed in order to commune with the spirits and their animals and to pray for good and worthwhile hunting.

Epaulette of a Northern Cree shirt, decorated with stitched beads and bead and quill fringing.

Cree woman's cape with bright geometric design. The background beads are attached by long stitches.

The design on this belt has been inspired by the headband of a Sioux chief's headdress. The geometric pattern is strikingly simple, allowing scope for variation in colour combinations from one motif to the next. The lines of beads are held down onto the denim with couching.

Beadwork Belt

You will need:

approx. 28 g (1 oz) no. 7
  glass rocaille beads in
  the following colours:
red
white
royal blue
pale blue
green
orange
6 or more larger beads to
  decorate the fastening
2 strips of denim 7.5 cm (3 in)
  wide and the length of your
  waist measurement
6.25 cm (2½ in) wide belt
  stiffening the length of your
  waist measurement
  less 5 cm (2 in)
1.5 m (1¾ yd) piping cord
a reel of blue button thread
a reel of blue sewing cotton
a piece of cotton sheeting or
  similar for backing
dressmaker's white chalk
ruler
old wooden picture frame
drawing pins (thumbtacks)
crewel needle
stiletto or large chenille
  needle

1 Working the embroidery.

drawing pins (thumbtacks)

cotton backing

frame

2 Threading the beads.

basting

denim

3 Couching the beads.

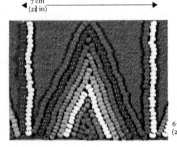

7 cm
(2¾ in)

6·3 cm
(2½ in)

4 Lacing the denim on the wrong side.

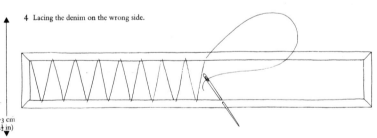

5 The oversewn eyelets.

Preparing the Fabric

Mark out the repeating pattern on one of the denim strips using a ruler and dressmaker's chalk. Baste it onto the cotton sheeting. Pin the sheeting to the picture frame, pulling it taut as you do so. (As the work progresses, move the sheeting further up the frame.)

Embroidery

Beginning at the outer edge of a motif, thread sufficient beads onto a length of buttonhole thread to cover the distance from the base to the apex of the triangle.

Take the needle through to the back and bring it up again at almost the same spot. Then work the second side of the triangle in the same way.

Work two or more lines of beads, making sure they lie flat on the surface of the fabric.

Couch the lines of beads to the denim with sewing cotton. Space the stitches two or three beads apart, keeping the tension even.

Add more lines of beads until the triangle has been filled and then work the other triangles and verticals.

Making the Belt

Cut the denim away from the cotton backing, trimming neatly round the strip, then lace it onto the belt stiffening. Turn in the edges of the second denim strip and slipstitch it to the back of the belt.

Pierce two eyelets in each end of the belt with the stiletto or chenille needle and closely oversew them with button thread.

Thread the cord through the eyelets, unravel the ends, and knot a large bead onto each strand.

Eskimo

Feather stitch.

Tlingit hanging blanket is decorated with buttons stitched on as beads to form an eagle motif.

An Eskimo girl's traditional costume is made from pieces of fabric and fur which are carefully hemmed together and then embroidered, often with running and double running stitch worked in zigzags.

Appliqué, popular with many Eskimo peoples, is used here by Tlingits for a ceremonial dance apron fringed with puffin beaks.

Two related Arctic cultures of North America are those of the Aleut of the Aleutian archipelago and the 40,000-50,000 Eskimos who live in the far north. The Aleut also have much in common with the neighbouring Tlingit who inhabit the coastal lands from Yakutat Bay north to the Fox Islands.

Some Tlingit and Aleut women still use fish skin and seal skin as ground fabric for warm waterproof clothing. They embroider the finished items with moose or caribou hair, which is brought from more easterly regions. Hair was also sometimes used as an edge binding as well as for cross braiding.

Unlike Aleut embroidery, which has much in common with Indian work, that of the true Eskimo is unique.

North American Eskimo women have a long tradition of needlecraft. Because of the rigours of the Arctic winter, clothing was always made of fur, caribou being the most popular. Pieces were carefully stitched together with oversewing. Costume styles of the Eskimos were to some extent regional, but in the main everyone, men and women, wore two coats, two pairs of trousers and two pairs of stockings with shoes or boots. Today much clothing is of the universal 20th-century anorak/parka variety.

In the early 1960s Gabriel Gély introduced some of the inland Eskimo women from the Baker Lake district, centred round the lake of that name, to the working of appliqué wall hangings. Cut-out devices of imported woollen cloth were stitched to different coloured grounds and applied pieces were held in place with buttonhole stitch. Details of faces and patterns on the clothing of the people shown in the hangings were superimposed, using running stitch, chain stitch and feather stitch.

Designs on Baker Lake hangings are generally in spot-motif form, with one applied device not necessarily either related to or in proportion with its neighbour. Some of the hangings show Eskimo men hunting, others show women cleaning fish, or animals of many different types. In Eskimo lore all animals are endowed with human characteristics, and some shown on the Baker Lake hangings have remarkably human faces. Other animals are entirely imaginary.

The European Tradition

Since the 17th century settlers from all over western Europe have introduced their own styles of embroidery to North America.

Among the earliest settlers were the Pilgrims from England who arrived in Plymouth, Massachusetts, in 1620. The original group of 120 persons included 'one fustian (linen and cotton fabric) worker and one silk dyer'. Their clothing was often rather plain, the black fabric being relieved only by tiny embroidered buttons and in 1634 the Massachusetts Court, composed of Puritans, even forbade all 'cutt works, imbroid'd or needle work'd capps'.

Contemporary Dutch settlers, however, were more liberal in their attitude to dress decoration. The Dutch women of New Amsterdam taught their maids how to spin and weave, and they sold whatever surplus fabrics they had in the Saturday markets which were trading centres for all sorts of materials.

In the 18th century flax was cultivated, and after being prepared and spun into linen thread, it was sometimes made into linsey-woolsey, a coarse cloth woven with linen warp and wool weft. There were also all-wool fabrics of local origin, cotton cloth and imported silk.

The women of New Amsterdam learned dyeing skills from the Indians, and in addition they developed their own natural dyestuffs. They extracted red from madder, yellow and brown from butternut bark, red oak and hickory,

crimson from pokeberry juice boiled with alum, and yellow and orange from sassafras bark. They bought indigo, either from pedlars or from local stores.

Embroidery was worked on many items. Ladies wore morning caps made of fine handkerchief linen and embroidered in whitework with imported floss-silk thread. They also wore embroidered skirts, stomachers, aprons, muffs and mittens and, sometimes, knitted silk stockings.

Embroidery on men's costume was found on waistcoats (vests), handkerchiefs and gloves. Sometimes gloves were made of fine skin from sheep, lamb, stag, kid or doe. Imported Spanish leather was

A husif—an apron like a large pocket—might have a stitched floral motif on the front panel.

the most expensive, luxurious material.

Many early American embroiderers used a crimped floss-silk thread, possibly imported from the Far East, which was seldom used by embroiderers in Europe. Stem stitch, satin stitch, coral stitch and bullion knots were worked in silk.

Most embroidery motifs were floral. Roses, lilies, harebells, tulips, hyacinths, honeysuckle, Indian pinks, and many other flowers were worked in arrangements of bunches, cornucopias and vases. Birds, animals and people were rarer.

Husifs

Aprons were a standard feature of the dress of early American women. For Sundays and festive occasions aprons were of muslin, silk or wool. Everyday aprons were made of one length of linen fastened to a waistband.

The apron was in constant use, which led to the evolution of a characteristic North American embroidered item, the husif (housewife), an apron formed from two identical pieces of fabric joined round all outer edges. The front piece of fabric was slit vertically in the centre to provide a large pocket, in which the wearer could store keys and other items that she wanted to carry around with her. The husif, in fact, fulfilled the role of the purse of today.

Husifs were generally made from a ground of cotton or wool and embroidered with crewel work, patchwork and quilting.

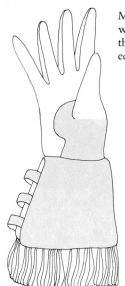

Men's gloves, lined with silk, would be embroidered below the thumb and on the cuff with an edging of gold silk fringe.

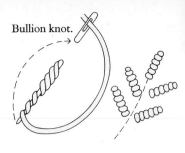

Samplers

As well as the traditional alphabet and numbers, young American girls commemorated family occasions on samplers.

Girls in the American colonies learned embroidery, and needlework in general, through the medium of the sampler or test piece. The word comes from the Latin *exemplum*, a pattern.

American samplers were generally worked on square or rectangular pieces of single-weave linen, cotton or wool fabric. Cotton, silk and wool yarn were used, with the material held taut on a wooden frame. Some of the major early American sampler stitches were back stitch, chain stitch, cross stitch, eyelet stitch, feather stitch, herringbone stitch (known as cat stitch), split stitch, stem stitch and french and bullion knots.

Texts were often included as a lettering exercise, and the resulting embroidery was sometimes known as a lettering sampler. Other popular forms of sampler were the band or border sampler, with stitches and patterns worked in horizontal bands across the sampler; whitework samplers, with exercises in embroidered cutwork and other whitework embroidered in white on a white ground fabric; and darning samplers, which contained many different darning stitches. There were also map or globe samplers portraying local or more wide-ranging maps in intricate detail.

Styles of sampler embroidery kept up with general fashions in needlework. By the middle of the 19th century Berlin woolwork samplers were being embroidered in many parts of North America. As in other parts of the world, sampler embroidery largely ceased at the beginning of the 20th century. With a relaxation in domestic education, it was no longer the norm for young girls to spend many months, if not years, working intricate embroidery stitches and patterns on what was, after all, generally intended to be only a test piece.

Star eyelet.

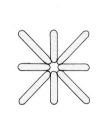

Cross stitch.

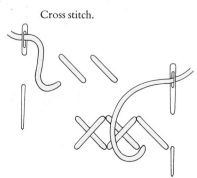

Herringbone stitch.

Split stitch.

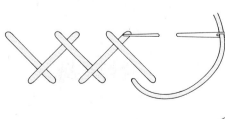

Crewel

Many crewel embroideries, worked with vegetable-dyed wools on linen grounds, had lively tree of life designs.

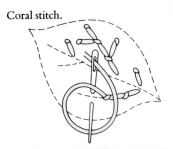
Coral stitch.

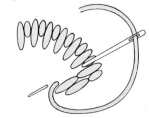
Long-and-short stitch.

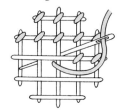
Trellis couching.

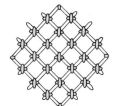

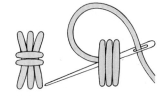
Sheaf stitch.

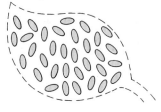
Seeding.

Crewel is a twisted two-ply woollen yarn. Early North American crewel embroidery used crewel yarn on a ground of unbleached home-produced linen or wool or of imported linen, cotton or wool.

Crewel embroidery was worked by women, who dyed much of their yarn at home, using indigo, either alone or with tag locks, the ends of sheep's wool, to produce a green-blue. Other dyes used by later crewel embroiderers included sumach and golden rod to produce a yellow, logwood and madder to achieve pink or red, and black walnut bark to give brown.

Crewel embroidery was particularly popular in New England. The early colonists had brought with them embroidered items that they could copy, and thus many English and other designs were adopted by the embroiderers.

The stitches used were one-sided satin stitch (known locally as New England economy stitch because less yarn was used than in the usual European method), herringbone stitch, running stitch and french and bullion knots. Design infilling was often done with long-and-short stitch, trellis couching, sheaf stitch and seeding (random straight stitches).

Early North American crewel embroidery designs were invariably floral, often simpler variants of the imported pieces. Because the embroiderers had little leisure time, their designs were less heavy than European equivalents, with more ground fabric left unworked. Designs had more coiling stems and fewer heavy flowers than English and other crewel pieces. North American stitches, too, tended to be lighter in effect.

A few examples of bed-sets worked in early North American crewel embroidery have survived. A bed-set was designed to provide privacy in small houses and warmth in unheated bedrooms. It consisted of two linen curtains that hung from the top of the four-poster rail to the floor at either side of the head of the bed, a headpiece, a tester (the overhead canopy, usually covered with a short curtain all the way round), valances (short floorlength curtains hanging beneath the mattress) and the main bedspread, covering the mattress. Many American women worked crewel embroidery for their own use. Sometimes families would work together to produce one bed-set.

Today crewel embroidery is enjoying a widespread revival among North American embroiderers.

Deerfield

In 1896 a temporary revival of the American crewel tradition took place in the town of Deerfield in western Massachusetts where the women took to making blue and white needlework.

Deerfield blue and white was crewel embroidery worked with imported linen threads on a natural linen ground. The first ground fabrics were mostly brought from Russia, and the linen yarn came undyed from Scotland.

The earliest examples of Deerfield embroidery used linen yarn dyed with Bengali indigo. Later, Mesopotamian madder was used to prepare a red yarn, bark of the South American acacia for a beige, fustic to produce yellow, and barks of local walnut, butternut, maple and sumach to obtain greys and browns.

Deerfield blue and white needlework was the inspiration of two local women,

Ellen Miller and Margaret Whiting. In 1896 both were in their thirties and intensely interested in local and social history. They started collecting examples and patterns of old crewel embroidery. They carefully unpicked some of the fragments of pockets they had discovered and by doing this learned the methods of construction and stitching which had been used. At first the two women simply wanted to copy some of the older pieces so that the heritage of Massachusetts needlework might be recorded in the Deerfield Museum. But then they began to teach some of the other ladies of Deerfield how to work crewel embroidery, and finally they established the Society of Deerfield Blue and White Needlework.

Embroidery patterns were drawn on heavy brown paper, sometimes old

paper bags. Then the pattern, a piece of linen ground fabric and necessary threads and working drawings were delivered to out-workers, who worked alone or in collaboration with friends. The main stitches used were cross stitch, feather stitch, herringbone stitch, romanian stitch, stem stitch and french knots.

The first examples of Deerfield blue and white embroidery were small mats (doilies). As the designers and their embroiderers became more ambitious and confident, they produced complete bed-sets, coverlets, curtains and many examples of table linen.

The Society was disbanded in 1926 when Margaret Whiting was losing her sight, and both she and Ellen Miller felt that they had achieved their original aim, the recording of the heritage of crewel embroidery in their area.

Quilting

The re-cycling of fabric scraps by settlers led to lively quilt designs in patchwork and appliqué, now American traditions.

Quilting has always been a popular pastime with North American women, and items have been worked both for home use and for sale.

It can be said with justification that quilting is today as popular as it has ever been, and groups of ladies meet in each other's houses to quilt. Quilted coverlets are popular though expensive items in boutiques and stores.

Quilting consists of two or more layers of ground fabric stitched together and padded with wadding or fleece. This gives a three-dimensional effect to the finished item and provides insulation (a necessity both in the case of padded petticoats and coats worn by American ladies of former times and for the quilted bed coverlets so popular today).

Three main methods of quilting are used in North America:

English quilting: running stitches are worked right through a top ground layer of fabric, a layer of wadding (possibly carded lamb's wool), and a layer of backing (lining) fabric.

Italian quilting: running stitches are worked in two parallel lines through a layer of top ground fabric and a layer of thin backing (lining) fabric, possibly of butter muslin. From the back, a thicker cord or thread is then threaded through the butter muslin and along the tramways produced by the two parallel lines of running stitch. This results in a finished item with relief outlining of the design motifs.

Trapunto: like Italian quilting, this is worked with running stitch taken through only two layers of fabric, the upper ground layer and a layer of thin backing (lining), possibly of butter muslin. But with trapunto only one line of running stitches is worked around the edge of the motifs. The whole is then padded, from the back, with small wads of cotton or other padding pushed through the butter-muslin lining.

When referring to American quilting today one invariably thinks of the bed-cover quilt, usually of cotton, worked in English quilting. A full-size bed quilt is normally worked on a frame, with one or two horizontal rollers holding it in place and exposing only the part of the design currently being worked. The layers of fabric (upper ground, inner

wadding and under lining) are first basted with large running stitches, and then the design is worked with small running stitches.

Sometimes the top layer of ground fabric is decorated with appliqué before being quilted. Motifs, usually of cotton, are applied to the ground fabric. Some of the most striking American quilts are those worked with symmetrical one-colour applied designs worked in a similar way to Hawaiian designs.

Alternatively, instead of superimposing motifs on the top layer of ground fabric, an entire ground fabric can, before quilting, be constructed from patchwork.

Patching, or piecing, can legitimately be considered embroidery when there is subsequent stitched decoration either with running stitches of quilting or with some other embroidery.

Patchwork in North America dates back to the settlers of the early 17th century. Because of the paucity and irregularity of supplies of ground fabric, resourceful women used and re-used the garments they had to hand. Old clothes were cut up and pieced together in patchwork.

Card templates were cut to the required sizes and shapes. A patch was made by basting a piece of fabric, with turnings, over the card. Two patches were sewn together with oversewing on the wrong sides of the patches. Different template shapes produced a variety of patchwork patterns.

A terminology of patched quilt designs evolved. Many of the names were

Pineapple design is a variation of log cabin, one of the most popular forms of American patchwork. The fabric strips are built up from the centre and stitched to a ground fabric.

Crazy patchwork is a form of appliqué, with the shapes stitched to a ground fabric and edged with embroidery. This late-19th-century quilt is of embroidered silk, brocades and ribbon.

taken from American themes. The 'log cabin' design was built up of rectangular patchwork shapes of varying lengths. Working from the middle of a design, and using the shortest pieces of the puzzle first, a four-sided pattern was achieved that was reminiscent of the construction of log cabins. Variations of this pattern were developed. Other patchwork forms used in quilting included 'the road to Oklahoma' and 'house on the hill'.

During the 19th century there was a fashion for crazy or kaleidoscope quilting. This consisted of a ground fabric made from irregularly shaped patches sewn at random to form one piece. The outlining of each patch was often subsequently embroidered on the right side with lines of herringbone stitch or feather stitch worked in various colours.

Quilting can be a communal affair, with groups of women meeting for a quilting bee. Each participant works one piece of a quilt, decorating it with appliqué or with plain embroidery. Each section is then pieced to the others and the whole is quilted. A friendship quilt, worked by many women in this way, is presented to its recipient by the makers. Communal quilting today produces items for friendship and for commemorative purposes.

'Stained Glass' Quilt

The quilting technique used on this baby's coverlet is of Mormon origin and has become very popular throughout the United States. It differs from other patchwork quilts in that it requires no padding and no actual quilting stitches are used. It is constructed from folded and stitched calico squares which are folded and sewn together to form an almost three-dimensional lattice pattern. Into this are sewn small patches of coloured or patterned fabric giving a cathedral window effect, after which the design is sometimes named.

You will need:
2.1 m (2¼ yd) unbleached calico 90 cm (36 in) wide
58 squares of plain coloured or patterned cotton fabric with 6.25 cm (2½ in) sides
needle
white cotton

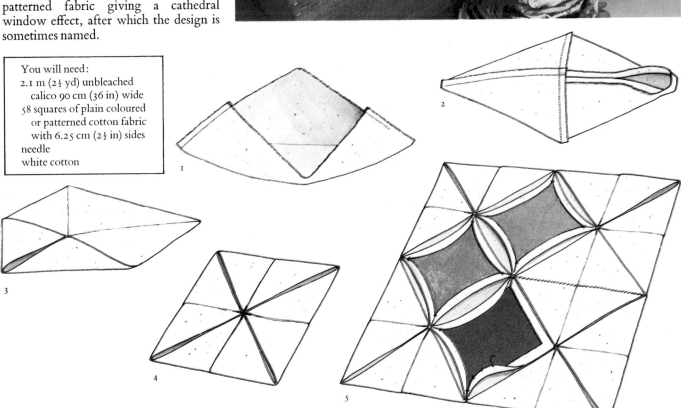

Preparing the Fabric
Shrink the calico by washing and ironing it and cut out 35 squares with sides measuring 22.5 cm (9 in). Use a card template to ensure accuracy (see page 272).

Fold one of the calico squares in half and sew in running stitch along the two short sides taking 6 mm (¼ in) turnings (diagram 1).

Take hold of the middle of each of the unsewn edges and pull them apart so that the two seams meet. Sew right across the unsewn edges, leaving a 5 cm (2 in) gap at one end (diagram 2).

Pull the rectangle inside out through the unsewn corner and press it flat. You now have a square with sides 14 cm (5½ in) long (diagram 3).

Turn it over, fold the corners in to the centre, and catch them together securely with a few stitches (diagram 4). Make 34 more calico squares in the same way.

Patchwork
Hold two calico squares together, the folded edges facing, and oversew them along one edge. Join a second pair of squares in the same way and then join both pairs of squares to make a larger square shape. Look at it carefully and you will see four diamond shapes inside this large square.

Pin a piece of cotton fabric onto each diamond. Fold the edges of the calico diamond shapes over those of the coloured fabric pieces and hem them down. Stitch adjacent folded edges together at each corner (diagram 5).

Build up the coverlet by attaching more squares of folded calico to the original four and fill the resulting diamond shapes with cotton pieces. Make it as large as you wish: this one is 5 squares by 7. The pattern leaves a row of plain calico triangles along each edge.

Needlepoint

Needlepoint can be used like painting when tent stitch is worked on a fine canvas. This piece, taken from a 16th-century Moghul painting, is worked in French silk and metal thread.

Another continuing North American stitchery field is that of needlepoint. Although needlepoint also refers to a type of needle-made lace, the term is used in North America, and increasingly elsewhere, for canvas-work embroidery, occasionally erroneously called tapestry.

Needlepoint is a counted-thread embroidery usually worked on a canvas of linen, cotton or wool. In the 19th century a wire canvas was sometimes used, and recently polyester fibre and plastic versions have become popular. The canvas has either single warp and weft threads (mono canvas) or two warp and weft threads woven together (Penelope canvas). The canvas forms a framework and the embroidery yarn is worked through the holes of the mesh.

Early North American settlers brought with them some of the needlepoint pictures that were popular with 17th-century European embroiderers. They were worked on a ground of single-weave canvas of linen or cotton. The yarn used was cotton, wool or silk and the main stitches were tent stitch and half-cross stitch, then known as petit point and gros point respectively.

In the first few decades of settlement North American women did not have much time for working any embroidery that was not functional. This is why hardly any examples of early North American needlepoint survive. The few existing pieces include chair covers, carpets, bell-pulls and other useful household items.

One exception to the functional character of early North American needlepoint is the 'fishing lady' or 'Boston Common' series. During the 18th century a few American embroiderers took designs for pictorial embroideries from contemporary engravings, and as a result many of the same themes appeared again and again, worked by different embroiderers. At least sixty-five variants of the 'fishing lady' have been recorded. Each of the pictures showed at least one lady fishing and a view of Boston Common in the background. The embroideries were worked in silks and wools on a ground of fine mesh canvas. Tent stitch was often used.

By the middle of the 19th century more North American ladies had time

Trammed gros point.

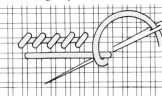

Rice stitch.

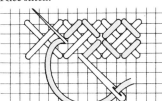

Parisian stitch.

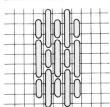

Horizontal tent stitch.

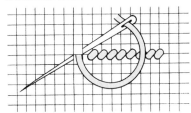

Vertical tent stitch.

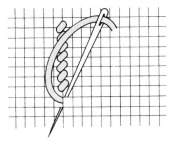

Diagonal tent stitch (A and B) has a basketweave effect on the reverse side (C).

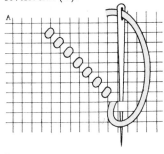

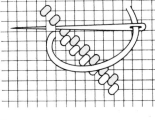

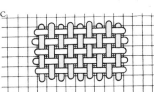

Early-19th-century needlepoint carpet from New Orleans.

to produce non-functional needlepoint. Many of them were enthusiastic Berlin woolwork embroiderers. The Berlin woolwork craze lasted in North America from about 1820 to 1880.

Today needlepoint in general enjoys the largest following of any American embroidery. There are national organizations devoted purely to needlepoint and its variants such as Florentine or bargello. Needlepoint is still worked primarily by women, but an increasing number of American men are enthusiastic needle-pointers. The geometry of fitting a pattern onto the canvas graph seems to make it particularly attractive to men of all ages and temperaments.

The main needlepoint stitches in use today include all forms of tent stitch (basketweave or diagonal tent stitch, horizontal tent stitch and vertical tent stitch), cross stitch, double cross stitch, long-legged or long-armed cross stitch, rice stitch, eyelet stitch, gobelin stitch, brick stitch and parisian stitch.

Needlepoint today is generally worked on canvas with a thread count of 10 to 18 to 2.5 cm (1 in). The most versatile thread is the all-wool three-strand 'persian' or crewel yarn; however, a good many man-made fibres are also used.

When working needlepoint, a blunt embroidery needle is used in order not to pierce the threads of the ground canvas. Since pulling the embroidery yarn in one direction through the canvas can lead to distortion in a finished work, this may be counteracted by working needlepoint on a frame.

Needlepoint can be given extra depth by tramming. This entails taking long running stitches across the canvas, parallel to the weft. Subsequent stitching is then worked over the trammed thread and the canvas thread.

Patterns taken from a woven 19th-century Navajo blanket and an Alaskan Indian basketwork border combine to make a shoulder bag and coin purse in colours matching the original natural cream and the blue and red produced by indigo and cochineal dyes.

Indian Needlepoint Bag

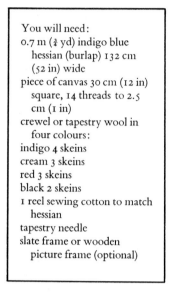

You will need:
0.7 m (¾ yd) indigo blue
   hessian (burlap) 132 cm
   (52 in) wide
piece of canvas 30 cm (12 in)
   square, 14 threads to 2.5
   cm (1 in)
crewel or tapestry wool in
   four colours:
indigo 4 skeins
cream 3 skeins
red 3 skeins
black 2 skeins
1 reel sewing cotton to match
   hessian
tapestry needle
slate frame or wooden
   picture frame (optional)

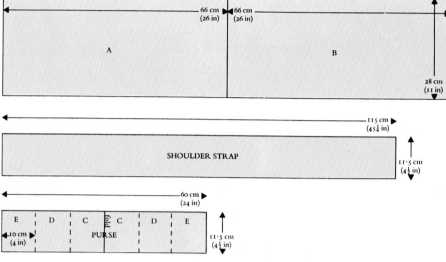

Preparing the Canvas

Embroidery is worked on one side of the bag only. Cut the canvas in half down the middle and set one piece aside for the purse.

Make a full-size drawing of the pattern 25 cm (9¾ in) across, lay the canvas over it, and trace off the design with a fine felt-tipped pen.

Bind the edges of the canvas to prevent fraying and pin it to the frame. The canvas should be taut, with the threads running parallel to the edge of the frame.

Embroidery

Work in tent stitch, starting with the central zigzag motif. Keep the tension even and cover the canvas ground completely. Three strands of crewel wool should be sufficient to cover it.

Work the band for the purse on a canvas strip 13 x 5 cm (5 x 2 in). The actual embroidery should measure 9 x 2 cm (3½ x ¾ in).

Making the Bag

Cut out the hessian (burlap) according to the pattern layout, withdrawing threads to make cutting lines. Oversew all edges to prevent fraying .

Trim round the needlepoint band leaving a canvas border approx. 1.5 cm (⅝ in) wide.

Lay the needlepoint band face up on the wrong side of panel A, 25 cm (10 in) up from the bottom.

Fold the upper section of the hessian

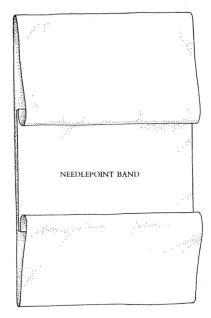

NEEDLEPOINT BAND

The completed needlepoint band is placed on the hessian which is folded over to enclose the raw edges of the canvas.

The back section of the bag is doubled over to form a lining and to make a neat finish to the seams inside the bag.

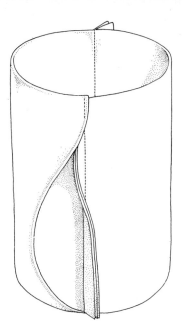

over to meet the band, turn in the raw edge 1.5 cm ($\frac{5}{8}$ in) and slipstitch it to the edge of the needlepoint (see diagram). Repeat this with the section of hessian below the band and press the folds.

Work a row of black stem stitch across the hessian 1 cm ($\frac{3}{8}$ in) above the band, and two rows 3 mm and 12 mm ($\frac{1}{8}$ and $\frac{1}{2}$ in) below it.

Lay section A on section B, right sides together so that three edges meet and the extra area of section B protrudes at the top. Stitch them together down the sides, stitching through all layers.

Fold section B back on itself to match A. Turn in the edges, and slipstitch them to the machine stitching to hide the seams.

Turn the bag right side out and machine across the bottom approx 4 cm (1$\frac{1}{2}$ in) below the band. Disguise the stitching with a line of stem stitch and withdraw the fabric threads to make a fringe below it.

Oversew the raw edges of the shoulder strap. Fold it in half lengthwise, right sides together, and stitch the seam. Turn it right side out and press.

Sew the strap to the top of the bag, giving an overlap of approx. 8 cm (3 in) each side to make a fringe.

Making the Purse

Fold the strip as shown, right sides together, and stitch the side seams, tapering them in section E. Turn it right side out and press. If you wish to stiffen the purse, slip a strip of canvas between the two layers.

Turn in and slipstitch the raw edges. Cover the stitching with a line of stem stitch.

Fold section C against section D and join the seams with black faggoting.

Back the needlepoint band with hessian and oversew it firmly in position.

Scandinavia

Cross stitch is one of the most popular Scandinavian stitches. These wild flowers are from Denmark.

Making a broad interpretation of the term Scandinavia, this chapter is concerned with the embroidery of Denmark, Norway, Sweden and Finland. It includes the embroidery of Lappland, in the north of the region and straddling the last three countries, and also of the North Atlantic islands of Iceland, which was at one time a Danish possession, and Greenland, which still is. Embroidery has been a traditional craft throughout Scandinavia for many centuries and has usually been worked by women in their own homes.

A high percentage of the population have always been farmers with a high degree of self-sufficiency, growing their own food and the raw materials from which to make their own clothing. Most farms had enough sheep to provide all the wool that a family required, and most of them also grew flax from which to make linen. Each year, generally after Christmas, the farmer's wife and daughters would spin linen thread.

Linen fabric was often left in its natural colour. Woollen fabric was dyed with vegetable dyes, among them cudbear, a compound extracted from lichens that grow throughout Norway and Sweden, which produced a shade of purple that was peculiar to the region. Flax is still farmed commercially in Denmark, and there is intensive sheep farming in western Norway, eastern Sweden and areas of Greenland, Iceland and Finland. Scandinavia is too far north for cotton growing and the little cotton that is used for embroidery is imported, in either thread or woven form. Silk thread and velvet fabric have also to be imported, usually from France or Italy.

The peoples of Scandinavia have enjoyed a great deal of political and cultural interaction and it is therefore not surprising to find the same embroidery techniques and stitches throughout the region. Pulled- and drawn-thread work, and also whitework, which are discussed in detail in the section on Denmark, are not restricted to one particular country or area.

Cross stitch is frequently seen in embroideries, designs of flowers being particularly popular in Denmark. 'Danish cross stitch' is practised in many other parts of the world.

The other main stitches employed in Scandinavian embroidery are back stitch, chain stitch (either tamboured or worked with a needle), running and double running stitch, satin stitch (known in some forms of Scandinavian embroidery as *kløster* stitch) and stem stitch.

Design motifs also cross national barriers, and there are some which may be thought of as typically Scandinavian. They include the square shaping found in blocks of hardanger, Amager and other drawn-thread embroideries; the geometric shapes of pulled- and drawn-thread works, and floral designs ranging from the recognizable flower devices of Danish cross stitch to the imaginative sprays of hedebo. Pictorial themes include earth mother motifs from central Sweden and Finland and religious devices on early Icelandic wall hangings.

Costume embroidery is found mainly on items of women's national dress which has changed little over the last three centuries. The only typical items of men's clothing that are decorated with stitching are the outfits of the Eskimo of Greenland and of the Lapps.

Other embroideries include household table linen, and wall hangings and cushion covers.

Many of the wall hangings of the past were *tjells*, elongated rectangular pieces of linen ground fabric decorated with embroidery. Cushion covers for the passenger seats of horse-drawn carriages were worked either for the embroiderers themselves or as special commissions. Some of the most beautiful examples, embroidered in wool or imported silk thread on a ground of mixed local wool and linen fabric, were worked in Götaland in the years between the mid-18th and mid-19th centuries.

Today the most popular forms of Scandinavian embroidery are cross-stitch work, hardanger and other drawn-thread embroideries, hedebo and pulled-thread work. Whitework embroidery is still practised throughout the region, and so is embroidery worked in one colour thread on a contrasting ground fabric. Blue thread on a white ground fabric is a much-used colour scheme. Appliqué, which was in the past worked particularly in Greenland, Iceland, parts of Sweden and Lappland, is also now popular in Scandinavia generally.

Embroidered carriage seat covers were worked in Götaland, southern Sweden, in the late 18th and early 19th centuries. This 'Adam and Eve' design, a popular theme, was worked in the region of Skåne in 1814.

Charming floral border decorating a woollen skirt from southern Iceland. The embroidery, stem stitch worked in multi-coloured wools, was executed in 1806 by Gudrun Sküladottír, who was renowned for her skill.

Greenland

Typical petalled flower motif sometimes worked as appliqué on women's hooded tunics.

As part of their traditional costume Greenland Eskimo girls wear leather boots over long stockings edged with bands of embroidery and lace.

A link between the embroideries of North America and Scandinavia is provided by Greenland. The majority of Greenlanders today are of mixed Eskimo and European descent. It is thought that the Eskimo people crossed to northern Greenland from North America. The few remaining pure-blood Eskimos live in the more northerly part of the island and it is they who still work embroidery similar to that of the North American Eskimos.

The Greenlanders raise some sheep in the more southerly parts of their region and hunt seal, arctic fox and polar bear. Keeping warm is a major consideration in Greenland, and clothing is made from woollen felt or from animal or seal skin. Even in summer both men and women wear fur trousers, but over them they wear parka-type tunics of heavy white cotton fabric, often imported from Venezuela. In winter the cotton tunic is replaced by, or worn underneath, a heavy fur coat.

The tunics are knee-length in front and slightly longer at the back. They are slit almost to the waist at either side and two

bands of a bright-coloured plain cotton fabric, each about 2.5 cm (1 in) wide, are sewn one above the other round the hem. The bands are applied to the ground fabric with hemming and are sometimes embroidered. The tunics have inset sleeves and a hood of the same fabric. Round the hood is an applied band of black cotton fabric, hemmed down. Embroidery is sometimes worked on the applied band in repeating motif designs, like a flower with five petals worked in concentric lines of chain stitch and with an eyelet wheel for the centre.

With this summer outfit Greenland Eskimos wear leather boots over lace-edged long stockings which extend over the bottom of the fur trousers. Between the lace and the stocking is a 5 cm (2 in) wide band of cotton fabric embroidered with bright-coloured silks in herringbone stitch worked in lines, and in straight stitch sometimes worked in stars.

Although no longer as plentiful as it once was, Greenland Eskimo embroidery is still sometimes worked by women for their own families' use. It is not produced commercially.

Iceland

The original settlers in Iceland were northern Europeans, mostly Vikings from Norway with some Celtic peoples from the British Isles who arrived from the 9th century onwards. Christianity was adopted in Iceland in the year 1000 and the country remained Catholic until 1550 when the last bishop, Jon Arason of Holar, was executed. Until this date Icelandic embroidery was almost exclusively religious.

Icelandic Catholic Church embroideries included frontals, altar cloths, chasubles, burses and chalice veils. They were often worked in local woollen yarn by professional women embroiderers. The yarns were either left their natural colour or dyed in soft blues, pinks and greens with lichen and other vegetable dyestuff. The ground was either local woollen fabric

Three bishops feature on this famous 15th-century church frontal from Holar, in the north.

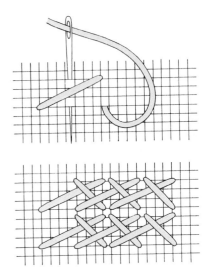

The horse and rider (below) are worked in horizontal lines of closely placed long-legged cross stitch (above) in woollen thread on a woollen ground so that the fabric is completely hidden.

or imported linen. Silk and velvet were occasionally used as ground fabrics, but these were expensive.

The medieval Icelandic embroiderers worked in five main forms of stitching. The first, *refilsaumur*, consisted of design motifs infilled with couching which was worked over a layer of satin stitches and executed in close parallel formation. The completed motifs were sometimes outlined with chain stitch, split stitch or stem stitch. *Refilsaumur* was generally executed on a ground of imported linen but local wool might be used instead.

Skorningur, appliqué, first mentioned in records dating back to 1394, was also popular with Icelandic embroiderers. Pieces of gilt leather, wool, linen or silk fabric were applied to the ground with

Pattern darning, one of the most popular Icelandic techniques, produces a woven effect on this piece of Church embroidery.

hemming in white linen thread.

Glitsaumur, pattern darning, sometimes known simply as *glit*, was used in parallel lines of horizontal stitching, and *krossaumur*, cross stitch, was generally worked in its long-legged form. It, too, was often executed in horizontal lines.

The most unusual Icelandic embroidery technique was *augnasaumur*, eye stitch. It was worked all over the ground fabric in repeating form. Each eye of *augnasaumur* generally made a square, with sixteen stitches to each hub of the eye. Occasionally lozenge-shaped eyes

were worked, with only twelve radial stitches to each hub. Eyelet stitching was also used for designs like the *attabladaros*, an eight-pointed star, which was later to be particularly popular in 18th- and 19th-century Icelandic folk art.

One of the distinguishing factors in Icelandic Church embroidery was the dominance of circles, or roundels, hexagons and octagons in many of the designs. These shapes would be worked as borders round individual motifs, or as sub-plots of a complex design. It is thought that the predilection for outlining the motifs may

All-over eyelet stitching is an Icelandic speciality. As many as sixteen stitches are worked through the same point to produce an eyelet hole. Eyelet stitching is combined with cross stitch in the early 19th-century wall hanging (right) but used alone on the cushion cover (below).

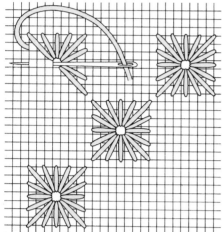

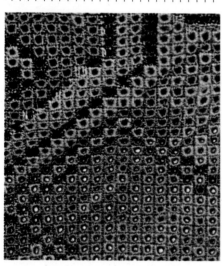

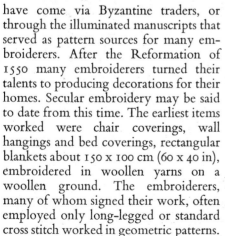

have come via Byzantine traders, or through the illuminated manuscripts that served as pattern sources for many embroiderers. After the Reformation of 1550 many embroiderers turned their talents to producing decorations for their homes. Secular embroidery may be said to date from this time. The earliest items worked were chair coverings, wall hangings and bed coverings, rectangular blankets about 150 x 100 cm (60 x 40 in), embroidered in woollen yarns on a woollen ground. The embroiderers, many of whom signed their work, often employed only long-legged or standard cross stitch worked in geometric patterns.

Floral designs were popular from the end of the 17th to the end of the 18th century. Motifs were executed in split stitch and patterns were taken from illuminated manuscripts or copied from embroidered items brought from Denmark.

Icelandic women's national dress has many variations, some of which have embroidered decoration. The main festive costume, which stems from a design executed in the 1860s by a local artist, Sigurður Gúomondsson, was quickly adopted as a national costume. It comprises a black woollen jacket with long tight-fitting sleeves worn over a full-length black woollen skirt that has wool or silk satin-stitch embroidery round the hem. The front opening, neckline and cuffs of the jacket are trimmed with black velvet and embroidered with silver or gilt thread, which is manufactured locally. The main stitch employed is satin stitch worked in close parallel blocks. Sometimes the satin stitch is given a three-dimensional effect by padding. The metal thread is laid in zigzag formation over a wadding of card and subsequently couched. Other stitches

used for embroidery on women's bodices include bullion knots and single straight lines of laid and couched work.

The designs on the long-sleeved bodice, and also on a sleeveless variation of the costume, are usually floral, comprising simple petalled motifs with pointed leaves and curved stems. The effect of the metal-thread embroidery on a ground of black woollen fabric, which might otherwise seem a little heavy, is balanced by drawn- or pulled-thread work stitched in horizontal bands on a long white linen apron.

Today traditional costume is worn in Iceland only on festive occasions, but the women still work embroidery for their own families' use. They decorate table linen, blouses and other costume items and wall hangings, using many patterns and stitches from elsewhere in Scandinavia.

Denmark

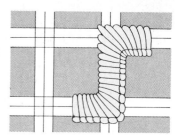

Festooning. After withdrawing threads buttonhole stitch is worked closely in step formation over the grid of remaining threads. To give extra bulk the buttonhole stitch may be worked over laid running stitches.

The three most important styles of Scandinavian embroidery—drawn-thread work, pulled-thread work and whitework—are practised throughout the region and cannot by any means be attributed to Denmark alone.

Pulled-thread Work

As its name implies, in this kind of embroidery the stitches are pulled very tight as they are worked, resulting in a lacy effect as the fabric threads are drawn together. It is worked with a blunt needle so as not to pierce the threads of the ground fabric, which is usually linen with a single-thread loose weave or an evenly woven fabric with easily counted threads. It is not necessary to work pulled-thread embroidery on a frame, although some embroiderers prefer to do so.

Pulled-thread work is a form of counted-thread embroidery and design motifs are frequently geometric. Outlines of devices can be worked in any suitable stitches such as four-sided stitch, punch stitch, ringed back stitch, satin stitch, three-sided stitch and so forth. The motifs may then be infilled with a variety of pulled filling stitches, including honeycomb stitch and wave stitch.

Drawn-thread Work

In this popular kind of embroidery some of the warp and weft threads are actually withdrawn from a ground fabric of loose-weave linen or other suitable fabric. In some cases, entire lengths of thread are carefully extracted from the ground fabric with a needle before any embroidery is worked, giving a web of single threads in the warp or the weft. Where threads are removed in both directions a void is created where they once crossed.

The resulting areas of exposed threads can be worked over in a number of ways. They may be secured with double hem stitch, interlaced hem stitch, ladder hem stitch, pin stitch, zigzag hem stitch or any similar stitch that is worked on a mesh ground. Sometimes two or more exposed threads are bound together with overcast

Black velvet caps richly decorated with metallic threads and spangles were worn by Zealand women in the 19th century.

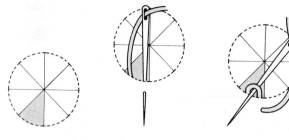

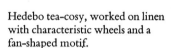

Hedebo buttonhole stitch. The motif is outlined with small running stitches. A series of cuts is then made inside it. One segment of this 'wheel' is turned back at a time and hedebo buttonhole stitch, in which the needle passes behind the loop of the last stitch giving an extra twist to the knot, is worked over the fold to hold it down. When all the segments have been turned back loose threads of ground fabric are trimmed off from the back.

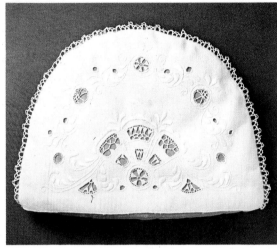

Hedebo tea-cosy, worked on linen with characteristic wheels and a fan-shaped motif.

bar stitch or needleweaving and sometimes they are festooned.

Drawn-thread embroidery has been worked in Scandinavia since the 17th century. It was at that time sometimes stitched with the ground fabric held taut on a birchbark frame and it was alternatively called 'birchbark embroidery'. Unless the bands are very narrow, it is impossible to do good drawn-thread work without having the fabric taut. Today it is held in a frame or basted over stout paper or architect's linen.

Whitework

Much of the embroidery of Scandinavia has in the past been worked in white threads on a white ground fabric. Some Scandinavian whitework embroidery is erroneously called 'Tønder work' after the city of Tønder in south-western Denmark, but in fact whitework has been practised in all parts of Scandinavia. Technically 'Tønder work' is a pillow lace, but in embroidery the term usually refers to 'Dresden work'.

The great era of Scandinavian whitework was from the late 17th to the early 19th century. Women embroidered on a ground of locally produced fine lawn, a semi-transparent linen cloth. The embroidery was worked with local white linen or imported white cotton thread. Whitework was executed in pulled-thread work or with buttonhole stitch and satin stitch. It was generally used for decorating women's sleeves, handkerchiefs, aprons and, from about 1790, as decoration on fichus, large shawls worn round the shoulders.

Whitework designs were usually floral and many of the motifs were similar to those found on bobbin laces. Scandinavian lacemakers took many of their designs from laces originating in Mechlin and other German towns, which is why Scandinavian whitework designs are similar to some German embroideries.

Hedebo

One of the most popular embroideries from Scandinavia is hedebo, which developed from ordinary drawn-thread embroidery, and which is named after heath lands south of Copenhagen (*hede* being the Danish for 'heath' and *bo* meaning 'to live').

In about 1760 the women living in the heath area near Copenhagen started to embroider on grounds of linen they had woven themselves from locally grown flax. They made up their own simple floral designs, sometimes adapted from carved and painted patterns on furniture in their homes, and outlined them with chain stitch. Infilling of motifs was done with geometric bands of drawn-thread work, in which lengths of warp and weft threads were carefully cut and removed with a needle, and the remaining threads held with needleweaving or bound with overcast stitching.

Early hedebo embroidery was worked on towels and pillowcases, and when a heath girl became engaged she embroidered a special nightgown for her own future use and also a shirt for her husband-to-be.

Not all hedebo work is whitework as this 19th-century wagon seat cushion worked in brightly coloured wools demonstrates.

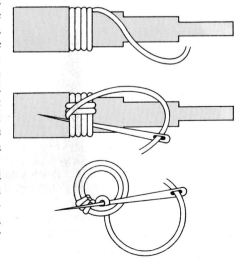

A hedebo 'ring' is formed with the help of a stepped gauge or stiletto (below). The thread is wrapped round the required width of the gauge several times and then secured with one or two over-stitches. The 'ring' is then slipped off the gauge and the threads worked over with hedebo buttonhole stitch. A finished 'ring' is set inside a worked hole of ground fabric and held in place by long straight stitches which are themselves then worked with hedebo buttonhole stitch.

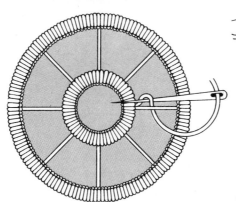

Three-sided stitch.

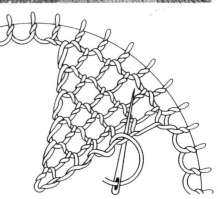

The 'pyramid' shape, worked in hedebo buttonhole stitch.

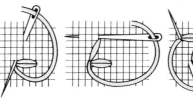

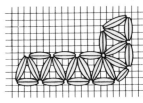

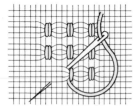

Punch stitch.

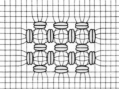

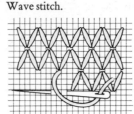

Wave stitch.

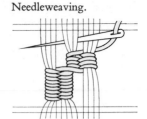

Needleweaving.

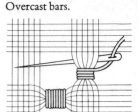

Overcast bars.

18th-century Amager sampler with stylized spot motifs of birds, trees and crowns worked in imported coloured silks on a ground of local linen.

By about 1840 actual cuts, rather than simply the withdrawal of certain threads, began to be used in hedebo embroidery. The appearance of the finished item was therefore much lighter than in earlier pieces. The trend towards a delicate design continued, and the form of hedebo embroidery as worked today was first apparent about 1850, at the same time as dealers began to export the embroidery throughout Europe.

Today hedebo embroidery is worked with natural-coloured two-stranded linen thread on a ground of single evenweave linen. It must be worked on a frame, preferably with a short length of thread to avoid knotting.

The outline of each device is marked with a circle of small running stitches. Radial slits are then cut to make a wheel and one section at a time is turned under. Embroidery is worked over the running stitch and over the turned-under section of the wheel and any untidy ends on the reverse are trimmed off when the embroidery is finished.

The main hedebo stitch is a variant of buttonhole stitch, with the needle passing behind the loop of the last stitch and through to the front, giving an extra twist to the buttonhole knot. Hedebo stitch, as it is universally known, is usually worked from left to right.

When a hole has been completely bordered by hedebo stitch, it may be divided into segments with long straight stitches of embroidery yarn stretched from one side of the hole to the other.

Several of these stitches are then bound together with hedebo stitch

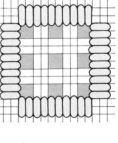

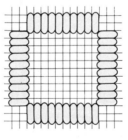

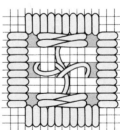

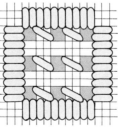

Amager drawn-thread work. First outline the motif with parallel satin stitches, usually worked over three or four threads. Two stitches should be worked into the same hole of the ground fabric when turning corners. Cut and withdraw the threads inside the motif as required. Bind the remaining threads with overcast stitching worked in one direction only. Subsequent decoration may be provided by needleweaving two blocks of the trellis or by working lace filling stitch over one of the interstices.

A typical lace filling stitch used to decorate the holes in drawn-thread work.

66

Pin stitch.	Hem stitch.	Ladder hem stitch.	Zigzag hem stitch.	Double hem stitch.

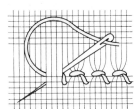 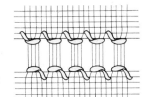 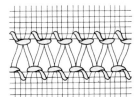 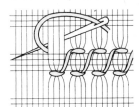

worked from one end of the bundle to the other to produce straight 'dividers'.

Circular 'dividers' can be made using a hedebo 'ring', formed on a short stepped rod (see page 64). The embroidery yarn is wrapped several times round the required width of the gauge and secured with a couple of over-stitches. The 'ring' is then slipped off the rod, and worked with hedebo stitch all round its circumference. The finished 'ring' is held in place in a spider's web of long straight stitches which are themselves then worked with hedebo stitch.

When a main hole has been partitioned, either with straight or circular 'dividers', each resulting small segment may be either left empty or infilled with hedebo stitch worked in lines forming pyramid shapes. Sometimes the infilling is so dense and intricate that the effect is that of lace.

Using the same method, leaf and other curved shapes can also be worked in hedebo embroidery. When all the cutwork is finished, surface embroidery is added to the ground, generally in the form of eyelet stitch and satin stitch. Flower stems were invariably worked in satin stitch.

It is this form of cutwork embroidery, with its emphasis on curvilinear cutwork and floral designs, that is now known as hedebo, not only in Denmark but throughout the world, and is generally worked for the embroiderer's own use, although in some periods of the 19th century hedebo embroidery was sold.

Amager

From 1760 to 1840 the women of Amager, an island near Copenhagen, were producing some of the most beautiful of any Scandinavian whitework embroideries. These were executed with linen thread on a ground of locally produced evenweave linen fabric.

Amager whitework, which is still worked in many parts of the world, is at the same time a form of drawn-thread embroidery. The outline of each device in a design is worked with blocks of satin stitches covering three or four threads of the ground. Two satin stitches are executed at right angles to each other at the corner of each motif, with both corner stitches worked through the same hole of the ground fabric. When the complete motif has been framed with satin stitches, some of the interior threads are cut close to the stitching and withdrawn in a regular pattern—perhaps alternately two threads withdrawn and two remaining. The resulting mesh is then decorated with needleweaving and lace filling stitch.

During the main peak of local Amager embroidery production at the beginning of the 19th century, embroiderers worked table and other household linens for their own use as well as for commercial purposes. Earlier they had also decorated cushion covers, usually working with imported silk thread on a ground of locally produced linen. Designs were sometimes copied from woven tapestries from Italy, Flanders or the Far East, or were stylized versions of local trees and plants. Because of its proximity to other parts of Europe, Amager was able to import embroidery materials more easily than some of the other Scandinavian regions. Silk thread was accessible, although expensive, and Amager needlewomen exercised economy when stitching with it. They would, for example, embroider a square scarf with two main designs in diagonally opposite corners. One design might be colourful and the other more subdued. When the scarf was folded diagonally, it accordingly served either a festive or a sombre occasion. The surrounding border embroidery accompanied both 'sides' of the scarf.

Amager silk-thread embroidery usually has floral motifs in chain stitch, cretan stitch, herringbone stitch and satin stitch. It is still worked today with commercial silk thread, but embroidered scarves, dirndl skirts and aprons, which are worn as regional costume on festive occasions only, are not generally executed. Amager embroiderers now work cushion covers and wall hangings, and most of their output is embroidered with woollen yarns on a ground of evenweave linen.

Danish cross-stitch floral motifs are sometimes worked in repeating formation like this modern leaf design.

Pulled-work Mats

You will need:
0.5 m (⅝ yd) white evenweave
    linen 140 cm (56 in) wide,
    10 threads to 1 cm (25
    threads to 1 in)
4 skeins white coton à broder
1 ball fine white crochet cotton
tapestry needle

Preparing the Fabric
Cut the fabric into four pieces 35 x 50 cm (14 x 20 in) and overcast all the raw edges with crochet cotton to avoid fraying.

Embroidery
Starting at one corner of one of the mats, measure 6 cm (2⅜ in) in from a short side and 4 cm (1⅝ in) in from a long side.

Using coton à broder work cross-stitch motifs parallel to the short side, starting at the point marked in the diagram. Work all the stitches of one type before starting another in order to keep the tension even. Work all the stitches over three threads in each direction and pull each tightly. Work the rows of cross stitch framing the motifs.

Leave 33 cm (13 in) along the long side of the mat and repeat the cross-stitch frame and then the motifs down the second short side.

Using crochet cotton work the triangles between the rows and motifs of cross stitch with four-sided stitch. Fill in the centres of the motifs with buttonhole-stitch stars.

Work all round the edges of the mat in squared edging stitch using coton à broder. (See description of stitch for turning the hem.)

Work the other mats in the same way.

Finishing
Trim all the raw edges as close as possible to the edging stitches.

Press the mats with a damp cloth, stretching them slightly.

Pulled-thread work is traditionally worked in a colour to match the ground fabric so that the pattern created by the pulled stitches shows more than the stitches themselves. However, the technique is effective if worked in a contrast thread—a typically Scandinavian scheme might be blue on a white ground.

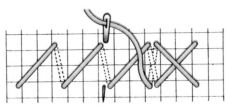

Cross stitch.
Sew a complete row of diagonal stitches from left to right, then work back along the row from right to left.

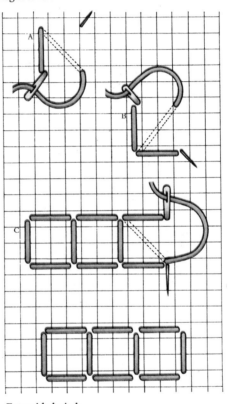

Four-sided stitch.
Each side of the square is worked over three threads. Start at the bottom left-hand corner and make the first stitch, A, taking the thread behind the fabric to the bottom right-hand corner. Make the second stitch along the bottom, B, bringing the thread out at the top right-hand corner. Make the third stitch along the top, C, bringing the thread out at the bottom right-hand corner. (There will be three diagonal stitches on the reverse side.) The fourth side of the square is filled by the first stitch of the square next to it.

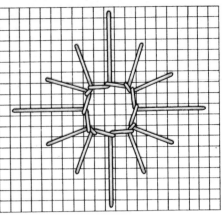

Buttonhole-stitch stars.
Fill the cross-stitch motifs with stars of buttonhole stitches of different lengths worked round in a circle in a clockwise direction. Pull the threads slightly to make a hole at the end of each stitch.

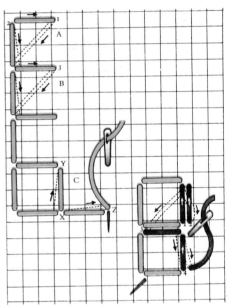

Squared edging stitch.
Leaving the hem allowance which will be turned in later, work a row of half four-sided stitches so that the closed side of the stitches lies on the hem line, A, B. At the corners, C, insert the needle at X, bring it out at Y, insert at X and bring it out at Z. Re-insert at X and bring out at Z to begin the next stitch.

Turn under the hem along one edge. Work a second row of half four-sided stitches through the double thickness and facing the opposite direction, D. Work all the vertical stitches twice to define the pulled holes and start the row four vertical stitches from the corner. Interrupt it the same number of stitches from the next corner, trim the fabric along the completed side, fold under the next side and continue.

Cross stitch.

Four-sided stitch.

Buttonhole-stitch stars.

Squared edging stitch.

The design on this table mat—the materials are given for a set of four—is worked in Danish pulled-thread work. The border could easily be translated to decorate a tablecloth or even the hem of a linen skirt.

Interlaced hem stitch.

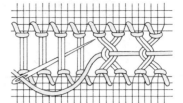 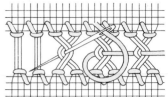

Norway

Like Denmark and the rest of Scandinavia, Norway has a strong tradition of pulled-thread work, drawn-thread work and whitework, and has also developed distinctive local styles.

Hardanger

Hardanger, precursor of many forms of whitework now being practised in other countries, came originally from the area around the Hardanger Fjord. It is a drawn-thread embroidery worked with white cotton or linen thread on a matching ground of double-weave linen. Blocks of parallel satin stitch, here especially called *kløster* stitch, are worked close together over four threads of the ground fabric, usually with five stitches to one block. As with Amager drawn-thread work, right-angle turns are executed with two corner stitches worked through the same hole of the ground.

Basic outlines of hardanger are thus made up by working right-angle designs, which can be extended by omitting four threads and continuing to work the next five threads before turning at right angles. When the stepped outline of a hardanger design is finished, the interior threads are cut as close as possible to the satin stitching. Threads that were originally left unworked are not cut. The cut threads are then carefully withdrawn, and the resulting mesh may be decorated in a variety of ways, perhaps overcast or interwoven with needleweaving and further embellished with picots. The interstices of the mesh may be infilled with lace filling stitch or built up with extra radial stitches to form a spider's web, which may in turn be decorated with overcast stitch or needleweaving.

The history of hardanger embroidery is not well documented, but the style has changed little since the end of the 18th century. At that time women in the Hardanger area were spinning their own flax and weaving it into double-weave linen which they embroidered and made into household linen, aprons and blouses.

Hardanger women's traditional dress consists of a red woollen sleeveless bodice worn over a white long-sleeved blouse with high collar and a full-length black woollen skirt with a mid-calf-length apron made of one width of white linen. Hardanger bands are embroidered round the cuffs of the blouse and also horizontally across the bottom and vertically up the sides of the apron. There may be an additional horizontal band of embroidery, perhaps as much as 30 cm (12 in) wide, a quarter of the way up the apron. The costume is worn with a cap of red wool edged with black velvet and outlined with beads. Motifs of linen and black velvet fabric, cut in star shapes, are applied to the ground with hemming stitches.

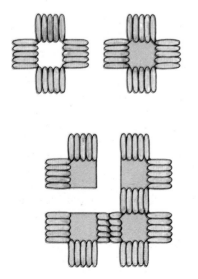 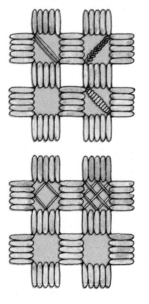 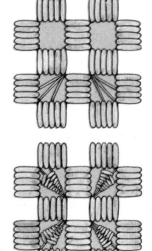

Traditional hardanger embroidery is worked with a natural-coloured thread and ground fabric combination. This modern example uses silk thread on a linen ground and the cutwork designs are surrounded by satin-stitch surface embroidery.

The finished effect of hardanger cutwork is similar to that of Amager drawn-thread work. Blocks of parallel satin stitches known as *kløster* blocks, usually with five stitches to a block and a double stitch in each corner, are worked round a square of threads which are then cut. The blocks are sometimes filled with needleweaving.

The Norwegian province of Telemark is famous for floral embroidery designs worked with polychrome wools on a plain woven ground. The sleeveless bodice (above) with deeply cut armholes is decorated with a typical satin-stitch motif.

Perhaps less typical is the asymmetrical design (right).

A cross-stitch motif taken from a linen mat worked completely in black cotton. The design is typical of the west coast of Norway around Trondheim.

Telemark

Telemark is famous both for its drawn-thread work and for its floral embroidery designs.

These are worked in bright-coloured wool thread on a ground of plain black or red woollen cloth or felt. Orange, purple and green are popular thread colours, and the predominating stitches are chain stitch, satin stitch and stem stitch.

Motifs are curvilinear and seem to flow from one spray of flowers to the next. The design is usually symmetrical, and blocks of satin stitch are carefully worked so as to separate quite distinctly one colour from the next. There is no 'voiding', as in oriental embroidery, where a thin line is sometimes left between colours.

Telemark embroiderers today work cushion covers and wall hangings, and also caps, bodices and other items for their regional costume. The designs show the floral motifs that have been worked for at least a hundred years.

From Telemark also comes a second, quite different style of embroidery in the form of drawn-thread work or other counted-thread embroidery worked in cross stitch, running stitch and double running stitch. These embroideries are generally made into traycloths and other household linens. Many of the designs are monochrome, executed in black or blue commercial silk threads on a ground of natural or white evenweave linen.

Telemark Bolero

This richly embroidered bolero will transform the plainest of dresses or add the finishing touch to a peasant-style blouse and skirt. The boldly swirling design, worked completely in satin stitch, can be embroidered in just an evening or two.

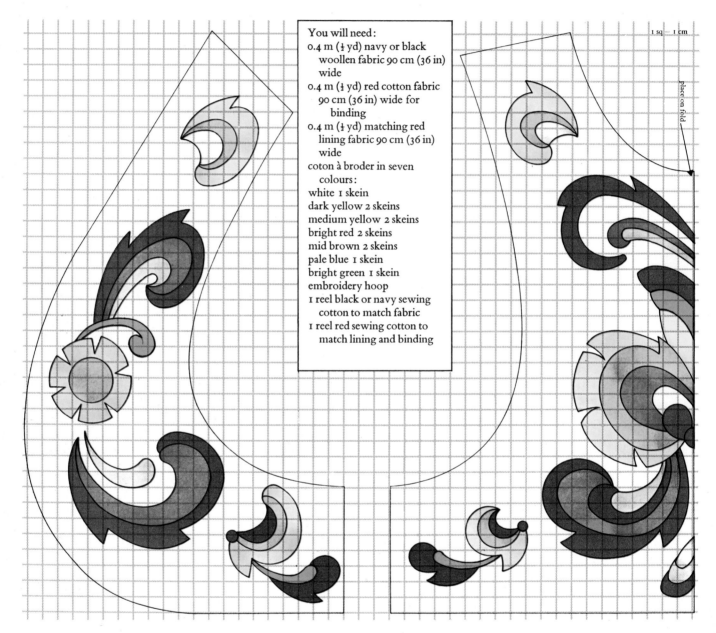

1 sq = 1 cm

place on fold

You will need:
0.4 m (½ yd) navy or black woollen fabric 90 cm (36 in) wide
0.4 m (½ yd) red cotton fabric 90 cm (36 in) wide for binding
0.4 m (½ yd) matching red lining fabric 90 cm (36 in) wide
coton à broder in seven colours:
white 1 skein
dark yellow 2 skeins
medium yellow 2 skeins
bright red 2 skeins
mid brown 2 skeins
pale blue 1 skein
bright green 1 skein
embroidery hoop
1 reel black or navy sewing cotton to match fabric
1 reel red sewing cotton to match lining and binding

Preparing the Fabric

Scale up the two pattern pieces and the embroidery design (see page 272), allowing 12 mm (½ in) for seams on the shoulders and at the sides only. Transfer the pattern outlines to the dark fabric. Open out the pieces and transfer the floral design, making sure to reverse it for left and right. Do not cut out the pieces yet.

Transfer the outlines only to the lining fabric and cut out the pieces.

Cut the binding fabric into bias strips 4 cm (1½ in) wide.

Embroidery

With the fabric still in one piece, mount the fabric in the hoop to keep the tension even. Work the design in satin stitch in the colours shown. Form the stitches so that they fan out from the centre of the motifs, spacing them closely on the inside edge of each curve.

Making the Bolero

Damp stretch the embroidery (see page 272).

Cut round the outlines of the bolero and join the shoulders and sides. Join the seams of the lining and press all the seams open.

Pin the lining to the bolero, wrong sides together, and pin and baste round all the edges.

Join several strips of binding and pin it round the outer and armhole edges, stretching it slightly. Stitch one edge to the right side of the bolero by machine, taking 6 mm (¼ in) turnings. Fold the opposite edge under for 6 mm (¼ in) and slipstitch the fold to the stitching line on the wrong side.

Press the finished bolero.

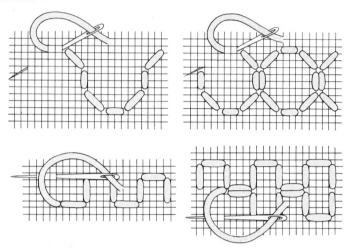

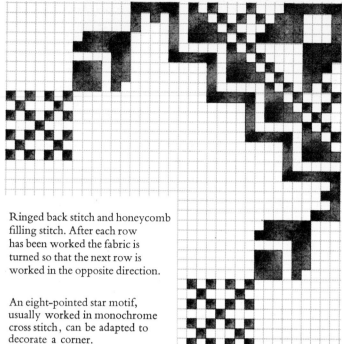

Ringed back stitch and honeycomb filling stitch. After each row has been worked the fabric is turned so that the next row is worked in the opposite direction.

An eight-pointed star motif, usually worked in monochrome cross stitch, can be adapted to decorate a corner.

Motifs, often symmetrical, may be based on star shapes, like a simple grouping of four small stars with antennae at each corner. The devices are worked either as spot motifs or as a repeating border pattern. Some of these border embroidery patterns are very complex and require concentration to execute, especially when worked in several colours.

Detail, worked in double running stitch, from the Hoyland 'tapestry' dating from about A.D. 1200.

Trøndelag

Trøndelag, the central region of Norway, is also known for floral embroidery designs worked in woollen threads on a ground of locally produced thick woollen fabric or imported velvet. Their colouring is more subdued than that of Telemark, and various shades of one colour are often worked next to one another. The finished appearance of the embroidery is sometimes heavier than that of areas further south.

Trøndelag embroidery is worked mainly in satin stitch with minor use of chain stitch, sometimes executed with single links (detached chain stitch), and straight stitch. Designs, which are usually symmetrical and worked in repeating form, are carefully aligned on the fabric.

In this region too, floral embroidery is used for costume items such as bodices, skirts, caps and belts, and also for cushion covers and hangings. Some hangings date from the 13th century and show religious themes worked on local linen with running stitches outlining the motifs.

Sweden

Although most of Sweden shares the embroidery traditions of the rest of Scandinavia, it also produces some distinctive and individual styles which come from the southern and central regions.

Götaland

Götaland, a province in southern Sweden, was in the past a centre of prolific production of flax and wool. Women spun and wove, and embroidered items for their own families' use and also for sale. Today wool and some flax are still farmed, but most embroidery materials are commercially produced.

Götaland is the home of many beautiful *tjell* wall hangings. They were often longer than the rectangular embroideries from other parts of Scandinavia, perhaps because many of the Götaland log cabins were also longer than other kinds of houses in Scandinavia.

Götaland wall hangings, which are not now usually worked in such exaggerated proportions, were generally executed in rose or blue linen or wool thread on a ground of local linen. The main stitching was chain stitch, cross stitch, hemming and satin stitch. Among the many popular spot-motif devices were birds, pomegranates and other fruits, and cross and wheel shapes. These last two motifs were

particularly associated with wall hangings from Halland, in the west.

Some of the embroidery styles and designs of Götaland are characteristic of one small part of the province. In general the most popular stitches continue to be cross stitch, pattern darning and the drawn-thread embroideries that have been worked by Götaland women for many centuries.

The region of Skåne is centred around the seaport of that name in the south-west of Götaland. It was Danish until

A 12th-century stitched wall hanging from a church in Skog in central Sweden. Early wall hangings, often worked in running stitch on a natural linen ground, usually had religious themes.

'Adam and Eve', executed on a 19th-century carriage seat cover from Skåne. The embroidery is worked in blocks of chain stitch, cross stitch and seeding on a wool and linen ground.

In Halland, in the west of Götaland, heart and wheel designs are particularly popular, either as spot or repeating motifs. They are traditionally worked in rose-coloured thread on a natural linen ground.

ceded to Sweden in the middle of the 17th century and many characteristics distinguish it from the rest of Sweden.

Skåne women have long been prolific needlewomen. One of the most popular stitches, still in use today, was cross stitch, which was often worked in linen thread on a linen ground in tulip, acorn and cone shapes. Motifs were frequently worked in neat, square compartments as borders for sheets, pillowcases and towels.

In the past Skåne embroiderers produced some of the most beautiful of all carriage seat covers. Christianity has always been important in Götaland and religious themes are evident in many of the covers embroidered between the middle of the 18th and the middle of the 19th century. These were sometimes embroidered in chain stitch, cross stitch and seeding on a ground of wool and linen fabric. Other motifs included lions and stars, and the embroiderer often dated her work, outlining the letters in running stitch.

Secular pictorial motifs have been worked by embroiderers in many areas of Götaland. Blekinge, on the east coast, gave its name to a form of embroidery with a design of local birds and flowers executed in satin stitch and stem stitch, usually worked with linen thread on a ground of linen. A distinguishing feature of all Blekinge embroidery was its colouring, with its preponderance of muted old rose, light blue and yellow on a natural ground.

Flax cultivation is still extensive in the Blekinge area and women continue to embroider prolifically. It is said that in the past many Blekinge women spun flax, wove it into linen fabric and embroidered items for sale in order to meet their taxes. They also continue a tradition of economical embroidery, for satin stitch is

Detail of an elaborate 18th-century whitework design from Sweden. The floral motifs are outlined with chain stitch and infilled with a wide variety of pulled-thread stitches.

usually worked in the one-sided economy form, and the overall design is less heavy than in other parts of Sweden, with more of the ground fabric between motifs left unworked.

Blekinge embroidery today, which is brighter than that of the past, is made into wall hangings, table napkins and similar items. It is generally worked either in satin stitch, with floral and bird designs the most popular themes, or in cross-stitch designs which often include hearts, flowers and birds.

Svealand

Svealand, the central area of Sweden, was once noted for intensive flax cultivation and for the spinning and weaving of linen. Much of the locally produced linen fabric was then embroidered, often in individual styles, since communication

Red and blue hearts and flowers (above) are recurring motifs in Swedish embroidery, often worked in Delsbo cross stitch (below).

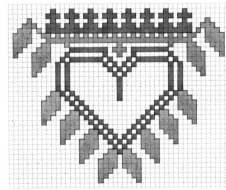

Järvsö cross-stitch motifs are sometimes decorated with small tassels to match the embroidery.

between parts of Svealand was usually limited.

One of the most famous embroidery centres today is Hudiksvall, in north-eastern Svealand. It is known for Delsbo work, a cross-stitch embroidery with stars and hearts worked in blue and red thread on natural or white linen. Delsbo embroidery is found on large tablecloths and cushion covers as well as on smaller items of costume such as collars and cuffs.

The history of early Delsbo work is not clear. Hudiksvall women were prolific and sociable embroiderers and they liked to take their work to one another's houses to embroider while they talked. Some of them designed as they embroidered, but others preferred to copy existing pieces of work. Cross stitch was the most popular stitch, but sometimes the Hudiksvall women worked one-sided satin stitch, which they called 'Delsbo stitch', which should not be confused with the term 'Delsbo work' that is used today.

Another Hudiksvall embroidery which is still practised is 'Järvsö' work. Like Delsbo work it is executed in cross stitch, but it is distinguished by the rose-coloured thread worked on a ground of white or natural linen. Sometimes there are little tassels of the thread hanging freely from the embroidered design, the motifs of which are similar to those of Delsbo work.

Cross stitching in Dalarna, a region in the centre of Svealand, is still worked the traditional way, in black cotton or linen thread on a white linen ground. It is known as *svartstickskläna*. Generally in repeating motif form, it sometimes has a little satin stitch incorporated into the design.

Satin stitch is also worked into some of the cross-stitch designs of Gävle, an important seaport and commercial centre on the east coast of Svealand. Gävle women have for many years embroidered blue, white and rose-coloured geometric motifs on a ground of locally produced linen fabric. Many of the designs, which are invariably geometric, are made up of repeating motifs. A popular device is a solid-looking eight-pointed star surrounded by a frame of cross stitches.

Suede Appliqué Bag

You will need:
0.7 m (¾ yd) firm linen fabric 90 cm (36 in) wide
0.9 m (1 yd) firm interfacing 90 cm (36 in) wide
0.9 m (1 yd) cotton gabardine 90 cm (36 in) wide
rubber-based fabric adhesive
leather pieces in two colours
sewing cotton to match linen and leather
1 skein coton à broder to match the linen
1.7 m (1⅞ yd) braid or even-weave linen 8 cm (3⅛ in) wide
firm card 40 x 8 cm (16 x 3⅛ in)

Preparing the Fabric

Make a scaled-up drawing of the complete design to 40 x 40 cm (15¾ x 15¾ in) — see page 272. Trace the motifs, make card templates for each one, and cut out the leather pieces.

Cut out the linen and overcast the edges to prevent fraying. Use carbon paper and the original drawing to mark the position of the leather motifs on the front of the bag.

Starting in the centre and working outwards, glue the leather pieces in place with small spots of adhesive before sewing round the edge with a medium-sized zigzag machine stitch.

Embroidery

Work the stitching in the centre of each of the leather motifs. Use the coton à broder and work in long straight stitches. If you are not using braid for the strap, work pattern darning on the evenweave linen.

Making the Bag

Use a 2 cm (¾ in) seam allowance throughout.

Cut out the cotton lining and interfacing. Baste the interfacing to the corresponding pieces of the bag, leaving the seam open 2 cm (¾ in) at each end. Stitch the side pieces to the front and back in the same way. Sew the short corner seams. Trim the interfacing close to the stitching and press all seams open.

Trim 2 cm (¾ in) from the top edge of both front and back interfacings and also from each long edge of the shoulder straps.

Turn a 2 cm (¾ in) hem round the top of the bag and sew it down with herring-bone stitch. Turn the bag right side out and glue the piece of card inside to form the base.

Make up the lining as for the bag. The side pieces will be twice as long, forming the shoulder strap. Press all seams open.

Without turning it right side out, fit the lining inside the bag. Turn in a 2.5 cm (1 in) hem and slipstitch the top of the lining to the bag.

Join the ends of the strap interfacings and then the ends of the strap linings. Snip the seam allowance of the lining on a level with the rim of the bag, fold it round the interfacing, and baste.

Pin and baste the embroidered even-weave linen or braid to the shoulder strap lining, taking it down the sides of the bag and onto the base. Turn in the raw edges.

Stitch the linen or braid to the strap by machine and to the sides and base by hand. Remove the basting and press.

Stitched motifs.

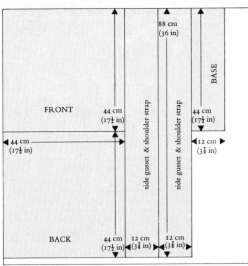

Pattern layout for lining and interfacing.

Pattern layout for bag.

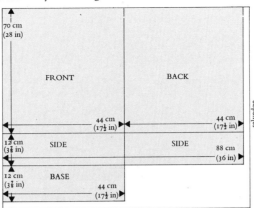

Embroidered suede-leather shapes of machine appliqué add striking decoration to a large shoulder bag useful for carrying books or shopping or even for weekends away. The stitched motifs give it a decidedly Scandinavian flavour. As an alternative to leather you could use felt.

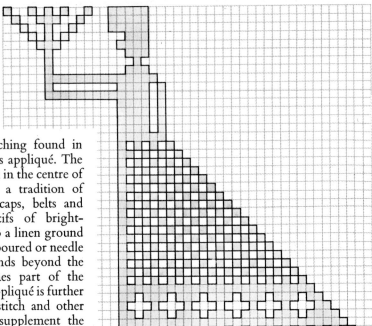

Another form of stitching found in some areas of Svealand is appliqué. The women of Floda, a parish in the centre of Dalarna province, have a tradition of working gloves, bags, caps, belts and other items with motifs of bright-coloured linen applied to a linen ground fabric with a line of tamboured or needle chain stitch which extends beyond the motif itself and becomes part of the design. Sometimes the appliqué is further embellished with satin stitch and other surface embroidery to supplement the chain-stitch decoration. Motifs are floral, and the density of appliqué and subsequent embroidery is such that little of the ground fabric is left without some form of decoration.

Floda appliqué has sometimes been executed for commercial purposes, but today much of the embroidery of the area is worked for home use.

Jämtland

Embroidery has been most widely practised in the southern parts of Sweden. The more central and northern areas have not enjoyed such extensive flax production, and consequently women have had fewer materials with which to embroider. Jämtland, north of Svealand, is one of the few areas in central Sweden which has given its name to a form of embroidery, which is traditionally worked in back stitch or cross stitch.

In the middle of the 18th century, farming of flax was specifically encouraged in the area and much of the embroidery dates from shortly after this time. It was then worked mainly as whitework, with white linen thread on a white ground, although coloured threads were used later.

One design particularly associated with Jämtland is the earth mother figure that is found in many embroideries of northern and eastern Europe. The Jämtland version sometimes has the earth mother wearing a full-length full skirt. She wears a large hat or crown and carries a branched candlestick or twig. Sometimes the motif is worked in repeating form, and sometimes the earth mother is accompanied by a dog.

The women of Jämtland still embroider many of the traditional designs on table and other household linens.

Typical cross-stitch floral motif from Bleckinge.

The Jämtland version of the earth mother with branched candlestick.

Leather bag decorated with felt motifs applied with double running stitch and subsequently decorated with satin stitch and buttons sewn on as spangles.

Lappland

Mostly lying within the Arctic Circle, Lappland is a region which straddles northern Norway, Sweden, Finland and extends into the extreme north-western part of the Soviet Union.

There are about a quarter of a million native Lapps today, although most have discontinued their traditional nomadic pursuits of fishing, herding reindeer and hunting elk. Reindeer were extensively used by the Lapps to provide food and clothing. Hides were made into coats, trousers and hats, but any kind of stitched decoration was rare.

The main form of Lapp stitched decoration was appliqué, used for decorating clothing as well as for making wall hangings to put inside the round tents of reindeer skin. Bright, plain-coloured strips of woollen cloth were applied to a ground of thick woollen fabric, often dyed a deep indigo. Woollen fabric, both for applied motifs and for the

Lapp men sometimes still wear traditional costume, their tunics and hats decorated with applied braids and bands of wool fabric.

Typical northern European motifs are these mating animals and earth mother figures from Lappland, worked in pattern darning.

ground, was usually bought commercially, although Lapps also have a tradition of weaving narrow widths of cloth which were then used for appliqué.

Lapp appliqué was worked by women for their own families' use, but little is being done today. Costume decoration in the form of stitching with tin or pewter bullion (purl), another traditional kind of Lapp embroidery, has all but disappeared too. Although the Lapps themselves do not now generally use it, a few embroidery shops in Scandinavia still stock the thread which is made of tin or pewter strips. These are heated and stretched through holes like knitting needle or spaghetti gauges to work them down to the desired diameter. The strip is then coiled round a central core of multi-stranded white thread. The threads used to be laid on a woollen ground and couched with cotton thread into floral and other curvilinear designs.

Finland

The embroidery of Finland has in some ways more in common with that of eastern Europe and the Soviet Union than with that of the rest of Scandinavia. Most Finns today are descended from the Finno-Ugric people who came from central Russia between 100 B.C. and A.D. 100. Some of them settled in what was to become Estonia and others displaced some of the nomadic Lapps in what is now Finland.

Much of the counted-thread embroidery worked by Finnish women for their own families' use is similar to that of the Archangel region and the Baltic states of the Soviet Union. Repeating designs of a plump-chested bird are seen in embroideries from all these areas, the Finnish version sometimes having a full tail display and plumes on the top of its head.

Finnish counted-thread work is executed in cross stitch, running stitch and double running stitch on a ground of evenweave linen, imported from Denmark or the Soviet Union. The ground fabric is often white and popular colours for embroidery thread are red and blue.

Finnish women once executed complicated whitework designs as costume

Finnish embroidery has much in common with that of the Soviet Union, as this detail from an 18th-century pillowcase shows.

Embroidery was often worked as costume decoration. This section of an 18th-century woollen winter apron from the Karelian Isthmus is richly decorated with bands of cross stitch and braiding.

decoration. They embroidered blouses, hats and aprons, often on a ground fabric of fine lawn, using continuous chain stitch, worked either with a tambour hook or with a needle, and satin stitch. Designs were flowing, with floral motifs, scrolls and curving leaves.

Whitework embroidery in Finland is now not as popular as counted-thread work. Today, however, both are still produced together with creative embroideries that demonstrate a high standard of design.

Birds, with full tail display and plumes on their heads, are popular counted-thread motifs.

Finnish Pouch Bag

You will need:
0.6 m (⅝ yd) silk or satin
   90 cm (36 in) wide
matching sewing cotton
3 skeins embroidery silk to
   tone
stiff card 14.75 cm (5⅞ in)
   square
2 m (2⅛ yd) thin cord

Preparing the Fabric
Cut out a rectangle 58 x 62.5 cm (23 x 25 in) and two 18 cm (7 in) squares. Mark the centre fold line across the width of the rectangle with basting.

   Scale up the design to 20.5 x 15 cm (8 x 6 in). Transfer it to the fabric (see page 272) in four repeats below the basting, allowing 12 mm (½ in) seams at each edge.

Embroidery
Work in chain stitch using three strands of thread. Damp stretch the embroidery.

Making the Bag
Fold the fabric in half lengthwise with right sides together and stitch the side seam. Trim the seam and press it open.

   Fold the fabric along the line of basting stitches, wrong sides together, and press. Sew two lines of machine stitching, 2 cm (¾ in) apart, 4 cm (1½ in) below the folded edge, to make a channel.

   Turn the bag right side out and fold it so that the seam is down the centre. Cutting through one thickness of the fabric only, make slits between the two lines of stitches on each side fold. Oversew the slits with double sewing cotton.

   Cut the cord in half. Thread in one piece from the right slit and join the ends securely. Slip the cord along the channel to hide the join. Repeat this from the left with the other piece of cord.

   Pin the squares of fabric right sides together and machine round three sides to make them exactly 15 cm (6 in) square. Trim the seams and corners, turn right side out and press. Slide in the card, turn in the raw edges and slipstitch.

   Turn the bag wrong side out and pin the base to it so that the seam comes at one corner. Taking a 6 mm (¼ in) turning on the bag, oversew it to the edge of the base using double sewing cotton and tiny stitches. Turn the bag right side out and draw up the cords.

1 sq = 1 cm

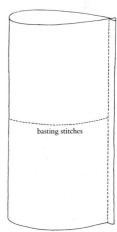

basting stitches

make slit here

seam

Western Europe

Much of western Europe has a strong embroidery tradition. One of the oldest embroideries of western Europe, and one of the most famous wall hangings of all time, is the late 11th-century Bayeux 'tapestry', a *tjell*-shaped embroidery that was probably on a larger scale than most of its contemporaries.

Early western European embroideries were usually executed with wool threads on a ground of local linen, often left undyed or bleached. Dyeing was carried out by a skilled dyer or by the embroiderers themselves using local plants. By the 17th century imported dyes such as cochineal, chips of fustic (*Chlorophora tinctoria*) and red brazilwood were commonly available.

The future of embroidery colours in Europe, and eventually the world, changed dramatically when, in 1856, an 18-year-old chemist, William Perkin, took out the patent for an aniline mauve which he had discovered while experimenting with the synthesis of quinine. Thereafter a whole range of chemical dyes became the norm and colouring was much brighter and less natural in appearance.

Apart from Andalusia in southern Spain and a small part of southern Italy, western Europe is too far north for cotton growing. Flax is grown now in north-east Ireland, Belgium, the Netherlands, Brittany, the Braganza area of Portugal and adjacent parts of northern Spain. Silk worms were clandestinely brought to Constantinople from China in the 6th century. Silk is now farmed in the Almería area of Spain, along the Rhône Valley, in the north-east of Sicily, in various coastal regions of Italy and especially along the Po valley. Sheep are raised extensively throughout the British Isles, the Iberian peninsula and Italy and to a lesser extent in most other western European areas. Wool output is not, however, sufficient to meet the needs of western Europe and much is imported.

The Church has been an important patron of embroidery since the 10th century. Church embroidery was at its peak from the middle of the 13th century until the middle of the 14th century, producing some of the most sophisticated and intricate work of western Europe. Church embroidery was generally worked by male professionals, crossed all frontiers of style and fashion and is, for this reason, not described here as part of the popular embroidery tradition of each country.

Typical European embroidery forms are whitework, blackwork, drawn fabric and cutwork. Tambouring, which involves producing a line of linked chain stitches with a hook, has also been an important technique for two hundred years. All kinds of European embroidery techniques were demonstrated by enthusiastic amateurs on test-piece samplers, the fashion for which began in the 17th century and spread throughout Europe, especially in the Netherlands, England, Germany and Spain, lasting until the beginning of the present century.

Regional costumes from many parts of western Europe were decorated with embroidery that was typical of the area, and in some instances, as in the case of Ayrshire whitework, an indigenous form of costume embroidery was exported or copied elsewhere. Embroidery motifs of western Europe are frequently floral, copying local species. Other recurring devices include eight-pointed stars, birds, trees in more or less stylized form, and the ubiquitous cone shape.

Many designs were copied from printed patterns. The first books of engravings were published in Germany and Italy in the first half of the 17th century and English and French publications appeared soon after. In the 19th century Berlin woolwork reached the height of popularity and as many as 14,000 different designs were printed within thirty years.

With the introduction of machines for weaving, lace making and embroidery came a decline in embroidery and other forms of hand stitched decoration which lasted from the mid-19th century until after World War II. Then came the great revival, with a strong trend towards simplification of traditional designs. Modern fabrics have also opened the door to new techniques, producing a fresh approach to traditional methods.

NORTH SEA

ATLANTIC OCEAN

Paisley •
• Edinburgh
AYRSHIRE

Carrickmacross •
• Dublin
Mountmellick •

British Isles

Coggeshall •
London •
DORSET

SAXONY
Berlin •

• MARKEN
Amsterdam •
Netherlands

Germany
Dresden •

Bonn •
Rhine

BAVARIA

Bayeux •
NORMANDY
• Paris

BRITTANY

France

Saône

Switzerland
ST GALLEN
VORARLBERG
TIROL

Vienna •

Austria

MADEIRA

BASQUE

Rhône

Lyon •

Po

Venice •

Bologna •

• Florence

Assisi •

Portugal

Braganza •

• Madrid
• Toledo

Spain

ANDALUSIA

Almeria •

SARDINIA

MEDITERRANEAN SEA

• Rome

Italy

Palermo •
SICILY

Tambouring (far left),
continuous chain stitch worked
with a hook, was an important
18th- and 19th-century European
technique originating in China.

Metal-thread work from Assisi
(left) laid and couched with silver
threads and embroidered with
silk stem stitch.

Sampler embroidery has always
been popular in north-western
Europe. In this 18th-century
Dutch example (right) a variety
of spot motifs are worked in
silk cross stitch on linen.

British Isles

The earliest known piece of English embroidery still in existence dates from the late 9th century. It is beautifully worked and clearly the result of a strong embroidery tradition, proving that the art must have been practised in the British Isles long before the Norman Conquest. Since then, many distinctive styles have been produced throughout the region. One such style, Opus Anglicanum or English work, was produced particularly from the middle of the 13th century to the end of the 14th century. Famous throughout western Europe, it was executed generally in workshops in London, by professional embroiderers, mostly men. Polychrome silks and metal threads were used, and the stitching was sometimes highlighted by seed pearls and semi-precious stones.

Orphreys, exquisite panels of gold needlework, were a common feature of ecclesiastical embroidery in medieval England. Thomas à Becket owned a set of robes made from them. The work was usually executed on rich silk or velvet ground fabric. This 15th-century panel depicts St Lawrence.

Items decorated with Opus Anglicanum were keenly sought after by monarchs and churches throughout Europe. Copes, chasubles and other vestments were embroidered with complex designs, often taken from the Old and New Testaments. Some designs were copied from contemporary miniatures.

Although production of Opus Anglicanum ceased in the London workshops at the time of the Black Death and the wars at the end of the 14th century, many exquisite copes and other items have survived, and are now in museum collections in Europe and America.

Amateur Techniques

Samplers were the traditional 'test-pieces' worked by women and young girls all over north-west Europe. The

The 14th-century Syon cope, a superb example of Opus Anglicanum. This detail depicts Christ and Mary in silk, silver and silver-gilt thread and uses split stitch and laid and couched work.

The earliest dated English sampler was made by Jane Bostocke who 'signed' it in 1598. She used silk, silver-gilt and gilt thread and an impressive variety of stitches, including algerian eye stitch, buttonhole stitch, two-sided italian stitch, ladder stitch, speckling, french knots and couching.

most prolific sampler workers lived in the Netherlands (see pages 92-93) but the art was also very popular in England. Early English samplers were executed in silk, silver-gilt and silver thread, and sometimes highlighted with pearls and beads, on a rectangular ground of linen. Back stitch, buttonhole stitch, chain stitch, cross stitch, ladder stitch, satin stitch and stem stitch were primarily used. Designs were both naturalistic, with flowers, fruit and animals worked in spot or repeating form, and geometric, with intertwined scrolls and zigzag formations.

In the 17th and 18th centuries white-work samplers were popular and in the 18th century intricately embroidered 'texts' were first incorporated into samplers, with homilies or biblical verses worked in minute detail, generally in cross stitch. From the early 19th century Berlin woolwork samplers became popular using wool threads, chenille, beads and ribbons worked on linen canvas ground fabrics in typical 'Berlin' stitches and patterns. (See pages 112-113.)

Few English samplers have been embroidered since the beginning of the 20th century, but early examples, now framed and glazed, have become increasingly popular with collectors.

Another technique popular with women amateur embroiderers, particularly from the beginning of the 16th century, was blackwork. Back stitch, braid stitch, buttonhole stitch, coral stitch, double running, or holbein, stitch and seeding, or speckling, were executed in black on white or bleached linen, and sometimes highlighted with silver-gilt and silver thread.

English blackwork is sometimes called 'Spanish work' (see page 101) since it is often assumed that it was introduced to England by Catherine of Aragon. It was in fact already known in England before she arrived in 1501.

From the early 17th century, crewel, or Jacobean, embroidery was particularly popular in England. It was worked by women for their own families' use, using ground fabrics of cotton and linen twill weave.

Typical stitches were stem stitch, long-and-short stitch, coral stitch, speckling and french knots, and designs took the form of repeating intertwined motifs, spot motifs such as flowers or animals, or pictorial motifs such as the tree of life.

An embroidery technique peculiar to the late 18th and the 19th century was needle-painting. Details of a design were painted in watercolour on a silk or cotton ground, and the main pattern was worked in silk or wool. Themes were romantic or floral and the finished pieces were purely decorative and not intended for use on clothing or domestic articles. In the late 19th century, amateur embroiderers turned to art needlework, a self-conscious term given to work executed

Idyllic hunting scene in crewel work (top) executed in coral stitch, stem stitch, long-and-short stitch, french knots and speckling. More peaceful floral themes and trees of life were also popular.

One of two prodigious needle-women, either Mary Queen of Scots or Bess of Hardwick, produced this handsome bed hanging (detail above), now at Hardwick Hall. Embroidery of this kind, worked with tent stitch or one of the many variants of cross stitch on a stiff linen canvas ground, came into particular prominence in the middle of the 16th century.

Characteristic Ayrshire whitework motif, worked with white cotton thread on a white cotton ground. Parallel flat satin stitches make up the leaves, padded satin stitches give body to the flower petals and the stems are worked with minute parallel satin stitches. Each flower centre is an eyelet hole.

French designs. These adaptations soon became popular with sewed-muslin producers. Pieces of cotton ground printed with outline designs, first with a wood block and later with a lithograph press, were delivered to the workers. Those pieces that were up to the manufacturers' high standards were collected from the out-workers and taken to a central depot, usually in Glasgow or Paisley, made up, washed, packed and sold throughout the British Isles or exported to Europe or America—an expanding market.

The decline of commercial Ayrshire whitework was signalled when the American Civil War interrupted the trade in cotton with the southern states. In addition machine embroidery had become feasible and this was soon taken up by manufacturers.

One of the drawbacks to Ayrshire-whitework production was the relatively high labour costs. In some instances the Glasgow manufacturers sent their agents to look for out-workers in Ireland where costs were lower. This led to other forms of whitework being established. The Scottish work was thus partly responsible for the evolution of the 'Irish flowering', the term sometimes used to describe the work of women who made various whitework embroideries with floral designs executed in cotton thread in tamboured chain stitch, satin stitch and knots on a ground of local linen. Although the greatest part of Irish-flowering embroidery was worked during the 19th century, some forms of the technique are still practised today.

Women throughout Ireland had been sewing for themselves for centuries, but as a result of potato famines in the first half of the 19th century, many embroiderers were prepared to work in their own homes for little remuneration.

Although the designs of Irish whitework were generally floral, distinctive styles developed in particular areas. Two of the most famous are Mountmellick and Carrickmacross work.

Mountmellick, a rural district of County Laois in central Ireland, has given its name to whitework characterized by designs worked in a soft unmercerized cotton sometimes known as 'knitting cotton' on a ground of white jean sateen, cotton with a shiny satin-like

to the designs of such eminent persons as William Morris and Burne-Jones. Pieces were also made commercially and were often used as firescreens, wall hangings, chair covers and so forth.

Ayrshire

Ayrshire whitework, known alternatively as 'sewed muslin' or 'Scottish flowering', takes its name from a county in south-west Scotland.

The embroidery was worked in fine cotton thread on a cotton ground with characteristic floral and scrolled designs executed in padded satin stitch and stem stitch and with fine needlepoint infilling or drawn-thread embroidery cut-out designs that were sometimes so intricate that they looked like fine lace.

Ayrshire whitework was used to decorate babies' christening and other robes, caps, ladies' dresses, cuffs, collars, shawls, petticoats and caps, and men's shirt frills.

Advances in weaving techniques in the 18th century led to the increased production of fabrics, and raw cotton was imported from the southern states of America. The mechanization of textile production in Scotland coincided with the development of a large horizontal embroidery frame which allowed several embroiderers to work simultaneously on one piece. Sewed-muslin production was soon established, with workshops in the cities and agents who kept the employers in touch with embroiderers who worked in their own homes.

During the Napoleonic wars, hitherto prized French laces were difficult to get, so one of the sewed-muslin agents, a Mrs Jamieson of Ayr, began to copy the

Carrickmacross work (right) looks like lace. It is achieved (below) by placing a layer of net under the linen ground. The motif is worked in running stitch through both layers, the reserves of the linen are cut away and it is reworked with tamboured chain stitch and further decorated.

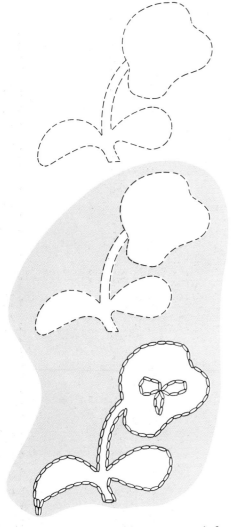

Mountmellick work (below) is more robust in appearance than Carrickmacross, being heavily fringed and worked on a thick shiny cotton ground. The petals and leaves of the typical floral motifs are made up of padded satin stitch with french knots and bullion knots forming the flower centre and buds.

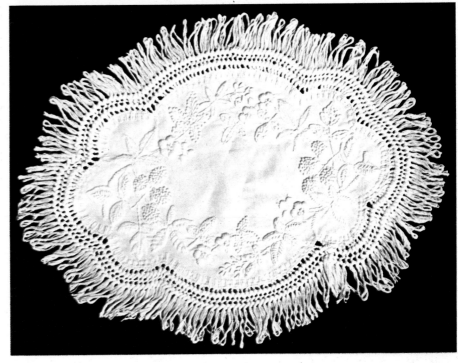

face. Finer ground fabric was used for working babyclothes and underwear. Motifs such as blackberries, passion flowers, oak leaves and berries were worked mainly in satin stitch, sometimes padded, and in bullion and french knots. Cable, chain, coral and herringbone stitches were also used, and the pieces were characteristically edged with buttonhole stitch and a knitted fringe.

Mountmellick work began about 1825 at a time when weaving mills in the area began to lose orders due to a slowing of trade with England. A local lady, Mrs Johanna Carter, diverted the skills of some of the weavers to using their cotton yarn for embroidery. The work is not now generally executed in its home area, but heavy white cotton embroidery on a white cotton ground is still popular in many other parts of the world and is

sometimes known as 'Mountmellick work'.

Another form of Irish-flowering embroidery is Carrickmacross, named after a market town in Monaghan, in central Ireland. The embroidery usually consists of a layer of cambric laid on a ground of hexagonal net. The outline of the design is stitched through the cambric and the net with cotton thread in running stitch. By cutting only through the cambric, reserves of the design are carefully removed to reveal the net beneath. The running stitch is then bound with over-stitching to prevent the edges of the cambric from fraying. Subsequent embroidery is worked in running stitch or tamboured chain stitch.

Many pieces of Carrickmacross embroidery are so intricate that they look like needle-made lace. Designs are

usually floral, and sometimes derived from Brussels lace patterns or from Italian whitework. A variant of Carrickmacross exists in the form of a basic cutwork embroidery. The design is worked on a ground of fine cambric with no net backing and the reserves of the design are then cut away in the usual manner.

Carrickmacross embroidery was taught at the Bath and Shirley School, Carrickmacross, until the end of the 19th century when the Sisters of St Louis, a Catholic order, established a convent in the town. The embroidery that is still worked today is executed by outworkers and the operation is managed by Sisters at the convent. Among the articles produced and sold by the convent are wedding veils, table linens, handkerchiefs, collars and cuffs.

English Whitework

One of the few forms of 'English-flowering' embroideries of the 19th century was Coggeshall work, named after a village in Essex. Used to decorate wedding capes, shawls, flounces and similar costume items, it is distinguished by tamboured chain stitch worked in white cotton thread on a muslin ground. Sometimes the centre of a flower is worked in buttonhole stitch. Designs are invariably floral, showing cow parsley, bluebells, ivy and primroses, all with long graceful stalks and often worked in repeating form.

Coggeshall embroidery had a productive lifetime of just over a century. Some time around 1823 a French immigrant established a tambour workshop in the town, employing girls from eight years old. Later, when the girls married, they worked at home, supplied by agents with unstamped fabric and thread. The embroiderers copied designs from card patterns which they either propped up in front of them as they embroidered or placed under the ground fabric so that the inked designs on the card showed through the muslin.

The Coggeshall tambour 'factory' reached its peak in 1851 when there was a total of nearly four hundred factory- and out-workers. Thereafter production gradually decreased. It stopped altogether with the outbreak of war in 1939, and no Coggeshall embroidery is worked today.

Another English whitework embroidery, broderie anglaise—English embroidery—was first introduced in the 1820s, and replaced the Ayrshire whitework that had until then been practised, particularly in the north of England.

Broderie anglaise, with cut holes subsequently worked round in buttonhole stitch, is executed in white silk or cotton thread on a ground of fine white cotton. Designs are either geometric or highly stylized floral themes.

Broderie anglaise was at first extensively worked by women out-workers in their own homes to decorate babies' garments, women's blouses and other items for commercial purposes. After the introduction of machine embroidery in the middle of the 19th century, it became primarily an amateur art, and thus it has remained to this day.

A 19th-century whitework wedding cape from the Essex village of Coggeshall. The repetition of the characteristic simple floral motif, worked in tamboured chain stitch on muslin, makes a charming and effective overall pattern.

Smocking

Embroidered smocks were worn by men in many country areas of England and Wales until the early 20th century. They were made of a heavy cotton or linen ground fabric, with a front opening, front and back panels gathered at the yoke, two shoulder panels, an inset collar and long sleeves, gathered at the shoulders and at the wrists, where they were attached to tight-fitting cuffs. The distinctive feature of this kind of shirt was the stitched smocking on the 'tubing', those parts of the garment which were gathered to give extra thickness.

By the 17th century, men's shirts in many parts of the British Isles had smocked neckbands, but the smock as it is best remembered today did not evolve until the 18th century. It was then worn regularly in many rural areas.

Smocks were made and embroidered by women, who usually bought ground fabrics, generally a natural or bleached linen, at local markets. As well as the smocked decoration they sometimes worked surface embroidery in chain stitch, feather stitch and french knots on the collars, cuffs and shoulder panels of the smocks, which they generally made for their own families' use but sometimes sold at fairs and markets.

Different regions had individual traditions. In some areas natural-coloured smocks were worn on days of work but brown, indigo or black garments were worn on Sundays. Certain embroidery motifs were similarly regional, such as a quartet of hearts worked in feather stitch on some Shropshire smocks. It was once thought that other motifs indicated the wearer's trade: for instance a shepherd's smock sometimes had a repeating design of swirls rather like his crook; a gardener's smock could hint of flowers and winding paths; and a ploughman's smock was frequently embroidered with repeating seed-shaped motifs. Recently, however, this theory of the meaning of motifs has been disputed.

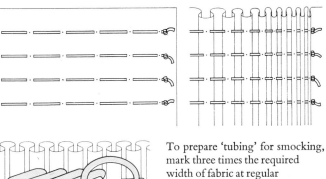

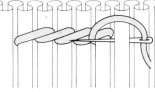

Rope stitch.

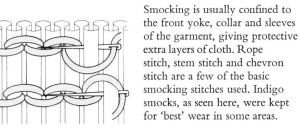

Stem stitch.

To prepare 'tubing' for smocking, mark three times the required width of fabric at regular intervals; work long running stitches through the marks from the back of the fabric; then pull all threads tight. The pleats are now ready to be smocked.

Smocking is usually confined to the front yoke, collar and sleeves of the garment, giving protective extra layers of cloth. Rope stitch, stem stitch and chevron stitch are a few of the basic smocking stitches used. Indigo smocks, as seen here, were kept for 'best' wear in some areas.

Dorset feather stitchery, worked on this apron (below), features applied felt motifs, buttonhole stitch, feather stitch and wheatear stitch.

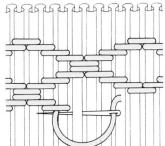

Chevron stitch.

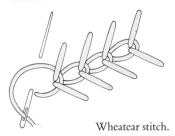

Wheatear stitch.

The production of British country smocks declined at the end of the 19th century, but the art of smocking and many of the designs found on traditional shirts have been adapted to other uses, particularly on baby clothes. Smocking is popular today with women in many parts of the world.

One modern adaptation of traditional smock designs is Dorset feather stitchery, which is generally found on table linens, aprons, blouses, skirts and caps. This work is executed in buttonhole, chain, feather and wheatear stitches with commercial silk threads on a ground of plain felt or linen. Zigzag or ric-rac braid is frequently laid on the ground fabric and couched with large running stitches in thread of a contrasting colour.

Designs of Dorset feather stitchery include wagon wheels copied from smocks, and repeating cone shapes. Sometimes the embroidery is worked with only one colour of thread throughout, but more often many different colours are used.

Netherlands

Some of the most beautiful of all western European samplers were those worked by women and young girls in the Netherlands. They sometimes wove their own ground fabric, which was usually of white linen or, occasionally, cream wool. Embroidery was executed in imported silk thread, often dyed red with madder, which had been extensively cultivated in the Netherlands since the 15th century. Ordinary cross stitch was predominant and other stitches frequently employed included back stitch, italian cross stitch and long-legged cross stitch.

The earliest surviving Dutch samplers, worked at the beginning of the 17th century, were about 62 x 30 cm (25 x 12 in), the width of the fabric being governed by the loom size. The ground fabric was generally a long thin shape, worked in a horizontal design. Later, when wider looms were available, samplers tended to be square, with sizes about 45 x 45 cm (18 x 18 in).

Dutch samplers frequently had a narrow border surround. The main part of the ground fabric was worked in spot motifs, the devices sometimes unrelated and certainly not aligned with each other. By using this method of 'spotting' the ground fabric rather than covering it with repeats of one pattern, it was possible to include many more motifs.

Dutch sampler embroiderers included themes of contemporary fashion. Tulips, for instance, are shown in some of the early samplers. At that time a novelty in western Europe, the bulbs had been introduced from Constantinople only a few years before. More homely motifs of tables and other household items were embroidered as close to the original shape as the use of cross stitch would allow. There were also flowers, windmills, animals, biblical themes and a variety of lettering forms. Sometimes the letters 'x', 'y' and 'z' were omitted from the alphabet. Occasionally the embroiderer had miscalculated and obviously did not have enough ground fabric left for these letters, but sometimes she deliberately left them off this test piece as she thought she would have little use for them later. In other instances, 'q' is left out, possibly since the embroiderer assumed she could always reverse a 'p' if necessary. And in other cases 'u' and 'v' were omitted, perhaps with the excuse that the embroiderer could work half a 'w'.

One much-practised variant of Dutch sampler embroidery was the darning sampler, sometimes so beautifully executed that it was difficult to distinguish one side of the work from the other. Patterns were worked in different colours to show the clever blending of stitches.

Although Dutch samplers ceased to be made at the beginning of the 20th century, the study of original motifs and their adaptation to other forms of embroidery is now popular with embroiderers in many parts of the world.

Marken

A part of the Netherlands where embroidery is still prolific is the island of Marken, immediately north-east of Amsterdam. Women there embroider both for their own use and for sale.

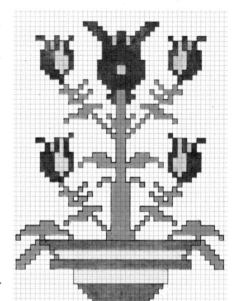

Tulips, the quintessentially Dutch motif, worked in cross stitch.

Sometimes darning samplers were so carefully embroidered that it is difficult to tell which is the right side of the work. This item, finished in 1803 and worked in silk on linen, includes eyelets and cross stitch as well as many different darning forms.

Jannetje Maas, a seemingly indefatigable sampler-worker, embroidered this piece at the end of the 18th century, using silk cross stitch on a linen ground fabric.

There is extensive flax farming in the western Netherlands and much use is made of linen thread and linen fabric.

Some Marken embroidery is found on costume items, worked in floral themes in chain stitch, tamboured or with a needle, buttonhole stitch and satin stitch.

Marken women's traditional costume consists of a linen bodice with a long-sleeved blouse, sometimes striped, and a mid-calf plain skirt. The bodice is either sleeveless or has long inset sleeves. It can be waist-length or slightly longer, with the two front panels sometimes held together with lacing. The edges are generally bound with braid and silk, and linen or wool embroidery is worked down either side of the front opening and across the back. Individual motifs may be bordered with square lines of chain stitching. Border designs tend to be vertical rather than horizontal.

Another type of Marken embroidery, a whitework, is sometimes found on women's caps. There is a wide variety of Marken caps, all made from a ground of fine white linen and most with a chin strap of the same fabric. Some versions are helmet-shaped with a tiny upturned brim all round. Others consist of a baggy 'pudding basin' hat with no brim and yet another form has a front brim visor but part of the back of the crown is

Sampler worked in 1764 with silks and silver thread on a linen ground. Cross stitch, eye stitch and satin stitch are used.

Monochrome cross-stitch sampler motif depicting hawking royalty.

A feature of Marken whitework is the seven-stitch block. When the centres of each block are cut and withdrawn, the remaining threads can be needlewoven. Such work often decorates borders, positioned alternately with diamond-shaped blocks of satin stitch and eyelets, and separated by bands of four-sided stitch.

Back view of a heavily
embroidered sleeveless bodice
made in about 1910. Using wool
on a wool ground, the maker has
worked buttonhole stitch, chain
stitch, detached chain stitch,
cross stitch and running stitch.

cut away. This may be for ventilation, or
perhaps so that the cap may be flattened
out for laundering.

Many of these hats are embroidered
with fine whitework stitching in drawn-
thread work and cutwork. Unlike
hardanger drawn-thread work (see pages
70-71) which has a similar appearance,
blocks of seven satin stitches are usually
worked before a corner is turned. After
the required threads are withdrawn, the
centre of a device is infilled and surface
embroidery worked in the reserves,
usually with eyelet stitch and satin stitch.

Cross stitch is worked on Marken table
and other linens, often with a single
colour of woollen thread, sometimes
yellow, on a ground of natural linen. Men
and women on horseback and complicated boat shapes are embroidered in spot
motifs and there is often a small repeating
pattern round the border of a cloth.

Dutch Sampler Designs

Samplers, originally worked by
young girls learning the gentle art
of embroidery, provided a
reference for stitches and patterns
that would be used on personal
and household linens. The
motifs and borders worked in
18th-century Dutch samplers still
retain their charm and may be
adapted to modern use in an
exciting variety of ways.

Suggested Fabrics

Linen is an obvious choice for working
traditional articles such as traycloths, and
it is also very useful as a base fabric for
motifs that can later be applied to other
fabrics.

Hessian (burlap), worked with thicker
thread such as pearl cotton or soft embroidery cotton, is ideal for casual bags
or for a stout apron.

Binca (Aida cloth), cotton woven in square
blocks of threads, can be worked with any
type of embroidery thread to make a
whole range of articles from shoulder
bags to cushion covers.

Gingham, or any other evenly checked
fabric, is particularly pretty for this kind
of work. Decorate the corner of a headscarf or the yoke of a blouse. Make an
embroidered shawl or stitch large patch
pockets on aprons or children's skirts.
And how about some country-style
check curtains for the kitchen?

Stitch Variations

Cross stitch is the obvious choice, but any
counted-thread stitch may be used.

Smocking is particularly effective. Fill in
the spaces between motifs with plain
honeycomb to ensure a good tension.
Work the patterns on little girls' dresses,
smocked cuffs and yokes.

Knitting is an exciting way of using the
motifs. Try working them on mittens,
scarves and hats. Let one knitted stitch
represent one square of the chart and
work over the V shape of the knitted
stitch using either a different-coloured
wool or any embroidery thread.

Stitches based on gingham squares.

Using the border designs
Use the designs as vertical borders for bag straps, trouser stripes, or to hold box pleats in place on a full blouse or skirt. Alternatively, use them as horizontal strips for trimming hems, cuffs and waistbands. Sew the required length of design on linen fabric and then slipstitch it to the garment. Use the narrower borders for hairbands or bracelets and chokers and make soft belts of hessian (burlap) or binca. Work the same border in rows of different colours or stitch different borders side by side. Border designs can also be used with motifs on napery and cushions.

Method of Working

Whatever fabric you use (with the exceptions of smocking and knitting), it is best to use a hoop and to damp stretch the work afterwards (see page 272). If using a loosely woven fabric such as hessian (burlap), add a calico or cotton lining and work through both layers.

Using the single motifs
A very effective method is to work the same design in different sizes. If you are using an evenweave fabric, first work the design over two fabric threads per chart square, and then work it again over three or even four threads.

Try an embroidered patchwork pattern on gingham using different sized checks for different sized motifs. When using the large 2.5 cm (1 in) checks, one stitch will not be sufficient to fill the square. Fill it instead with several stitches, still regarding it as one square on the chart.

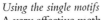

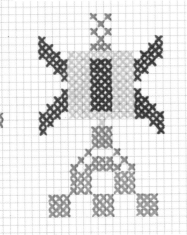

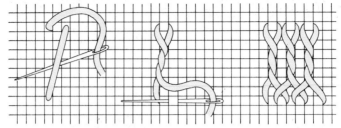

France

Repeating floral pattern in satin stitch and chain stitch used to decorate scarves and borders.

One of the most important techniques that France has given to western embroidery is tambouring. The method was introduced to France from China in the 1760s and derives its name from the french *tambour*, a drum, because the ground fabric is always stretched taut in a frame. The thread is held underneath the ground fabric with one hand while the other hand pushes the tambour hook down through the ground fabric and brings back, through the same hole, a loop of thread which forms the first link of the chain. The next stitch is made through this link.

French embroidery styles are for the most part regional, however. Many of the most beautiful embroideries from Normandy, on the northern coast of France, have been worked as women's costume embellishment. In the past women embroidered on white linen brought from neighbouring Brittany. Cotton was seldom used as a ground fabric. Silk in fabric and thread form was obtained from the Rhône Valley. It was dyed yellow with weld or 'French berries', a member of the *Rhamnus* family, blue with woad, or red with madder which was usually brought from Holland.

A traditional Normandy woman's costume consists of a triangular shawl worn round the shoulder, an ankle-length full-skirted dress with short inset sleeves, and a long apron with a front yoke bib. The shawl is often embroidered with a border of solid block design worked with silks in buttonhole stitch, chain stitch or satin stitch. The main ground might be infilled with floral spot motifs or left plain.

From the 14th century it was customary for every woman to receive a whitework embroidered bonnet when she got married. No unmarried woman wore such a bonnet. The shape of the Normandy bonnet was highly regionalized. In places a simple semi-circular crown of fine linen was attached to an arched brim of the same fabric. Elsewhere a tall tubular hat might have a turned-up brim and a neck flap.

Embroidery was worked on various parts of the cap. The designs on the crown, always symmetrical, were executed in buttonhole stitch, needle or tamboured chain stitch or stem stitch,

Careful shading gave naturalism to many beautiful floral embroideries. This detail from a 17th-century chair back is worked with silk and metal threads on a silk ground.

and many were floral. Sometimes motifs were copied from fine needle laces from Flanders or Italy, in which case the outlines of motifs were worked exclusively in buttonhole stitch and then infilled with a variety of pulled-thread stitches including honeycomb stitch, punch stitch and wave filling stitch.

Women of Normandy embroidered costume items for their own use and to make presents for family and friends. Costume embroidery is not now worked, and traditional Normandy dress is rarely seen today.

Brittany, the north-western peninsula of France, has given its name to breton stitch, a twisted stitch worked in horizontal lines and with an overall appearance of vertical spindles.

Breton stitch was in the past employed by women as decoration for costume items. Traditional Breton women's dress consisted of a stiff white linen cap with widely extended flaps to either side of the crown, a black bodice of local wool with a yellow, green or scarlet neck scarf, sometimes made of silk from the Rhône

Valley, and a long full skirt in bright plain-coloured wool, with a white or black linen apron worn over it. Breton stitch, chain stitch, satin stitch and stem stitch were sometimes worked on the apron and on the scarf. Motifs were usually floral, with emphasis on repeating designs showing ears of corn and similar everyday subjects. Sometimes the embroiderers adapted patterns found on carved wooden objects and other decorative items. Flax is still extensively farmed throughout Brittany, and this is the basis of France's linen exports. Traditional costume is not now generally worn, however, and women of Brittany prefer to embroider items such as table linens and similar household requisites.

At the confluence of the Rhône and Saône rivers stands Lyon, the centre of the French silk industry. Until the 16th century the town served as a market for imported Italian silks. In 1536 it began to produce silk in its own right. The zenith of Lyon silk embroidery was reached in the middle of the 18th century. At that time more than 20,000 embroiderers,

St Tropez ladies in their traditional costume which includes fine whitework bonnets.

19th-century repeating motif in two-colour cross stitch.

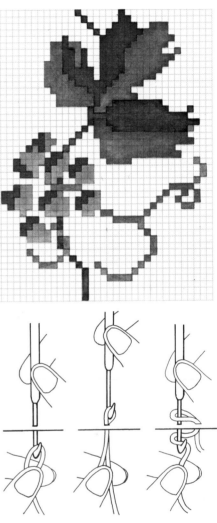

Tambouring employs a hook to work continuous chain stitch, pulling thread through the ground fabric.

men and women, were employed in the district, producing items such as men's single- or double-breasted waistcoats and outer coats.

Sometimes the embroiderers worked on a ground woven with a velvet void, which meant that part of the resulting ground fabric had cut velvet pile and other areas did not. This was one of the many complicated silk weaves used by French embroiderers. Satin stitch, known as flat stitch since it was unpadded, was the most popular embroidery stitch. French knots were widely used, and tamboured chain stitch was later taken up. Untwisted floss thread, silk thread, metal threads and silk chenille were the favourite embroidery yarns for this work.

There was careful shading of silks to give naturalism to the devices, which were usually very elaborate, with flowers, leaves and berries arranged in cornucopias or individual sprays, or with classical or rural themes. The embroidery was worked on each separate panel of ground fabric, carefully arranged so that when the garment was sewn together some motifs appeared to extend from one piece of ground fabric to another. The high standards of the embroiderers also required that embroidery designs be continued right under the pocket flaps.

In the years following the French Revolution and the decline of silk

Opulent 18th-century tamboured silk on a satin ground.

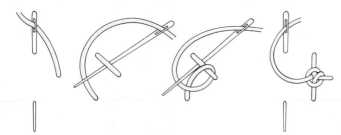

Basque knot, also known as knotted loop stitch. The thread is pulled tight at the third stage.

Basque stitch (right).

Manufacturer's sample showing the superb craftsmanship the discriminating customer could expect from Lyon workshops.

production in Lyon, fashionable costume simultaneously turned away from silk embroidered decoration. Many exquisite examples of Lyon silk waistcoats and other costume items are now treasured in museum and private collections around the world.

The scroll-like basque stitch and basque knot, although sometimes found on embroideries elsewhere in southern France and throughout the Iberian peninsula, are usually associated with the lands of the Basques, which lie on both sides of the Franco-Spanish border.

Traditionally many Basques were farmers who grew their own flax. Sometimes a little wool was mixed with the flax before it was woven into cloth, usually 50 cm (20 in) in width.

Basque women generally embroidered with thread of linen or wool dyed blue either with imported indigo or with local plants. They decorated shirts for their men and items such as aprons for their own use with geometric designs often worked in lines of basque stitch.

Breton Skirt

A pretty idea for summer—a full Breton skirt in crisp white poplin, the hem embroidered with suitable 'hot' colours of deep red, flame and orange.

You will need:
1.6 m (1¾ yd) white poplin 120 cm (48 in) wide
0.7 m (¾ yd) waistband interfacing 3.5 cm (1½ in) wide
18 cm (7 in) zip fastener
1 reel white sewing cotton
coton à broder in three colours:
nasturtium 1 skein
flame 3 skeins
cardinal red 3 skeins
crewel needle
18 cm (7 in) embroidery hoop
hook and bar skirt fastening

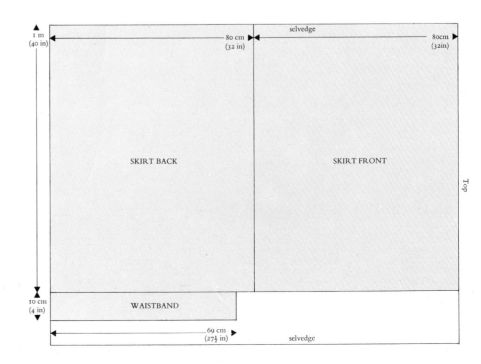

Size

This skirt is 71 cm (28 in) long and has a waist measurement of 64 cm (25½ in). Cut a longer waistband for a larger waist measurement. To make the skirt longer, double the additional length needed and buy that much more fabric.

Preparing the Fabric

Cut out the three pattern pieces as shown. Mark the centre of the lower edge of the skirt back. Scale up the design (see page 272) to 32 cm (12½ in) across and transfer it to the fabric (see page 272) so that its centre matches the centre mark on the fabric. Repeat the design once more on either side to give three repeats.

Prepare the skirt front in the same way.

Making the Skirt

Use a seam allowance of 1.5 cm (⅝ in) throughout. With right sides facing, baste and stitch the side seams, leaving the top 20 cm (8 in) of the left side open for the zip. Check that the embroidery is in line across the joins.

Press the seams open and insert the zip according to the instructions on the packet.

Run two gathering lines round the top edge of the skirt 1 cm (⅜ in) and 1.5 cm (⅝ in) from the top. Pull up the gathers evenly to a measure of 64 cm (25½ in).

Fold the waistband in half lengthwise and machine the short ends. Baste the long edge of the interfacing in place along the fold.

Baste and then stitch the waistband to the skirt, right sides facing, leaving the extra length of waistband at the back of the skirt.

Turn the waistband right side out, turn the seam allowance under, and hem it in place.

Stitch on a hook and bar fastening, lapping the front of the waistband over the back.

Turn up a 10 cm (4 in) hem. Press the completed hem.

Use the chart as a guide to both stitches and colours. Hold the fabric in the hoop to avoid puckering. The satin stitches of the small circles should be vertical and those of the flower and crescent shapes should radiate outwards.

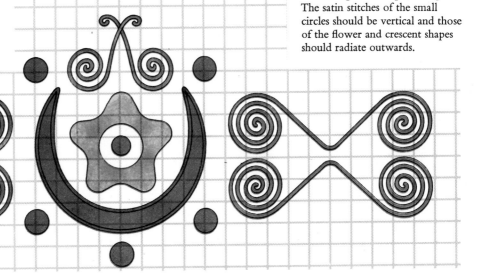

1 sq = 1 cm

Spain

Early 18th-century sampler worked in silks and silver-gilt thread using such stitches as back stitch, twisted chain stitch, fern stitch and others, with drawn-thread work and french knots.

'Spanish-work' double-headed bird design.

Various provinces of Spain have their own embroidery traditions but there are some universal forms, the most popular of which is cross stitch. Other commonly used Spanish embroidery stitches include basque stitch, buttonhole stitch, chain stitch, running stitch, long-legged cross stitch and french knots. Frequent design motifs include cocks with antler-like combs, an ancient symbol, and double-headed eagles.

Cotton is grown in southern Andalusia. Silk is produced to the north-east of Almería and also further up the east coast. There is flax production in north-western Spain and wool production is scattered throughout the country.

In the past embroiderers in Spain often worked on a natural-coloured ground fabric. They dyed their threads red with cochineal, an art learned from Mexico at the beginning of the 16th century, blue or black with logwood also brought from Latin America, and yellow or red with safflower, sometimes grown in their own gardens. Sometimes wool from black sheep was spun and used as embroidery thread.

An Islamic influence in Spanish embroidery is particularly evident in Toledo, Almería and Andalusia, the most southern region of Spain to which the Moors first came when they crossed from North Africa in the 8th century. Andalusia retained particularly close links with the Moors and even converted to Islam for a period during the 17th century.

Much of Andalusian embroidery was geometric, with one colour of silk thread worked on a ground of local cotton in running, double running or cross stitch. This is what is sometimes known generally as 'Spanish work' or 'black-work' even though the one-colour thread is not necessarily black. The idea of one-colour geometric design was possibly introduced by the Moors.

Some of the most beautiful gold and silver work in the world comes from Spain. This detail from a border is 17th-century work using predominantly gold threads and a variety of laid and couched work techniques.

Exquisite Spanish shawls are much sought after today. They are almost the only Spanish women's garment that is traditionally decorated with embroidery. This heavily fringed, creamy silk example is lavishly worked in satin stitch and stem stitch. Flowers and leaves are popular themes.

Some of the most beautiful one-colour Spanish embroideries were worked as samplers, usually with silk thread on a linen ground. They are often identifiable by the silk tassels attached to each corner and by the frequent use of satin stitch. Other stitches included back stitch, stem stitch, italian cross stitch and bullion and french knots. Floral and geometric designs were worked in repeating form.

Embroiderers in many parts of Spain have used their talents for costume embellishment. A typical man's shirt, with long sleeves gathered at the shoulder and cuff, is embroidered solely with flat non-smocked embroidery. The shape, colouring and decoration varies with the region, although generally the shirt is embroidered on the collar and cuffs, down either side of the front neck opening and in a narrow border round the hem. Variants are found in former Spanish colonies in Latin America, modelled on those worn by soldiers and colonists.

Late 16th-century blackwork coif embroidered in silk braid using double running stitch and stem stitch. Catherine of Aragon was popularly but erroneously supposed to have introduced blackwork to England from Spain, where it was widely practised.

Repeating blackwork motif to be worked in chain stitch and french knots.

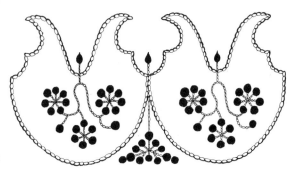

Toledo, a province in south-central Spain, was once famous for whitework decoration on men's shirts. Another form of popular decoration was honey-coloured or blue embroidery worked on a natural linen ground. Toledo is also exceptional for its traditional embroidery of women's clothes, not usually decorated elsewhere in Spain. Women sometimes wore black or white flannel sleeveless bodices with lines of basque stitch embroidered in black thread down either side of the front opening. The bodices were worn with white linen long-sleeved shirts, knee-length full skirts of red flannel, woollen stockings which were sometimes embroidered and with scarves printed or embroidered with floral designs.

As in the rest of Spain, Toledo men and women today wear regional costume only for festive occasions. Spanish scarves, sometimes in the form of large square shawls, are popular with fashionable women in many parts of the world. The scarves are usually embroidered in silks on a silk ground. The edges are deeply fringed and the embroidery appears either in one corner or repeated in spot form all over the ground fabric, usually worked in large floral satin-stitch motifs.

Filet work and satin stitch in blue thread constitutes the local variety of whitework in Madeira.

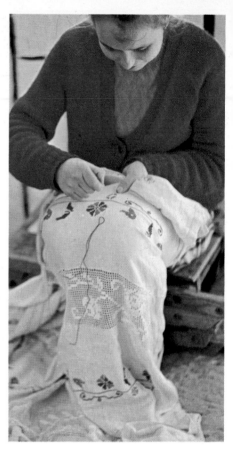

Portugal

A small amount of flax is farmed today in the north-east of Portugal, around Braganza. Sheep are raised in the hills on the eastern border with Spain, and some of the wool was in former times used for embroidery on the aprons and skirts of women's regional costume. The costume consisted of a large scarf, often undecorated, worn round the shoulders with the two front ends passed across the wearer's chest and tied behind her back; a sleeveless bodice worn over a long-sleeved white blouse, and an ankle-length skirt decorated with horizontal bands of embroidery worked in chain stitch or satin stitch. The apron, worn over the skirt, was brightly coloured and sometimes worked with applied motifs of linen or cotton, cut in zigzag or square shapes, to a ground of red cotton. As in most parts of western Europe, however, this traditional dress is now rarely worn.

Some of the locally produced wool is used today for Portuguese rug embroidery, with symmetrical and geometric designs worked in long-legged cross stitch on a ground of sacking or linen. Much of the work is actually done in women's prisons and destined for sale. Custom-made carpets, rugs, cushion covers and other small pieces are finding a ready market in North America and in many other parts of the world.

One type of embroidery still popular with Portuguese women is filet work, which consists of running stitch and buttonhole stitch worked on a ground of square mesh, with each hole of the mesh about 3 mm ($\frac{1}{8}$ in) square. Both mesh and embroidery thread are made of linen.

Portuguese filet work is made into table mats and other domestic linens as well as into collars and cuffs. Larger items are worked on a frame which is usually supported horizontally. The embroiderers' standard patterns include bunches of grapes, flowers and stars.

Unlike the embroideries of Spain, which show design links with North Africa and Latin America, those of Portugal have more affinity with work of the Indian sub-continent. Portuguese explorers opened the sea route round Africa to India during the 15th century, and by 1505 the first Portuguese vice-regency in India was established.

Embroideries worked in India for a Portuguese market are known as Indo-Portuguese, the first examples of which were worked in Bengal. They were usually executed with yellow silk thread on a ground of white cotton. Later, when Indo-Portuguese work was embroidered in Goa, red and blue were added to the colour scheme.

Traditional dress is rather plain except for the blouse cuffs and apron. The cuffs are decorated with narrow garlands of chain stitch crosses and the apron with applied cotton shapes and with silk chain-stitch embroidery.

Distinguishing between embroideries worked overseas for a Portuguese market, those worked overseas for a local market and those worked in Portugal is sometimes difficult. Often items worked by Indian embroiderers for their own use were more intricate in execution but simple in design. Items worked in Portugal, sometimes by immigrants from the Indian sub-continent, usually have more complex designs but often the natural curving scrolls of indigenous Indian patterns have been lost.

The supply of Indo-Portuguese embroideries began to diminish in the 17th century. Fortunately many fine examples of Indo-Portuguese bedcovers and other items such as aprons and altar-cloths survive today in collections.

Madeira

The archipelago of Madeira, off the Atlantic coast of Portugal, is still a prolific centre for the output of embroidery. Thousands of women embroider towels, table mats and other domestic items for sale not only in Madeira and mainland Portugal but also overseas, particularly in America.

Although the term 'Madeira work' sometimes refers to English broderie anglaise, Madeira embroidery is rather different. It is usually worked in pale blue cotton thread on a ground of white or bleached Portuguese cotton fabric. Buttonhole stitch and satin stitch are worked

Small filet-work mat from Madeira, the mesh surround interlaced and bordered with closed buttonhole stitch.

Long-legged cross stitch worked in wool on a linen or sacking ground is often used to cover cushions.

in scallop shapes and also, as in Ayrshire and other British cutwork forms, in cut-out floral and scrolled designs. Madeira cutwork was introduced to the islands in 1850 by a philanthropic Englishwoman, Mrs Phelps, but because of the islands' climate, blue thread was substituted for the more easily soiled white.

Sometimes Madeira work includes appliqué, with small pieces of cotton fabric hemmed to the main ground, which is then embroidered.

Another form of embroidery popular in Madeira now is filet work similar to that of the Portuguese mainland. Table mats and collars and cuffs are executed by women, generally in their own homes for commercial purposes.

Appliqué work is popular in Madeira. Floral or other motifs are either hemmed or attached with buttonhole stitch to the ground fabric, and the design is then decorated with satin stitch and stem stitch embroidery.

Italy

Cross stitch is one of the most popular forms of embroidery throughout mainland Italy today. Ordinary cross stitch is sometimes known as written stitch. There is also a special Italian cross stitch, alternatively called arrowhead cross stitch, in which each cross is bordered by a square surround. Both forms of cross stitch are often worked in coarse red cotton thread on imported linen.

Other forms of embroidery worked in Italy include drawn-thread work, smocking, whitework which is sometimes decorated with sorbello stitch, a knot filling stitch, and cutworks.

Some of the cutwork embroideries of Italy were worked with so much of the ground fabric cut away that eventually no ground fabric was required, and lace evolved. Some needle lace or 'needlepoint', in the original sense of the word, was incorporated with other forms of embroidery. Some Italian samplers, for instance, worked with linen threads on a linen ground and usually somewhat wider than Dutch contemporary versions, included needle lace as well as drawn-thread work with surface stitching such as eye stitch and satin stitch.

Another technique often associated with Italy in the past was metal-thread embroidery. The city of Venice inspired much of the early use of metal thread, a term which now encompasses real gold, gilt, silver-gilt, silver, lurex and other artificial substances as well as the tin and pewter threads of the Lapps.

Metal thread is produced in wires or coiled into bullion, or purl, thread, sometimes around a core of yellow floss-silk thread. The thread is generally laid on the ground fabric and couched, often with silk. Sometimes the laid thread is pulled sharply through to the reverse of the fabric with each couching stitch, resulting in underside couching, the couching stitches being invisible from the obverse of the ground. Any untidy ends of laid metal thread, whether superficially or underside-couched, can similarly be pulled through to the reverse so that they do not spoil the look of the finished piece.

Metal can also be used in embroidery in the form of spangles or sequins. A spangle is attached to the ground fabric with long straight stitches worked

'St John the Baptist', a 'silk picture' worked in the 17th century, using silks and metal threads in long-and-short stitch, split stitch and couching.

Early 19th-century design from Abruzzi, worked in cross stitch and double running stitch and featuring acanthus motifs.

Sorbello stitch.

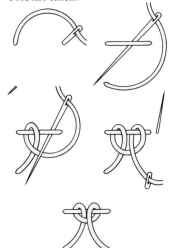

from the centre hole to the edge.

Embroidery throughout Italy is worked mainly by women, usually for their own household decoration. Italian regional costumes do not generally include embroidered items.

One of the main regional forms of Italian embroidery is Assisi work, named after the town in Umbria, a province in central Italy. It consists of an outline motif worked in double running stitch, traditionally executed in black or dark brown thread, with reserves filled in with cross stitch in bright red or blue. This results in a negative-image appearance, with the main feature of the design left unworked, as in Sicilian embroidery. Sometimes a device worked in Assisi embroidery is subsequently bordered with a design worked in double running stitch.

Assisi work possibly originated with nuns at a convent in the town. The first definite records of it indicate that by the 14th century the designs were of simple animal shapes, similar to wood carvings and other local decorative art forms.

Assisi embroidery enjoyed a great revival at the end of the 19th century. Needlewomen copied older pieces and

Assisi work is characterized by the use of monochrome (usually red) thread and cross stitch in some form. Assisi-work motifs are outlined in black double running stitch; the reserves are infilled with red cross stitch, and the motif border is then reworked. Flower and pomegranates (left) and birds (below) are typical motifs.

also adapted other designs to counted-thread work. Today it is popular throughout the world in the form of household linens and small decorative panels on blouses and other costume items. It is usually worked on a ground of even-weave linen with a standard thread or coton à broder.

Another form of local Italian embroidery was the late-19th-century *Aemilia Ars* work from Bologna. It was a whitework embroidery, executed on a ground of local linen. Much of the decoration was worked with reticella, a cutwork in which the outline of a square motif was first worked in running stitch, and was then cut away leaving a few warp and weft threads to form vertical and horizontal bars. The edge of the motif was then overcast and the bars held together either with needleweaving or with overcast stitching. Each segment of

the cut-out device was rebuilt as required with diagonal and other 'bars' formed as in hardanger and other cutworks, with several long straight stitches bound together with overcast stitching, and sometimes further decorated with picots. The work was also embellished with drawn-thread work and with surface embroidery executed in buttonhole stitch and french knots.

Production was organized partly by a society formed in Bologna at the end of the 19th century to give employment to local women. Work ceased with the outbreak of World War I.

Some of the most skilled dyers in medieval Italy were those in Florence. A local merchant by the name of Federico introduced a purple dye executed from the lichen *Roccella tinctorius*. He had discovered the art of making this dye while travelling in Asia Minor, and the secret of it became for many years a monopoly of the powerful Florentine dyers. In general, however, it was woad dyers who were among the most respected craftsmen of their Wool Guild. They were able to produce more shades of any one colour than other contemporary dyers. The more shades of embroidery thread to hand, the more carefully shaded the resulting embroidery could be.

Florentine embroidery is an alternative name for bargello, known also as hungarian point and flame work.

Bargello is named after the Bargello, or Podestà Palace, in Florence, which was turned into a museum in 1857 and in which were housed four 17th-century

Reticella is Italian cutwork. Small running stitches are worked around the required shape. Inside the stitched areas, the threads are cut and withdrawn, leaving two or four intact as cross bars. The cut edges are carefully overcast and the remaining threads are worked with needleweaving. The bars can then be worked or added to as required.

Detail of a flounce worked in reticella with flower and wheatear designs. The work possibly dates from the late 16th century.

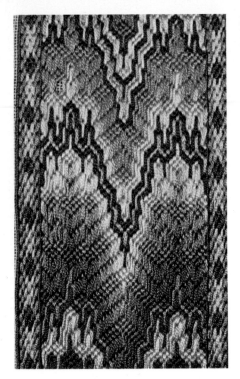

chairs with the stitching now known by the name of the museum.

Bargello is usually executed with wool or silk thread on a single canvas ground. It is worked with vertical parallel straight stitches which rise or descend according to the pattern being followed. Each line is generally worked in a shade or colour different from the one before. Lines of stitches therefore form points ('flames') or curves, depending on the pattern, at regular intervals.

Now a popular form of embroidery with men and women in many parts of the world, it is made into wall hangings, chair seats, purses, bags and belts. Some embroiderers are experimenting with free-form bargello which does not adhere to the repeating motif format.

Sardinia

The Mediterranean island of Sardinia is noted for appliqué, worked by women and usually made up into costume items.

There is no local textile production and much of the embroidery is therefore worked on a ground of imported cotton. The embroiderers apply bright plain-coloured motifs in triangles and other geometric shapes to a ground fabric of black or red cotton. Sometimes the edges of the applied motifs are covered with loosely worked lines of romanian stitch in commercial silk thread.

Satin stitch is also much used in Sardinian embroidery, worked as in-filling for segments of symmetrical designs which may be outlined in double running stitch. This type of embroidery is executed on aprons and other items of women's costume.

Bargello work, the traditional Florentine embroidery method. This is a typical design, although unfinished, with lightning and mosaic patterns in multicoloured silks on a cotton canvas ground fabric.

Sicily

The island of Sicily has a long history of sumptuous silk embroidery, particularly during the 12th century, when professional male craftsmen at the Royal Workshop of Palermo produced exquisite regal and other court robes. Production ceased when the French captured Sicily in 1266 and many of the most skilled embroiderers fled to Italy. Embroidery in Sicily was thereafter confined to domestic purposes.

One form popular today is a drawn-thread work in which the reserve of the ground fabric, usually evenweave linen, is worked into a square mesh, the bars of which are overcast. This net-like ground fabric acts as background.

Most Sicilian embroidery today is worked in cross stitch, sometimes in one colour thread on a ground of linen.

Decorative motif worked for the traditional calf-length black apron worn by Sardinian women. The design is outlined in silk double running stitch and infilled with satin stitch in various colours.

In Sicilian whitework the chosen motif —here a goat— is outlined in small running stitches. Cut-out holes are overcast, and drawn-thread work forms the background.

Unfortunately, Sicily has lost most of its ancient embroidery techniques. Quilting worked with fine back stitches was once practised, as can be seen from this 13th-century, crusader-patterned bed covering.

Bargello Cushion

One theory holds that bargello florentine work was brought to Italy by the Hungarian bride of one of the Medici but its true origins have been lost in the mists of time. This cushion cover worked in four shades of greenish blue has the characteristic rich look of florentine embroidery.

You will need:
a square of canvas 45 x 45 cm (18 x 18 in), 18 threads to 2.5 cm (1 in)
tapestry wool in four shades: 5 skeins each of light, pale, mid and dark greenish blue
a cushion pad 35 cm (14 in) square
0.5 m (½ yd) firm woollen fabric for backing
tapestry needle

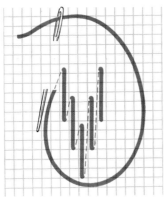

Florentine stitch.

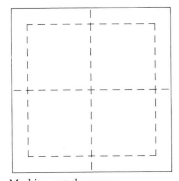

Marking out the canvas.

Preparing the Canvas

Mark the area of the cushion and also the centre of the canvas with basting stitches (see diagram).

Embroidery

If an embroidery frame is used it should be of the rectangular variety.

Begin at the centre of the canvas at the point indicated on the chart. Work outwards in both directions along the base line. Fill the blocks of the curved pattern with satin stitch and work the rest in florentine stitch. Continue two or three stitches beyond the cushion area to ensure that no canvas is visible when the cushion is made up. Work each stitch over six threads of the canvas using a rise or drop of three threads throughout.

Check the base line carefully before continuing. A mistake at this stage will spoil the pattern. All subsequent rows are identical to this first one and the shades of wool should be used in order from very light to dark.

Making the Cushion

Damp stretch the canvas (see page 272), being very careful not to distort it. Trim the backing fabric to the same size as the canvas. Baste canvas and backing together, right sides facing. Stitch along three sides, leaving the fourth side open. Trim the corners diagonally.

Turn the cushion cover right side out and insert the cushion pad. Turn in the raw edges and close the fourth side with slipstitch.

Start here

Stitch and colour chart.

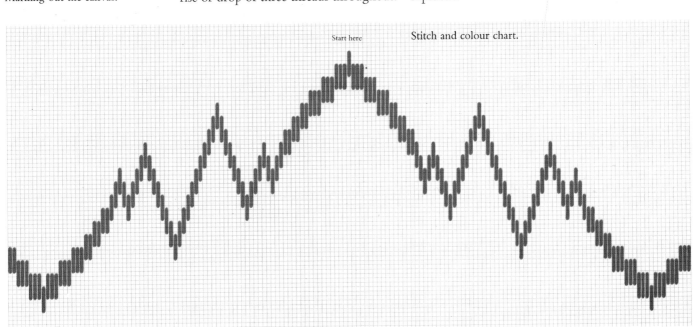

Austria

Vorarlberg, a province of neighbouring Austria, has embroidery similar to that of St Gallen, for when commercial embroidery was first established in Vorarlberg in 1753 women from St Gallen were brought in as instructors. It was executed by out-workers embroidering by hand in their own homes. In 1868 the first manually operated embroidery machines were installed in factories in Vorarlberg.

Machine embroidery generally, as worked by the individual embroiderer, now consists of one of three forms. There is 'straight stitch' worked on an ordinary domestic sewing machine with two threads, one above and one below the ground fabric. This can result in identical two-sided embroidery. Another form is worked on a Cornely sewing machine which has only one thread, the needle fulfilling the role of the hand-held tambour hook and producing a line of continuous chain stitch. The third form of domestic machine embroidery is done with a machine which has built-in embroidery patterns that can be worked by the embroiderer simply pressing an appropriate button on the machine.

Although much of the embroidery now produced in St Gallen and Vorarlberg for export uses a combination of

Exquisite Viennese evening bag worked in petit point. This technique is still very popular in Austria, and is used for purses, cushions and other articles.

Beautiful effects can also be achieved with machines. This magnificent net embroidery was worked on a Cornely machine.

colours, there is still a substantial commercial output of whitework, some of which is worked by hand but most of which is executed by machine on a ground of fine linen. Exquisite handkerchiefs and other costume items and fine table linens are sold in many countries.

The Alpine province of Tirol lies mostly in western Austria, with a smaller southern part that was annexed to Italy in 1919. Sheep are farmed on many of the lower mountain slopes and much of the embroidery of the region was worked on a ground of thick woven wool. The embroiderers, who were always women, usually worked embroidery for their own families' use but sometimes also for commercial purposes. They spun thread using an upright spindle on a stand and wove it into fabric on horizontal looms. The fabric was then made into coats and trousers for men or bodices, skirts or coats for the women of the family. Embroidery was worked after the garment was made up. Today much less traditional costume is worn and correspondingly little is made and embroidered.

Traditional dress for a Tirol man consists of a long-sleeved jacket of thick wool yarn over a white shirt and trousers

Hearts and flowers in red back stitch and blue cross stitch, using wool on a linen ground fabric. This motif is often found in the Tirol region.

Austrian whitework is mostly decorated with laid and couched work. Cutwork is rare. An interesting shadow effect is created on this piece with bands of black embroidery framing the central white motif.

A spectacular halo-shaped bonnet worn on festive occasions in Vorarlberg. The metal-thread-work hat is entirely hand-made, an unusual departure for the region which specializes in high-quality machine embroidery.

which are sometimes made of leather. Embroidery can be worked on both jacket and trousers and despite the possible difference of ground fabric the design of stitching may be the same. It is often worked as floral motifs in monochrome chain stitch outlining which is infilled with blocks of satin stitch. Colouring is always bright.

Tirol women's costume is highly regional. Basically it consists of a bodice worn over a white blouse, either short- or long-sleeved, and a calf-length full dirndl skirt with a front apron. The bodice is a sleeveless *mieder* or it has full-length inset sleeves. In either case it is made of wool or velvet, and sometimes has a band of lace as well as embroidered decoration. The embroidery, which is executed in monochrome or in many bright colours, is stitched round the neck and to both sides of the front opening and also round the wrists of a sleeved bodice. It is worked in silk or wool threads, usually in chain stitch, herringbone stitch, satin stitch and french knots. Patterns are generally floral, with sprays of local flowers worked either in spotmotif or repeating form.

Since the front opening is often laced, a small decorative pad is sometimes inserted behind the lacing. This pad is usually made of velvet backed with card and is sometimes embroidered with silk thread worked, as on the bodice, in chain stitch and satin stitch to a floral design.

Older women in Tirol used to wear hats that identified the region of the wearer. Sometimes these were of black velvet with large brims of stiff white linen embroidered with eyelet work and satin stitch.

Another regional hat consisted of a round 'top knot' crown that was purely decorative, with a brim that fitted the woman's forehead fairly tightly. It swept up and away from her head at the back, and the stiff net ground fabric was completely worked with gold thread in satin stitch and bullion knots and laid and couched work. Sometimes spangles were sewn to the ground with long straight stitches.

Regional dress is today worn generally only on festive occasions, although more often than in most of western Europe.

Women of Tirol are still keen embroiderers, but their output consists mainly of household items such as table and other linens. Much of the work is done on a ground of cream linen and with wool or commercial stranded cotton. Colouring is often monochrome, generally red, and embroidery is executed in back stitch, chain stitch and cross stitch. Popular designs include figures of men and women, sometimes with an accompanying child, and heart shapes, worked either in spot motif or repeating form.

Knotted insertion stitch.   Twisted insertion stitch.

Buttonhole insertion stitch.

Switzerland

The region of St Gallen in north-east Switzerland is famous for whitework embroidery on a ground of fine cambric, with floral and other curvilinear designs worked in buttonhole stitch, chain stitch, eyelet stitch, seeding and satin stitch.

The first examples of St Gallen whitework, which evolved from polychrome work on a ground of local linen, date from the 16th century. Many early pieces were worked with one whole width of narrow linen cloth and one half-width, held together by a network of interlacing, in the form of buttonhole, knotted and twisted insertion stitches or a similar 'joining' stitch. Embroidery might then be worked over the insertion stitching.

A Swiss businessman, François Mange, perfected the newly invented sewing machine in the middle of the 19th century and this was to play a large role in Swiss whitework production. St Gallen became a centre of Swiss machine whitework with scalloping and, after 1863, cutwork, and remains so today.

St Gallen whitework gazebo motif outlined in chain stitch and infilled with pulled-thread work and closely packed vertical rows of more chain stitch.

Velvet bodice worn for festive occasions, vividly embroidered with double running stitch, zigzag and satin stitch. The matching sash is also worked in satin stitch.

Swiss mountain farmer in a traditional shirt decorated with bands of satin-stitch edelweiss.

Germany

Typical bird motif worked in cross stitch, usually silk on linen.

The story of Tobit, told on the panels of a delightfully embroidered 18th-century satchel, worked in silk long-and-short stitch and split stitch on a silk ground (below left).

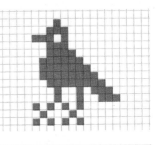

Bavaria in southern Germany has a long embroidery tradition. Women spun local flax and wool and wove some of the thread into fabric. They embroidered with convent stitch which took the form of laid threads couched with the same coloured thread, and with other laid and couched work and buttonhole stitch. Their designs were often pictorial, with themes sometimes taken from contemporary woodcuts.

Many German embroiderers in the past worked samplers. In format and design these were similar to those from the Netherlands. Early German samplers, worked with imported silk threads on a linen ground, were often long and narrow with proportions about 110 x 23 cm (43 x 9 in). As wider material became available samplers tended to be square, about 43 x 43 cm (17 x 17 in). Colouring was sometimes restricted to two shades of thread, and designs, often in spot-motif form, were usually executed in cross stitch but also in satin stitch and stem stitch. An eight-pointed star was one of the most popular devices. As with the rest of Europe, the practice of working samplers largely ceased by the beginning of the 20th century.

Much of the more recent output of Bavarian embroidery is found on traditional dress, embroidered by women for their families' use. Women's traditional dress consists, as in the Tirol, of a sleeveless front-lacing bodice worn over a white long-sleeved cotton blouse which is sometimes attached to its own linen skirt-petticoat. The skirt is a calf-length dirndl with a front apron.

Double-headed eagle in the national colours worked in long-legged cross stitch on a sampler made in 1685 (top).

Repeating pattern in brick stitch, worked with silk on a linen ground.

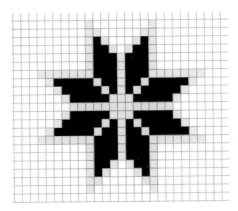

Eight-pointed star motif worked in black and cream cross stitch.

The Bavarian bodice is made from three pieces of fabric, usually wool or velvet joined together with underarm seams and buttoned at the shoulders. It is often boned for extra support. Embroidery is worked on both front panels and in the centre of the back panel with wool or silk thread, usually in satin stitch. Sometimes laid and couched metal thread is worked as an extra embellishment, either in zigzag formation or in large, swirling coil patterns.

Embroidery may also be worked on the apron, which is usually formed of one length of white cotton fabric, sometimes with a frilled border round the edge,

embroidered with scalloped cutwork. Decoration of the main panel of the apron is often worked with tiny stitches in repeating designs such as arrows.

Around the neck the Bavarian women might traditionally wear a square shawl made of silk and sometimes embroidered in silk thread. Devices are outlined in buttonhole stitch and infilled with gold thread laid diagonally and couched at junctions with tiny cross stitches in silk.

There is a variety of different Bavarian headdresses, the most common of which is a headscarf formed of one triangular piece of white linen. The scarf has panels of embroidery over the centre of the

forehead, as it is worn, and also in the corner hanging down at the back. Embroidery is geometric or floral with symmetrical devices worked in black or white silk in buttonhole stitch, satin stitch and stem stitch. Other forms of Bavarian women's headdress include complicated hats formed on frames of wire or card and embroidered with silver thread, spangles and beads.

Bavarian women also like to do counted-thread work in the form of cross-stitch embroidery, often working repeating motifs as borders to traycloths and similar items.

The tradition of various kinds of woolwork associated with many areas of northern Germany dates back to the 12th century. Women spun fleece into thread which they then sometimes used to embroider on grounds of locally produced linen in brick stitch, chain stitch, convent stitch, satin stitch and stem stitch.

Dyeing has generally been a man's skill in northern Germany. One of the most popular dyes was Saxon blue produced with chemic, a combination of sulphuric acid and powdered indigo, discovered by Herr Seidelman from Altenburg in Saxony in the middle of the 18th century.

Many of the woolwork embroideries were made into wall hangings and floor or table carpets, the last being essential furnishings of many German homes. Ground fabrics of linen were embroidered, generally with wool, sometimes using cross stitch and tent stitch. Designs were often pictorial or armorial.

Northern German embroiderers also used imported silk thread for some items of decoration as in the case of hats from Hesse. These hats take the form of small bonnets, often made of black silk formed over a card frame, with two long black streamers hanging down the back. The crown and brim were embroidered with silk or wool, with floral and diamond motifs in chain stitch and satin stitch.

Northern German traditional costumes are not now generally worn and embroiderers, usually women, work on household items and creative wall hangings. Needlepoint is popular and continues the long heritage of woolwork.

Undoubtedly the best-known and

Black silk satin-stitch flower motif to decorate a headscarf, and a cross-stitch lozenge for a shawl.

Bavarian traditional dress is possibly the most spectacular in Germany and there are many variations on the regional theme. The sleeves on the girl's bodice are unusually decorated with diamond-shaped smocking.

Late 17th-century woolwork table cover richly decorated with laid oriental, or romanian, stitch (below).

One of the ever-popular floral designs (below right), this motif is usually worked in cream and black silk cross stitch on linen.

most universally popular of all German woolwork forms is Berlin woolwork, a form of embroidery worked with bright-coloured wool, silk, chenille, beads and ribbons on a ground of single-weave canvas. The main stitches are cross stitch and tent stitch, with some use of bargello.

Berlin woolwork is so called because at the beginning of the 19th century a print seller in that city first produced hand-coloured paper graph patterns for embroiderers to transpose to their canvases. Ordinary engraved graphs with suggested motifs had been popular for many years, but the innovation of colour suggestions was well received by embroiderers in Berlin and soon the fashion for this easy embroidery spread throughout Europe and even to America.

Berlin woolwork was executed by

women generally for their own amusement. Although the paper patterns were produced commercially, many thousands of them being available from printsellers and other establishments in big cities, the actual embroidery was usually worked by amateurs. People practising Berlin woolwork would either transpose designs from a paper pattern or copy a motif already embroidered.

Designs were geometric, floral or pictorial. The geometric themes included many tartan-type designs offering a challenge to the embroiderers who wanted to work a complicated 'plaid'. Floral designs frequently had bunches of assorted flowers in cornucopias or in cone shapes. Pictorial themes, particularly from the middle of the 19th century, either stressed the exaggerated emotion

Sinuous floral motifs worked on fine cotton ground characterize Dresden whitework (above).

One of the first hand-coloured 'woolwork' paper patterns produced for sale (far left).

Berlin woolwork kettle boiling on the hob—a typically homely theme.

that was commonplace in much of Europe at that time or depicted pet dogs, parrots, hens on nests and homely kettles on the hearth. In the 1860s colouring became even more vivid than before with the advent of synthetic dyes.

Berlin woolwork lost its popularity during the late 19th century, although it is now enjoying a revival in some other countries, notably America. The collecting of old paper patterns and of actual examples of this and other Victorian embroidery reflects this interest.

Dresden

Another form of embroidery which takes its name from a German city is Dresden work. This is a whitework pulled-thread embroidery which is characterized by floral devices with flowing stems worked in cotton in a variety of stitches on a fine cotton ground.

Dresden work is sometimes wrongly called Tønder work, possibly because some of the early designs were copied from pillow laces from Jutland. It is not known whether Dresden work was in fact first worked in Germany, although Dresden had been producing pillow laces since the 16th century. The earliest examples of Dresden-work embroidery surviving today were worked in the late 17th century and by the middle of the 18th century the embroidery was international, being practised not only throughout Europe but also in New

England. It was sometimes taught in girls' schools.

Dresden work, made into caps, shirts and ruffles, fichus and aprons, was always worked by women, either for their own use or for sale. They embroidered with cotton thread on a cotton ground which was sometimes imported from India. Stitches include back stitch, coral stitch and various pulled-thread stitches. After the 1760s tamboured chain stitch was employed both for outlining devices and also for infilling leaves and other motifs.

Dresden work lost popularity in the middle of the 19th century and there is now no substantial commercial or domestic production of this form of needlework in Germany or elsewhere.

Bavarian Blouse

Inspired by the traditional costume of Bavaria, this cotton summer blouse has a flattering neckline and delicate smocking on the sleeves.

> You will need:
> 1.2 m (1⅜ yd) cotton fabric 112 cm (45 in) wide. Choose a tiny pattern in deep colours with a little white to match trim.
> 0.25 m (⅜ yd) broderie anglaise 3 cm (1¼ in) wide
> 1.1 m (1¼ yd) broderie anglaise 7 cm (2¾ in) wide
> 1 reel sewing cotton to tone
> 2 skeins pearl cotton to tone
> smocking transfer with dots 12 mm (½ in) apart
> 40 cm (16 in) zip fastener

Preparing the Fabric

Scale up the pattern pieces on paper (see page 272) and cut them out. Pin them to the fabric as shown in the layout. Cut four strips 26 x 3.3 cm (10¼ x 1⅜ in) for sleeve bands. Trim off L-shaped pieces of paper pattern from the neck and shoulder edge of both front and back of the bodice, making them 7.5 cm (3 in) wide. These will be the facings. Cut them out of the

waste fabric, remembering to place the centre front on a fold. Mark the centre fronts, centres of sleeves and the positions of the darts.

Use the smocking transfer to mark dots over the shaded area on the wrong side of the sleeves.

Preparing Sleeves for Smocking

Run gathering threads of sewing cotton along horizontal lines of dots, taking a tiny stitch at each dot. Set a pin alongside each pair of threads and pull up the threads to form regular pleats, winding the spare thread round the pins. Work the smocking as shown.

Making the Blouse

Baste and stitch the darts in both front and back. Slash the front darts and press them open.

Insert the zip fastener and sew the remainder of the centre back seam.

Join the shoulder seams and press them open. Join the shoulders of the facings and press them open. Sew a narrow single hem round the outer edges of the facings.

Pin and baste the narrow trimming right sides together to the right side of the fabric along the back sides of the neck opening. Add the wider trim across

the front edge (see diagram). Baste and stitch the facings to the neck edge, right sides together. Trim the seam. Reinforce the corners with a second line of stitching alongside the first and clip in towards the stitching (see diagram). Turn the facings to the inside and press. Fold under the short ends of the wide trimming and slip stitch.

Sew the side seams, neaten with zigzag machine stitch, and press them open.

Lay the sleeve bands together in pairs, right sides facing. Sandwich a piece of narrow trim between them along one long side, as for the neck edge, and stitch.

Sew the sleeve seams, neaten and press them open. Attach a sleeve band to the lower edge of each.

Pin the sleeves into the armholes matching the centres of the sleeves to the shoulder seams. Stitch, trim, neaten and press the seams towards the garment.

Turn up a narrow hem at the bottom edge of the blouse and press.

Pattern sizes	
————————	81 cm (32 in)
– – – – – – – –	91 cm (36 in)
— — — — — —	96 cm (38 in)

For size 86 cm (34 in) split the difference between sizes 81-91 cm (32-36 in).

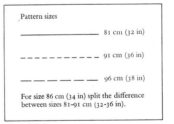

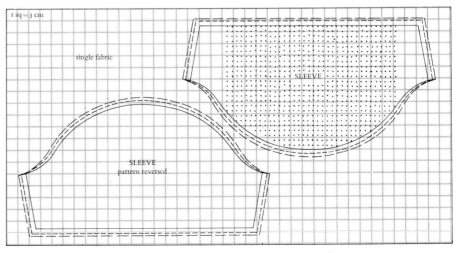

Smocking.

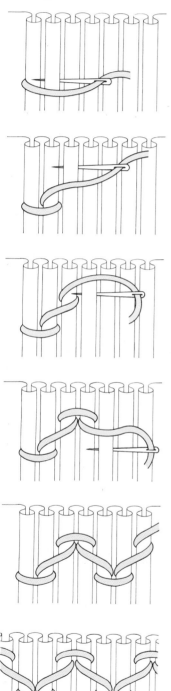

Eastern Europe and the Balkans

The embroidery of eastern Europe and the Balkans is characterized by a predominance of red stitching on a ground of natural or bleached single open-weave linen, a fabric that is still widely used in embroidery. Flax is cultivated in Poland, Czechoslovakia, Hungary, eastern Yugoslavia and inland Romania. There is some silk farming in western Yugoslavia and in Bulgaria and Romania and cotton is grown extensively in southern Macedonia but neither is used very much in embroidery. Sheep are farmed throughout eastern Europe and the Balkans and embroidery on sheepskin, fur or hide is carried out in Hungary and Romania.

In the past some embroidery was worked with natural-coloured linen thread on a ground of the same colour linen, sometimes woven by the embroiderers themselves. When natural dyestuffs began to be used red was obtained from florets of madder or dried bodies of kermes insects from the Mediterranean areas; yellow from dried weld or onion peel; blue from woad plants; and black from oak or alder bark.

Then as now embroidery was worked by women. They were taught at home, or, in Christian areas, in convents. In contrast to western Europe, novice embroiderers did not practise on samplers. Men do occasionally embroider, however, producing the woolwork of Carpathia, the leather work of the Magyars of Hungary and the costume decoration of the Ghegs and Tosks of Albania.

The stitch most frequently met with in the embroidery of eastern Europe is cross stitch. There are many varieties, including ordinary diagonal cross stitch and long-legged cross stitch. In Hungary particularly, vertical cross stitches are worked on a trellis of laid threads. In Montenegro an exaggeratedly long-legged cross stitch is employed. Other stitch forms include needle or tamboured chain stitch, festoon stitch, slanting Slav stitch, flat or padded satin stitch and needleweaving. Drawn-thread work is practised to a small degree in the Carpathian mountains and in Croatia, and cutwork is particularly associated with Czechoslovakia. Appliqué is found in Hungary and also in Bulgaria and Romania. Whitework is executed in Krakow, Croatia and Wallachia and blackwork is associated primarily with Bohemia, Montenegro and Transylvania. Metal-thread work is practised today in Silesia, Serbia, Montenegro and Albania.

The long Turkish occupation until recent times of Bulgaria, part of Romania and Yugoslavia, including Macedonia, means that Islam has played a dominant role in embroidery design in those areas. There are also strong Catholic and Orthodox Christian traditions, particularly in Yugoslavia, but these

have not resulted in measurable influence in embroidery design. Although eastern Europe has been a bridge between the west and Asia, few embroidery designs, religious or secular, have been introduced from western Europe. In the main the flow of motifs and patterns has been from the east.

Eastern European embroidery is often worked in band form, in narrow borders of repeating motifs. These are extensively used to decorate the edges of household pieces such as towels and table linens. Embroidery is still used in some areas for costume decoration, mainly embellishing women's scarves and caps, blouses, petticoats and aprons. It is also sometimes employed to decorate men's shirts and trousers.

Colours sometimes had particular meanings in different areas. Bright red, for instance, signified innocence and contentment with life, as in Croatia and Serbia, or it was thought to be appropriate for younger women, as in Silesia. Older women tended to wear more sombre embroidered decoration. Apart from the now more limited working of costume embroidery for their own use, women in many parts of eastern Europe decorate blouses and other garments for sale in western Europe and America. They use commercial threads on grounds often of natural-coloured linen and work cross stitch in repeating or spot motifs of floral or geometric patterns.

Many forms of headdress are worn by Hungarian women. This cap is decorated with applied pieces of ribbon, spangles sewn on with radial retaining stitches and with long tubular beads.

In Romania, double running stitch is sometimes worked in step formation, in two different coloured threads.

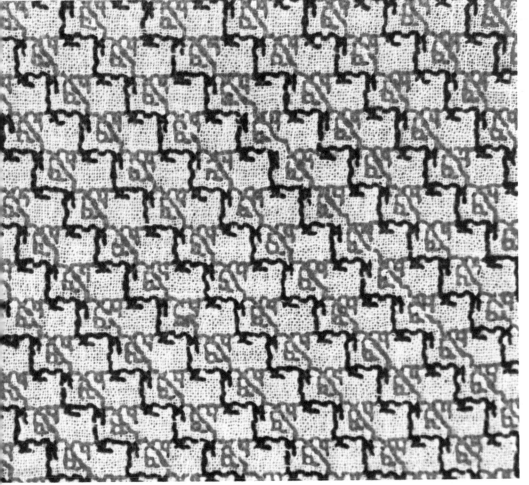

Poland

Women of Poland have a tradition of embroidery which they work for their own families' use and for sale. Much of the most beautiful work has been used to embellish women's traditional costume, which is highly localized in the detail of its design but in general similar to that of many areas of western Europe. It consists of a white blouse with puffed sleeves, a wool or velvet front-lacing bodice, a mid-calf skirt and white linen apron. Embroidery is found on the blouse cuffs and on the front panels and shoulder straps of the bodice.

Since traditional costume is now generally worn only by a few older people, some of the women of Poland today work cross stitch and other forms of embroidery on domestic items. They use a natural-coloured linen ground with a monochrome thread, often of deep red, or with two or more colours. Designs are often worked in repeating form, with eight-pointed stars and other geometric devices.

Silesia, a region in the south-west of Poland, has its own distinctive style of embroidery, silesian cross stitch. This is often worked in narrow bands with the reserves of the motifs embroidered and the devices themselves, in star or floral shapes, left unworked, giving a negative pattern similar to Assisi work. Although ordinary diagonal cross stitch is most often employed, long-legged cross stitch is sometimes preferred, with red the most popular colour.

A distinguishing feature of traditional Silesian embroidery is the goldwork decoration found particularly in the

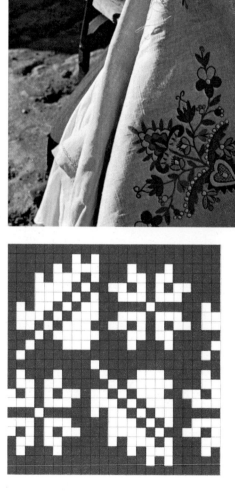

This Polish lady, wearing a sleeveless bolero and matching cap embroidered with gold thread laid over card and couched, is working satin stitch and stem stitch on a linen ground fabric.

Silesian cross-stitch designs which could be used for a repeating border. Dark red is the traditional colour.

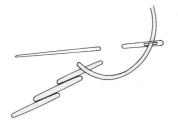

Slanting slav stitch can be worked in diagonal or horizontal alignment.

southern part of the region on women's bonnets and bodices. Gold thread and gold-coloured silks are either couched or worked in satin stitch, and patterns often consist of simple floral devices with oval leaves. The centres of the flowers are sometimes infilled with gold-coloured spangles, each held in place with a large french knot.

Whitework, with chain stitching on a ground of fine linen, was formerly worked in the Poznań region of western central Poland but today it is generally associated with the Krakow area where women decorate table linens and similar household items. Krakow whitework is a cutwork embroidery, and surface stitching is worked in padded or flat satin stitch. Design motifs are floral with great swirling blooms formed of round or oval holes which are made with a stiletto or with scissors and are then bound with closely worked small overcast stitches.

A strong tradition of sheep rearing exists in the Carpathian Mountains, which straddle parts of Poland, Czechoslovakia, Hungary, Romania and the Soviet Union. This area today is one of the few enclaves in eastern Europe where men embroider. They sew and embroider men's coats and trousers for sale, decorating local woollen fabric with woollen threads which they usually dye themselves.

Nearly a hundred years ago trousers with two front openings became fashionable. Embroidery round the openings became more and more elaborate until what are known as *parzenice* evolved. These are complicated knot and scroll embroidery devices worked in U-shapes down either edge and round the bottom of the vertical openings. The main stitches are chain, herringbone and flat satin as well as laid and couched work, in the form of commercial twisted braid coiled into arched, scrolled and knot shapes and couched with small hemming stitches.

Carpathian men's trousers also have embroidery worked in a narrow vertical band covering the outer leg seams. This embroidery frequently matches that on the long coats formerly worn with them.

While Carpathian men's coats and trousers are professionally embroidered, their shirts are generally worked by women at home. Made of white linen, the shirts have stand-up collar bands and flared wrist-length sleeves. Bands of embroidery are worked on the collar and round the sleeves, below the shoulder and round the wrists. Embroidery is executed in drawn-thread work and satin stitch, with repeating patterns of triangles and zigzags.

The petals and leaves of this Silesian motif are worked with close parallel satin stitches, and the stamens are spangles held with french knots. The stems are gold cord laid and couched with tiny hem stitches. The ground is of deep purple velvet.

Carpathian men's traditional dress includes front double-opening trousers decorated with *parzenice*, complicated scroll and floral designs of twisted and couched braid.

Czechoslovakia

Three main styles of embroidery can be found in Czechoslovakia, and these correspond to the geographical regions of Bohemia, Moravia and Slovakia although many stitches and techniques are practised throughout the country.

Flax is grown in many parts of Czechoslovakia but most embroidery is now worked on a commercially produced linen fabric, with traditional motifs in counted-thread or free-form floral styles mainly executed as decoration on household linens.

Ordinary or long-legged cross stitch is found in the north of the country. Narrow bands of embroidery are worked in such a way that the background is embroidered in one colour and repeating motifs of eight-pointed stars and other devices are left unworked, as in Silesia.

Embroidered bands may alternatively be worked in satin stitch, the stitches worked vertically, horizontally or diagonally to form triangles and stars. Both threads and ground are usually of natural-coloured linen.

Cutwork embroidery is popular in many parts of Czechoslovakia. As in hardanger work and related forms, the outlines of the devices are worked with tiny running stitches. A series of radial cuts is made inside the outlines to allow one segment at a time to be turned back and overstitched. In Czechoslovak cutwork, motifs, which may be of circular, arc or leaf shape, are sometimes so closely aligned that after the centres of the devices have been cut and worked none of the original ground remains and the result resembles lace.

Traditional costume in Czechoslovakia was often richly embroidered. It is now worn only on special occasions, and the brightest embroidery is worn by unmarried girls or brides.

Bohemia and Moravia, the western and central regions of Czechoslovakia, have

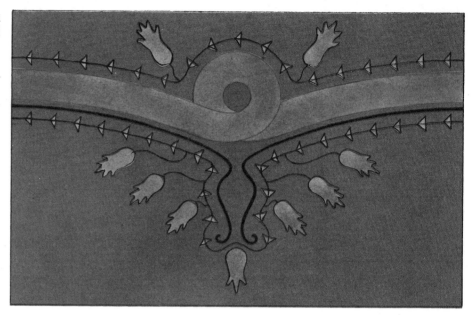

Detail of a Moravian *parzenice* motif in applied braid surrounded by laid and couched work,

very similar costumes. Women wear a front-lacing bodice, often stiffly boned, over a white full-sleeved blouse. In Bohemia the sleeves and collar may be decorated with fine needle or pillow lace and in Moravia with deep indigo satin stitch in a complicated design of flowers or square blocks representing grapes. In Moravia the hems of the elbow-length sleeves are also embroidered with back stitch and satin stitch worked in metal thread to form complex scroll patterns.

The women also wear a full skirt of thick wool over several petticoats and a front apron tied round the waist. In Bohemia the aprons are embroidered with buttonhole stitch, satin stitch, french knots and some drawn- and pulled-thread work. Colouring is often monochrome, with golden, indigo or black thread worked in solid blocks of satin stitch to form repeating floral devices.

A distinguishing feature of Moravian costume is tamboured chain stitch, which is sometimes used to outline flower and leaf designs embroidered in woollen thread on a linen apron.

The costume is completed with a linen cap, sometimes embroidered with eyelet stitch, but younger girls may prefer a white linen headscarf, its edges decorated with white or black repeating designs in satin stitch and cutwork. These are sometimes embellished with spangles, each one sewn on with a french knot through the centre, and the main corner of the scarf is often filled with a similar motif.

The embroidery and costume decoration of Slovakia, the south-eastern area of Czechoslovakia, are more similar to those of northern Hungary than to the rest of Czechoslovakia.

A Slovak woman's traditional costume consists of a sleeveless dress worn under a short-sleeved white linen blouse and a sleeveless front-lacing bodice. Two aprons are worn, one at the back and one at the front, and frequently they are both embroidered with cross-stitch spot motifs

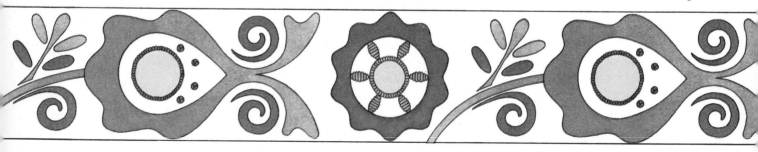

Silesian cross-stitch motif.

of birds, flowers and people, worked in red and black throughout.

A married Slovak woman used never to go outside without covering her head. One form of traditional hat, made of white linen, consists of a square crown with gathered brim about 19 cm (7½ in) deep, embroidered all over in orange, black and green silk threads with four-sided stitch, satin stitch and needle-weaving.

Slovak women prefer today to embroider household items such as table linens and bed hangings. A typical border for a bed hanging might be made up of outline devices of plant forms in brown back stitch infilled with cream-coloured silk thread. The reserves of the design would be pulled-thread work.

A popular form of decoration in Slovakia is complex knot stitching, with french knots worked close together to cover the reserves of a design which is itself left unworked. This produces a variation of the Assisi-type 'negative motif' found in the cross stitching of Silesia and in other parts of Czechoslovakia. When executed in white on white, this Slovak knot stitching has a very subtle effect.

Bohemian repeating design worked on linen, with satin stitch, stem stitch and french knots. Overcast stitching is worked round the cutwork holes.

Czechoslovak cutwork is similar to Danish hedebo (see page 64), the folded edges stitched with overcasting instead of buttonhole stitch.

Hungary

The embroidery that is characteristic of Hungary is mainly the work of the Magyars, who make up the vast majority of the population. It may be divided into embroidery on linen and embroidery on fur or thick wool, often decorating the traditional coats worn by Magyar men.

Flax is farmed throughout Hungary, and there is a strong tradition of embroidering on local linen. Women used to spin and weave flax which they then decorated and made into household items such as bedcovers, which were also used as funerary cloths or as screens when women were in childbirth. The covers were made of two widths of linen cloth joined by interlacing and embroidered at one end, which was often fringed.

Linen embroidery today is decorated with either counted-thread or free-form designs. Counted-thread techniques include alternating satin stitch, two-sided stitch, whipped stitch, open chain stitch, and satin stitch with each stitch worked over a designated number of warp or weft threads to contribute to a geometric pattern such as a diamond. An unusual version of cross stitch is also used, in which vertical crosses are formed on a lattice of threads laid on the ground fabric. Each cross is subsequently couched with a small diagonal stitch.

Free-form embroidery is worked with needle chain stitch, feather stitch,

Detail of modern Hungarian embroidery worked in woollen satin stitch.

satin stitch or stem stitch. Open chain stitch is worked in scrolled lines, hence its local name of small writing stitch. Devices are sometimes first outlined with chain stitch or stem stitch, then infilled with alternating satin stitch or ordinary satin stitch. This is worked over the stem stitch, or through half the chain stitch, without entering the ground fabric, and then into the ground at the opposite side of the motif.

Embroidery designs are truly cosmopolitan, illustrating the fact that Hungary has been a crossroads in Europe. The Magyars are thought to be a blend of Ugric and Turkish peoples who came from western Siberia in about the 5th century and there are, certainly, elements of Turkish design in some Magyar linen

Hungarian satin stitch is sometimes worked in carefully counted blocks to produce geometric shapes.

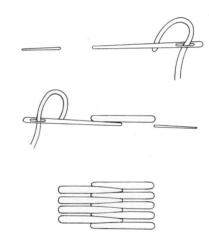

Alternating satin stitch.

Whipped stitch (or alternating back stitch).

Hungarian wool embroidery, with densely worked chain stitch, plait stitch, satin stitch and stem stitch.

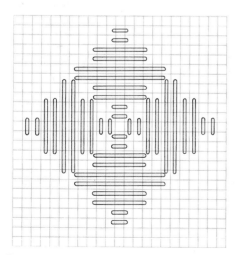

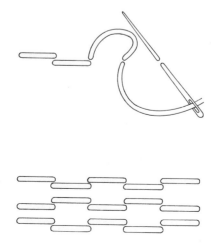

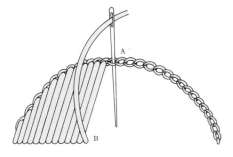

Sometimes satin stitch is worked over an outline of chain stitches. The needle goes through the chain, but not the ground fabric, at A, and then makes a tiny stitch at B.

Hungarian satin stitch worked in combination with white cut-work on a white linen ground.

Repeating floral design worked in buttonhole stitch, chain stitch, cross stitch and satin stitch.

Hungarian cross stitch worked on a lattice of laid threads.

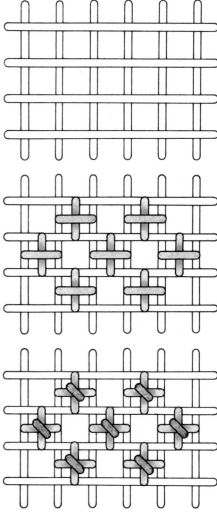

embroideries. One example is a cypress tree, or tree of life, embroidered in red cotton cross stitch in repeating form. From more recent times, trade with the Far East has undoubtedly introduced an element of Chinese 'voiding' in much solid-block satin-stitch embroidery.

As well as household items, Magyar women used to embroider traditional costume, but very little is worked today. Details vary according to the region, but the costume generally consists of a bodice, sometimes with a concealed fastening rather than the usual eastern European open lacing, worn over a short-sleeved blouse and very full, below-the-knee skirt with front apron. In some regions embroidery is worked on front yokes and around the bottom of the sleeves of the blouses, all over the bodices, and in horizontal bands at the bottom of the aprons.

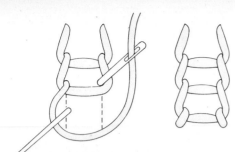

Open chain stitch.

In winter some men and women wear traditional sheepskin cloaks, coats and jackets, decorated with leather appliqué or with direct embroidery. Applied devices of bright-coloured leather, held in place with small cotton hem stitches, are found round the shoulders of the cloak and on the front and back panels of women's jackets. The stylized floral devices are sometimes embellished with silk satin-stitch embroidery and buttons held in place with french knots or running stitch.

Appliqué on leather is still worked by male embroiderers in many parts of Hungary today. Appliqué of fine linen or silk on a linen ground is, on the other hand, traditionally a woman's skill in the west of Hungary.

Male embroiderers also decorate *szürs*, the thick coats worn by many Magyar men. The coats have full-length inset sleeves and wide collars that extend at the back to form small square capes. The skirts of the coats reach below the knee and have back and two side slits from the hips down. Sometimes all the outer edges of the *szür*, round the vertical front opening, round the cuffs, either side of all three skirt slits and round the hem, are decorated with appliqué in plain-coloured wool. The appliqué serves the duty of giving binding support as well as being decorative. The applied binding is held in place with back stitch or chain stitch or by laid cord couched with small hem stitches. Embroidery is subsequently worked on the appliqué, and also on other parts of the coat which are subject

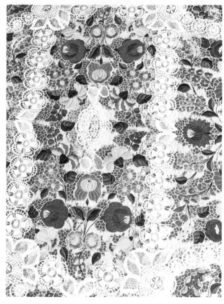

Polychrome satin stitch is sometimes worked on a ground fabric of fine white needle or bobbin lace.

to extra wear or strain, notably under the arms. One characteristic of *szür* embroidery is a tendency to crowd all the areas of ground with stitching, leaving very little of the fabric unworked.

Beneath his *szür* a Magyar man traditionally wears a tunic of natural-coloured linen reaching below the knee. It has inset sleeves and a vertical front opening down to the waist and is tied at the neck with a bow. Embroidered borders are worked over the seams, round the hems of the sleeves and round the main hem of the tunic. They are repeating patterns worked in cross stitch, often in red and featuring floral motifs.

Although traditional costume is now rarely used for everyday wear, embroidered items are still being produced by both men and women.

Szür floral border design in satin stitch on a white wool ground. A wavy line of back stitch is worked on the applied red wool edging.

Yugoslavia

The embroidery of Yugoslavia falls into four subdivisions according to the geographical regions of Croatia, Montenegro, Serbia and Macedonia.

Croatia is the northern central area of Yugoslavia around Zagreb, now also including the Dalmatian coast, where cross-stitch embroidery is predominant. It is usually worked with a silk thread which is sometimes locally produced in Dalmatia. Ground fabrics are linen, some of which is spun in the home, and wool. The most popular embroidery colour scheme is red on a natural-coloured ground.

Although cross stitch is predominant in coloured-thread embroidery, other stitches are also used. Towards the north of the region buttonhole stitch and free-form satin stitch are popular. Further south, counted-thread satin stitch and drawn-thread work are preferred. White thread is sometimes used, particularly in Dalmatia where women's blouses are decorated with eyelet stitch, satin stitch and stem stitch worked in floral designs similar to some Italian embroideries.

Montenegro, a constituent republic of southern Yugoslavia, was for a long time fiercely independent. The area is rugged and is largely agricultural and pastoral. Local wool is used for both embroidery thread and ground fabric. Blackwork is sometimes executed, with woollen thread from black sheep used to decorate white woven wool or felt fabric.

The stitching is sometimes so dense that none of the ground fabric shows through. Embroidery is done in montenegrin stitch, a long-legged cross with a vertical stitch, and also in buttonhole stitch, chain stitch, satin stitch and pattern darning.

Bosnia stitch.

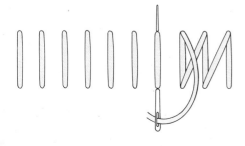

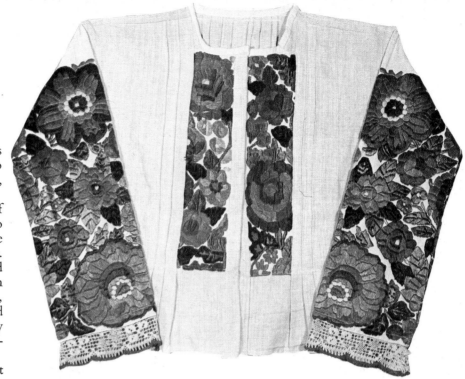

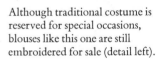

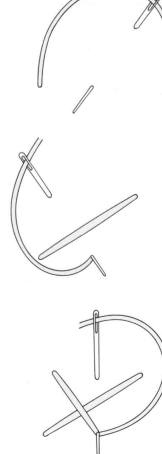

Although traditional costume is reserved for special occasions, blouses like this one are still embroidered for sale (detail left).

Montenegro cross stitch.

Cross stitch is popular throughout Yugoslavia, sometimes worked in black silks on a white linen ground.

Yugoslavian Blouse

You will need:

2.8 m (3 yd) fine white
cotton lawn 90 cm (36 in)
wide

3 m (3¼ yd) nainsook bias
binding 12 mm (½ in) wide

0.5 m (½ yd) rolled elastic
for the cuffs

14 skeins stranded
embroidery cotton in the
following colours:

red 6 skeins

black 4 skeins

yellow 2 skeins

green 2 skeins

bright-coloured basting
cotton

2 reels white sewing cotton

Zigzag chain stitch.
Work as for ordinary chain
stitch, slanting the stitches
alternately to right and left.

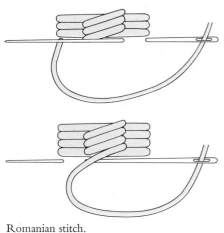

Romanian stitch.
Start as if for a satin stitch, but
bring the needle up one-third of
the way back along the stitch and
above it. Bring the thread over
the stitch, push the needle down
through the fabric two-thirds of
the way along the first stitch and
bring it up as if ready to start
another satin stitch.

Preparing the Fabric

Draw the pattern pieces to size on thin
white paper and mark the position
of the embroidery on them.

Pin the pattern pieces on the fabric.
Do not cut out the sleeve top panels. Instead
of cutting, baste round the edges and
mark the position of the embroidery with
tailor tacks. Cut out the pieces, leaving
as much fabric as possible round the
sleeve tops. Mark points a, b, c and d.
Do not split the neck opening.

Neaten all the edges with zigzag
machining or overcasting.

Transfer the embroidery design to the
fabric pieces (see page 272).

Embroidery

Use two strands of embroidery cotton
throughout. If you do not use an
embroidery hoop, take care not to pull
the stitches too tight.

Work the embroidery using the diagram as a guide to both stitches and
colours.

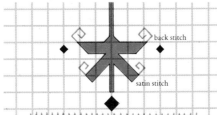

Scale up the motifs for the cuffs
(left) to 7 cm (2¾ in) wide and for
the centre front (above) to 11 cm
(4¼ in) wide. Work the stitches
as shown in the diagrams.
Scale up the motifs for the upper
sleeves (below) to 27 cm (10½ in)
wide. Work the black and gold
petals in romanian stitch, the red
and yellow petals, the green stems
and the red and black sections of
the border in satin stitch. Work the
remaining areas in close rows of
chain stitch and outline the
centre red motif in back stitch.

A pretty adaptation of a traditional east European style with a versatile drawstring neckline and elasticated cuffs. The unusual cut was originally dictated by the size of traditional looms which produced fabric only 45 cm (18 in) wide.

Making the Blouse

Damp press the embroidery (see page 272).

Trim off the extra fabric round the sleeve tops and neaten the edges.

Slit the neck opening and roll the smallest double hem possible. Baste this in place and work over it in a buttonhole stitch, taking care that the lower end of the slit is firmly stitched.

Roll narrow hems at the bottom edges of the cuffs and work over them with the same buttonhole stitch. Make a casing 8 cm (3¼ in) above the hems by stitching bias binding to the wrong side.

Gather the top of the lower sleeves between points a and match them to the points marked a on the top sleeve. Seam the two parts together and press.

Sew the gussets to the sleeves, matching points b and c (see diagram).

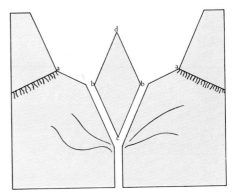

Sew the sleeve seams and press.

Seam the sleeves and gussets between side fronts and side backs, matching points a, b and d, and press. Then sew the side seams from d to hem and press.

Sew the side fronts to the front and side backs to the back.

Turn in 6 mm (¼ in) round the neck and finish with binding.

Turn in a 2 cm (¾ in) double hem round the bottom of the blouse and hem it with white cotton.

Thread elastic through the cuffs and adjust it to size.

Using black embroidery cotton work zigzag chain stitch down the seam lines of front and back and either side of the sleeve tops.

Make a drawstring 1.5 m (1⅝ yd) long with three strands of embroidery cotton and thread it through the neck. (If preferred, the neck may be elasticated.)

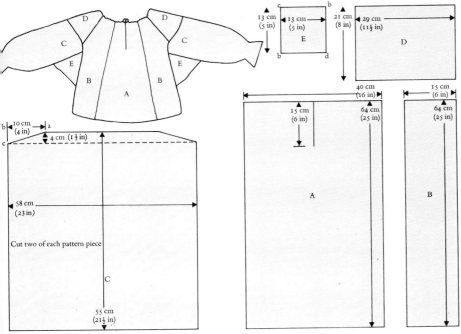

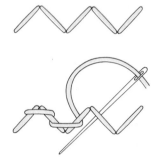

Yugoslav border stitch (laced zigzags of straight stitches).

Macedonian stitch (lines of tent stitch worked in alternating directions).

Trees of life are particularly evident as a repeating motif in Serbian embroidery design, a direct result of strong Turkish influence.

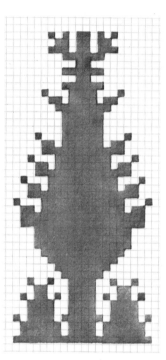

Geometric cross-stitch design worked round the edge of a sleeve. Tassels are frequently added to complement the design.

Serbia, the central region of Yugoslavia, is the home of most of the minority of Moslems in Yugoslavia. Turkish influence is therefore particularly prominent in embroidery design, with mosques and cypress trees or trees of life recurring.

The colouring of the embroidery, worked usually in silk or wool thread on a ground of natural-coloured linen or wool, is often red. It is brighter towards the north of Serbia, where the colour is associated with happiness. In the south, dark colours such as black, green and dark red are popular. Predominant among Serbian embroideries are repeating bands worked, for example, as borders for long tablecloths. The main motifs are often crosses or eight-pointed stars, which may be flanked by scrolls and squares.

The southernmost part of Yugoslavia is Macedonia, a region which extends across northern Greece and south-western Bulgaria. Some cotton and flax are grown in this area and both cotton and linen are used as embroidery grounds.

Much of the embroidery of Macedonia is worked solely in red thread, and generally in wool. Motifs are sometimes outlined in chain stitch and subsequently infilled with tent stitch, which may be worked from the reverse of the fabric. Horizontal lines of tent stitch, with diagonal lines facing alternately to the left and to the right, may be called macedonian stitch. Cross stitch and pattern darning are also used.

Traditional costumes in Yugoslavia vary a little from one area to the next. In the north a woman's costume generally consists of a long-sleeved white linen blouse worn under a bodice which is usually attached to its own full skirt. An embroidered front apron is worn by women throughout Yugoslavia.

To the south of Zagreb the skirt and bodice are replaced by a linen tunic decorated with wool embroidery in cross stitch and stem stitch on the sleeves and front yoke.

In Macedonia a woman's long-sleeved white linen dress is sometimes decorated with applied bands of black cotton embroidered with diamond shapes of pattern darning. In Serbia, however, the costume is Turkish in origin. It often takes the form of a natural linen dress embroidered with woollen, linen or cotton thread, often worked in bosnia, chain and cross stitches. Sometimes it is made of dark-coloured velvet decorated with metallic braid or thread laid and couched or worked direct to the fabric with chain stitch.

A Yugoslavian man's costume generally consists of a white linen shirt, embroidered either side of the neck opening, a sleeveless jacket, and trousers with two vertical front openings decorated with laid and couched cord in a similar fashion to Carpathian trousers.

With the exception of parts of Serbia, traditional costume is little worn today and not much costume embroidery is practised.

Bulgaria

The embroidery of Bulgaria is characterized by motifs outlined in black silk with either back stitch or cross stitch, with black hooks coming off at a tangent from the main motif. The motifs are usually stylized floral devices worked in repeating form and infilled with reds, dark blue or green.

Embroidery is worked by women on a ground of wool or linen, often locally produced. Much of the silk thread comes from the eastern coastal region.

Traditional costume for a woman consists of a full-length white linen dress with long sleeves worn under a woollen or linen skirt with a matching short or hip-length bolero or jacket. There is a front waist apron, which sometimes has woven decoration, and a headscarf.

The main embroidery embellishes the sleeves, front neck opening and hem. In the north-west of the country, vertical strips of linen about 30 x 12 cm (12 x 5 in) are first embroidered and then applied to women's jackets. In the Sofia region embroidery is worked on woollen skirts and jackets.

Embroidery is sometimes executed on the woollen jackets traditionally worn by Bulgarian men. White cord is laid on the ground fabric and couched with small stitches. White silk thread is subsequently worked in satin stitch to form half-circle and diamond shapes.

Traditional dress from Burgas on the Black Sea Coast of Bulgaria includes a black velvet bolero decorated with spangles.

Bulgarian motif with an outline worked in black back stitch and a device infilled in dark red cross stitch.

Detail of a Bulgarian 'modesty vest', the repeating motifs outlined with back stitch with cross-stitch infilling.

Albania

Fertile but surrounded by mountains, Albania is the most politically inaccessible country in Europe. It is home to two major language groups, the Ghegs to the north and the Tosks to the south. Five hundred years of Turkish rule before the beginning of this century influenced Albanian embroidery in the use of unusually delicate ground fabrics and various Turkish metal-thread techniques.

Silk is sometimes locally produced but Albania has no local flax or cotton farming and some embroidery ground fabric must therefore be imported, now mainly from its major trading partner, China. There is, however, sheep farming in the mountainous inland areas, and wool is used for both ground fabric and embroidery thread. As well as vegetable dyes such as sumach and madder, Albanian women use green walnuts to obtain brown, ash bark for black and copper sulphate for blue. Traditionally women embroider on linen or cotton, whereas professional men work embroidery on wool.

Embroidery includes gold or silver thread or fine flat strips of either metal laid on the ground fabric and couched with large stitches. Sometimes the laid metal is coiled in circles, with one retaining stitch in the middle of each circle, giving the effect of a wheel hub. Other designs include long straight stitches worked as radii to form a wheel. Spherical and tubular glass or plastic beads are sometimes attached to the ground fabric with straight stitches.

Most Albanian embroidery is found as costume decoration. A Gheg man traditionally wears a loose shirt of linen, a

tight low-necked waistcoat, and tight woollen trousers embellished with embroidery. A Gheg woman wears a full-length long-sleeved dress of linen or black wool with a sleeveless bodice and a small waist apron. On her head she wears a small skull cap with a shoulder-length white veil. Embroidery is worked in bands round the opening of the bodice and at the cuffs, round the hem of the dress, on the hem of the trouser legs and on the cap.

A Tosk man wears a long-sleeved shirt with a thick waist cummerbund, either a knee-length kilt or calf-length baggy pants, and one or two jackets, one on top of the other, of wool or velvet, generally one with sleeves and the other sleeveless.

Embroidery is usually worked only on the jackets. A Tosk woman wears a full-length sleeved dress, a short sleeveless bodice, long tight trousers and a large muslin waist apron, which is sometimes two layers thick with scalloped edges. On the head she wears a pillbox cap, sometimes with coins attached round the brim. Embroidery is executed on the bodice, round the sleeves of the dress, on the trousers and on the apron.

No Gheg or Tosk embroidered costume is produced commercially for export. Unlike their counterparts in other areas of eastern Europe and the Balkans, Albanians have scarcely begun to appreciate the potential overseas market.

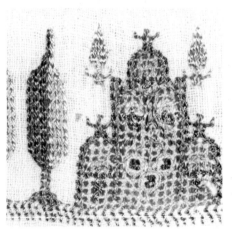

Albanian silk embroidery, worked with chain stitch and overcast filling and other pulled-thread techniques.

Albanian embroidery on cotton is traditionally worked by women, sometimes using both silk and metal threads to execute satin stitch, stem stitch and straight stitch.

Romania

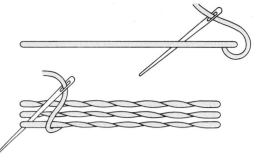

Romanian couching. Small stitches are taken from right to left over the laid thread.

Whitework design with blocks of satin stitch and regularly positioned eyelets.

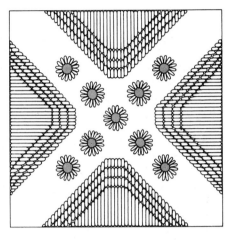

Locally produced ground fabrics and threads are in greater supply in Romania than in any other eastern European country. Cotton, linen and silk are all produced in localized areas and sheep are farmed extensively throughout. Embroidery is often worked on a ground of natural-coloured *pansa*, a fabric woven loosely of cotton or linen with the appearance of thin crepe.

One frequently encountered technique now popular in many countries of the world is romanian stitch, worked either as an infilling or couching. Other stitches employed in Romanian embroidery include back stitch, buttonhole stitch, chain stitch, cross stitch, eyelet stitch, double running stitch and straight stitch.

Romanian women usually embroider motifs in repeating form. Complex crosses, stylized flowers and simple zigzags are aligned vertically, horizontally or diagonally. Many motifs are embellished with scrolls or hooks, as in Bulgaria.

A man's traditional costume consists of a long white linen shirt, with embroidery sometimes on both the front yoke and sleeves. Motifs are outlined in

black and frequently infilled with green, red or blue. The shirt is worn outside white linen trousers and with a sleeveless bolero or sleeved jacket of either wool or leather.

Particularly in Transylvania, the northwestern area of Romania, black sheep's wool is embroidered in satin stitch on white woven or felt jackets giving them the appearance of blackwork. Leather jackets are sometimes embroidered by men, who apply rectangles of cotton to the main ground with slipstitch and then cover the edges of the motifs with laid and couched white cord. Surface embroidery is then worked in romanian stitch and satin stitch in circles, half-circles and diamonds.

A woman's traditional costume includes either a white blouse, generally with a full yoke gathered into a waistband and full-length raglan sleeves, or a long tunic worn under a full-length gathered or wrap-round skirt of wool or linen. Tunics and blouses are embroidered round the neckband and waistband, across the shoulders and in horizontal and diagonal bands on the sleeves. All embroidered decoration is worked either in

colour, with red and black dominating, or, especially in Wallachia to the south, in whitework, with eyelet stitch, satin stitch and pulled-thread work executed in diagonal crosses and other geometric patterns.

Embroidery is still worked in many areas and traditional dress is occasionally to be seen in daily use. Some blouses and other costume items are produced for commercial purposes and traditional designs are also transposed to household linens, and are sold in markets.

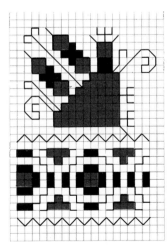

Romanian whitework quilt.

Traditional table runner incorporating a wide variety of stitches and spangles and bugle beads.

Many Romanian embroidery motifs are outlined in back stitch and infilled with cross stitch.

Romanian Apron

You will need:
1.25 m (1⅜ yd) white cotton
    lawn 90 cm (36 in) wide
soft embroidery threads in
    three colours:
blue 1 skein
yellow 1 skein
red 2 skeins
coton à broder in three
    colours:
red 1 skein
black 1 skein
green 1 skein
1 reel white sewing cotton
embroidery hoop (optional)

The bold designs and strong
primary colours stitched on skirts
and aprons in the Balkans are just
right for decorating a pretty
pinafore.

Preparing the Fabric

Open the fabric out flat. Measure and
mark out the pattern pieces with pins or
tailor's chalk (see diagram). Cut out the
pieces.

Taking a 2 cm (¾ in) seam allowance,
turn in and machine a narrow hem down
each side of the apron skirt.

Turn the bottom edge under 6 mm
(¼ in) and then another 4 cm (1½ in).
Machine the hem in place.

Scale up the embroidery motif to an
area 16 x 25 cm (6½ x 9¾ in) and transfer it
(see page 272) so that it repeats three and
a half times across the skirt. The base line
of the pattern should lie 3 mm (⅛ in)
below the line of machine stitching and
the left-hand edge should lie just outside
the side hem.

Embroidery

It is advisable to hold the work in an
embroidery hoop to avoid puckering.

Work the skirt embroidery using
colours and stitches as shown in the
diagram.

Use soft embroidery thread for all the
stitching except fly stitch and detached
chain motifs, which should be worked in
the thinner coton à broder.

Use fairly short back stitches for the
blue and yellow scrolls and large ones
(about 6 mm or ¼ in) long for the red
lines.

Work herringbone stitch in two bands

so that the bottoms of the stitches in
the upper band align exactly with the
tops of the stitches in the lower one.
Work the blue stitches first and then
space the yellow ones evenly between
them.

Work a row of running stitches across
the middle of each herringbone band so
that the stitches hold down the two
colours of herringbone threads where
they cross.

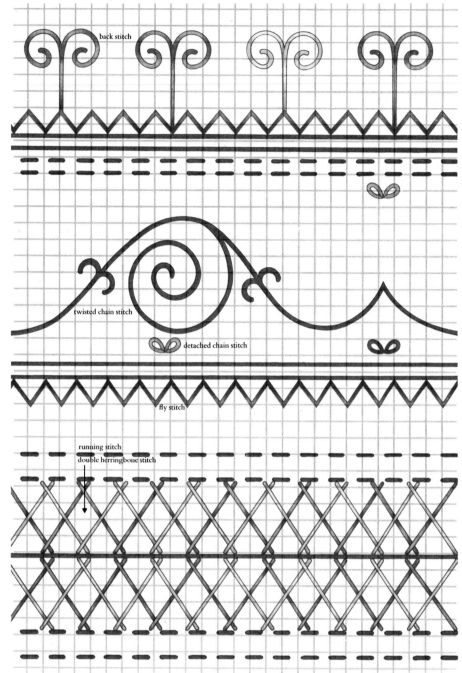

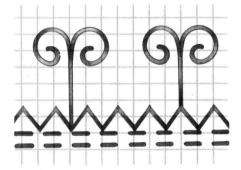

Herringbone stitch.

Double herringbone stitch.

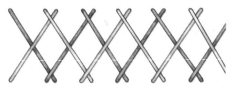

Making the Apron

Make a line of gathering stitches 6 mm (¼ in) from the top of the apron, leaving 12.5 cm (5 in) free at each side. Draw up the gathers so that the top measures 42.5 cm (17 in).

Machine a narrow hem down each side of the bib and a wider one (4.5 cm or 1¾ in) across the top. Baste the bib to the skirt gathers, wrong sides together.

Machine the ties together to make one long strip. Fold the strip in half lengthwise. Machine the ends and along the long edge towards the centre taking a 6 mm (¼ in) seam. Leave a gap equal to the waist measurement of the skirt. Turn it right side out and press, turning the remaining raw edges to the inside along the seam line.

Fit the top edge of the apron into the gap in the tie. Baste and machine through all thicknesses. Fold the bib up and top-stitch it to the waistband.

Fold the neckband in half lengthwise and stitch the long edge taking a 6 mm (¼ in) seam. Turn it right side out and press. Turn in the ends and baste. Machine the ends of the neckband to the bib, overlapping the bib by 12 mm (½ in).

Transfer the embroidery motif to the bib to fit the width, placing it 3 mm (⅛ in) down from the hem and then work the embroidery.

Fly stitch.

Twisted chain stitch.

Detached chain stitch.

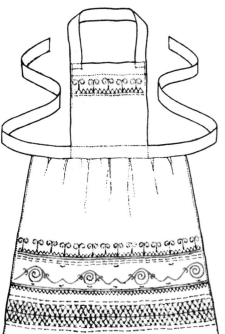

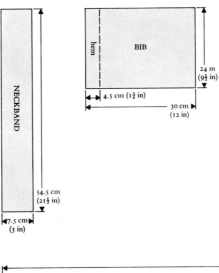

NECKBAND

hem

BIB

4.5 cm (1¾ in)

24 m (9½ in)

30 cm (12 in)

54.5 cm (21½ in)

7.5 cm (3 in)

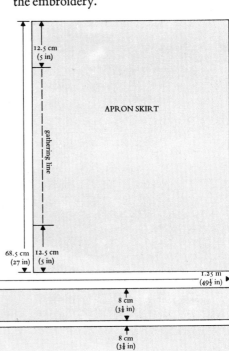

12.5 cm (5 in)

APRON SKIRT

gathering line

68.5 cm (27 in)

12.5 cm (5 in)

1.25 m (49½ in)

TIE

8 cm (3½ in)

TIE

8 cm (3½ in)

The Soviet Union

The Soviet Union covers a vast land mass stretching from Europe in the west right across Asia to the Pacific, separated from North America by only the Bering Strait. The embroidery of the area has a correspondingly large range.

Of the fifteen republics and numerous autonomous regions of the Soviet Union, the main embroidery centres are western Russia, including Belorussia, the Baltic Republics of Estonia, Latvia and Lithuania, the Ukraine, the Caucasian Republics of Georgia and Armenia, the Central Asian Republics of Turkmenistan and Uzbekistan, and Siberia, technically part of Russia but with a separate embroidery tradition.

The known history of embroidery in the area begins with Siberian burial treasures of the 5th century B.C. More recent styles and forms can be traced directly back for several hundred years.

The area is rich in embroidery materials. The Soviet Union provides seventy per cent of the world's flax. Sheep are raised in many southern areas and cotton is grown particularly in the Ukraine, southern Georgia, Turkmenistan and Uzbekistan. Metal thread is associated particularly with Russia, Georgia and the Tatars of Siberia, and leather is used as embroidery ground in some regions. North of about 65° latitude reindeer are herded and their skins used for ground fabric. Until recent times their hairs were used for embroidery thread. Occasionally fish skins have been used as an embroidery ground in these northern areas.

Red monochrome stitching is particularly associated with Russia and the Baltic Republics. There is no blackwork, but whitework is found particularly in the Vologda region of northern Russia and in Estonia.

The most popular embroidery technique in the Soviet Union is cross stitch. Other universally popular stitches include back

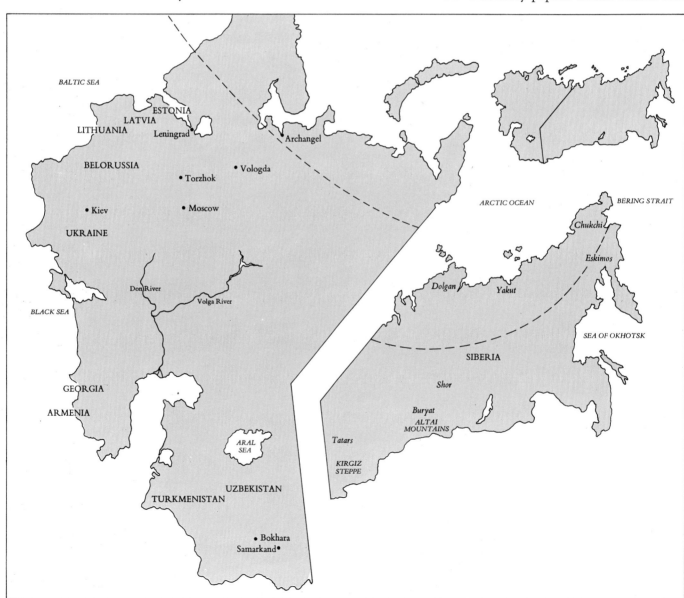

Eight-pointed stars are popular embroidery motifs in many parts of the world. This Ukrainian repeating design is worked in satin stitch and straight stitch.

stitch, buttonhole stitch, chain stitch and satin stitch. Pattern darning is particularly evident in the Ukraine, and Armenia has a unique surface interlacing. Pulled- and drawn-thread work embroidery are found in Russia and in the Ukraine. Appliqué is worked primarily in the Baltic Republics, in the Ukraine, in Turkmenistan and in Siberia.

In the west the predominant religion has in the past been Christianity. Many sumptuous vestments were embroidered, particularly in Armenia, with silk threads and pearls and precious stones applied to ground fabrics of silk or velvet. These ecclesiastical articles were embroidered by professional artists. In Russia, Georgia and Armenia, areas which embraced the Russian Orthodox or another branch of the Eastern Church, some private houses had embroidered icons or covers for painted icons embroidered by a female member of the family which were set up on a wall or flat surface as a religious focal point for believers. Icons are not now generally embroidered.

Secular embroiderers in western areas of the Soviet Union have generally been women. Taught by their mothers or, before the revolution, in convents and church schools, they embroidered towels, tablecloths, sheets and other linen and costume items. Depending on the region, they executed designs such as the earth mother, eagles and other birds, sometimes with complex tail and wing forms, and narrow borders of geometric repeating motifs.

Embroidery is found on traditional national and regional costumes, especially on women's outfits in Russia, the Baltic Republics, the Ukraine and Turkmenistan, and on men's hats and men's costumes in parts of Siberia. Traditional costumes are not now generally worn, although they may be brought out for weddings and other special occasions, particularly in the villages and in country areas.

Quarter segment of a Russian eight-pointed star motif (right). This would be outlined with chain stitch and infilled with cross stitch.

Similar motifs appear on this woman's headscarf from Siberia (detailed below).

Russia

One of the most popular techniques in Russia proper, including Belorussia, is cross stitch, often worked in red silk thread on a ground of natural-coloured linen. A great deal of flax is still produced throughout the area. The only other textile fabric produced is wool, in the more temperate parts of Russia. Wool is, however, used as ground fabric for embroidery only in the north and near the Baltic, where it is sometimes employed for clothing items. Embroidery is usually worked with commercial silk thread.

As well as ordinary cross stitch, Russian embroidery includes montenegrin cross stitch and back stitch, buttonhole stitch, satin stitch, split stitch and chain stitch, which is either tamboured or worked with a needle, when three detached chain links are sometimes grouped together. Popular designs, all worked either in repeating or spot form, include eight-pointed stars, particularly in the

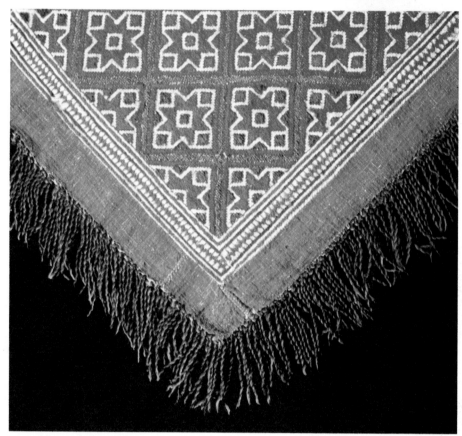

Individual or detached chain stitches are often worked in groups of three, and may be aligned horizontally or vertically.

Moscow region, diamond shapes, pomegranates and other fruits, flowers often shown in pots, birds and people.

Another form of Russian embroidery, usually worked on a natural linen ground, consists of free-form curvilinear motifs. Embroidered in one colour or polychrome, they are outlined with a single line of chain stitch and sometimes infilled with cross stitch or satin stitch.

Monochrome embroidery, generally worked in red silk thread on a natural linen ground, and polychrome embroidery, worked in similar styles and patterns, are both traditionally employed to decorate table and bed covers and clothing items.

Generalization about Russian traditional dress is difficult because of regional differences within the vast geographical area. The embroidered items include men's summer shirts, white hip-length tunics with inset sleeves and a narrow embroidered neck band; women's blouses, embroidered particularly on the sleeves; and *sarafans*, overskirts that were sometimes attached to bodices

Russian overcast filling stitch. Threads are withdrawn to leave a mesh of two warp and two weft threads. Starting at A, remaining threads are overcast in step fashion. At junctions of the mesh, both warp and weft threads are overcast. The next step line of overcast stitching begins at B, and the process is continued until the entire mesh is covered with stitching.

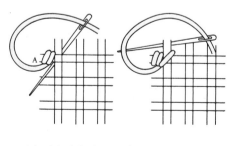

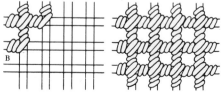

without sleeves and suspended from simple shoulder straps. All these garments are embroidered with cross stitch and other counted-thread stitches, usually in repeating motifs of flowers, animals and people.

Women also wear velvet headdresses embroidered with gold and silver thread and embellished with spangles, beads or pearls, and small pieces of foil.

Traditional costume is now worn only on special occasions, particularly in some northern villages, and little costume embroidery is worked today.

Whitework is especially associated with the Archangel and Vologda districts of northern Russia. Sometimes devices are worked on a ground of square net but generally white linen material is preferred. Designs may be free-form, curvilinear, similar to those of polychrome embroidery, or pictorial, with men on horseback or in carriages. Motifs are sometimes outlined with chain stitch and then infilled with russian overcast filling, also known as russian drawn ground. This is worked on a trellis

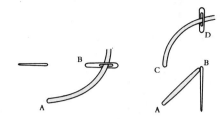

Reversed faggot stitch. Each stitch should be pulled tight to form parallel lines of stitches.

formed by withdrawing two warp and weft threads, the junctions being closely bound with overcast stitching. Alternatively, the trellis is left unworked but selected interstices are infilled with russian drawn filling, similar to lace filling stitch but with an added central diagonal tie stitch.

Another popular whitework motif infilling is russian filling stitch, a pulled-thread form in which no threads are cut or withdrawn, worked with parallel lines of diagonal reversed faggot stitch executed in cross directions.

Russian whitework is often employed to decorate sheets and towels which are made of lengths of bleached linen with a narrow length of lace, net or woven white linen fabric joined along one edge with interlacing or hem stitch. A joined band is often decorated with dense embroidery worked in white silk thread in typical whitework forms.

Torzhok, one third of the way from Moscow on the road north to Leningrad, formerly St Petersburg, was for a long time associated with the making of embroidered leather boots for women. The boots were decorated with silks in

Russian drawn filling. After working lace filling stitch (see page 66), two further stages are executed to form a 'knot' in the centre of each stitch.

many colours worked in symmetrical satin-stitch floral motifs round the top of the leg and in single motifs on the upper.

The boots were made by men, but in the main the embroidery of Russia was executed by women, usually for their own families' use. The peak of domestic embroidery was in the early 19th century.

Not many young Russians in the Soviet Union today have time to embroider or easy access to materials, although some do continue to work traditional stitches and designs, usually in polychrome colouring, as decoration for household items or for garments.

Counted-thread border design worked on linen in a combination of cross stitch and montenegrin cross stitch.

A linen cloth from the Moscow area, with characteristic floral and eight-pointed star designs in closely worked satin stitch.

Russian filling. Parallel lines of reversed faggot stitch are worked, starting at A. The fabric is then turned through 90° and, starting at B, parallel lines of reversed faggot stitch are worked as before.

Russian cross-stitch design, with flowers worked as variants of the eight-pointed star theme.

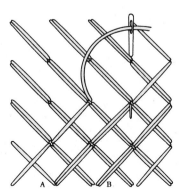

Baltic Republics

The embroidery of the Baltic Republics of Estonia, Latvia and Lithuania is often worked in red silk thread, generally on a ground of white or natural linen which is sometimes produced locally. In the Baltic Republics, satin stitch predominates, but other techniques include cross stitch, eye stitch, punch stitch and tent stitch. A popular device in all these techniques is a snowflake, an adaptation of the eight-pointed star. There is much whitework, with designs sometimes similar to those of neighbouring northern Russia. Drawn-thread work is practised, as is some appliqué, usually in the form of linen motifs for woollen winter coats.

Embroidery in the Baltic Republics has generally been worked by women for their own families' use. They decorate fine table and other cloths as well as costume items for themselves and for their daughters. In Estonia, for instance, women work drawn-thread work as narrow borders to table and other linens, using overcast stitching with many picots and alternating the drawn thread with occasional pattern darning.

An Estonian girl's traditional costume includes a white linen blouse with inset full sleeves gathered into the cuffs. Horizontal bands of drawn-thread or polychrome surface embroidery are set below the shoulder and above the cuffs. The blouse is worn with a sleeveless overdress of linen or local wool and a plain white linen apron. A Latvian girl's costume, on the other hand, is less similar to other eastern European costumes. A long-sleeved blouse with front button opening and little collar is embroidered in wide horizontal bands, usually just below the shoulders on the sleeves, and on the collar. The blouse is worn under a sleeveless overdress and with a large shawl wrapped round the body and held in place with a metal clasp attached to one shoulder of the overdress. Sometimes the overdress is striped and the embroidery on the blouse reflects the colouring of those woven stripes.

National costumes are still worn, especially by expatriates, for special occasions. Although few costumes are now produced, some embroidery designs and styles are worked as decoration on household linens and similar items.

Latvian girls' traditional dress includes long-sleeved blouses with embroidery on the collars, shoulders and cuffs, worked in satin stitch, drawn-thread work and needleweaving.

Embroidery is still worked throughout the Baltic Republics.

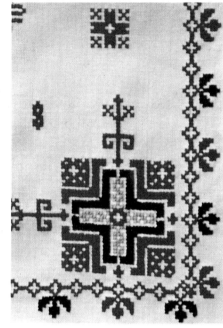

Corner motif, worked in cross stitch, of a woman's kerchief from the Nica district of Latvia.

Caucasian Republics

The Caucasian mountains, stretching from the Black Sea to the Caspian Sea, give their name to an area which includes the Republics of Georgia and Armenia.

Silk, cotton and wool are all produced in the area and it is known that spinning and weaving were well developed by about 1000 B.C. In the Middle Ages, dyeing was a particular Caucasian professional speciality. Roots of madder were being exported to Turkey and further afield, and the bodies of kermes insects were used to produce an alternative red dye. It is not surprising, with such a wealth of materials to hand, that

embroidery also has a long history. At home, it was worked by gentlewomen and their servants, who often learned their skills in monastery workshops where weavers, dyers, tailors and needlewomen all worked together.

Embroidery was in the past particularly to embellish household linen cloths. It was worked with spot and repeating flower designs and geometric patterns in needle or tamboured chain stitch, cross stitch, satin stitch and other universal stitch forms. More elaborate forms were sometimes unique to one specific region. In Georgia, for example, women sometimes used embroidery

Armenian drawn-thread-work tablecloth. Several warp and weft threads are withdrawn, and those remaining are bound with needleweaving. Here satin stitch has been used to complete the design and the edges are bordered with buttonhole stitch.

Drawn- and pulled-thread techniques are combined in this unfinished Armenian tablecloth (left).

Complicated surface interlacing is characteristic of Armenian embroidery. Worked on a trellis of long diagonal straight stitches, Armenian interlacing produces a castellated line of stitches. It is usually worked in diamond, square and rectangular motifs (see page 140).

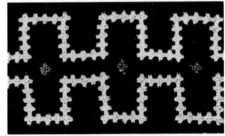

to decorate such items as book bindings as well as velvet covers for pistols or food. Silk and metal threads were worked in chain stitch or satin stitch or laid and couched with designs such as cones or cypress trees, indicative of the constant trade with both Turkey to the south-west and Iran to the south-east.

Traditional embroidery of the Caucasian Republics is less in evidence today than in some other areas of the Soviet Union. With the exception of armenian interlacing, which is still worked by Armenian women, embroidery in Georgia and Armenia is an art that is seldom practised nowadays.

Armenian Skirt

You will need:
1.2 m (1⅜ yd) black woollen
    fabric 140 cm (54 in) wide
18 cm (7 in) zip fastener
interfacing 5 cm (2 in) wide by
    length of waistband
tapestry (or 4-ply) wool in
    four colours:
red 2 skeins
light green 2 skeins
dark green 1 skein
mid blue 1 skein
1 reel black sewing cotton
crewel embroidery needles
blunt-ended bodkin
large embroidery hoop
button

interfacing | 10 cm (4 in)
waistband

gathering line

zip opening

19.5 cm (7¾ in)

seam allowance 12 mm (½ in)

1.20 m (1⅜ yd)

seam

140 cm (54 in)

basting line for edge of embroidery pattern

hemline   5 cm (2 in)
                            7.5 cm (3 in)

Size
Adjust the waist measurement by altering the waistband length. Make it your waist measurement plus 3.5 cm (1½ in). Adjust the hem line to the required length. Mark the edge of the embroidery 5 cm (2 in) above it.

Preparing the Fabric
Mark and cut out the two pattern pieces. Mark the hem line and bottom edge of the embroidery pattern with basting stitches.

Scale up the embroidery design to 23 cm (9 in) across and transfer it to the fabric so that it sits on the basted line.

Repeat the pattern six times across the fabric, matching the base lines.

Armenian interlacing.
Work a row of herringbone stitch, A. Work a second row on top of it, B, threading the down-slanting stitches underneath the others. Work a row of interlacing through the bottom of the stitches, C, and then a second row through the top.

The positions for the foundation stitches of the interlacing (below).

Detail from the skirt with the finished interlacing (below right).

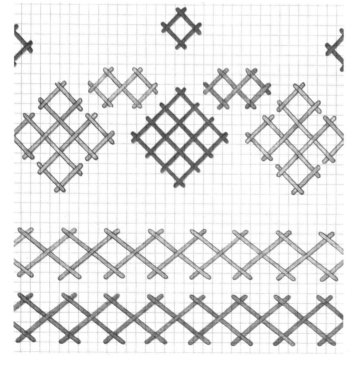

Armenian interlacing, named after the region in the U.S.S.R. where it is practised, is based on bands of double herringbone stitch which are interlaced by a matching or contrasting colour. Maltese interlacing is similar, but the herringbone stitching is worked in motifs like Maltese crosses. Interlacing gives an unusual ethnic finish to a cosy woollen skirt for winter evenings if worked in soft wools using traditional Armenian colours.

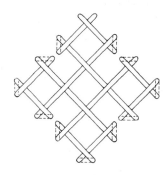

Maltese interlacing foundation. Work as shown, following the direction of the arrows which show where the thread goes underneath the fabric. The long stitches weave over and under each other without penetrating the fabric.

Maltese interlacing, A. Work over and under the foundation as shown without penetrating the ground fabric. Work each complete diamond before passing on to the next.

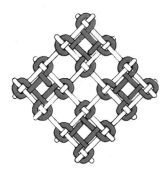

Maltese interlacing, B. Work as above, but stitch each cross separately, starting at its inner corner and using no connecting threads through the centre of the motif.

Embroidery

Work the two base lines of the design in armenian interlacing, the top row in light green and the bottom row in dark green. Work the foundation stitch the whole width of each row before starting the interlacing. Check that the foundation has been interwoven correctly, for otherwise the interlacing will not work.

When a length of thread has been used up, take it through to the back of the fabric at a point where the interlacing passes under a foundation thread and finish off neatly. Bring the new thread up in the same position and continue the interlacing. Begin and end each row of interlacing in the same way.

Work the rest of the design as shown, interlacing each cross with its own colour. Work the small red motifs like one corner of the larger one.

Making the Skirt

Damp press the embroidery (see page 272).

Run a gathering thread along the waist edge. Join the centre back seam leaving the top open for the zip, and press the seam open. Insert the zip.

Cut interfacing to half the width of the waistband but the same length. Baste it to the wrong side of the waistband along the fold line. Stitch the ends through both thicknesses of the band, taking a 5 mm (¼ in) seam. Turn the waistband right side out and press.

Pull up the gathers to fit the waist and baste them to the waistband, right sides together, allowing a 2.5 cm (1 in) overlap at one end. Stitch and trim the seam. Press it towards the waistband.

Turn the waistband up, baste the remaining raw edge under, and topstitch all round the waistband 3 mm (⅛ in) from the edges.

Work a buttonhole on the overlap and sew on a button.

Turn up a hem and press it lightly.

Ukraine

Rooshniks, made of long rectangular pieces of linen, may be embroidered at either end with rich bands of pattern darning or cross stitch.

The Ukraine is one of the leading embroidery areas of the Soviet Union. Many Ukrainian women are still prolific embroiderers, generally working on a ground of loose-weave linen or cotton, usually white, natural or grey. Both textiles are produced in inland areas in the east of the Republic, but most of the fabric used in Ukrainian embroidery today is brought from other parts of the Soviet Union. Commercial silk or cotton thread is used, and popular colours include bright shades of maroon, red, orange, yellow, green, gold and violet, and black. Pastel shades are seldom seen.

Techniques frequently used include back stitch, buttonhole stitch, needle chain stitch, cross stitch and long-legged stitch, eyelet stitch, interlaced or whipped running stitch, ladder stitch, satin stitch, stem stitch and needleweaving, pattern darning and drawn- and pulled-thread work. Traditional embroidery of

Ukrainian eyelet stitching. Groups of 'eyes' may form square or triangular motifs as required.

Ukrainian woman's apron, with carefully aligned diamond motifs worked in cross stitch.

Ukrainian pattern darning. Parallel lines of vertical running stitches (A) are worked on the reverse of the ground (B). Then, on the right side of the fabric, the interstices are filled with a different-coloured thread (C).

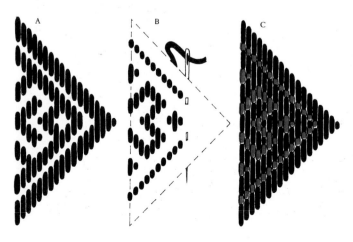

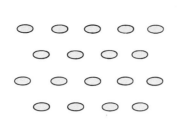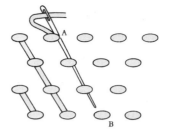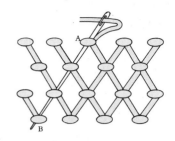

Ukrainian interlaced running stitch. The interlacing is worked under the running stitches without entering the ground fabric.

the Ukraine is still vigorously practised both at home and by expatriates.

Ukrainian pattern darning is sometimes known as tweed replica. It is worked with close parallel lines of long vertical darning stitches, usually black or maroon, executed from the reverse of the fabric. When all the vertical darning stitches have been completed, the fabric is turned over and the gaps in the design are filled with straight stitches, in bright colours, from the right side.

Ukrainian drawn-thread work is similar to hardanger, with five parallel satin stitches worked over four threads of fabric to form one kløster block. In Ukrainian drawn work, however, the corners of the blocks are sometimes filled with a large cross stitch.

Pulled-thread work makes frequent use of eyelet stitching. Ukrainian eyelets are often worked in close formation to form triangles, squares, diagonal lines

and other groupings. Spaces between eyelets are filled with cross stitches.

Ukrainian embroidery is worked by women, usually for their own household and clothing decoration. Blouses are embroidered with floral or geometric motifs worked round the neck opening and on the sleeves either in horizontal bands or in one solid block down the outer arm. Ukrainian household embroideries include *rooshniks*, ceremonial towels made of long rectangular pieces of linen. These are embroidered at either end with pattern darning and other Ukrainian stitch forms worked in symmetrical motifs, often in repeating form, in narrow horizontal bands. Embroidered towels were at first executed by women to decorate family icons set up in the home, or to use at christenings, engagements, weddings and burials. More recently, Ukrainian women have begun to use towels as table runners.

Detail of a woman's blouse from the western Ukraine. Embroidery is worked in bands round the neck and sleeves.

Turkmenistan

Although some of them live in northern Iran, Afghanistan, Iraq, and Syria, the majority of Turkmen now live within the confines of the Soviet Union, mainly in Turkmenistan, a rugged area of deserts and mountains. The principal embroidery groups are the Teke and Yomut.

In the past Turkmen took wool, sheepskins, horses and prisoners to markets such as those in Bokhara and Samarkand and exchanged them for silk and cotton or wool fabric.

Turkmen women embroider for their own families' use. The main stitches are back stitch, worked in continuous lines or isolated stitches in small clusters; buttonhole stitch; needle chain stitch, usually in close parallel lines; cross stitch; plait stitch; a unique Turkmen lacing stitch; appliqué and laid and couched work.

Turkmen embroidery is distinguished by the careful geometric proportions and alignment of its repeating angular or

Turkmen geometric design worked in double running stitch in silks on a cotton ground.

Turkmen stitch.

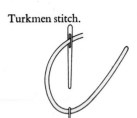  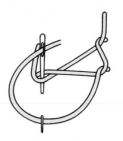

Turkmen horse and other animal trappings are sometimes lavishly embroidered.

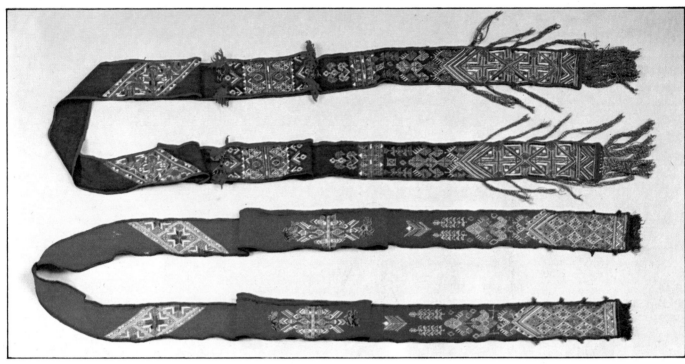

curvilinear devices. Turkmen were converted to the Sunni form of Islam by Tatars and there is, therefore, little direct pictorial representation in embroidery. Geometric motifs are, however, sometimes named, with a four-armed cross known as a ram's head and a hooked motif called a chicken's beak. Another device characteristic of much Turkmen embroidery is a Teke hook, an antenna to a main design, worked with either sharp or curved outlines.

Turkmen have traditionally been nomads whose embroideries were worked as tent furnishings and animal covers and trappings. Sometimes the tents have an elaborate door hanging, often with a fringed bottom consisting of vertical tabs of material, the whole made of pieces of bright-coloured cotton fabric cut in repeating triangular and other geometric shapes and applied to ground fabric with hemming. Subsequent embroidery is worked in satin stitch and open turkmen stitch. Other embroidered items inside a tent include gun cases, pot holders and mirror and comb bags, all made of white felt and decorated with silk thread.

Embroidery on Turkmen costume is always worked after a garment is made up. If a piece of clothing is lined, subsequent embroidery, executed from the

Plait stitch.

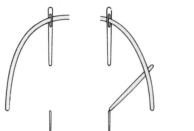

right side of the main ground fabric, is carefully worked so that no stitches pierce the lining.

Turkmen women traditionally wear a cotton or silk ankle-length dress with long sleeves. It is embroidered with repeating designs on the cuffs, the small upright collar, round the vertical front neck opening and sometimes round the hem. Underneath, the women wear baggy full-length pants, supported from the hips by drawstrings, and tapering at the ankles to tight-fitting cuffs which are often elaborately embroidered. When the main body of the pants, usually constructed from cheap cotton fabric, wears out, the cuffs are attached to another 'upper'. A coat is worn over the dress and pants, generally decorated with both silver coins and narrow border embroidery round all the outer edges.

Turkmen embroidery worked in silks in chain stitch, satin stitch and turkmen stitch on a cotton ground.

Uzbekistan

A stitch form particularly associated with Uzbek embroidery is bokhara stitch, also known as bokhara couching. It is traditionally used as filling for large floral motifs. These are worked in repeating form, surrounded by scrolled foliage embroidered in silk in back stitch and chain stitch on a cotton ground. Silk and cotton are still produced in Uzbekistan, but recent bokhara embroidery has been worked with commercial threads and ground fabrics.

Popular thread colours are maroon, beige, green and black. Embroidery is worked on long lengths of natural cotton fabric, usually about 23-30 cm (9-12 in) wide, which are then joined together along the selvedges. Sometimes two adjacent panels may not be meticulously aligned and a fine hair-line of ground fabric selvedge is revealed, bisecting a stitched motif.

Panels are joined together to form wall hangings, usually about 250 x 185 cm (100 x 74 in). They sometimes have a repeating floral motif border about 20 cm (8 in) deep round all four edges and a dozen or so big motifs covering the main ground. A panel about the same size may alternatively be used as a prayer mat, with a *mihrab* design embroidered round three sides and in the two upper diagonals of the main ground.

Some other embroideries of Uzbekistan are similar to those of neighbouring Turkmenistan, a not surprising feature since they were both part of the former region of Turkestan. Uzbek embroidery employs back stitch, buttonhole stitch, chain stitch, cross stitch, and appliqué and it is used for tent decoration, animal trappings and costume similar to those of Turkmenistan. Designs are geometric or floral, often worked in repeating form on narrow bands bordering men's and women's coats.

Skull caps, usually made of black cotton decorated with silk chain stitch, are still made by Uzbek men for everyday wear. Apart from this, Bokhara and other Uzbek embroidery is now less often practised than that of other areas of central Asia. Old embroidered wall hangings are, however, becoming increasingly popular with foreign collectors, notably with those of western Europe and North America.

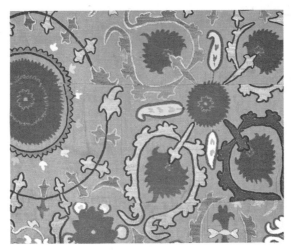

Detail of a large hanging from Bokhara, with characteristic large floral motifs surrounded by scrolled foliage, worked in back stitch and chain stitch on a cotton ground fabric.

Typical Uzbek embroidery designs include flowers and cone shapes, here outlined in open chain stitch and densely infilled.

Bokhara couching.

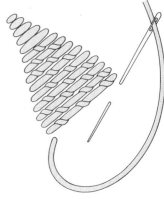

Although many Uzbek men's caps are today decorated with machine stitching, this velvet cap is embellished with gold laid and couched work.

145

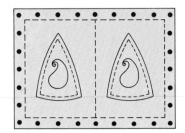

Uzbek Cap

You will need:

0.3 m ($\frac{3}{8}$ yd) velvet 90 cm (36 in) wide

0.3 m ($\frac{3}{8}$ yd) soft non-woven interfacing 90 cm (36 in) wide

0.3 m ($\frac{3}{8}$ yd) lining 90 cm (36 in) wide

1 ball gold lurex crochet yarn

1 spool gold untarnished metallic/nylon filler yarn

1 reel sewing cotton in gold

1 reel sewing cotton to match velvet

small box gold sequins

small box gold beads

slate embroidery frame

Fabric prepared for embroidery, which is worked before the sections are put together.

Attaching a sequin with a bead.

Size
To fit an average-size head. Adjust the size by taking larger or smaller seams.

The ancient cities of Tashkent and Samarkand, the wonder of travellers from the west and prize of conquerors from the east, are both in the Soviet Republic of Uzbekistan. The Uzbeks are Moslems, whose culture and dress, of which the richly embroidered caps are a part, reflect the influence of Islam.

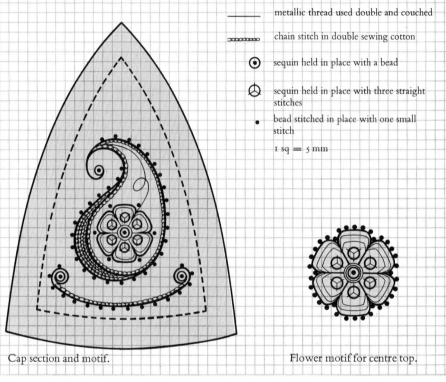

——— gold lurex crochet yarn

——— metallic thread used double and couched

⨯⨯⨯⨯⨯ chain stitch in double sewing cotton

⊙ sequin held in place with a bead

⊕ sequin held in place with three straight stitches

· bead stitched in place with one small stitch

1 sq = 5 mm

Cap section and motif.

Flower motif for centre top.

Preparing the Fabric
Cut the velvet into three pieces, each 30 cm (12 in) square. (Each piece will make two cap panels.) Back each piece with interfacing. Be careful when basting the edges together that no stitches mark the velvet where they will be visible later.

Mount each piece, one at a time, in the slate frame. (An embroidery hoop will mark the velvet. If no slate frame is available, use any open wooden frame and pin the fabric to it with drawing pins or thumbtacks.)

Make six tracings on tissue paper of the cutting and seam lines and main outline of the motif. Making sure that the pile is running in the same direction on each piece, place the tracings on the velvet.

Stitch along the lines with small running stitches and then tear the tracings away.

Embroidery
Embroider each section of the cap using the diagram as a guide to both threads and stitches. Sew on the beads and sequins with gold sewing cotton and work the couching in sewing cotton also. (N.B. The flower motif is worked, off the frame, after making up but before stitching in the lining.)

Making the Cap
Cut out the six sections of the cap along the cutting lines. Cut six sections the same size in lining fabric.

Machine the six cap sections along the seam lines, reducing the pressure of the pressure foot if necessary to avoid marking the velvet. The stitch tension may also need loosening. Trim and clip the seams. It may be more satisfactory to finish the seams by hand where they meet in the centre.

Stand a warm iron on end and cover it with a damp cloth. Press the seams by passing them gently over the tip.

Embroider the flower motif in the centre of the crown.

Seam the cap lining, trim the seams and press them open.

Turn in the seam allowance round the edges of both cap and lining. Place lining inside the cap, wrong sides facing, and slipstitch the two together.

Siberia

The vast land mass of Siberia, comprising most of Russia and the largest region of the U.S.S.R., stretches from the Ural Mountains east to the Bering Strait.

Appliqué dominates Siberian embroidery. Leather or wool motifs or lengths of ribbon are applied with hemming to ground fabrics of linen, wool, sheepskin, reindeer skin or fish skin. Designs are usually symmetrical and abstract, and often exaggeratedly curvilinear or angular.

The Soviet flax-growing belt reaches from the west eastwards to Lake Baikal.

Sheep are raised in various regions in the south and reindeer are herded in the north. Reindeer skin is used as embroidery ground and the hairs were once used as thread. Siberian hair embroidery took the form either of undyed reindeer hairs laid and couched as in Alaska, or of individual hairs used as thread.

The area has seen a rapid increase in population in recent years. Mining, hydroelectric schemes and industrial expansion have resulted in an influx of people from many other parts of the Soviet Union, but embroidery in Siberia

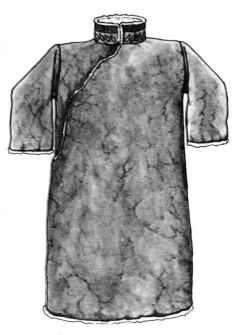

Winter coat worn by the nomadic Buryat people of Eastern Siberia. Continual trade with China has influenced some of their costume design.

Woman's shirt from western Siberia, the region immediately east of the Urals, mostly embroidered in satin stitch, with swastika and other repeating geometric motifs.

is mainly done by indigenous peoples, particularly the Buryat, Tatars, Dolgan, Yakut and Chukchi. The Eskimo, the most eastern and a primarily maritime group, practise embroidery that is closely related to that of the North American Tlingit. Embroidery is traditionally worked variously by men or women for costume decoration and few ceremonial garments or hangings.

Many groups adhere to Shamanism, a religious phenomenon of north-east Asia in which a central witch doctor figure, the shaman, is believed to have direct communication with a spirit world. This enables the shaman to act as healer, advisor and general leader. Some shamans' traditional robes are decorated with ritual leather motifs hemmed to a leather ground.

The oldest surviving Siberian embroidery pieces date back to the 5th century B.C. and were found in the Altaian-Scythian burial chambers at Pazyryk in the Altai Mountains. Included in the treasures are fragments of a felt appliqué picture, with motifs of red, blue, yellow and black attached to the beige ground with horsehair hemming. A reconstruction of the hanging, which shows a rider on horseback, can be seen in the Hermitage Museum in Leningrad.

Appliqué is found on the traditional costume of the Shor, another Siberian tribe living to the north of the Buryat. Sometimes embroidered costume items

Linen shirt richly embroidered with geometric motifs in surface stitching and beadwork (opposite, with a detail below). Although from western Siberia, the sharply outlined motifs are similar to those of the Central Asian Republics of Turkmenistan and Uzbekistan.

Yakut motif with crescent moon and characteristic of appliqué and surface embroidery throughout northern Siberia.

Drawing of a Chukchi boot, from north-eastern Siberia, made of sealskin and decorated with reindeer hair.

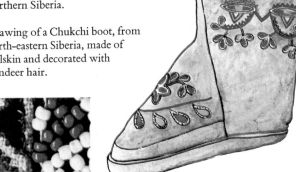

of wool or leather appliqué hemmed to the ground with hair and embroidered in silk or wool satin stitch. Another Dolgan embroidery ground, also used for warm clothing, is de-haired reindeer skin. It is sometimes painted and decorated with hair embroidery, leather appliqué and beads stitched to the fabric with straight stitches in diagonal lines.

Traditional costume is still more generally worn in north-eastern Siberia than in some other areas. Both men's and women's boots, made of reindeer skin or seal or wool, are embroidered with hair and cotton stitching in satin stitch and laid and couched work, sometimes with appliqué of leather motifs.

Some Siberian women used in the past to wear moccasin-type shoes decorated with stitched beadwork.

are embellished with cowrie shells, brought by traders and travellers, and pierced and sewn on as spangles with long straight stitches.

Contacts with other parts of Asia and regions even further afield meant that embroidery designs were sometimes transported from one area to another. The Tatars, for instance, generally associated today with the northern areas of the Kirghiz Steppe, were particularly wide-ranging traders in the 18th and 19th centuries. Tatar embroidered costume makes use of silk from various regions of central Asia embroidered with gold and silver thread laid on a ground fabric of silk. Particularly sumptuous examples of Tatar women's traditional clothing are their headcoverings.

In northern Siberia traditional clothing is practical as well as decorative. A Dolgan man's coat, for instance, is sometimes made of fish skin, the skins sewn together with hair or cotton to form a ground fabric. Round all the edges of the front-opening sleeved coat are bands

Eastern Mediterranean

Detail of a lavishly worked skirt border from Crete, featuring the native cretan stitch, chain stitch and stem stitch. Flower motifs, especially tulips and carnations, and vivid colours are extremely popular. Richly decorated skirts are part of the Cretan traditional costume.

In the eastern Mediterranean region the main embroidery areas are not governed by the national boundaries of Greece, Turkey, Syria, Lebanon, Israel and Jordan, and many of the most interesting examples come from the Greek Islands.

The climate of much of the area is ideally suited to the cultivation of cotton, and it is grown today throughout Greece, in Thrace and on the Anatolian coast, and in northern Syria. Flax is now grown only on the southern Anatolian coast. Silk is produced in eastern mainland Greece, in Crete and the Cyclades, in Gallipoli and north-western Anatolia, and in some areas of the Syrian coast. Sheep are extensively farmed in Greece and inland Turkey but wool is used as embroidery ground material only in northern Greece and occasionally in Turkey. Sheepskin is sometimes used as an embroidery ground in the sheep-farming areas of Turkey.

The area is rich in sources of dyes. Tyre, on the Levantine coast, was a centre for the production of a rich red-purple dye from the shellfish of the *Murex* family. It took nearly 9,000 shells to produce 1 gramme of pure dye and its use was consequently strictly controlled. Blue was achieved with indigo; red was obtained from madder; yellow from buckthorn berries, sumach or the root of kirkum plants, *Curcuma;* and black from iron and vinegar.

Both spinning and weaving were, in most areas, traditionally held to be women's work. A hand spindle was frequently used, and the fabric was woven on horizontal looms. Apart from work produced by professional male embroiderers in Turkey,

embroidery is generally traditionally worked by women. They learnt the art from their mothers or, in Christian areas, in convents and church schools.

Much of the embroidery design has been relayed from one people to another through constant interaction, although many eastern Mediterranean techniques are unique. Cross stitch is the dominant stitch among embroideries of the whole region. It is worked in red monochrome or polychrome silk threads on natural, bleached, indigo or black linen, cotton or silk fabric.

Other popular stitches found throughout the whole area include chain stitch, satin stitch, pattern darning and laid and couched work. Nowadays, most embroidery is worked with commercially produced silk thread on bought ground fabric except for that produced by the Bedouin of the Levant.

Metal thread is used in many areas to highlight silk embroidery. It was also used for lavish court costumes and animal trappings, particularly in Turkey and areas of former Turkish domination such as Syria, during the 18th and 19th centuries. Imitation 'goldwork' is executed in Damascus where a monochrome embroidery with gold-coloured silk thread is worked on a ground of linen or cotton. Other eastern Mediterranean techniques include cutwork, especially in Cyprus, whitework in the Ionian islands and Cyprus, drawn-thread work in Ipiros, and appliqué in the Levant.

The whole of the eastern Mediterranean area came under Turkish rule for several centuries. Greece regained its long-lost independence during the 19th and early 20th centuries and

at the end of World War I the Levant was detached from Turkey. After elaborate re-drawing of boundaries and population exchanges, Greece today is very largely a Greek Orthodox Christian nation, and Turkey is Sunni Moslem, as are most of the peoples of the Levant. There are important Christian communities of many different sects in Lebanon and Israel, although in the latter, Judaism is the religion of the largest group. The emigration of Jewish people to Israel has been significant in introducing the embroidery of their former homes, such as Morocco and Yemen.

As befits a maritime area on international trading routes, the eastern Mediterranean shares many universal embroidery designs. The tree of life or cypress tree and other naturalistic motifs are popular throughout the entire region. Specific foreign influences have been Italian whitework designs in the Ionian islands, and the Iranian or Indian cone shape popular in Turkish goldwork and in silk embroideries elsewhere. Influences have also spread in the other direction. Turkish floral designs and other eastern Mediterranean themes such as 'king' and 'queen' leaf designs found in many Greek island groups and the double-headed eagle once associated with Byzantium have

been copied by embroiderers all over the world, notably in western Europe.

Embroidery is worked primarily on women's costumes, the most beautiful of which are marriage outfits. Traditionally cut dresses, many of them now decorated with machine stitched embroidery, are still worn, principally in the Levant, though headdresses are only worn on special occasions. Men's costume is not generally embroidered, except in the Ionian islands, in Turkey, where it took the form of court dress, and in Damascus. Such pieces are hardly ever worn today.

Domestic embroidery is employed to decorate bed covers and hangings, particularly in Greece and Turkey; towels and 'show towels', especially in Turkey; and cushions.

With the political upheavals of the 20th century, many local embroidery styles, notably those in the Levant, have been discontinued. However, throughout the eastern Mediterranean in general women still practise embroidery for their own purposes, and work blouses, dresses and other costume items for sale locally or for export. In Greece and Turkey commercial designers are incorporating small scraps of old or new 'traditional' embroidery into fashion garments.

Greece

The embroidery of Greece is probably more strongly associated with particular islands and island groups than with the mainland. Particularly interesting island embroidery comes from the Ionian islands, including Corfu; Crete; the Dodecanese, including Rhodes and Astipalaia; the Cyclades and the Northern Sporades; on the mainland the most interesting region is Ipiros. Polychrome silk borders worked on costume items are characteristic of all areas.

Greek embroidery is typified by silk stitching on a ground of white cotton or linen. More than one colour is generally used, with a predominance of red. One of the main stitches is pattern darning or patiti stitch. Especially in Ipiros and the Cyclades, pattern darning is executed with long stitches worked over five threads and under one. Other popular stitches include astipalaia stitch, byzantine stitch, chain stitch, cretan stitch, cross stitch, herringbone stitch, rhodes stitch and satin stitch.

Counted-thread work is dominant throughout the area with the exception of Ipiros and the Sporades and whitework is popular in the Ionian island of Levkás. Metal thread is sometimes worked in

Turkish fashion, with flat strips of thread forced right through the ground fabric, sometimes splitting both warp and weft.

Popular designs found in many Greek embroideries include the double-headed eagle and peacock, both examples of Byzantine influence, pomegranates and floral motifs similar to many found in Turkey, the ubiquitous tree of life and winged animals. Except in the Ionian islands and Crete, there is little western influence in embroidery design. Narrow borders, for clothing and household items, are sometimes worked with repeating geometric satin-stitch motifs such as zigzag lines or eight-pointed stars.

Greek women usually embroider for their own purposes but sometimes, especially in Ipiros and the Dodecanese, where professional embroiderers are known to have been working in the 16th century, there is a history of items being produced for sale. Girls learn embroidery at home, but only in the Dodecanese have they practised on samplers.

Greek embroidery is used for costume and household items. Most of the costume decoration is polychrome, worked on women's white linen or cotton skirts or full-length under-dresses worn beneath dresses of coloured cotton or silk. The main items of embroidered costume for men are whitework shirts from Levkás.

Greek girls traditionally include

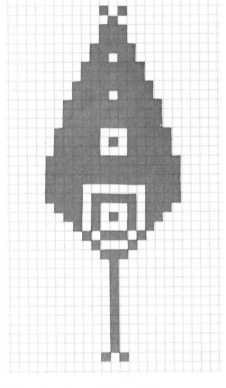

The universal tree of life motif would be worked in solid green cross stitch.

Gold- and silver-thread work on a cushion cover from Ioannina reflects the influence of the region's former Turkish overlords.

As popular in Greece as elsewhere, the double-headed symmetrical bird is usually worked in silk cross stitch.

various embroidered dresses in their dowries, and they also decorate furnishings for the marriage bed. In some areas of Greece, notably the eastern islands, a bed consists simply of a raised platform in the living room. To afford privacy, it is surrounded by curtains which are often embroidered. In all areas, Greek beds are liberally piled with embroidered cushions and pillows.

Embroidery in Greece began many centuries ago. A Hellenistic fragment remains from the 4th or 5th century, worked with wool and linen threads on a woollen twill ground fabric, and embroidered in chain stitch and satin stitch. There follows a gap in the known history of Greek embroidery. The earliest surviving items from island groups are generally from the 16th century. Many 'old' Greek island embroideries are thought to date from the 18th century and there was certainly a decline in embroidery throughout the 19th century concurrent with a fall in silk production and with the introduction of the power loom.

Women in some areas of Greece still embroider, usually decorating household items for their own use. Sometimes fragments of old embroidery and new items specially worked with traditional stitches and designs are used by dress designers as patchwork pieces to be incorporated into high fashion garments.

A Thracian wedding guest displaying the beautifully embroidered traditional costume of the mainland.

Embroidered bands repeat the familiar birds and trees theme in cross stitch and buttonhole stitch. Such bands decorate dress and blouse sleeves on both the mainland and the islands.

Greek Shawl

This pretty fringed shawl for chilly days is made of fine wool with a characteristic Greek chain-stitch design worked in one corner.

You will need:
1.2 m (1⅜ yd) fine woollen fabric 115 cm (45 in) wide
1 reel sewing cotton to match
6 skeins coton à broder to match
stranded embroidery cotton in three colours:
dull gold 3 skeins
brick red 1 skein
pinkish beige 2 skeins
crewel needle
fine crochet hook

Preparing the Fabric

Trim the fabric to 115 cm (45 in) square. Cut it in half diagonally and use one piece for the shawl.

Turn and stitch a narrow hem about 6 mm (¼ in) wide round all three edges.

Trace and scale up the complete motif to measure 30 cm (12 in) from top to bottom. Transfer it to the square corner of the fabric (see page 272), setting it about 5 cm (2 in) from the edges.

Repeat the spiral shape from the top of the motif all over the shawl so that the spirals seem to radiate from the design.

Embroidery

Work all embroidery in chain stitch using two strands of cotton. Begin by outlining the large central shape and work towards the centre, filling it completely with lines of stitching. Complete the rest of the design in the same way, but working the scroll and spiral shapes in single lines of chain stitch.

Making the Fringe

Cut the skeins of coton à broder into three lengths which will measure about 34 cm (13½ in). With the right side of the shawl facing, pierce the single thickness of fabric close to the hem with the crochet hook. Fold two threads in half, loop them over the hook and pull them through the fabric. Pass the four ends through the loop and pull them tight. Work the fringe along the two short edges of the shawl spacing the loops 1 cm (⅜ in) apart. Press the work lightly.

Ipiros

Ioannina, capital of the region of Ipiros, belonged to Turkey from 1430-1912 and there was considerable Turkish influence on the embroidery. Professional embroiderers in the capital decorated sleeveless woollen jackets with gold thread laid and couched with silk retaining stitches, executed in scrolled designs similar to those of Turkey. Amateur embroiderers, working in their own homes, worked Turkish motifs such as pomegranates, lilies, tulips and hyacinths, often enclosed in an arched shape composed of two leaves. Patterns were executed so skilfully that this type of floss-silk 'Joannina' or 'Jannina' work, usually in strong tones of blue, green and red on a white linen ground fabric, was much sought after.

Ipiros embroidery may take the form of Ipiros pattern darning in monochrome red silk thread, in zigzag and other simple diagonal repeating motifs. Sometimes it is worked from the wrong side of the fabric as in the Ukraine. Other popular stitches include double running stitch and herringbone stitch, worked in repeating floral patterns similar to Turkish motifs.

Some of the most beautiful Ipiros embroidery is executed on marriage cushions, usually about 118 x 50 cm (47 x 20 in), made of linen and embroidered with repeating floral motifs round all the edges. Corner devices are sometimes worked in chain stitch, herringbone stitch and outline stitch. Ipiros marriage cushions and bedcover decoration sometimes include stylized brides in Turkish-type court dress, with elaborate full-length coats worn over long-sleeved dresses and with large balloon-shaped hats. Such devices are

Braids and beads traditionally adorn Ipiros work. Additional decoration on this man's waistcoat is worked in fishbone stitch, satin stitch and straight stitch.

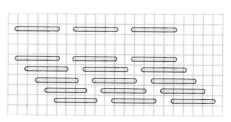

Ipiros pattern darning: stitches cover five threads and miss one.

Embroidered aprons with thin cord hemmed to the ground fabric.

sometimes outlined in black split stitch or stem stitch.

Other household embroidered items include show towels similar to those of Turkey and wall hangings, generally about 90 x 60 cm (36 x 24 in), which are hung above the mantelpiece in the living room. Bed 'tents' are also embroidered here.

Women's under-dresses are sometimes more elaborately embroidered in Ipiros than elsewhere in Greece. As well as narrow repeating borders around the neck, cuffs and hem, there is sometimes a vertical block of embroidery about 30 x 10 cm (12 x 4 in), generally set centrally at the outer edge of each full-length sleeve.

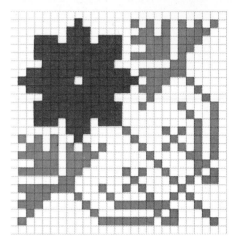

Ionian flower motif, usually worked as a repeating pattern in red and green cross stitch.

The Greek Islands

Ionian Islands

Distinguishing between the embroidery of mainland Ipiros and the western Ionian islands, excluding Corfu, is likely to lead to disputes even between acknowledged Greek embroidery experts. It is thought, however, that whereas pattern darning can possibly be associated mainly with Ipiros, cross stitch and drawn-thread work generally belong to the islands.

Ionian embroidery is worked on a white linen ground with silk thread using cross stitch, long-legged cross stitch and double running stitch. Metal thread is sometimes incorporated into the design, and is either laid on the ground fabric and couched with retaining stitches or, in typically Greek style, worked straight through the fabric in double-sided satin stitch.

Peacocks, fountains, flowers and trees are popular themes, all of which are worked either in monochrome (usually

Section of a fringed linen bedcover from the Ionian Islands. The dense border design of stylized motifs is worked in cross stitch in silk.

red) or polychrome threads. One design associated primarily with Corfu is a symmetrical four-stemmed flower with diagonal axillary buds.

Much Ionian embroidery shows considerable Italian influence, a heritage of the islands' past. In many Ionian border embroideries, for instance, the reserves to the design are stitched, as in Assisi, and the main motif is left unworked.

Another example of Italian influence is the whitework typical of the island of Levkás. Repeating geometric motifs such as diamonds are executed in satin stitch and drawn-thread work as edging decoration for men's and women's shirts. An alternative form of Levkás whitework is used to decorate items such as women's headscarves. Chain stitch is worked in gently flowing flower devices with connecting scrolls similar to the English Coggeshall work. This link with English embroidery is probably purely coincidental, although many of the islands, after being held variously by Venice and Turkey until the late 18th century, were under British rule until they became part of Greece in the middle of the 19th century.

Peacock motif from Corfu, worked in deep red cross stitch.

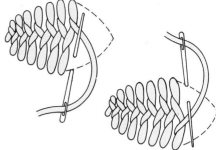

Cretan stitch.

Stylized border design
worked in straight stitches
on an apron.

Embroidered in cretan stitch,
this urn would be used as a
repeating border motif on skirts,
shawls and other costume items.

Crete

The island of Crete has given its name to a stitch known as cretan stitch or cretan feather stitch. It can be worked in closed or open form and it is found only in Crete and occasionally in Ipiros. Other stitches frequently used in Cretan embroidery include back stitch, chain stitch, cross stitch, herringbone stitch, ladder stitch, satin stitch, split stitch and french knots. Embroidery is often worked in monochrome silks, either blue or red, on a white linen, linen and cotton or silk ground. Sometimes cross-stitch motifs are outlined with green and infilled with red, and designs worked in cretan stitch often make use of many different bright-coloured silks.

Traditionally more embroidery is worked on clothing in Crete than in other areas of Greece. Surprisingly, there is less embroidery on household items.

A Cretan woman's traditional dress includes a skirt formed of five loom widths of white linen and cotton fabric suspended from below the bust by adjustable shoulder straps. The lower 30 cm (12 in) or so of the skirt is decorated with a repeating pattern, often in blue silk monochrome or alternatively in various bright colours. It is worked in cretan and other popular stitches, with devices such as urns, vases of flowers and tulips and carnations.

Over her bare shoulders a Cretan woman sometimes wears a cape of silk. Four panels of fabric are joined together with interlacing to form a curved shape which is then embroidered. Narrow borders of repeating motifs are worked round the outer edge of the arc of the

Open cretan stitch.

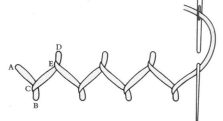

shawl or in blocks in the centre of each component panel.

Women's traditional clothing sometimes includes trousers, probably a result of past Turkish influence. Unlike women's trousers of, for instance, Turkmenistan, which have richly embroidered cuffs attached to main bodies of poor quality fabric, Cretan trousers are more likely to be made of linen or silk and embroidered not only round the cuffs but also up the outer edge of each leg.

The few examples of household embroideries include cushion covers which are often decorated with cretan stitch in marvellous curvilinear designs showing sirens or mermaids, a typical Cretan embroidery theme. Other motifs include double-headed eagles and the tulip and carnation forms found throughout Greek island embroidery.

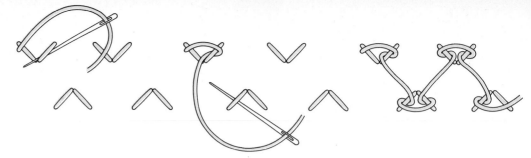

Astipalaia stitch. Parallel rows of chevrons are interlaced with a second thread. The needle does not penetrate the ground fabric during the interlacing.

Dodecanese

The Dodecanese, which today number rather more than the twelve islands that the name indicates, are the home of certain distinctive forms of embroidery.

In Rhodes, largest of the islands, a particularly thick floss-silk thread is worked on a linen ground. Cross stitch is popular, and so is double running stitch, which is often worked in parallel lines of step formation known as rhodes stitch. Horizontal 'treads' are incorporated in the first line of stitching, worked from top to bottom. The second line of stitching, worked from bottom to top, fills in the 'risers' of the steps.

Popular Rhodes embroidery designs include repeating motifs of water ewers looking rather like coffee pots; pairs of leaves, sometimes known as 'king' designs; and individual leaf motifs and flowers, sometimes known as 'queen' designs and worked next to or framing the 'king' motif.

In typical Greek island fashion, Rhodes decoration is worked on cushion covers, bedcoverings and hangings and women's traditional under-dresses, over-skirts, headscarves and belts.

Rhodes bed hangings are among the most exquisite in Greece. A 'tent' is constructed from tapering strips of linen which hang down from a wooden ring attached to the ceiling. There is sometimes an additional linen 'door' attached to the front opening of the tent. Each of the linen panels is lavishly embroidered, often with one of the variants of the repeating leaf motif.

In other Dodecanese islands, embroidery is sometimes worked with finer silk thread on a linen ground and in Astipalaia a twisted silk thread is popular. Red and green are the thread colours most often used throughout all the Dodecanese. They are worked predominantly in cross stitch, although back stitch, buttonhole stitch, darning stitch, running stitch and double running (rhodes) stitch, satin stitch and stem stitch are also employed. Parallel lines of individual running stitches are sometimes worked in alternating 'V' form and subsequently whipped, a technique

Tree of life richly worked in traditional red and green silk thread using cross stitch, part of the repeating pattern from a bedspread border.

The repeating pattern of paired leaves in a framework of individual leaves and flowers which decorates this bed hanging from Patmos is known as the 'king and queen' design and is worked in chain stitch, darning stitch and satin stitch.

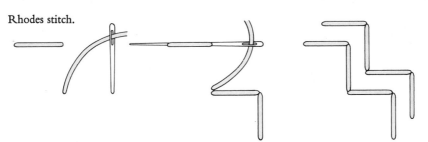

known as astipalaia stitch.

As well as floral and other motifs popular in Rhodes, Dodecanese embroideries include spot devices of men in ships, birds and abstract shapes distributed at random over a ground fabric, occasionally in sampler form.

Women's under-dresses throughout the Dodecanese are embroidered in typical Greek fashion. In Astipalaia over-dresses are generally sleeveless and embroidery is extensively worked on the wide sleeves of the linen underdresses. Motifs may be complex combinations of the 'king' and 'queen' patterns

17th-century table cover, worked in imitation of Venetian velvet.

carefully aligned up each sleeve and bordering the open cuff. Sometimes skirts, worn over under-dresses and made of heavy coarse cotton fabric, are decorated with horizontal borders worked in back stitch, buttonhole stitch and cross stitch with repeating designs of birds and flowers. The waist is covered with a belt, generally about 10 cm (4 in) wide, made of cotton gauze embroidered with metal threads laid and couched with retaining stitches and very often embellished with spangles.

On her head a woman sometimes wears a rectangular silk scarf with silk border embroidery and a motif such as a symmetrical double-headed eagle in the centre of the ground.

Cyclades

The embroidery of the Cyclades, to the west of the Dodecanese, is characterized by such motifs as intertwined squares, stylized animals which sometimes flank a tree of life, and peacocks. Designs, many of which are geometric, are more substantial in appearance than those of the Dodecanese.

Much Cyclades embroidery, worked in cross stitch, darning stitch and satin stitch, is used to decorate cushions and bed hangings. The traditional Cyclades bed consists of a raised platform with

storage beneath set in an alcove at one end of the room. The alcove is partitioned off by three or four widths of linen with elaborately embroidered vertical borders and sometimes joined by interlacing.

There is little evidence of embroidery in traditional Cyclades costume, apart from the border decoration round the edges of women's under-dresses found throughout Greece. This is often worked in satin stitch in repeating geometric motifs. Colours may be yellow, cream, blue and brown on white cotton or linen.

Angular 'threads' of unworked ground fabric are another characteristic of embroidery from the Cyclades.

Counted-thread techniques (cross stitch, darning stitch, satin stitch) typify Cyclades embroidery, as do intertwining squares with a symmetrical central motif.

Monochrome embroidery instantly identifies this Naxos cushion cover as Cyclades work.

Greek Island Dress

You will need:
3 m (3¼ yd) evenweave linen-type fabric with 24-30 threads to 2.5 cm (1 in)
matching sewing cotton
embroidery hoop (optional)

stranded embroidery cotton in four colours:
red 5 skeins
green 5 skeins
blue 5 skeins
yellow 5 skeins

This richly embroidered dress is designed to be worn either on its own or as an over-dress. It is a loose-fitting, off-the-shoulder garment with side slits and a front neck opening.

The dress is designed to be worn loosely but a tie belt may be added if you wish.

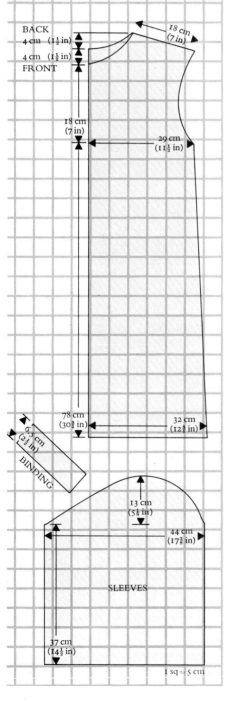

Preparing the Fabric

Draw the pattern pieces to the sizes shown on the cutting chart and cut out the fabric. Overcast or zigzag the edges.

If you are making a tie belt, cut two strips of fabric 55 cm (22 in) long and 10 cm (4 in) wide.

From the remaining fabric cut a bias strip 6.5 cm (2½ in) wide × 100 cm (40 in) for binding the neckline and front opening.

Embroidery

All the embroidery is worked in counted-thread cross stitch except for the two lines of blanket stitch round the edge of the neckline. Work from the diagram, using the colours indicated and forming each stitch over a unit of three threads (shown as a square on the diagram).

Start the embroidery about 8 cm (3¼ in) from the bottom edge of the sleeves and work the stitches across the edges of the border. Work the two colours of the blocks enclosed in the border in sequence with two needles (threaded with the appropriate colour), passing the threads under the backs of the adjacent blocks.

Stitch the figures one at a time, beginning at the bottom of each and working in rows to the top.

Join the centre-front seam, taking a turning of 12 mm (½ in) and leaving 20 cm (8 in) unstitched at the top for the neck opening.

Work the blue motif so that the centre line of stitches lies over the seam. Work the remaining motifs individually, row by row, from the bottom up.

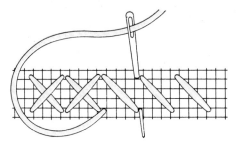

Making the Dress

Join the shoulder seams. Bind the front opening and neckline with the prepared bias strip, tapering the ends of the strip to a point at the centre front and mitring the corners at the top of the opening. Work blanket stitch round both edges of the binding.

Stitch the sleeves in position and then stitch the side and sleeve seams in one, leaving 25 cm (10 in) at the bottom of each seam for the side slits. Clip the seams over the crown of the sleeves and under the arms.

Check the length of the dress and turn up the hem. Work the border 5 cm (2 in) above the bottom edge and 1 cm (⅜ in) from the edge of the side slits.

Tie Belt

Join the strips together along one short end. Fold in half lengthwise and crease the fold lightly with your fingers. Open out the fabric and work a bird motif on one half, about 2.5 cm (1 in) from the ends of the strip.

Refold the strip in half lengthwise right sides together and stitch the long edges. Turn right side out, press and turn under and stitch the raw edges. Edge the tie with blanket stitch.

A free-form bird, worked in stem stitch, satin stitch and double darning stitch.

Northern Sporades

The embroidery of the Northern Sporades, the most northerly of the Greek island groups, is typified by many bright bold colours and often pictorial and asymmetrical motifs with curvilinear outlines.

Stitches such as brick stitch, chain stitch, double darning stitch, double running stitch and satin stitch are worked in blue, green, yellow, red, black, brown and cream silk on fine natural linen ground fabric.

Popular motifs are stylized flowers, men in ships, and a winged lion, an apocalyptic beast also associated with Venice. They are embroidered on household items such as cushions and bedcovers. The cushions have narrow embroidered borders on two or three sides only, since the fourth side does not show when many cushions are piled one on top of another. Bedcovers are composed

Stylized flower motif outlined in stem stitch and infilled with darning stitch. Such motifs would usually be worked on domestic items.

Fully manned ships are very popular decorative motifs. This example is from Skyros.

of three widths of linen joined together with interlacing and embroidered all round with narrow borders.

Women's under-dresses are decorated with bright border embroidery. For special occasions a woman wears a bolero of dark red or blue silk with elaborate laid and couched gold thread in scrolled designs, evidence of the proximity of Turkey and long Turkish rule over the area.

Cyprus

The island of Cyprus incorporates in its embroidery not only designs and techniques of Greece and Turkey but also some from further afield.

One of the main forms of Cyprus embroidery, traditionally worked in local red silk thread on a white linen or cotton ground, is an Assisi-type technique, with repeating motifs left unworked and reserves embroidered with cross stitch, long-legged cross stitch, two-sided italian stitch, double running stitch or satin stitch. This embroidery, generally worked as decorative borders for bedspreads and other household items, makes use of repeating scroll designs similar to those of Italy.

Another form of Cypriot embroidery, often known as Levkara work after a village south of Nicosia, is a whitework technique, with cotton thread on a cotton ground worked in repeating zigzag motifs of cutwork subsequently bordered by eyelet stitch and surface satin stitch.

Cypriot embroidery, worked by women for their own use, was seldom executed on costume items and today little embroidery is worked on the island for either dress or domestic purposes.

Traditional use of red silk thread in a repeating geometric pattern worked in double running stitch and long-legged cross stitch.

Table mats from the village of Levkara in whitework techniques with cutwork, eyelet holes and surface satin stitch.

Turkey

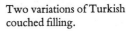

Turkish metal-thread embroidery, worked on silk with gold or silver-gilt thread, was often decorated with spangles or sequins which were sewn on with bullion knots.

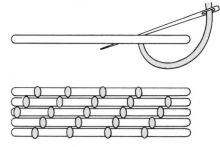

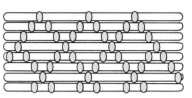

Diagonal couching (above), and diamond couching (below).

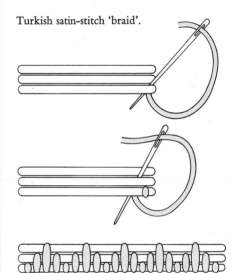

Turkish satin-stitch 'braid'.

L ike the country itself, the embroidery of Turkey offers a bridge between Europe and Asia, with the western, European, region of Thrace separated from Asian Anatolia by the narrow Bosporus. The religion of Turkey is predominantly Sunni Moslem, and consequently there are few embroidery devices depicting humans or animals.

Turkey has exerted a strong influence on embroidery since the 16th century, seen primarily in representations of flowers, cones and the tree of life, motifs which became popular in many other parts of the world. Another Turkish 'export' was madder, originally introduced to Turkey from India. The dye was exported in quantity from Turkey to western Europe where it was sometimes known as Turkey red. Other dyes used by Turkish embroiderers include indigo for blue and vinegar and iron for black. These colours were used to outline motifs and in the course of time have often become discoloured.

Turkish embroidery is generally worked with silk threads on a ground of cotton, linen, silk or velvet. Silk production was first established in Constantinople (Istanbul) in the 6th century and today silk is farmed in the Gallipoli peninsula and in north-western Anatolia. Cotton is grown in the west of Anatolia, in the Izmir area, and in the south, near Adana, where flax is also grown. There

Turkish diagonal stitching.

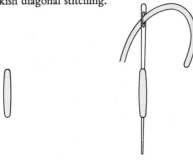

is intensive sheep farming in Thrace and, to a lesser extent, in many inland areas of Anatolia, but wool is generally used as embroidery ground fabric only for thick coats.

Turkish silk embroidery is typified by curvilinear floral motifs outlined in black, now sometimes faded to brown, and infilled with chain stitch, cross stitch, double running stitch, satin stitch and tent stitch. Also used are pattern darning, worked over three threads and

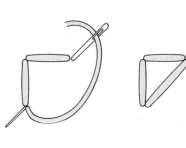

Superb silver-thread work on silk ground, a product of the 19th-century craftsmen of the Ottoman Empire.

under one, a diagonal stitch rather like an extended rhodes stitch, a diagonal couched filling stitch and a diamond couched filling stitch.

Main motifs are sometimes flanked by narrow borders, which may have similar floral devices worked in repeating form. Alternatively a narrow braid-like border can be formed using laid silk cord with satin stitch. The retaining stitches are worked in parallel lines at right angles to the laid cord, making a chevron-shaped pattern.

Turkish silk embroidery is traditionally worked by women for their own families' use. A great many samplers used to be worked, particularly during the 18th and 19th centuries. They were about 66 x 42 cm (26 x 16½ in), and were generally worked in silk thread on a linen ground. Floral and other motifs were executed in spot formation using eye stitch and double running stitch. As with samplers from other countries, Turkish samplers were worked not only as test pieces but also to provide patterns that could be copied or developed by other embroiderers.

Turkish embroiderers use their skills to decorate both household and costume items. The former include towels, pillow covers, prayer rugs and other floor coverings, bed tents similar to those of the Dodecanese and coverlets for day beds or divans.

Some of the most beautiful surviving domestic embroideries are 'show towels', long rectangular pieces of linen, usually about 113 x 50 cm (45 x 20 in), which were used to hide toilet requisites. Often they were embroidered as presents. Show towels generally have borders of embroidery worked at each end, either with the repeating floral devices used for other Turkish domestic embroideries or, less commonly, with a continuous pictorial design such as a row of arches or mosques or a stylized view of the Bosporus. The embroidery is often double-sided, with the outline of each motif worked in double running stitch or stem stitch and infilled with one of the many Turkish filling stitches. In Thrace infilling is definite and bold, the most popular colours being orange, blue and brown. In Anatolia colouring is more subdued, with peach and pale blue predominating.

The main items of Thracian and Anatolian women's traditional dress which have embroidery are trousers and headscarves, worn with long dresses which are generally not embroidered. Trousers are similar in cut to those of Crete and other eastern Mediterranean islands and are made of coarsely woven cotton or linen. They are embroidered in red, blue, green, yellow and black cotton or silk thread. Typical stitches are chain stitch, cross stitch, darning stitch and running stitch worked in repeating spot

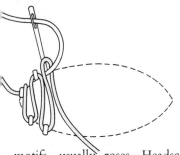

Various kinds of couching stitch can be used to hold down loosely laid threads. The design is bulked with a piece of card or padding; a single gold thread is then laid down in a zigzag pattern and couched at each bend with silk retaining thread.

motifs, usually roses. Headscarves are made of cotton, linen or silk and worked with silk thread, usually in green, gold, black or red, sometimes augmented with metal thread. Designs, which are less crude than those executed on the trousers, are stitched in double darning stitch and double running stitch, which are worked right through the ground fabric.

Men's coats, and many of the court costumes worn by both men and women, were in the past sometimes lavishly decorated with Turkish goldwork.

Turkish metal-thread embroidery was sometimes worked by professional male embroiderers, particularly in Thrace. It consists of gold, silver-gilt or silver thread in flat strip, round coil or purl (bullion) form laid on a ground of velvet, silk or, occasionally, soft leather. The thread is held to the ground fabric in a variety of ways. It is sometimes laid in simple zigzag form and couched with small silk retaining stitches at each junction, or it may be laid in longer zigzags with extra intermediary retaining stitches. If padding is required, the thread is laid over a card template and couched at either side of that padding. Alternatively, large areas of goldwork may be executed with parallel lines of metal thread. These are laid either directly onto the ground fabric or over an underlayer of a 'padding' of laid cords, and are couched, singly or in pairs, in basket-weave formation.

The designs often include cones and other scrolled motifs such as stylized peacocks, which are sometimes connected by repeating coils. Turkish goldwork, although no longer generally practised, was popular not only in Turkey but also in areas of the former

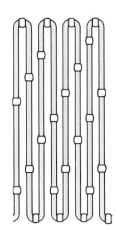

Metal thread laid in long zigzags couched at the bends and along the straight thread.

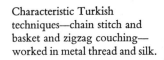

Small zigzags need only be couched at each bend of the laid thread.

A repeating pattern of trees worked in fishbone, satin and other stitches on cotton ground.

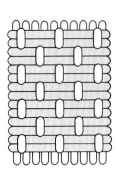

Characteristic Turkish techniques—chain stitch and basket and zigzag couching— worked in metal thread and silk.

Turkish Empire and many of the motifs have now been transposed to other embroidery techniques.

As could be expected from the work of such a busy crossroads, many diverse techniques are employed in the embroidery of Turkey. Whitework, for instance, is found both on the mainland and, more generally, in islands off the Anatolian coast. Some whitework is executed on a silk and cotton ground fabric, with silk thread worked in double running stitch, satin stitch and drawn-thread work to form repeating stars, leaves and zigzag motifs.

Turkish embroidery today consists mainly of traditional floral motifs worked in polychrome silk threads. It is used to embellish household items worked by women for their own use. As in neighbouring Greece, hand embroidery is sometimes employed commercially to decorate high fashion clothing.

Fishbone stitch.

Another method of couching is to lay down threads to form padding, then to lay metal threads over them in the other direction. The metal threads can be couched in pairs to look like basket work. A similar effect can be achieved without the base padding threads, but the result is not so textured.

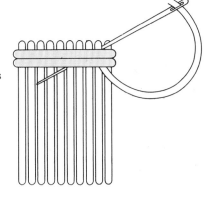

The Levant

When considering the embroidery of the eastern Mediterranean it is useful to define the Levant as the western part of Syria, Lebanon and Israel, including Palestine, and western Jordan. The indigenous embroidery of this area, which has large Christian, Moslem and Jewish communities, also includes decoration worked by some nomadic Bedouin tribes. Much of the work is known as 'Palestinian', although various related forms of decoration are worked in all the countries of the region.

Silk and cotton are both produced throughout the northern part of the Levant. Spinning and weaving are traditionally women's skills, although in some areas men weave, usually with an upright horizontal loom.

The Levant has a long history of embroidery, although, because of the Mediterranean climate and the fact that most embroideries have been in regular use, few examples survive that are over a hundred years old. Under Turkish rule, which lasted until the early 20th century, some pieces were made by professional men embroiderers. Today embroidery is worked by women, sometimes on household items such as marriage cushions but usually on costume and for their own families' use. Embroidery is often worked with red thread, which is sometimes associated with the costume of married women. Unmarried girls traditionally wear blue embroidered robes. Patterns are passed on from generation to generation, and are generally worked in silk thread on ground fabrics of cotton, linen or silk.

Traditionally, women wear full-length flowing dresses of black, indigo or white cotton, linen or silk. The fabric is doubled across the warp to form back and front of the dress which has a vertical neck opening at the front. The sleeves are straight pieces of fabric, sometimes with added wings extending downwards in points. Extra width is given to the body of the dress by inset triangular panels and since many dresses are handed down

Front panel of Palestinian dress, richly decorated in cross stitch.

from one generation to another, various extra panels are added or taken in depending on the girth of the current wearer. Embroidery is worked on one or two separate panels which are subsequently applied to the front yoke of the dress with chain stitch or hemming. In some regions, embroidery is also worked on panels applied at the back of the neck, vertically up the seams of the skirt and on

Traditional Palestinian dress, made about 1930 (front and back view), with appliqué and floss-silk embroidery.

'Chicken's feet', one of the repeating cross-stitch designs used to decorate narrow borders on garments.

the sleeves. Designs are often embroidered straight onto the ground fabric.

In Moslem areas, dresses are worn over trousers, which may have embroidered cuffs in the style of Turkmenistan. Full-length sleeved coats may also be worn. These are densely embroidered on the front yokes, all round the main hem and on the sleeves.

Like the dresses, head coverings are highly regionalized, and consist of various forms of scarves or caps. A scarf is usually made of two or more lengths of cotton sewn together to give an overall size of about 195 x 75 cm (78 x 30 in). They are frequently fringed, and embroidered with wide panels at either end and narrow borders along each side. Caps, made of linen or cotton and padded or moulded over cardboard templates, are embroidered and sometimes enriched with gold or silver coins and coral beads, pierced and sewn on as hanging spangles.

Wedding outfits are generally the most lavishly embroidered of all the costumes, and they are worked usually by the bride herself. In the past a bride's

trousseau could contain as many as thirteen exquisitely embroidered dresses.

Many women in both village and town are still to be seen wearing embroidered dresses and trousers, although today most are machine embroidered with Cornely machines. Headdresses and other embroidered costume items are not part of everyday wear.

Men of the Levant do not normally wear embroidered costume, although in some parts Druze men, who adhere to a little-known religion which separated from Islam a thousand years ago, wear white cotton shirts embroidered with silk thread. The shirts have gathered fronts similar to English smocks and double sleeves with one cuff extending from beneath the other.

Embroidery designs throughout the Levant are usually densely worked, often in repeating motifs such as eight-pointed stars known by local names such as 'wide open eye' or 'Bethlehem star', narrow borders called 'water melons' or 'chicken's feet'; and the universal tree of

Corner motif and border design from an Israeli tablecloth. Worked in counted-thread cross stitch on evenweave linen.

The basic Levant dress shape sometimes has long wing sleeves added to it. Embroidery is either worked directly onto or applied in panels to the areas indicated.

Israeli dress-panel design to be worked in cross stitch features the ubiquitous eight-pointed star motif.

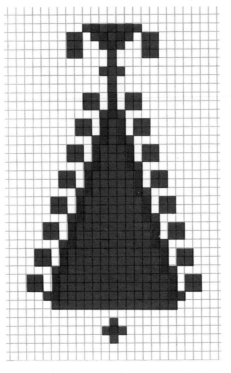

life. Repeating designs are sometimes purposely misaligned since it is considered unlucky to achieve perfect stitching. Superstition enters into much of the embroidery design of the Levant and, for instance, turquoise beads are sometimes sewn onto embroideries to ward off the 'evil eye'.

Counted-thread geometric work is popular throughout the Levant, usually executed in cross stitch, but sometimes in buttonhole stitch or tent stitch. Free-form embroidery is generally practised only in Bethlehem and Gaza, where the women also work appliqué.

One form of embroidery practised in Damascus is Damascus goldwork, which takes the form of gold-coloured silk thread worked on a white cotton ground. In the past there was substantial silk farming in the area and woven silk fabric and fine thread were sold to embroiderers throughout the Levant, but more recently commercial silks have been used. The embroidery is worked in intricate buttonhole stitch and cross stitch in repeating patterns of geometric motifs such as zigzags and floral devices. Damascus goldwork is traditionally used for such items as tablecloths and food covers, with embroidered outer surrounds and a main central motif such as a complex eight-pointed star. It may also be used to decorate Druze men's shirts.

Damascus goldwork is not now generally practised. Embroiderers in the city itself prefer to use Cornely machines to mass produce embroidered items for sale throughout the Levant and elsewhere. They execute scrolled designs of machine-tamboured chain stitching on table linen as well as women's robes.

Traditional embroidery continues to be practised around the Sea of Galilee where some of the people are still nomadic Bedouin. Women are more likely than men to be seen wearing traditional embroidered costume. Sometimes they have wide parallel bands of cross stitch worked in repeating geometric motifs round their skirt and sleeves; and sometimes their wing-sleeved and full-length dress is embroidered solely on the front yoke applied panels, at the back of the hem and in narrow vertical borders on the sleeves.

Ramallah, a town ten miles north of

Jerusalem whose name means 'hill of God', is particularly famous for embroidery. This is often worked in deep red monochrome silk thread on bleached cotton or linen ground, although black, orange, pink, turquoise and green threads are also used.

Ramallah embroidery designs, generally all executed in cross stitch and usually in repeating form, have such names as 'apples', 'old man's teeth', 'the baker's wife', 'road to Egypt' and 'chick peas and raisins'.

Much of the finest Ramallah work is

executed on women's dresses, usually made of white linen with an applied yoke panel. Embroidery is worked direct to the ground fabric in vertical panels on the skirt and on the cuffs of the full-length sleeves.

Ramallah embroidery is not now generally worked in the area itself, but American Quakers established a base there in 1868, and many Ramallah embroideries have been taken to North America. Ramallah designs are today popular with embroiderers in many parts of the world.

Embroidery of Bethlehem is typified by appliqué and laid and couched work on women's cotton and silk robes, sometimes called 'queenly dresses'. Panels of silk attached on either side of the vertical neck opening are sometimes known as a 'flower garden'. The panels are densely embroidered, with gold or silver thread laid and couched with silk worked in designs such as 'flower pots', with circles about 7.5 cm (3 in) in

Metal-thread work, laid and couched in the Turkish manner, decorates a 19th-century rabbi's gown.

diameter, outlined with laid and couched metal thread and infilled with small circles of parallel satin stitches. These are worked in pink, white, orange, black or green floss silk. Applied panels are also sewn to the sleeves and skirts of Bethlehem dresses, but embroidery is often confined simply to needle chain stitching or small blocks of parallel satin stitches worked in repeating floral devices.

Traditional short-sleeved velvet jackets have applied yoke and cuff panels of silk embroidered with laid and couched work and satin stitch. Linen caps are thickly padded, and have gold thread and polychrome floss-silk embroidery with added gold coins and coral beads.

In the hills south of Bethlehem, in Hebron and the surrounding villages, embroidery is characteristically in deep red silk cross stitch, with some running stitch and tent stitch, worked on a ground of indigo or black cotton. Devices such as S-shapes known as 'leeches', eight-pointed stars, apple trees and V-shapes known as 'necklaces' are worked mainly on women's wing-sleeved dresses. There are few Hebron domestic embroideries, although traditional designs are sometimes executed on wedding cushions made by brides as presents for their husbands' families.

The most southerly of the important embroidery centres is the coastal city of Gaza, where typical embroidery is worked on pieces of silk, either before or after they are applied to dresses. They are attached to the ground fabric, usually a black silk and cotton mixture, with chain stitch or slipstitch. Chain stitch is also used for outlining curvilinear floral motifs, generally worked in repeating form and infilled with satin stitch. Other repeating floral motifs are executed in cross stitch.

Little Gaza embroidery is now worked and in only a few parts of the Levant is embroidery being produced in any quantity. It is, nonetheless, still being practised in many areas by older women to decorate dresses, usually for their own use. These are worked mostly with machine stitching, but sometimes by hand. Embroidery is also enjoying a revival among some young people, who transpose traditional stitches and designs to more fashionable garments.

Modern Syrian woman's dress. The embroidery was worked by hand in cross stitch.

Palestinian motif worked in cross stitch consists of a stylized flower flanked by a geometric border.

Lavishly decorated velvet jacket from Bethlehem, a town traditionally noted for its sumptuous embroidery. The applied panels are embroidered with laid and couched threads and a variety of stitches.

Palestinian Smock

You will need:
3.4 m (3¾ yd) indigo cotton fabric 115 cm (45 in) wide
0.5 m (⅝ yd) magenta cotton fabric 90 cm (36 in) wide
0.3 m (⅜ yd) coarse linen or hessian (burlap) to tone with either colour, 18 threads to 2.5 cm (1 in)
0.3 m (⅜ yd) calico for backing
pearl cotton in five colours
1 reel each magenta and indigo sewing cotton
embroidery hoop (optional)

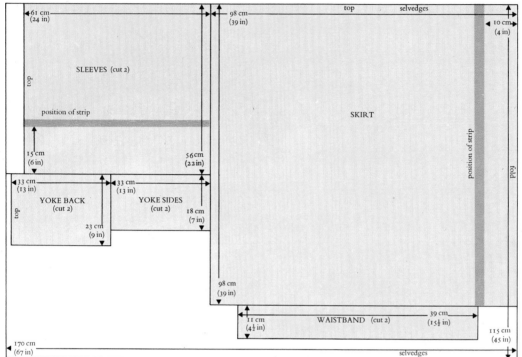

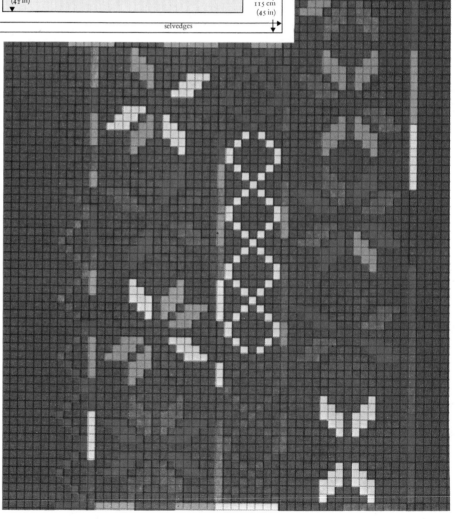

Preparing the Fabric

Cut out the hessian (burlap) and calico backing to the size shown plus 5 cm (2 in) all round for damp stretching. Baste the backing to the hessian and treat the two thicknesses as one.

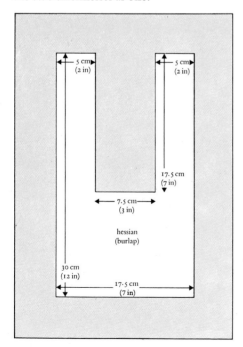

Size
To fit 81–86 cm (32–34 in) bust.

An unusual smock incorporating features of Palestinian embroidery.

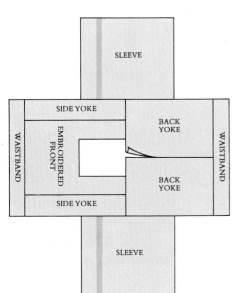

SLEEVE

SIDE YOKE

BACK YOKE

WAISTBAND

EMBROIDERED FRONT

WAISTBAND

BACK YOKE

SIDE YOKE

SLEEVE

Embroidery

This is a counted-thread design in which one stitch is worked over one thread of the hessian and marked as one square on the chart. Work in tent stitch, changing and arranging the colours as you wish, without following a rigid pattern. (Restrict yourself to two or three colours per flower for a more lively design.)

Starting at the centre thread of the yoke, and using the chart as a guide, work the design in strips. Continue one panel of flowers and a narrow strip right up the yoke to the shoulder and reverse the design from left to right for the opposite side of the yoke.

Damp stretch the embroidery (see page 272) and trim the yoke to size.

Making the Smock

Use 12 mm ($\frac{1}{2}$ in) seams throughout.

Cut four strips 5 cm (2 in) wide across the full width of the magenta fabric.

Turn in the raw edges and machine the strips in position on the sleeves and skirt, sewing close to the edges (see cutting layout for placing).

Join the centre-back seam of the yoke leaving it open 16 cm ($6\frac{1}{2}$ in) at the neck edge. Stitch the side yokes to the embroidered front and then join back and front yokes at the shoulders. Open the pieces out flat and add the sleeves and waistbands (see diagram). Join the sleeve and side seams as one continuous seam from wrist to waistband.

Run two lines of gathers round the skirt top inside the seam allowance. Draw up the gathers and stitch the skirt to the waistband.

Turn up a hem round the skirt and sleeves. Cut bias strips of magenta cotton 2.5 cm (1 in) wide and use them to bind the back opening and then the neck edge. Extend the ends 15 cm (6 in) each side of the neck to act as ties for fastening.

Sub-Saharan Africa

This gown from Liberia, with its square neck hole and applied chest panel, is typical of the men's robes of West Africa.

The Tharaka of East Africa are renowned for their stitched beadwork. This girl's leather tunic has panels of stitched beads.

Some of the most decorative ceremonial embroidery in sub-Saharan Africa is worked by Hausa men of Nigeria and Niger.

Women in Dakar, Senegal, wear white cotton dresses embroidered with swirling patterns, typical of West Africa.

In the part of Africa which lies south of the Sahara desert, embroidery is practised by comparatively few of the groups that make up the complex tribal mosaic of the population. Those who do embroider are scattered widely throughout the continent. Except in western Africa there has been little or no contact between the various groups with the result that disparate and unrelated techniques have developed in several separate areas.

One of the most popular West African embroidery motifs is an intertwined knot, a geometric form often found on tiles and in calligraphic art. Other typical West African embroidery motifs include Catherine-wheel swirls, the outlines of jagged teeth, and the crescent moon of Islam.

Although it is impossible to generalize about the embroidery motifs of the whole of sub-Saharan Africa, indigenous styles are usually non-pictorial, influenced in part by the Sunni faction of the Islam religion. Pictorial embroidery is often the result of foreign influences. There is, for example, a keen following of needlepoint in some parts of the country, particularly in eastern and southern Africa and among the Mende of Sierra Leone. Needlepoint has in each instance been introduced by settlers.

Embroidery in sub-Saharan Africa has been used mainly for costume decoration or, where few clothes are worn, for accessories such as necklaces and bracelets.

Men do a great deal of the indigenous embroidery, particularly in western Africa, designing the motifs and executing the stitchery. Much of the finest embroidery is worn by men, especially in West Africa. Elsewhere in sub-Saharan Africa embroidery is more usually women's work. Many of the men embroiderers are professionals but the women embroiderers usually work pieces for their own use or for their families'.

Cotton is the most important textile material in Africa. It is grown in many parts of the continent, with significant concentrations near Lake Victoria and in West Africa, especially in Cameroun, Chad, Mali and Nigeria.

Sub-Saharan Africa is climatically unsuited for growing flax and hemp, and silk farming has been of no importance. The raffia palm yields the raffia fibres used by the Bakuba of Zaire. Although sisal is grown throughout eastern Africa, it is seldom used for embroidery. Sheep are raised in many places, but wool is infrequent in indigenous embroidery, and the yarns needed for needlepoint are generally imported, usually from Britain or from Scandinavia.

Weaving is an old native occupation in the northern areas adjacent to the Sahara and several types of traditional loom are employed in western and eastern Africa. Women in the west of the continent still sometimes use a vertical mat loom which produces cloth one metre or more wide. Other women in the same area weave more elaborate materials on a horizontal loom, the setting up of which is done by the men.

Another loom found throughout western Africa today is the strip loom, also known as a Sudanese men's loom. Cotton cloth woven on a strip loom is narrow. Widths as little as 2.5 cm (1 in) have been recorded, although most strips are between 8 and 26 cm (3 and 10½ in).

There are practical reasons for producing such narrow strips

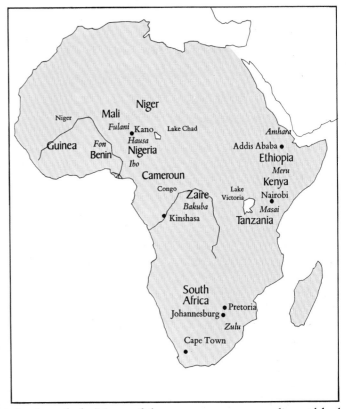

of cotton cloth. Many of the weavers were nomadic, and had to be able to carry their looms when they moved. It was also desirable from an economic point of view not to invest in too many warp threads at one time.

Woven strips of cloth are oversewn, selvedge to selvedge, to produce the width of ground fabric required. Sometimes as many as a hundred strips are used, although the number of widths in most of the embroidered strip–cloth costumes is considerably less than that.

As in many other areas of the world, the most common natural dye used is indigo. Other natural dyes for both grounds and threads have included the acacia, *Acacia senegal* (the same tree which produces gum arabic), which yields a brown; the kola nut, which produces a beige, and dried flowers of the safflower, *Carthamus tinctorius*, which produce a red.

Imported embroidery threads are more commonly used today. Bright emerald green, scarlet, yellow and black are popular shades.

One unusual material sometimes used in embroidery in sub-Saharan Africa is the cowrie shell, a marine snail of the *Cypraeidae* family. It has a thick humped shell, and those used in embroidery are about 2.5 cm (1 in) in length. They are pierced with a strong needle and sewn to a ground fabric with two long running stitches.

Cowrie shells used sometimes to form part of a woman's marriage price, and today they are still used by a few embroiderers in western and eastern Africa, primarily for decorative rather than nuptial purposes. They are often mixed with beads which are also popular in other areas.

Eastern Africa

Amhara

Embroidery is still favoured by several groups of peoples in eastern Africa, each of whom uses it in a distinctive way.

The Amhara people of the northern highlands of Ethiopia are descendants of Semitic tribes who crossed the Red Sea from Arabia between the 6th century B.C. and the 1st century A.D.

Some cotton is grown in Ethiopia today, but most of it is imported, much of it in the form of white yarn. The thread is woven into a loose-mesh fabric about 82 cm (32 in) wide. It is left undyed and is bleached in the sun.

This muslin-like material is used for making women's skirts and shawls. The skirts consist of one piece of the cotton fabric gathered round the waist. One selvedge is at the waist, and the other forms the hem of the skirt. A band of pattern darning is worked round the hem in imported silk thread. Stitches are generally about 2.5 cm (1 in) long and colouring is bright. A turquoise, red and yellow combination is typical. Designs are simple and geometric, with lozenges and triangles divided into smaller, still regular, shapes. Sometimes they are further embellished with metal thread.

Around her shoulders an Amhara woman wears a *shamma*, a shawl made of a 2.4 m (2⅝ yd) length of the same open-weave white cotton. A band of pattern darning is embroidered across

Detail of Amhara pattern darning worked on loosely woven cotton in a typical pattern of diamonds and lozenges.

each fringed end of the shawl.

The stitching is sometimes rather crudely executed, with loose ends of embroidery yarn and knots visible on the reverse. It is obvious that most skirts and *shammas* are not expected to last a long time; the poor quality of the ground fabric certainly does not suggest durability. In some instances, however, metal thread is incorporated with silk stitching.

Amhara pattern darning is worked by professional embroiderers, and the shawls and skirts are offered for sale in the markets to local women and visitors.

Dignitaries of the Ethiopian Church carry ceremonial umbrellas decorated with metal thread laid and couched with silk.

This Amhara woman at the market in Gondar is wearing a cotton shawl decorated with colourful pattern darning.

Meru

Some of the Meru people of Kenya also employ stitched beadwork decoration. Imported plastic beads are used, sometimes mixed with cowrie shells. Married women of the Tharaka tribe, a subdivision of the Meru living to the north east of Nairobi, sometimes wore triangular leather bodices decorated with horizontal rows of plastic beads and cowrie shells. The bodices were stitched by women for their own use and are not generally worked today.

Another Meru tribe, the Tigania, has in the past used cowrie-shell embroidery to decorate quivers, harness aprons and other war apparel.

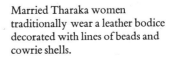

Kurya women sometimes embroider leather belts with beads stitched in coils and other geometric designs.

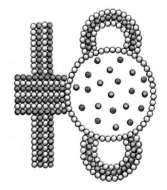

Married Tharaka women traditionally wear a leather bodice decorated with lines of beads and cowrie shells.

175

Masai

The Masai, nomadic pastoralists who live mainly in Kenya and Tanzania, are recognizable by the completely shaved heads of the women and uninitiated boys and also of some married men.

Many Masai still wear leather costume accessories decorated with brightly coloured beads stitched to the leather, often in geometric patterns. Although Masai women are quick to offer threaded bead items such as necklaces and hoop earrings for sale to visitors to the game parks of eastern Africa and to travellers crossing the Kenyan-Tanzanian border, some stitched bead items are also available.

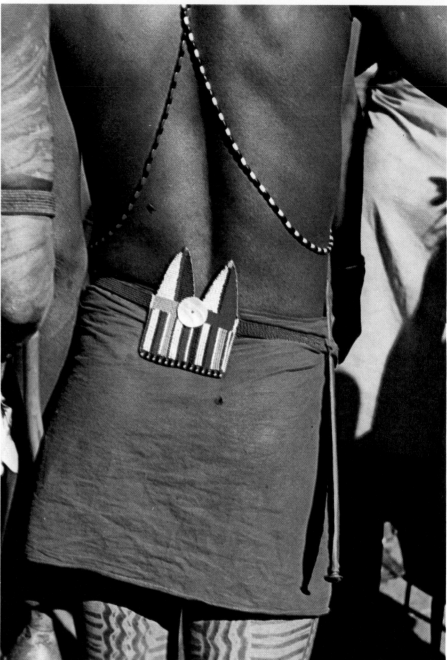

Masai hand ornament. The loops, which are embellished with beads and buttons, fit over the wearer's fingers.

East coast stitched beadwork is used to decorate a variety of costume accessories such as this Masai leather belt.

Although much of their bead decoration takes the form of beads threaded on wire, this Masai leather bracelet has beads stitched to the ground fabric.

Embroideries from the east coast sometimes incorporate cowrie shells and glass beads into their designs, as on this Masai apron.

Southern Africa

Southern Africa has very little indigenous embroidery other than the stitched bead-work of the Zulu.

The tribal homeland of the Zulus is in the north-eastern part of the Republic of South Africa. Many men have, however, temporarily left Zululand to work in the cities and the mines of the Republic. Thus, in the main, the Zulu homeland is a female-oriented society. The women are left to look after the children and they stitch beadwork.

Plastic beads are stitched to a ground of leather or plastic, with cotton thread worked in long running stitches. One of the many popular geometric designs is a recurrent pattern of a circle cut into many segments.

The Zulu traditional dress consists of a heavy two-piece leather harness and some of the most beautiful examples of beadwork are seen on belts worn by Zulu men. These belts are worn at regular Sunday morning tribal dances held at some of the gold mines around Johannesburg.

Zulu leather harness, sometimes decorated with plastic beadwork. The segmented circle is a popular Zulu motif.

Sometimes Zulu skirts made of woven fabric are decorated with stitched beadwork in repeating V and other geometric designs.

European Influence

Dutch settlers coming to South Africa brought with them their own embroidered costume and other items, and the women continued to embroider aprons, blouses, caps and other whitework items in the styles of the Netherlands. They worked with imported cotton yarn.

One form of traditional Dutch whitework was the *kappie*, a bonnet worn by women and girls. *Kappies* take various forms but all had a wide poke brim and a back neck flap. Many *kappies* were made of fine white cotton and embroidered with cutwork or other whitework stitching. Patterns were intricate and often took the form of floral sprays worked in buttonhole stitch, chain stitch, satin stitch and stem stitch.

Dutch and later English settlers often worked the flowers of southern Africa into their embroidery designs. The protea, today a national emblem of the Republic, still appears in embroideries.

As in eastern Africa, in the 19th century European nuns and missionaries introduced foreign styles of embroidery to African girl students. Today, however, European embroidery in southern Africa is more or less exclusively a white women's pastime.

The most popular forms of embroidery are hardanger, hedebo and other whiteworks and cutworks, blackwork, tambouring and needlepoint. Months, sometimes years, are spent working enormous tablecloths and domestic linens, dresses and babies' christening robes. All the fabrics and yarns are imported, usually from England or from Scandinavia.

Southern African embroidery designs today are usually composite patterns of recognized motifs. The combination of motifs is important; great attention is paid to the fact that in a particularly complex jigsaw of motifs that particular combination of shapes has never been worked before.

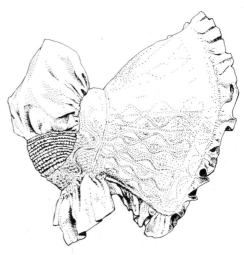

South African women made themselves *kappies*, bonnets with wide poke brims and back neck flaps. They were quilted and richly embroidered with whitework.

Western Africa

Bakuba

The Bakuba or Kuba people of Zaire are about sixteen small groups numbering some 75,000 in all. They produce a limited amount of cotton fibre and woven cotton textiles.

The Bakuba are chiefly known, however, for their unusual raffia embroidery. The raffia palm, *Raphia ruffia*, has feather-shaped leaves about 60 cm (24 in) long. The leaves are first pounded in water until they are supple and then they are split as finely as possible and worked in the hands until soft. Several strands are twisted together and woven into cloth or left as embroidery yarn. Bakuba men weave, but today women do the embroidery.

Bakuba embroidery was made into wall hangings or decorative covers for horizontal surfaces. They were embroidered with several strands of raffia yarn threaded through an iron needle and worked in chain stitch, stem stitch, tent stitch and a variety of drawn-thread stitches. Sometimes areas of embroidery were cut close to the surface of the

Bakuba stitching used for ceremonial masks, incorporating cowrie shells and beads sewn on with long straight stitches.

Bakuba intertwined knots and other geometric designs are worked on raffia matting made from the pounded and twisted strands of leaves gathered from the raffia palm.

ground fabric to give the effect of carpet-like pile. Subsequent infilling between the pile was worked with ordinary uncut embroidery. The effect could be further heightened by cutting tassels composed of long stitches to give a knobbly pile. Designs were usually geometric.

Although most of the traditional Bakuba raffia embroidery was done purely for decorative purposes, Bakuba women sometimes made wrap-around skirts of raffia cloth. A Bakuba skirt consisted of a length of raffia cloth about 70 cm × 5.25 m (28 in × 17 ft). The women would then work appliqué on the skirt, applying motifs cut from other pieces of raffia cloth with slipstitch.

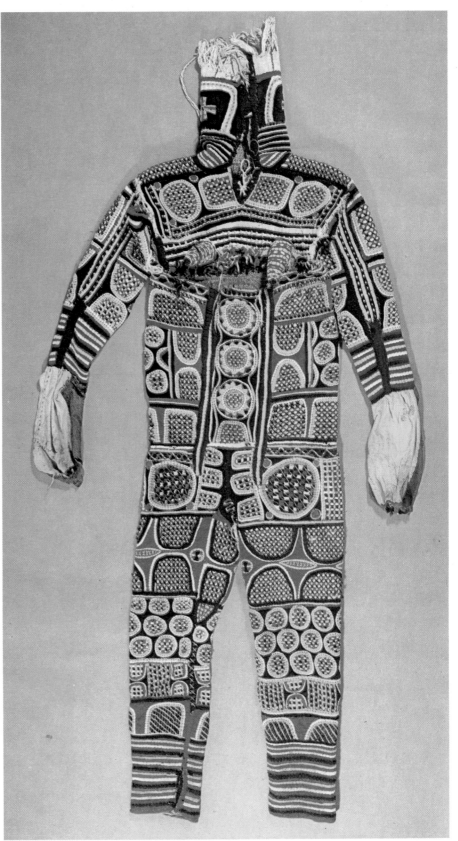

An Ibo man's ceremonial all-in-one costume with geometric cotton appliqué shapes stitched to a cotton ground.

Ibo

The Ibo of the delta of the Niger are now spread throughout Nigeria. Many are small traders and businessmen.

Traditional Ibo religion included in its pantheon a god of creation, a goddess of earth and innumerable other deities and spirits. Men participated in religious ceremonies wearing tightly fitting, complex all-in-one costumes made of cotton fabric and decorated with cotton appliqué attached with slipstitch and running stitch. The applied devices covered the entire surface. The overall design was geometric, with circles recurring in various forms on different parts of the costume, although the individual devices making up the design had apparently no religious significance.

The Ibo today have to a great extent given up their tribal religion for Christianity. They do not therefore normally make festival costumes, nor is appliqué worked for any other purpose.

The Ibo sometimes decorate plain woven cloth to great effect with appliqué, pattern darning and running stitch.

179

Hausa

The Hausa inhabit north-western Nigeria and southern Niger. As with other groups in western Africa, they adopted Islam from the 14th century onwards.

The Hausa have for many centuries practised intensive agriculture based on a strict rotation of crops. They produced more than enough food for their basic requirements and have therefore had time to devote to handicrafts.

The manufacture of woven fabric from locally grown cotton remains one of their main non-agricultural activities. Local cotton production is not enough, however, to satisfy current demand and additional supplies have to be imported. This heavy demand for cotton fabric is exacerbated by the fact that some items of Hausa men's clothing are enormous! They wear trousers, tight-fitting brimless caps and voluminous gowns, or *rigas*. Some of the gowns are full-length and consist of a tube of cotton fabric

Hausa cotton trousers with typical intertwined knot and jagged 'teeth' devices embroidered in silk and skilfully outlined in chain stitch (detail left). The other trouser leg (detail above) is worked in the favourite Hausa colour combination of bright red, purple, green and orange.

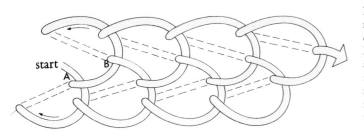

Kano chain stitch. Bring the needle up at 'start' and make a chain loop from right to left. Bring the needle back up at A and make a second chain loop from left to right. Bring the needle up at B. Make a chain loop from left to right, finishing inside the first chain.

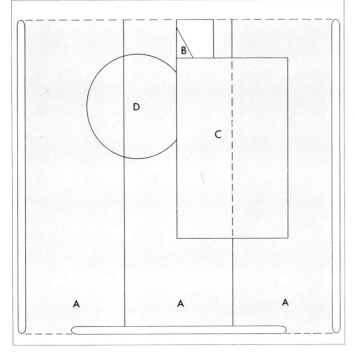

A Hausa man's robe is made from five pieces of fabric. Three long strips, A, are joined selvedge to selvedge. The fabric is folded over at the top and joined along the bottom edge, leaving a slit for the legs. The sides are left open to make long, cool armholes. A rectangular neck hole is cut and half filled with a triangular piece of fabric, B. The robe is then finished with a large patch, C, sewn onto the left side and often left open at the top to form a large pocket. Both this and the area marked D are embroidered with Hausa swirls and the traditional 'jagged teeth' motif.

The intertwined knot, a popular Hausa motif, is often worked in parallel lines of chain stitch. Sometimes it has eyelet infilling (detail below right), also called the 'thousand ant holes' pattern.

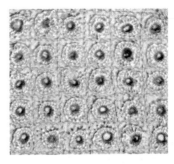

shaped like a roller-towel with part of the one seam left open for the wearer's legs to protrude. The selvedges at the sides form extended armholes, open from the shoulder to the hem of the gown. The tube is made with three widths of fabric and has an overall width of about 2.1 m (nearly 7 ft).

At the top of the gown, a rectangular neck hole is cut out and partly infilled with a triangular panel of needleweaving, which is inset to the wearer's right side. A large panel of cotton fabric, the same as the main ground of the gown, is added to the front. This applied panel is sometimes left open at the top to form a massive pocket. The panel is embroidered either before or after application to the main ground. A spiral or circular motif is embroidered on the front of the gown, below the right shoulder, with a similar embroidered motif at the centre back. Circular motifs are a prominent feature of Hausa design. They are made by cutting circles in the cloth, turning the cut edges under, and filling the spaces with needleweaving.

This crocodile with bared teeth is one of the typically humorous motifs embroidered by modern Hausa women on various household items.

Among the pastoral Hausa, men generally wear short tunics constructed in a similar way to an ordinary shirt. These short robes are about 75 cm (2½ ft) long and only slightly wider than the wearer. Three widths of striploom cotton, each about 15 cm (6 in) wide, are sewn together. Two elongated triangular panels of the same cloth are inserted at the back and the front,

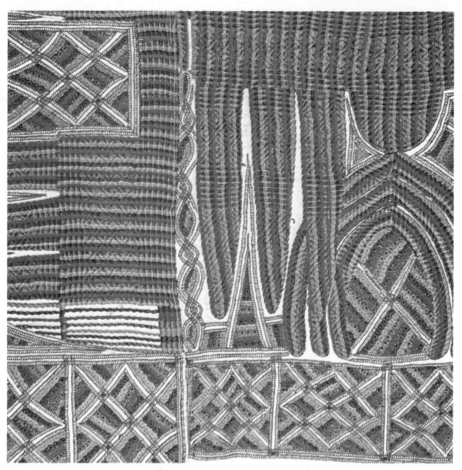

Brightly coloured jagged 'teeth' designs are often worked in buttonhole, eyelet and ladder stitches.

A circular swirl is often infilled with different-coloured blocks of stitching.

Hausa men sometimes wear beautiful slippers and shoes, embellished with typical local embroidery.

gowns. Herringbone stitch, locally designated as bulls' urine or fishbone, and buttonhole stitch are employed for caps. Running stitch appears on gowns and caps, as does wave stitch, known as earthworm or worm tracks. Laid and couched work, called grass or door covering, is found particularly on the front pocket panel of the full-length gown. Often machine stitching is incorporated into a design that is predominantly hand-embroidered.

Embroidery on Hausa men's robes is never pictorial in design. The Islamic intertwined knot, known locally as *dagi*, is one recurrent motif. It is often much more curvilinear than in Islamic embroidery of other areas, and its interstices are sometimes infilled with eyelet stitching. The knot is often worked next to the crescent moon.

One popular design is the two knives, or two needles, motif. Lines of parallel stitches are worked in exaggerated zigzag form so that the finished effect looks like two long teeth. *Yayin sharif* is the name for the combination of the two-teeth pattern with the intertwined knot and crescent moon motifs.

Clothing accessories are also embroidered by male professionals. These include boots of soft calf, sheep or goatskin, and bags and pouches decorated with applied leather motifs attached with hemming or slipstitch and embroidered with cotton thread.

Although embroidery has always been the province of professional male embroiderers, some Hausa women have recently begun to work it, generally as decoration on pillowcases and other household linen. Hausa women embroider their items for their own use, employing the same local and imported cotton ground fabrics as the men.

Unlike the professional male embroiderers, Hausa women work pictorial stitcheries. Their designs are their own creations and they do not adhere to traditional motifs. Often they portray local heroes, stitching, for example, the highly stylized portrait of a football star on a cotton pillowcase. Hausa women also embroider *bêtes noires* on their household linen, decorating it with scorpions, open-mouthed and about to devour flies, or ferocious crocodiles.

between the centre and side sections, with the widest part of the inserts at the bottom of the tunic.

Hausa embroidery is generally worked by professional male embroiderers. It is either specially commissioned or is available through local markets. The embroiderer often works his own original combination of recognized designs, using a reed pen to draw his pattern directly on a ground of local or imported cotton.

One of the most characteristic Hausa embroidery stitches on men's trousers, tunics and caps is double chain stitch, known locally as kano chain stitch. Groups of eyelet stitching, known locally as termite nests, wasps' nests or honeycombs, are embroidered mainly on robes. Fly stitch, called small fishbone or locusts' eggs, is used for trousers and

Hausa Motif

The design for this simple and attractive motif is an adaptation of a small repeating pattern which forms the main decoration on a pair of Hausa embroidered leather shoes. The motif is quick and easy to embroider and may be used to decorate a wide variety of accessories from bags to espadrilles.

Preparing the Fabric
Transfer the motif to each of the pieces of fabric (see page 272).

Embroidery
Start by cutting several lengths of embroidery silk and splitting them so as to work with three threads at a time. Embroider the petal shapes of the flower motif first, setting the stitches of each petal across it at an angle of 90° to the centre. Work the stitches close together to give a firm, neat edge.

Stitch two circles of chain stitch round each flower shape.

Complete the motifs with an outer band of closely worked buttonhole stitch to give a neat finish.

Finishing
Cut out the motifs, carefully trimming the fabric away close to the buttonhole-stitch edging.

Spread adhesive thinly over the back of each motif and right up to the edges. Press the motifs firmly into position on the espadrilles.

Work the satin stitches across each petal as shown and fill the outer rim with buttonhole stitch.

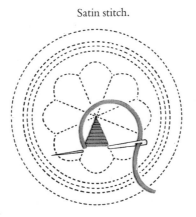

Satin stitch.

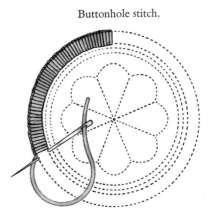

Buttonhole stitch.

Hausa Smock

You will need:
2 m (2¼ yd) white poplin or cotton fabric 90 cm (36 in) wide
coton à broder in two colours:
red 2 skeins
green 2 skeins

soft embroidery cotton in four colours:
red 3 skeins
green 4 skeins
blue 4 skeins
yellow 4 skeins
white sewing cotton

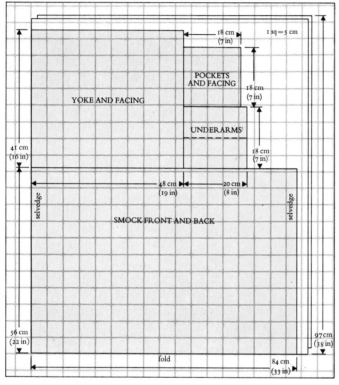

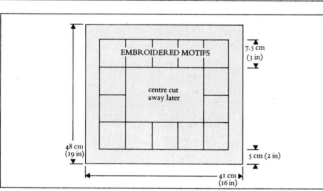

Size:
To fit a 81–91 cm (32–36 in) bust. Adjust underarm sections for other sizes.

Preparing the Fabric
Measure and cut out the four pattern pieces, cutting through two thicknesses to produce eight pieces of fabric. Transfer the design to one yoke and one pocket section (see page 272). Do not cut out the centre of the yokes at this stage.

Embroidery
Work in open chain stitch throughout. Begin by outlining the square motifs on the yoke with the two, thinner, coton à broder threads. Fill in the rest of the design with the four soft cotton threads.
Work the pocket in the same way.

Making the Smock
Damp stretch the embroidery (see page 272). Trim to within 1 cm (⅜ in) of the embroidery on both yoke and pocket.

Lay the second yoke section face down on the embroidery. Baste and machine stitch round the embroidery and cut away the centre section, leaving a 1 cm (⅜ in) margin. Clip into the corners right up to the stitching and turn the yoke facing to the wrong side. Turn in the edges and slipstitch the yoke and facing together over the shoulders.

Gather the front of the smock and set it into the yoke leaving enough fabric at the sides for gathering into the underarm sections. Set in the back of the yoke in the same way. Join the side seams.

Prepare the underarm sections by pressing a 1 cm (⅜ in) turning to the inside on all four edges. Press each section in half lengthwise, right sides out.

Ease the smock fullness into each of the underarm sections and sew them in place.

Lay the second pocket section face down on the embroidery. Machine stitch round the edge of the embroidery, leaving a small gap. Trim the seam, turn the pocket right side out and sew up the gap. Stitch the pocket to the smock.

Turn up and stitch the hem and press.

This light, summery smock is embroidered with some of the bright colours and the geometric patterns that are characteristic of Hausa designs. It is a simple garment to make and the embroidery is worked entirely in open chain stitch (see detail, left).

The Fulani Emir of Kano, Nigeria, wearing embroidered costume and riding in the shade of an embroidered ceremonial umbrella. The man in the foreground, right, is wearing a *gambari*, a short cotton tunic made with three widths of cloth with inset panels worked with machine embroidery.

Fulani

The Fulani, who are also known as the Fulbe, live in Cameroun, Guinea, Niger, Nigeria and Mali. Many Hausa traits are to be seen in Fulani design, particularly in Niger and Nigeria, which date back to the time when the Fulani ruled over part of Hausaland.

The Islamic faction of the Fulani are today principally found in the cities. Many of the pastoral Fulani have retained some of the pagan beliefs that were adhered to long before the advent of Islam. Most Fulani embroidery comes from the countryside, and the overall effect is similar to that of the neighbouring Hausa embroidery with motifs such as the intertwined knot and the crescent moon.

Fulani embroidery, like that of the Hausa, is worked by professional men embroiderers for men to wear. Today they use ground fabrics of local or imported cotton and usually work with commercial silk threads. Bright emerald green is a popular thread colour, and many items are worked in one colour on a bleached white cotton ground.

Fon

The Fon constitute approximately a third of the population of the republic of Benin (formerly Dahomey). Agriculture is the most important occupation of the Fon, and although they produce and export some cotton in the form of woven fabric, more cotton textiles are imported.

The men weave the cotton and design and execute appliqués on the fabric. They work sitting cross-legged on the floor, shaping their designs from cloth or paper templates. The motifs are stitched to a ground, usually of black cotton, with back stitch, chain stitch or running stitch, to create vivid and fascinating wall hangings.

Fon wall hangings often take the form of battle scenes, with appliqué figures hemmed to a plain black cotton ground. The Fon themselves are depicted with lighter-coloured skins than their Yoruba enemies.

A Fon chief's tunic decorated with ladder stitch, satin stitch and chain stitch.

Other Fon motifs are derived from the personal insignia of former kings. Among them are the boar of King Akaba, the ship of Agadja, the buffalo of Tegbessou, the shark and egg of Behanzin, the fish and trap of Houegbadja, the sparrow of Kpengla and the pineapple of Agonglo.

Akaba

Agadja

Tegbessou

Behanzin

Houegbadja

Kpengla

Agonglo

A lion, symbol of King Gelele (1858-1889), is frequently found on Fon appliqués.

Many of the motifs in Fon appliqués stem from their tribal history. At the beginning of the 17th century three brothers divided the Kingdom of Ardra among themselves. One of them called his territory Abomey, and this name was used until the French reunited the three territories as Dahomey in 1893. The Fon of Abomey were continually at war with the Yoruba to the east, often recorded in appliqué, in which the Fon are always shown with lighter skins than their enemies. The scale of the resulting trade in Yoruba slaves was cut down by the great Fon king Gezo (1818–58), who also greatly reduced the number of human sacrifices made at regular twice-yearly ceremonies and on the death of a king. These sacrifices are depicted many times on wall hangings in the form of caricatures of human beings slain with axes or shot with enormous guns. One of Gezo's personal insignia was a buffalo, a device shown on many stitcheries. Another of his special motifs was a spindle, signifying that people should look to the king for support.

Many of the devices found on Fon appliqués today were once royal insignia: a fish and a wicker fish trap (Houegbadja, 1645–85); a ferocious-looking boar (Akaba, 1685–1708); a ship (Agadja, 1708–40); another buffalo (Tegbessou, 1740–74); a sparrow (Kpengla, 1774–89); a pineapple (Agonglo, 1789–97); a lion (Gelele, 1858–89); a shark with an egg, representing the world, which the shark wants (Behanzin, 1889–92); and a foot and a pebble (Ago-li-Agbo, 1892–1900).

Although, like today, most appliqués were made into wall hangings, some use was made of applied decoration for royal costume and accessories. A king's outfit sometimes consisted of an *akansawu* (a sleeveless tunic) with *chokoto* (trousers) and *aza* (hat). Occasionally court officials were also allowed to wear the *akansawu*. All three items were decorated with Fon applied devices, often with pictorial themes similar to those found on wall hangings, and the same patterns were found on umbrellas worked for ceremonial occasions.

Fon appliqué today is worked by professional embroiderers catering for an increasingly large market in Europe and North America.

Fon Appliqué Hanging

You will need:
pale green or neutral cotton
    fabric for the background
    1.1 m x 75 cm (42 x 30 in)
felt in six colours:
    green 90 x 15 cm (36 x 6 in)
    red 25 x 10 cm (10 x 4 in)

brown 65 x 30 cm (26 x 12 in)
yellow 38 x 15 cm (15 x 6 in)
blue 45 x 25 cm (18 x 10 in)
black 5 x 3 cm (2 x 1 in)
sewing cottons to match
fabric adhesive

Preparing the Fabric

Draw out the design on squared paper and make an accurate tracing of it.

On the backcloth, mark the rectangular shape of the design in contrasting basting thread. Make sure that the top and bottom lines lie on the straight grain of the fabric.

Trace the crocodile and cut it out in brown felt.

Using a paper template cut out the 33 elliptical shapes for the back of the crocodile and also the stripes for the nose.

Embroidery

Fix each of the yellow pieces of felt on the crocodile with a tiny dab of adhesive. Sew in zigzag stitches, by hand or by machine, round all the edges. Thread the ends of the cotton through to the back and tie them off as you work.

Lay the crocodile in place on the backcloth, using the tracing to check its position. Hold it in place with pins or adhesive as you sew. Begin by working straight stitch all round the edges, then work round again in zigzag leaving the 'toes' and 'fingers' free.

Cut two eyes of blue felt and sew them in place with zigzag stitches. Cut two yellow eyelids and glue and sew them in place. Indicate the creases of the eyelids with lines of zigzag stitching in black and sew on tiny circles of black felt for nostrils.

Cut two strips of green felt for the short sides and sew them in place.

Cut two green rectangles for the other sides, making them 5 cm (2 in) wide and the length of the design. Lay them in position on the backcloth with the tracing over the top. Work the outline of the pattern in straight stitch, sewing through the tracing. Tear the paper away. Trim away the surplus felt and then zigzag all the way round.

Treat the rest of the design in the same way, cutting plain rectangles for the pattern areas. Sew them down with straight stitch, trim away the surplus fabric, and zigzag all the way round.

Finishing

Press the work on the wrong side using a medium-hot iron.

See page 272 for making up the appliqué into a wall hanging.

1 sq = 25 mm

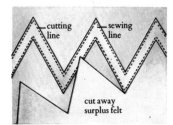

cutting line
sewing line
cut away surplus felt

Lay a felt rectangle on the fabric with the tracing on top. Sew through all layers, tear off the paper, and trim the edges.

Fon appliqués were often made as wall hangings. The bold traditional motifs lend themselves well to modern interiors.

Yoruba ceremonial headdresses are decorated with stitched beadwork and sometimes with long fringes. Beads are stitched to the ground fabric to form intricate geometric patterns and a wide variety of pictorial devices.

Yoruba

The Yoruba today live principally in south-western Nigeria, with smaller groups in Benin and northern Togo.

Although some are now Christian or Moslem, many Yoruba adhere to ancestor worship. Traditional ceremonies connected with their religion include the weaving of elaborate masks or conical headdresses with hanging beaded or leather fringing. The main crown may be decorated with stitched beadwork, with parallel lines of coloured beads forming a zigzag or other geometric motif, or portraying a grinning face. Ceremonial staves, leather bracelets and other accessories are also decorated with stitched beadwork.

North Africa

The rich and complex traditions of embroidery in the lands to the north of the Sahara Desert are centred on a relatively few peoples or areas.

One of the two countries specifically connected with embroidery is Morocco, especially in and near Casablanca, Rabat, Fès, Meknès and Tetuan. The other is Egypt, with its long history of Coptic embroidery going back at least as far as the 1st century A.D. There is also, to a lesser degree, a tradition of embroidery in both Algeria and Tunisia.

Cotton is grown extensively along the Nile and flax is farmed in limited quantities around its delta. Wool is produced in parts of northern Morocco, Algeria and Egypt. There is no indigenous silk production. Traditional dyes used throughout the area include madder and the shellac-producing *Coccus lacca* to obtain reds, indigo for blue and safflower for yellow. Many old textile fragments have retained their original colouring, for dyers, particularly in Egypt, have long known how to achieve colour fastness.

Nomadic groups throughout northern Africa often straddle political boundaries. Many tribes in the Sahara are Bedouin, mainly animal herders who traditionally despise agricultural work. The camel-herding Bedouin are among the élite of all such groups, generally more highly regarded than their sheep- and goat-herding cousins in the Levant and further east. Bedouin of northern Africa, Caucasian peoples scattered in tribes across Morocco, Algeria, Tunisia, Libya and Egypt, are sometimes referred to as Berber, and one group often associated with embroidery is the Tuareg.

Religion, and particularly the Sunni form of Islam, exerts a strong influence on embroidery design throughout northern Africa. Motifs, worked in imported cotton or silk thread generally on a ground of bleached or indigo cotton or linen, very rarely depict humans or animals, although peacocks and other birds are popular. Other embroidery motifs include candelabra, especially in Morocco, trees of life, flowers, eight-pointed stars and boxes, linked knots and other repeating geometric devices. The formerly large Jewish minorities, particularly in Morocco, have distinctive embroidery themes. Only the Copts, the main Christian group, have depicted human beings in their embroidery designs.

The influence of Moorish design, originating in the east of the area, travelled from east to west along northern Africa. The simple repeating step and box shapes adapted from 15th- and 16th-century Egyptian samplers were originally worked just before the upsurge of this black and white embroidery form in other parts of the world.

Blackwork is one technique that is historically connected with northern Africa. This is sometimes associated with the Moors (a term almost synonymous with Moroccans) who settled in southern Spain from A.D. 711 and introduced to the Iberian peninsula geometric motifs simply outlined in black on a white ground. Many of the Moorish, or Arabesque, designs were later adapted by Spanish, and subsequently by other western European, embroiderers in the form of 'Spanish work' or 'blackwork'.

Spanish and some Turkish influences are apparent in the embroideries of Morocco. Other foreign influences, such as the period of French rule in Morocco, Algeria and Tunisia, and the Turkish, French and British involvement in Egypt, have not had such outstanding effect on northern African embroidery.

Other techniques and stitch forms popular in northern Africa include buttonhole stitch, which is practised especially in Rabat; chain stitch, associated particularly with Tunisia and the Copts of Egypt; cross stitch in various forms; double and whipped running stitch; the satin stitch of the Tuareg; and the stem stitch of the Copts. Pattern darning is practised in Egypt, and laid and couched work is associated with Morocco and Algeria. Metal-thread work is executed in both Algeria and Egypt. Pulled-thread work is found in Algeria, and appliqué is worked among the Berbers and in Egypt. Samplers are recorded only from Morocco and Egypt.

Both men and women embroider, decorating costume items which usually consist of full-length cotton robes for men or, in some areas, for women. Household items such as show towels, tablecloths, pillow covers and wall hangings are also worked, and so are animal trappings. Embroidery is still extensively practised, usually for commercial purposes.

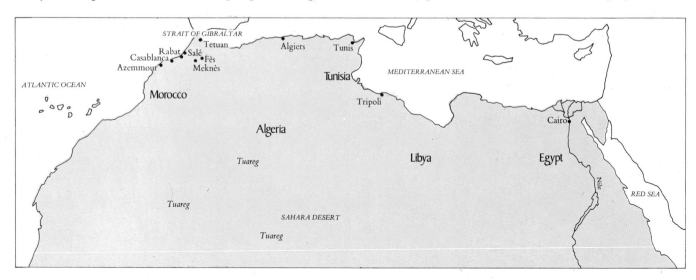

Morocco

The complex history of Morocco contributed various important international influences to the embroidery of the country. Many of the people, particularly those in the Rif Mountains area to the north of Fès, are either true Berbers or descended from them. Through intermarriage they have become closely linked with descendants of the Bedouin who entered the country in Islamic crusades in the 7th, 11th and 12th centuries.

Following the Moors' invasions of the Iberian peninsula, many Spaniards came to Morocco, especially to Salé, Rabat, Fès and Tetuan. They brought with them their embroidery heritage and designs. In return Moroccan embroidery, especially blackwork, has been extensively copied in Spain. The more recent emigration of much of the large Jewish minority to Israel since 1948 has meant that embroidered items and designs have been disseminated in that direction.

Traditional dress in Morocco reflects this diversity of style. Berber women wear white full-length sleeved dresses or white blouses with long baggy trousers and sleeveless wool or velvet boleros, often richly embroidered with laid and couched silk thread. The costume is highlighted with silver coins either attached as hanging spangles or worn as long necklaces or head circlets.

Another form of traditional costume includes a full-length dress, often of indigo cotton, worn over full-length cotton trousers. The fabric is finely woven, sometimes with as many as 20 threads to the centimetre (50 to the inch). The dress has a horizontal band of embroidery round each cuff, with repeating floral and tree of life designs in cross stitch, eyelet stitch, satin stitch and tent stitch.

A Moroccan Jewish woman's traditional dress includes an orange full-sleeved overblouse with black braid binding the seams and edges and the shoulders decorated with black silk cross stitch. Alternatively the blouse may have full-length sleeves decorated with braid and cross stitch embroidered round the cuffs.

Few items of a Moroccan man's traditional clothing are embroidered. Jewish men, however, most of them now in

Berber riders, with richly embroidered saddles, from southern Morocco. The central rider wears the traditional indigo robe decorated with narrow bands of cross stitch and satin stitch.

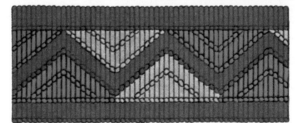

Chevron border design from Rabat, worked in close parallel buttonhole stitch.

The fine silk overdress of this Jewish 'baker' from the Atlas mountains is decorated with open satin-stitch stars in gold thread.

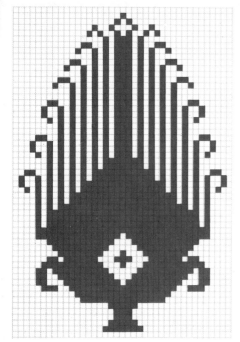

Exuberant tree of life motif from
Salé, worked in cross stitch.

More refined trees of life,
worked in blue silk satin stitch,
tent stitch and eyelets, decorate a
woman's linen trousers.

Israel, used to wear black woollen hooded
cloaks lined with orange wool and embroidered round the hem with repeating
geometric motifs in blue, red and white
cross stitch or pattern darning.

Moroccan girls embroider, usually
working with silk thread on ground
fabrics of imported cotton or linen. In
the 18th and 19th centuries embroidery
was practised on samplers, with several
lengths of linen sometimes joined along
the selvedges to form a ground about
105 x 75 cm (42 x 30 in). The ground was
neatly divided into rectangular segments,
aligned vertically or horizontally, each
one embroidered right to the edge of the
compartment so as not to waste any
ground space. Back stitch, buttonhole
stitch, cross stitch and long-legged cross
stitch, ladder stitch, plait stitch, double
and whipped running stitch, satin stitch
and stem stitch were worked in repeating
devices of candelabra, scrolls, eight-
pointed stars and cypress trees.

Moroccan embroidery is still extensively worked today, much of it for the
growing tourist trade. Traditional stitches
are worked in repeating patterns, with
monochrome or polychrome silks on
cotton ground fabrics. Many of the
embroiderers are out-workers, paid by
the amount of embroidery thread they
use. Consequently they will sometimes
use two-sided versions of stitches such as
satin stitch in order to use more thread.
This can result in the rather heavy
appearance of some of the modern items
such as kaftans and T-shaped robes which
are sold locally and also exported to
western Europe or North America.

The Atlantic coastal centres associated
with Moroccan embroidery are Azemmour, Casablanca, Rabat and Salé, all
international trading ports but with their
own distinctive embroideries.

Azemmour has a characteristic technique similar to Assisi work, the reserves
of the design embroidered in red silk
long-legged cross stitch. The motif itself,
either with or without a black silk outline in double running stitch, may be
either worked in black silk cross stitch
or left unworked. Designs used in
Azemmour 'Assisi work' include peacocks and other birds, some with single
or double crowns on their heads and with
branches in their beaks, and symmetrical
floral devices. All motifs are executed
individually or in Siamese-twin form,
with identical devices joined at their base.

Azemmour peacock motifs worked
in cross stitch on a background
of long-legged cross stitch.

Tall peacocks with elongated
tails are popular designs in
Azemmour embroidery.

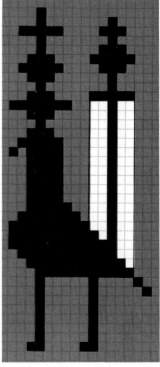

In Casablanca ordinary cross stitch is employed to work devices such as tall trees with feather-like branches, which are often executed in monochrome silk in repeating form. As with all Atlantic coast embroideries, Casablanca designs are used mainly to decorate show towels and other household cloths.

Rabat has a greater variety of stitches, including buttonhole stitch, ladder stitch, plait stitch and satin stitch. These are usually worked in adjacent blocks of parallel stitches, each block with its stitches set in a different direction from those of the neighbouring segment. Although Rabat infilling stitches are carefully worked to form complicated, and sometimes rather heavy, floral designs, trees of life and stylized mosques, there is no attempt at Chinese 'voiding' between blocks. Many devices appear in repeating form, sometimes bordered by a narrow band of triangles or other geometric shapes, usually worked in parallel vertical

buttonhole stitches with the 'knot' of each stitch at its base.

Rabat embroidery also shows a variety of colourings. Some work is executed in monochrome, deep purple or blue being popular colours, but much is worked in blocks of bright orange, beige, red, green and blue all used together on the same ground fabric. Gold, in the form of thread or braid, is also used.

Salé, the most northern of the embroidery centres of the Atlantic coast, has less variety in its embroidery. This is mostly worked in cross stitch either in one colour, often in salmon-coloured silk on a white cotton or linen ground, or in two colours. Devices often take the form of tall fountain-like variations of the tree of life.

Inland at Fès and nearby Meknès, cross

Beautiful wrap-over, full-length velvet skirt from Rabat. The decoration of gold braid applied in concentric curves is characteristic of the region.

stitch, plait stitch, double and whipped running stitch and stem stitch are popular, often worked in blackwork or other monochrome schemes on an unbleached cotton ground.

Fès embroidery designs are recognizable by their 'corner' motifs, composed of equal lengths of vertical and horizontal stitching forming an L-shaped right angle. Sometimes there are small repeating devices such as leaves outside the angle, which is worked with an exaggerated candelabra-shaped motif with diagonal alignment that is characteristic of much Fès embroidery. This 'corner candelabra' device was once worked on Fès samplers, particularly in the 19th century. Although the motif looks as if the two vertical and horizontal bands should be extended to fill a border, the device may be worked on a corner only on such items as fine linen handkerchiefs or tablecloths.

Bird and tree of life motifs, sometimes in the form of a bird perched on top of a tree, are also characteristic Fès designs that are still worked today. The trees, which are executed in cross stitch, sometimes have diagonal running stitching providing feathery 'leaves', continuing the diagonal theme that is found not only in Fès pictorial designs but also in purely geometric patterns where the diagonal is obvious in repeating parallel zigzags worked in whipped double running stitch.

Designed to fit a corner, a candelabra motif in blue cross stitch from Fès.

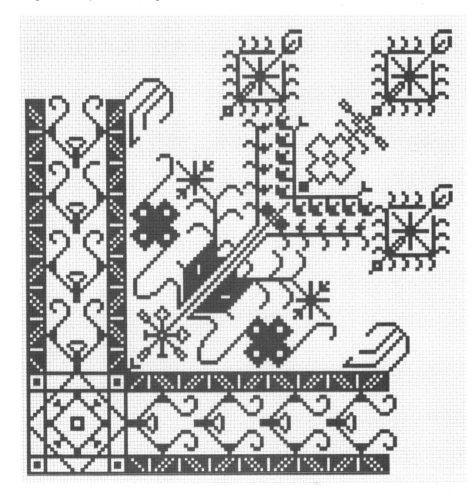

Panel from the front yoke of a velvet dress from Rabat, decorated with gold thread laid in zigzags over padding and couched with silk.

The edge of a silk hanging made in Fès in 1950. Cypress-shaped motifs, characteristic of the area, are worked in satin stitch and romanian stitch.

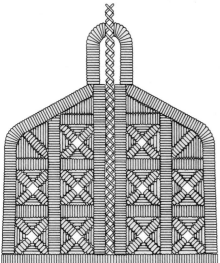

Sinuous and elegant Tetuan laid and couched work design, with white and golden cords laid on a green velvet ground fabric and couched with golden silk.

Rabat stylized mosque design worked in buttonhole stitch, ladder stitch and cross stitch.

Gaily coloured 19th-century Tetuan bolster cover, worked with silk thread on cotton.

In Tetuan, on the Mediterranean coast, Turkish influence is apparent in various embroidery designs such as repeating stylized floral devices. These are often outlined with black double running stitch and infilled with closely worked darning stitches in orange, yellow, red and brown and are used to embellish the ends of show towels and other household cloths.

Other Mediterranean influences can also be found in embroidery of the Tetuan area. Laid and couched work is, for instance, sometimes similar to Albanian work, with white or silver cord rather than gold thread. Tetuan laid and couched embroidery, often on a ground of dark green velvet, is generally used for embellishing women's boleros.

There is greater diversity in Tetuan embroidery than in that of other Moroccan centres and it is therefore sometimes difficult accurately to identify Tetuan work. Cross stitch is, for instance, sometimes worked in stepped blocks of different-coloured silks to achieve a geometric pattern that is hardly characteristic of Tetuan.

Moroccan Sundress

You will need:
2.5 m (2¾ yd) dress-weight
    calico 90 cm (36 in) wide
stranded embroidery cotton in
    seven colours, 1 skein each
    of:
dark green
blue
pale blue
orange
yellow
red
black
3.5 m (3⅞ yd) red ribbon
    12 mm (½ in) wide
1 reel sewing cotton to match
    calico
1 reel sewing cotton to match
    ribbon
2 large hooks and eyes
embroidery frame 10 cm (4 in)
    in diameter

Size: 81 cm (32 in) bust. Length
from centre back to hem 102 cm
(40 in). See page 272 for enlarging
patterns.

Couching
Use three strands of cotton for the
main thread and catch it down with
tiny stitches worked with a single
strand of the same colour.

Laid work
Using three strands of cotton,
fill in the shape with satin
stitches laid on the horizontal or
vertical weave of the fabric.
Leave gaps of one thread's width
between the stitches.
Work back, filling in the gaps with
more stitches. Using one strand of
cotton, catch the satin stitches
down with tiny stitches made at
right angles to the laid threads.

← centre front

Preparing the Fabric
Fold the fabric in half, selvedges together,
and cut out the pieces according to the
pattern layout. Cut an opening 14 cm
(5½ in) long from the top edge of the
centre back.

Oversew the edges of the band to
prevent fraying. Fold the band in half,
long edges together, and press. Open it
out and baste along the fold line.

Trace the border design and transfer it
to the bottom half of the band below the
line of basting (see page 272), starting at
the centre front. Treat it as a repeating
pattern and reverse it right to left at the
centre front.

Embroidery
Use a frame to prevent puckering and
work outwards from the centre front.

Fill the petal shapes with satin stitch
and the leaves and the remainder of the

circular motifs with laid work. Use the
colours as you wish, reserving the black
for outlining the motifs with couching.

Press the completed embroidery face
down on a folded towel using a damp
cloth and a medium-hot iron.

Making the Dress
Work a line of gathers along the seam
line on the top edge of both the front and
back sections of the dress.

Stitch the side seams and neaten the
edges. Press the seams open.

Baste the ribbon to the right side of
the embroidered band so that the bottom
edges are level. Stitch, taking 3 mm (⅛ in)
turnings. Turn the ribbon to the wrong
side of the band and hem the free edge
just below the stitched line.

Draw up the skirt gathers to fit the
band, concentrating the fullness in the
centre front. With the right sides facing

up, place the lower edge of the band on
to the gathering line, baste and topstitch
through the ribbon, using red thread.
Slipstitch the plain half of the band to the
stitched line on the inside of the dress.
Bind the top of the band to match the
bottom edge.

Fold the shoulder straps in half lengthwise with right sides facing. Stitch the
long edges together, taking 6 mm (¼ in)
turnings. Turn right side out and press.
Pin the straps to the inside of the band
and try on the dress to check their length
and position. Turn under the ends and
oversew the edges of the straps to the
band.

Bind the ends of the band and the
edges of the opening with a strip of calico.
Sew the hooks and eyes to the band.
Turn up the hem to the desired length.
Stitch a band of ribbon round the skirt
about 9 cm (3½ in) from the bottom edge.

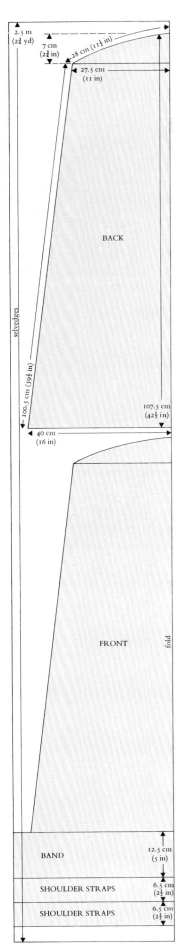

2.5 m
(2¾ yd)

7 cm
(2¾ in)

28 cm (11½ in)

27.5 cm
(11 in)

BACK

selvedges

100.5 cm (39½ in)

107.5 cm
(42½ in)

40 cm
(16 in)

FRONT

fold

BAND

12.5 cm
(5 in)

SHOULDER STRAPS

6.5 cm
(2½ in)

SHOULDER STRAPS

6.5 cm
(2½ in)

The embroidered design on this calico sundress was inspired by the bolster on page 195. The use of colour in the design is left to the embroiderer.

Algeria

Naturalistic Algerian floral motif, outlined in black stem stitch and infilled with silks and silver bullion worked in very large stem stitch.

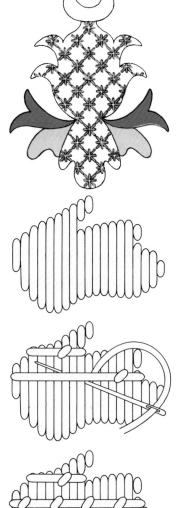

Techniques as varied as those of Morocco are found in northern Algeria, where embroidery is executed in monochrome or polychrome silks and silver thread on ground fabrics of linen or cotton. As well as ordinary cross stitch there are long-legged cross stitch, algerian cross stitch, a closely worked herringbone stitch, and a double algerian cross stitch which is most effective when worked with two different-coloured threads. Eyelet work is popular, sometimes with eight-pointed eyelet stars known as algerian eyelet stitch. All these stitches are commonly used in other countries, often on canvas.

Another form of pulled-thread work is known as algerian stitch, which is formed from horizontal satin stitches worked in close parallel formation. Stem stitch, another Algerian technique, is generally worked in black silk to outline devices which are sometimes infilled with stem stitch in brightly coloured silks or silver purl (bullion). Algerian couching may be employed as an alternative infilling. Vertical silk straight stitches are worked in close parallel lines and a long horizontal stitch is laid over the vertical stitches and couched before another horizontal thread is laid and couched at the required distance below it.

Algerian embroidery techniques, worked in zigzag and other geometric patterns or in floral devices, are used mainly to embellish towels, curtains and other household items, and also to decorate men's full-length cotton robes. These robes have sleeves inset or cut with the body of the garment, sometimes with borders of geometric cross stitch or other embroidery round the neck and vertical front opening. Increasingly today, however, continuous chain stitch worked on a Cornely machine is used to decorate robes for commercial purposes, mainly for export to western Europe and North America.

Motif for a linen towel (right) in stem stitch and eyelet stitch.

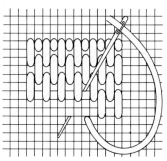

Brick stitch (above) closely resembles algerian stitch (below), where the thread is pulled tight for the best effect.

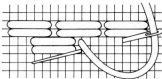

Double algerian cross stitch, also known as double herringbone stitch.

Cotton fabric intricately embroidered with silk cross stitch, satin stitch and stem stitch (left).

Algerian couching is also known as Iranian or Italian couching. Over a padding of parallel, vertically laid threads, single threads are laid horizontally and couched at regular intervals.

Tunisia

A great similarity can be found in the embroidery techniques and forms throughout the northern coastal areas of Algeria and Tunisia, although Tunisia, a much smaller country, has correspondingly fewer embroideries than Algeria.

Tunisian embroidery, generally in the form of repeating borders for the edges of men's full-length cotton robes, is executed primarily in hand chain stitch, cross stitch, straight stitch and laid and couched work, although now machine chain stitch is being increasingly employed. Robes are still produced, usually for sale, but the embroidery style is not instantly recognizable and it is accordingly difficult to distinguish Tunisian from other northern African garments offered for sale in boutiques and markets abroad.

Animal trappings such as saddle covers

Ceremonial velvet saddle cover, decorated in gold laid and couched work. Other such trappings and hangings are still worked today by professional male embroiderers.

Harness covers are often decorated with floral motifs such as this, worked in silk chain stitch and straight stitch on a heavy, usually red, cotton ground.

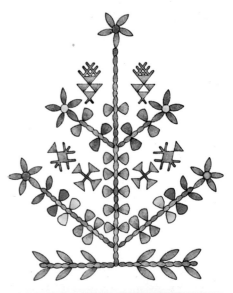

are also embroidered. They are often fashioned from red cotton fabric worked with brightly coloured yellow, orange, blue, red and green silk thread in needle chain stitch and straight stitch. Motifs, usually symmetrical, are often floral, with five-petalled flowers on long stalks branching diagonally from a main centre stem.

Tuareg

A predominantly fair-skinned Berber people, the Tuareg live in the south-central mountains of the Sahara desert, principally in southern Algeria. They are among the most settled of all desert Berbers, with home industries which include spinning, done with a hand-held spindle, and weaving. Since the mainstays of the desert people are sheep, goats and camels, cotton thread and material for costume embroidery have today to be imported, sometimes from Mali or Egypt.

Tuareg women do not usually wear embroidered clothing; the men, on the other hand, still wear decorated traditional dress. Their habit of veiling the face, particularly when travelling in the desert, has led to their being known as 'the people of the veil'. They use either a long indigo cotton scarf or a simple tubular head mask with one horizontal front slit to allow the wearer some air and a minimal view. Both are worn under flat cotton caps with circular, vertical brims, and are sometimes embroidered. More frequently the full-length indigo cotton robe of a man is embroidered, usually with designs in self-coloured thread. Needle chain stitch and eyelet stitch are worked in geometric patterns such as repeating diamonds or trellises bordering eyelet stars.

The Tuareg also use animal hide for embroidery, using the skins as ground fabrics for items such as saddlebags. These are decorated with applied leather strips sometimes laid in zigzag formation and couched with long running stitches. They are embroidered with cotton thread, mainly in romanian stitch, satin stitch and straight stitch.

Tuareg man wearing an indigo cotton robe decorated with self-coloured chain stitch and satin-stitch embroidery.

Egypt

The heritage of textiles in Egypt can be traced back to the 3rd millennium B.C. by which time it is thought that decorative needlework was known and certainly cotton, flax and sheep were being farmed. Linen thread was generally left its natural colour or bleached, but from early times wool was dyed with a variety of natural dyestuffs such as madder, safflower and indigo and, later, with lac insects. Yellow was obtained from safflower and blue from indigo. The earliest evidence of mordants, metallic salts whose affinity for both fibre and dyestuff improves the fastness of the dyes, has been found on textiles in tombs dating from before 1500 B.C.

Surviving embroidery in Egypt dates from as early as the 1st century A.D., the time of the first Egyptian Christians. These people were known as *qibt* (Arabic for Egyptians), later westernized to become 'Copt'.

Coptic embroidery, associated generally with the 3rd to 7th centuries, was used mainly for costume purposes. Linen or woollen material, usually left in its natural colouring, was woven on wide looms that produced weft measurements of about 2.5 m (99 in). A length of fabric was folded in half along the warp to make a man's sleeved robe, with the selvedge at the main hem.

Sometimes, particularly in early examples, coloured threads were incorporated into the weaving of the cloth to decorate the finished robe. In other examples, especially from the 5th century on, linen strips, squares or roundels, usually about 15 cm (6 in) in diameter and already embroidered with silk, wool or linen thread, were hemmed to the ground fabric of the finished garment. Appliqué was arranged in a variety of designs, sometimes with vertical bands to either side of the neck opening and with roundels on the shoulders.

Embroidery was executed principally in chain stitch, cross stitch, whipped running stitch, satin stitch, stem stitch and split stitch. Designs could be rudimentary, perhaps with the basic outlines of scrolls worked in natural linen thread stem stitch on a dark indigo linen ground fabric. Sometimes the reserves were worked in parallel horizontal lines of stem stitch. At other times designs could

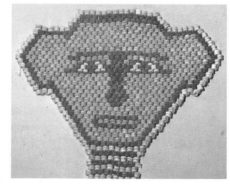

The splendid remains of a 5th-century Coptic portrait, worked in wool chain stitch on a wool ground fabric. The piece may have been used as a cushion cover or as a cover for the face in imitation of the contemporary vogue for painted plaster masks.

Face made up of stitched beadwork, thought to have been made between 1st century B.C. and 1st century A.D.

be complex, with every part of the ground fabric, including the reserves, completely covered with chain stitch.

Since the church in Egypt did not forbid the portrayal of human beings in art, Coptic embroidery sometimes illustrated stories from the Bible or classical myths. Hercules, personification of physical strength, was shown strangling the lion that terrorized the citizens of the Greek valley of Nemea and holding the animal's neck in an arm lock. Animal, flower and fruit themes were also popular, often

humorously portrayed with, for example, a hare chasing a ram.

Although most surviving Coptic embroidery, now fragments, decorated men's robes, it is thought that some was used on cushions and wall hangings.

Few Coptic embroideries were worked after the middle of the 9th century when members of the church, suffering Islamic repression following revolts, were required to wear special yellow robes. There are still about 90,000 Copts in Egypt today, but embroidery production

Running animals from a Coptic embroidery design worked on a ground of indigo cotton. The motifs would be outlined in natural-coloured linen stem stitch and the reserves filled with parallel horizontal rows of the same stitch.

Coptic men's robes were basically elongated linen T-shirts, decorated with bands, circles and squares of applied embroidery.

Modern Egyptian wall hanging of local cotton, decorated with hemmed appliqué and stem stitch.

is now no longer specifically connected with them.

Other embroidery in Egypt is of more indeterminate, though probably less ancient, lineage. From the 15th century, embroidery was sometimes practised in sampler form, with double running stitch, split stitch and pattern darning worked in silks on a linen ground fabric with geometric box designs typical of contemporary Islamic art. The main religion of Egypt today continues to be the Sunni form of Islam and embroidery therefore does not feature human themes.

Appliqué, usually produced for sale, is worked by men who collect old brightly coloured clothes, mostly of local cotton, and cut them into such motifs as palm trees and pyramids. These are hemmed

onto a ground fabric of new, sometimes local, cotton material, which is usually bleached. Appliqué designs, with motifs either aligned in imitation of wall paintings found in old Egyptian tombs, or worked in isolated spot form, are used to decorate colourful wall hangings, generally about 50 x 100 cm (20 x 40 in), and similar household items.

Net embroidery, also popular in Egypt today, is usually worked by women. On a ground of commercially produced net, flat strips of silver, ribbon or silk thread are used to work cross stitch, satin stitch and pattern darning to achieve repeating designs such as tall trees and pyramids. Net embroidery is generally used for scarf decoration and the finished item is often reversible.

Egyptian Kaftan

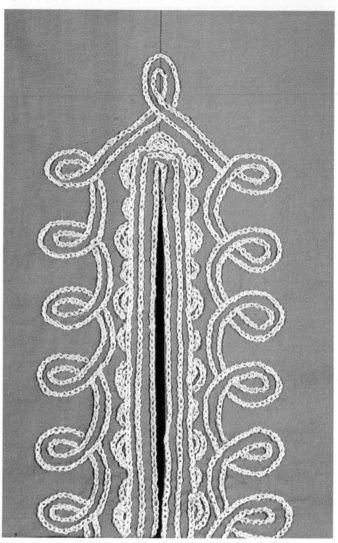

You will need:
2.1 m (2⅜ yd) blue cotton
    fabric 90 cm (36 in) wide
silky-textured crochet or
embroidery thread in two
    colours:
white 2 balls
cream 1 ball
1 reel blue sewing cotton
1 small white button

Size: 81 cm (32 in) bust. See page
272 for enlarging patterns.

Details of the embroidery round
side slits (right) and sleeves
(below). The motifs can be drawn
to scale from the graph pattern
for the neck facing or you could
draw the pattern with the aid of
circle and oval templates (available
in all sizes from art shops).
Draw the outlines of the embroidery on your pattern and mark the
positions of the ovals. Draw the
ovals and connect them with semi-
circles. Erase those sections crossed
by other lines. Then draw the
semi-circles along the edge.

Pattern layout.

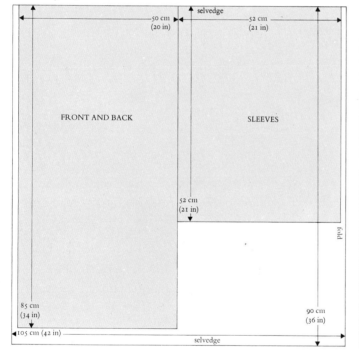

Both the design and colours of this loose-fitting blouse are strongly reminiscent of the embroidered robes worn throughout north-west Africa.

Preparing the Fabric

Cut out the fabric as shown. Mark the centre front and back and the centres of the sleeves with lines of basting stitches.

Make a scaled-up drawing of the combined neck facing and embroidery diagram (see page 272), so that the front motif measures 38 cm (15 in). Matching the centre lines on the drawing to the basted lines on the fabric, cut out the neck edge, but not the opening.

Make pattern pieces for the facings and cut them out of the surplus fabric, taking care to place both centre front and centre back on a fold. Mark the same looped design along a straight line 5 cm (2 in) from the bottom edge.

Embroidery

Work in single lines of chain stitch throughout, using a large-eyed needle.

Do not pull the thread tight and fasten the ends off well, sewing back through two or three stitches on the reverse. Use the photographs as a guide to colours.

Work the embroidery round the sleeves using the same colour key.

Making the Kaftan

Using a 1.5 cm (⅝ in) seam, join the front and back at the shoulders. Neaten the edges and press the seams open.

Join the shoulder seams of the facings, trim and press open. Machine a narrow hem round the outer edge of the facings. Stitch the facings to the neck edge, matching seams and centres, and stitching to a V from the neck to the base of the line for the front opening. Slash the opening, trim the turnings and press the facings to the inside.

Matching the centre of the sleeve to the shoulder seam, machine each sleeve in place taking a 4 cm (1½ in) seam. Join the side and sleeve seams as one, again taking a 4 cm (1½ in) seam, and leaving the side seams open 24 cm (9½ in) at the bottom for the slits. Trim and neaten the seams leaving the full seam allowance along the slits to act as facings.

Using the same scaled-up drawing as for the neck opening, mark the embroidery design round the sides and top of each slit leaving 5 cm (2 in) at the bottom for the hem. Work in chain stitch, using the same colour key as before.

Turn a narrow hem on the slit facings and press them to the inside. Turn up a 5 cm (2 in) hem round the sleeves and round the bottom of the blouse.

Sew the button to the top left-hand side of the neck slit and work a loop to match it on the right-hand side.

Western Asia

The prayer mat is a speciality of western Asian embroidery. The essential feature of the arch represents the mosque *mihrab* and faces Mecca at prayer times.

For the most part, embroidered costume is worn only by women and children (below).

The history of embroidery in western Asia can be traced from surving examples from 6th-century Persia (Iran) and 10th-century Yemen and Iraq. Apart from in the Arabian Peninsula, embroidery is still extensively practised throughout the entire area.

In western Asia, the lands between the Red Sea and the Khyber Pass, excluding those countries on the Mediterranean, the great majority of the people are Moslems who adhere to the Sunni form of Islam, derived from precedents laid down by early followers of the prophet Mohammed (c. 570-632 A.D.). One of their beliefs has led to the discouragement of animal portrayals in art and consequently few such themes are used in embroidery. The other main Moslem group, which predominates in southern Iraq and Iran, is that of the Shi'a, a faction which broke away from the main branch of the religion. The Shi'a are not dogmatic about artistic motifs and animal and even human forms are therefore found in embroideries of the Marsh Arabs and throughout Iran. Apart from Islam, Judaism has had a significant effect on embroidery in Yemen, and Zoroastrian symbols are found in parts of Iran.

Secular influences on the embroidery of western Asia have resulted from immigration, as in the case of Indians in Yemen and Oman, from trade, as evidenced by delicate floral designs reminiscent of Chinese embroideries perhaps brought to Iran along the silk route, and from past Turkish rule of most of the Arabian Peninsula and Iraq. Popular motifs are cone shapes and trees of life. Peacocks and other birds, and animal and floral themes are sometimes found in embroideries, and geometric repeating patterns are universal.

Embroidered Arabic lettering, usually words from the Koran, the holy Moslem book, is peculiar to western Asia. It is worked either in Kufic, a bold and angular script first developed in Mesopotamia, now Iraq, towards the end of the 7th century, or in the cursive Naskhi style.

The availability of embroidery materials varies greatly within the region. Little flax is now grown, but cotton is cultivated in

Yemen, Iraq, Iran and Afghanistan. Sheep are farmed in Yemen and in Iraq, Iran and Afghanistan. Silk, once only imported from China, is now produced in central Iraq and north-western Iran.

Much of the embroidery of western Asia is worked with silk or cotton thread on a cotton, woven wool or felt ground, although leather is occasionally used as a ground fabric in Yemen, Iran and Afghanistan. Cotton fabric is often left natural or bleached, or dyed with natural dyes such as indigo. Polychrome thread colouring is preferred, although whitework is found in Isfahan and Afghanistan.

One of the stitches found throughout western Asia is tamboured chain stitch, although needle chain stitch and stitching worked on a Cornely sewing machine are also popular. Other universal techniques include cross stitch, satin stitch, appliqué, pulled work, and laid and couched work.

Embroidery is worked by either men or women depending on the region. They decorate floor rugs and wall hangings, Koran covers, cushion covers and costume items.

Western Asia has produced many fine embroidered rugs. Some have a religious purpose, with decoration featuring an arch to one end of a rectangular ground, reminiscent of the *mihrab*, a niche in a mosque indicating the direction of Mecca. During the five daily periods of prayer, a Moslem believer puts down a rug with its *mihrab* pointing towards Mecca. Other forms of embroidered religious rugs, such as those in Hazarajat, show entire mosques and shrines.

Arabian Peninsula

The Kingdom of Saudi Arabia comprises the greater part of the Arabian Peninsula. The main centres of embroidery in the peninsula are Mecca, Yemen, Oman and Kuwait. Except in Yemen, local embroidery materials are practically non-existent, and cotton fabric and cotton and silk threads are imported.

Foreign influences in embroidery are many and varied. In Yemen, for instance, gold-thread embroidery and laid and couched work are in some cases similar to North African embroidery, a connection strengthened partly by early Arab colonization and also by the fact that both areas were once part of the Turkish empire. Indian influence is also apparent in some Yemeni embroideries and in those of Oman. In Kuwait there is a history of trade in both materials and ideas with the whole Gulf area.

In most of the peninsula it is still imperative for women to wear the veil, especially in public. Even in cities as large and modern as Riyadh, for instance, Saudi women cover themselves with heavy black full-length veils that completely obscure their faces, and it is impossible to see what they are wearing underneath.

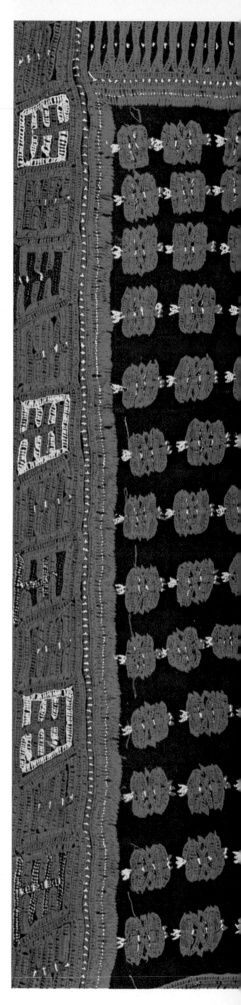

Nearly everywhere on the peninsula women must still wear the veil, especially in public. Underneath the 'shrouds' they wear out of doors many women have beautifully embroidered dresses, sometimes decorated with herringbone stitch, ladder stitch and with appliqué work.

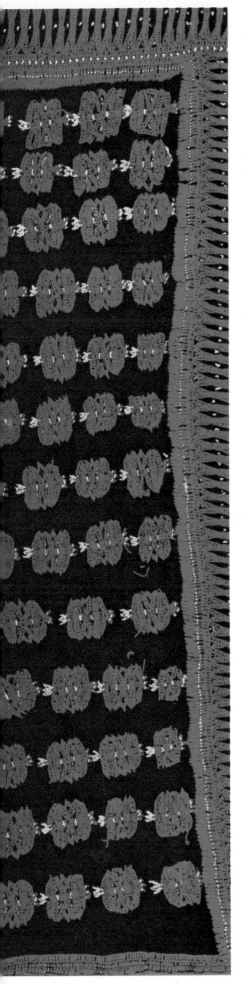

Detail of the embroidered *kiswa* (below), a rug covering the central *ka'ba* at Mecca, decorated with gold thread laid over cardboard templates and couched with small hemming stitches on a ground of black velvet.

Mecca

Mecca, the birthplace of Mohammed, is the religious centre to which Moslems aspire to make a pilgrimage, the *hajj*, at least once in their lives. At the time of this annual pilgrimage, hundreds of thousands of believers from all over the world travel to Jiddah and thence by an enormous fleet of special buses up the twisting mountain road to Mecca, a city forbidden to non-Moslems.

The focal point of much of the ceremony is a cube-shaped shrine called the *ka'ba*. The whole shrine is covered with a single embroidered rug known as the *kiswa*, made of black velvet and decorated with gold thread laid in zigzag formation over cardboard templates and couched with silk at each bend of the zigzag. The decoration, in Naskhi script, consists of verses from the Koran, two copies of which reside within the *ka'ba*.

A new *kiswa* is embroidered every year, for at the end of the *hajj* the local administrator, the Governor of the City of Mecca, cuts the embroidery into small pieces, giving them as mementoes to dignitaries among the pilgrims.

Yemen

The Yemen Arab Republic occupies an unusually fertile part of the Arabian Peninsula. In the coastal region, cotton is now grown, thanks partly to aid from the French and Lebanese, who built a cotton-spinning and weaving mill in 1966, and the Chinese, who built a big cotton factory in the same year. Sheep are also reared in the Yemen, particularly in the higher inland areas. Both sheepskins and cotton are now exported.

Yemeni menfolk are widely scattered. For centuries they have worked elsewhere in the Islamic world, supporting their families at home, and this tradition continues today.

There was a large Jewish complement in Yemen, almost all of whom have now emigrated to Israel, and it is sometimes hard to distinguish between Moslem and Jewish embroidery in the area. Both forms feature chain stitch, herringbone stitch, romanian stitch and straight stitch, often executed in zigzags or triangles.

Yemeni women work embroidered costume for their own use. One form is an indigo cotton calf-length sleeveless dress held in at the waist with a belt. The armholes, front vertical neck slit, hem and a necklace-shaped band are decorated with applied ric-rac braid and brightly coloured cotton thread worked in chain stitch and straight stitch in triangles and other geometric shapes. Another form of women's costume consists of a sleeved indigo cotton dress with vertical seams to either side of the centre of the front. The seams are subsequently decorated with silk thread worked in chain stitch, romanian stitch and straight stitch in tall, open 'ladder' repeating motifs. These motifs are flanked by diagonal branches of chain stitch, by cowrie shells which are held in place by two black straight stitches, and by small pieces of red felt hemmed to the ground fabric.

Underneath their dresses, some women wear full-length loose cotton trousers with tapered legs attached to narrow tight-fitting cuffs, usually of a more lasting material than the main part of the trousers. Cuffs can therefore be attached to another pair of trousers when the 'uppers' wear out. Some cuffs have intricate silk embroidery worked in parallel horizontal lines of chain stitch, ladder stitch and straight stitch, or in triangles and intertwined scrolls. Alternatively, metal thread, usually silver, is either laid on the ground fabric of the cuffs and couched with silk retaining stitches, or worked in long bullion knots in close parallel formation to form petals or flowers, sometimes with a spangle in the centre.

Metal thread is also used to decorate women's headdresses. One type is like a shoulder-length loose hood of black cotton. This is embellished with applied silver braid, silver beads and silver plaques which are attached with long straight stitches; it is also embroidered with neat parallel rows of small straight stitches worked in zigzags.

Yemeni men often wear a length of gingham-type cotton fabric loosely caught at the waist to form a knee-length kilt. With it they wear a cotton shirt, turban and heavy cotton hip belt about 10 cm (4 in) wide. The main ground of the belt is decorated with applied cotton bands and cotton thread worked in zigzags of straight stitches. The whole item is then edged with leather

Hand-embroidered or machine-stitched shawls sometimes augment the Yemeni man's wardrobe.

Underneath their dresses Yemeni women wear trousers with tight-fitting embroidered cuffs (below) sometimes decorated with metal spangles.

Yemeni border design in chain, herringbone and straight stitches on a cotton ground.

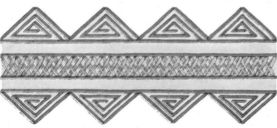

Leather belt (below) decorated with applied cotton pieces, running and straight stitches.

bands previously decorated with a leather strip threaded in and out and attached with running stitches.

The history of Yemeni embroidery is not known, although one of the earliest surviving examples is an embroidered Kufic inscription dating from the 10th or 11th century. The lettering, 5.8 cm (2¼ in) high, is worked in double running stitch in undyed cotton thread on a woven ground.

Yemeni embroidery from more recent years generally takes the form of costume decoration and little is produced today.

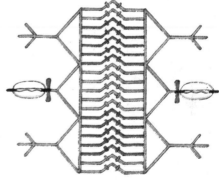

Basic Yemeni dress decorated with ric-rac braid, chain stitch and straight stitch.

Cowrie shells are used in a repeating motif to decorate vertical dress seams.

Metal thread is laid in a single line and couched with small stitches or worked in long bullion knots to floral designs.

Like the rest of the Islamic world, Oman produces sumptuous embroideries for religious and other festivals. This opulent piece (below left), worked in 1905, is embroidered with gold thread laid over cardboard templates.

Most Omani embroidery is worked to decorate women's costume. This girl's dress and the tight cuffs of her under-trousers are decorated with applied braid, chain stitch and with some pattern darning.

Oman

The independent Sultanate of Oman, in the south-east of the Arabian Peninsula, was for a long time a trading centre with few natural resources, although enough cotton was once grown for a small amount to be exported. Now, however, cotton material and thread, some of it subsequently woven on hand looms, has to be imported. Indigo, a plant which grows profusely in central Oman, was once used for dyeing purposes, but now chemical dyes are used.

Embroidery, worked by women, is usually employed as costume decoration. Particularly in Dhufar, in south-western Oman, women wear tent-shaped full-length cotton dresses with square necks, wide winged sleeves and a hem which is slightly raised in front. Dark plum and magenta are popular ground colours. The embroidery, worked on the front yoke, down the front vertical seam and round the main hem, is executed in brightly coloured silks, mostly in very

fine satin-stitch floral designs. Under the dresses, some Dhufar women wear full-length trousers with cuffs embroidered to match the dresses. The outfit is completed by a conical, flat-topped hat like the Turkish fez, decorated with coins and jewellery sewn on as spangles.

The population of Oman is of cosmopolitan origin, and today there are large numbers of Baluchi living in the area. As in other parts of western Asia, and further east in the Indian sub-continent, Baluchi women wear knee- or full-length robes with distinctive central stomach pockets. Horizontal and diagonal satin stitches are worked in orange, rust, dark green, black and white cotton or silk thread in repeating geometric motifs.

Omani men, irrespective of their ancestry, seldom wear embroidered costumes. Many wear a full-sleeved white cotton robe over a white cotton sarong or trousers. They do, however, wear a variety of embroidered headdresses, including the *dumma*, a skull cap made of

stiff white cotton fabric and elaborately decorated with white cotton eyelet stitching in an intricate and unique repeating pattern, possibly of cone shapes. Often in the past such caps were embroidered by the wife of the wearer. Today, however, many skull caps are commercially embroidered, usually by Indian or Pakistani immigrant male embroiderers, and patterns are repeated on more than one cap.

Another form of headcovering is the Kashmir shawl, decorated by immigrant embroiderers with monochrome or polychrome silks on a ground fabric of cotton or imported wool. Motifs are often repeating cones executed in minute stem stitches, and either worn as a turban or simply draped across the shoulders.

The glittering face mask is yet
another layer of protection
between Omani women and the
eyes of the world. Usually hidden
by a headscarf, the mask is
embroidered with buttonhole,
chain and cross stitches and with
spangles.

Kuwait

Kuwait, on the far north-east of the
Arabian Peninsula, has had less foreign
influence on its embroidery than some
other areas. This independent State is
mostly desert, and materials for embroidery have consequently to be imported.

Kuwaiti women once embroidered
costumes for their own use. They
traditionally wear full-length cotton
dresses, sometimes deep red, and loose
black shoulder-length headscarves joined
with front vertical seams, worn under
full-length black veils. Dresses and

scarves may be elaborately embroidered
with golden silk chain stitch worked in
repeating geometric patterns. Spangles
and tiny pieces of silvery metal, attached
as in mirror work, are occasionally added.

Kuwait is now one of the most
prosperous of the Arabian States and
many women prefer to buy dresses which
have been professionally embroidered,
sometimes with chain stitching worked
on a Cornely machine. As with modern
dresses of the rest of the Arab world, the
decoration frequently incorporates lurex
thread.

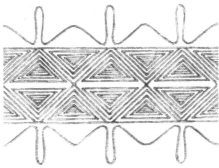

Repeating gold chain-stitch
pattern, traditionally part of the
decoration on a Kuwaiti dress.

Iraq

Older examples of Marsh Arab chain stitching, now eagerly sought by collectors, usually have more subdued colouring and more intricate design than modern pieces. Detail from a rug bought in a market in Baghdad.

The bright embroidery of the Marsh Arabs is worked in close-packed chain stitch on a dark loose-weave ground. Favourite themes are flowers and birds, often flitting through a landscape of geometric shapes (detail, bottom).

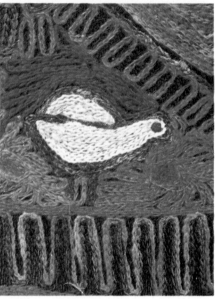

Most of the people of Iraq are Arabs, of whom the greater number, including the Marsh Arabs in the south-east of the country, are Shi'a rather than Sunni Moslem. There are also, as a result of successive migrations from central Asia, minority groups such as the Turkmen, especially in the north-east of the country, who have embroidery styles in common with those of their cousins now in Soviet Turkmenistan. The Kurds, who inhabit the mountainous regions of northern Iraq, as well as eastern Turkey, northern Syria, north-western Iran and parts of Soviet Armenia, are a warrior group not practising much embroidery. Kurdish women, often more emancipated than other rural peoples in western Asia, do, however, embellish their traditional full-length silk dresses with orange silk herringbone stitch or interlacing round the front vertical neck opening and covering some of the seams.

As in other areas of the Islamic world, the history of embroidery in Iraq generally dates back at least as far as the 10th century. Surviving fragments, with blue silk stitching worked in Kufic lettering on natural linen ground fabrics, have texts such as 'favours and glory to the Servant of Allah', eulogizing a contemporary caliph or ruler.

Sheep are farmed today in higher altitudes of the north and in the drier part south-west of the Euphrates, and wool is exported, especially to Europe. Flax is no longer generally produced. In the marshy lands round the confluence of the Tigris and Euphrates Rivers, some cotton is grown, although production is hampered by soil salinity.

Marsh Arabs

The Marsh Arabs, inhabitants of the marshy lands in the south of Iraq, have a distinctive form of embroidery, sometimes erroneously known as 'Kurdish work'. Continuous chain stitching of brightly coloured wools covers almost completely a rectangular ground fabric of loosely woven dark red wool.

The required length of ground is generally divided with lines of chain stitch into various segments. Borders about 15 cm (6 in) wide, edged with the selvedge of the ground fabric, are subsequently infilled with close parallel lines of chain stitch usually worked in diagonal formation. The rest of the ground, similarly divided by continuous chain stitching into triangular and other segments, is also infilled, sometimes with chain-stitch motifs of stylized camels, birds and men on horseback.

Marsh Arab embroidery, worked by men, is usually made into rugs or wall hangings and sold. Older examples, now eagerly sought by collectors, are sometimes rather subdued in colouring. Pieces worked recently tend to be almost garish, sometimes with pink and bright yellow thread predominating.

Marsh Arab Rug

A bold geometric pattern characteristic of the Marsh Arabs adapts well to an unusual chain-stitch rug to brighten the hall.

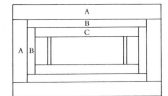

Border outlines.

You will need:
0.6 m (⅝ yd) dark-coloured hessian (burlap) 90 cm (36 in) wide
soft embroidery cotton in six colours:
off-white 2 skeins
red 16 skeins
green 14 skeins
orange 8 skeins
pink 10 skeins
blue 10 skeins
1 reel sewing cotton to match hessian
crewel needle

Preparing the Fabric

Machine round the edges of the hessian (burlap) using closely worked zigzag stitch to stop them fraying.

Use tailor's chalk or basting stitches to mark a rectangle 76 x 50 cm (30 x 20 in) in the centre of the hessian.

Make a scaled-up drawing of the design (see page 272), giving it the same dimensions. Transfer to the hessian the straight lines marking the outlines of the borders. There is no need to transfer every detail of the design, for embroidery without guidelines will add a 'peasant' quality to the mat.

Embroidery

Work in chain stitch throughout and fasten off the ends by sewing them neatly into the back of the last three or four stitches.

Begin by working all the marked border outlines in red. Fill in border A with slanting stripes filled with three rows of chain stitch using the colours in roughly this sequence: red, green, pink, blue, off-white, red, green, orange. Work border B in single lines of pink, green and orange and border C in single lines of red and green.

Fill in the centre panel with single lines and solid blocks of closely worked chain stitch using the chart as a colour guide.

Finishing

Leaving a small border round the embroidery, fold back the edges of the hessian (burlap) and hem them to the back of the mat.

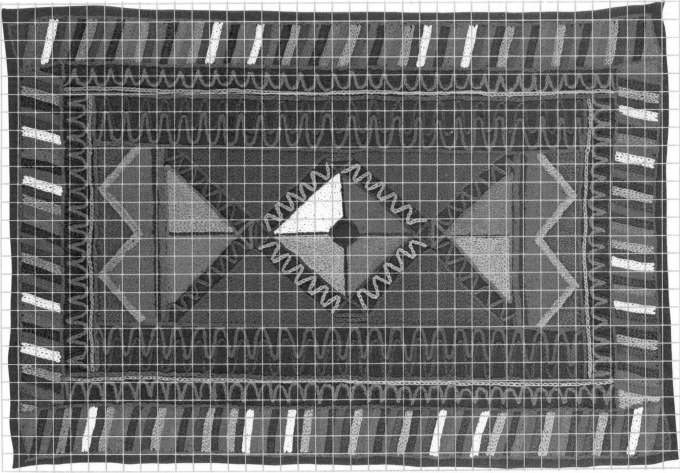

1 sq = 2 cm

Iran

Many Iranian dresses are decorated with applied panels of embroidery which can be removed and hemmed to another ground fabric when the original wears out.

Chequered or magic chain stitch.

Detail from 6th- or 7th-century embroidery, demonstrating the lasting popularity of chain stitch.

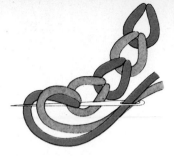

The documented history of Iranian embroidery dates from the time of the Sasanian Empire, between the 3rd and 7th centuries, and early work is typified by devices of birds, animals, men and trees worked in chain stitch in wool thread on a linen ground. In the late 13th century, Marco Polo mentioned that women in Kerman were producing excellent gold embroidery. Following Mongol invasions under Timur (Tamerlane) in 1393, when fresh impetus had been given to the re-opening of the silk route with China, silks and Chinese embroidery styles became popular in Iran. A couple of centuries later, under the Safavid dynasty, embroidery featured many 'garden scenes' with complex floral patterns. Ardabil, which has given its name to one of the most famous knotted carpets of all time, was one of the most important embroidery centres, although by the 17th century embroidery was being practised all over the country.

Iran has never been short of embroidery materials. Cotton is grown in many areas. Sheep are grazed at higher altitudes, especially on the slopes of the Zagros Mountains in the west of the country, and by various nomadic groups who do not usually embroider. Silk is produced in limited quantities in the north-west of Iran, around Rasht.

Buttonhole and cross stitches on a woman's trouser leg (below).

A narrow padded couched border.

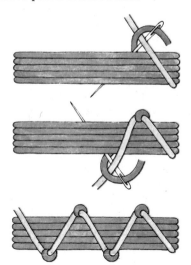

The abundance of embroidery stitches is striking. Universal forms include back stitch, whipped running stitch, satin stitch, split stitch, worked as outline or filling, stem stitch, tent stitch and pattern darning, generally used for in-filling motifs and worked in brick or diagonal formation. Other popular techniques include couching, pulled-thread work and tamboured chain stitch, sometimes combined with specific local techniques such as Azerbaijan appliqué or Isfahan whitework. Needle chain stitch is occasionally preferred, at times worked with two different-coloured threads, alternating the top thread to produce 'magic', or chequered, chain stitch.

Couching is used extensively for

Laid threads couched to produce zigzag or diamond patterns.

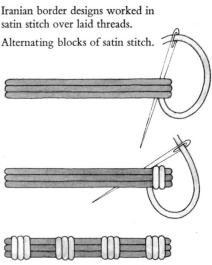

Delightful Persian embroidery of the 17th or 18th century, worked in silk on a silk fabric ground with split stitch and a variety of couched stitches.

Iranian border designs worked in satin stitch over laid threads.

Alternating blocks of satin stitch.

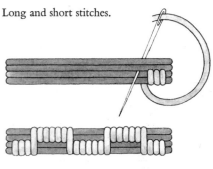

Long and short stitches.

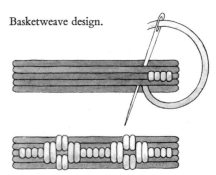

Basketweave design.

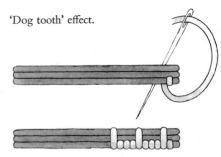

'Dog tooth' effect.

infilling motifs, taking the form of algerian couching or a denser version known as persian couched filling. Alternatively, chevron-couched filling stitch, diamond-couched filling stitch or one of the many Turkish goldwork couched fillings may be employed.

Couching is also used as the basis of some of the various narrow borders used in Iranian embroidery. Laid threads are couched with silk or gold thread worked in satin stitch either over the entire bundle of laid threads or over some of them to produce the required pattern. A bundle of laid threads can also be covered by a single thread itself laid in zigzag formation from side to side of the original bundle and couched at each bend. Narrow borders may be formed from parallel vertical satin stitches worked in repeating triangles, zigzags or other geometric shapes, or with back stitches worked twice through the same holes, with each pair of stitches slightly apart from its neighbours. Wider borders can be similarly executed, with parallel lines of back stitch or satin stitch.

Most Iranian Moslems adhere to the Shi'a rather than the Sunni form of their religion and therefore pictorial devices appear in some embroideries. Peacocks and other birds, figures of monarchs, hunters and other men, are often outlined with split stitch or stem stitch and infilled with one of the many forms of Iranian couching.

The tree of life, another popular Iranian motif, was possibly introduced from central Asia. It symbolizes a sacred tree of Paradise, and is generally represented in Iranian embroidery as a cypress tree, also a symbol of the sun, as a candelabra or as a palm bearing a cone-shaped fruit. The cone, which is known as a *buta*, *kulka* or *kalka*, is also worked by itself, and may be made up of various floral devices.

Sometimes abstract devices are chosen.

A variety of different narrow borders can be worked using parallel vertical satin stitches or by sewing small separated back stitches in pairs.

Drawn- and pulled-thread work and surface satin stitch are sometimes executed in silk and metal thread as in this Iranian wall hanging.

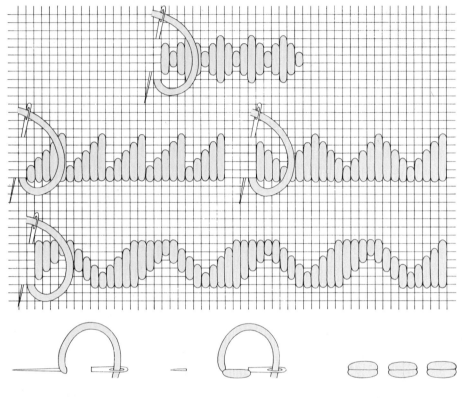

These may be eight-pointed stars, triangles and other geometric shapes reminiscent of the jigsaw complexity of the tesselated domes and walls of Iranian mosques.

Iranian embroidery is used for decorating hangings, rugs and small mats, cushion covers, Koran covers and costume. Traditional clothing varies with the region concerned, although throughout the country Moslem women wore, and some still wear, tunics or dresses over full-length cotton trousers. In typical Moslem style, many trousers have tight-fitting embroidered cuffs about 28 cm (11 in) deep, worked with polychrome silk satin stitch and stem stitch in diagonal bands of repeating motifs, usually floral.

In the past, court dresses were, as would be expected, lavishly embroidered with silk threads on a ground of silk brocade. The cut of some court coats, however, with tight-fitting waists and full-hipped skirts, and long sleeves joined under the arm only briefly at the elbows, did not provide proportions that were conducive to much decoration with embroidery stitches.

As well as universal Iranian techniques, individual ethnic and religious groups have their own peculiar styles of embroidery. The Turkmen employ techniques and styles similar to those of neighbouring Soviet Turkmenistan and north-western Iraq and the nomadic Baluchi of eastern Iran have embroideries that may be classified with those of the Indian sub-continent.

One minor cult with peculiar embroidery forms is Zoroastrianism, a pre-Islamic religion that today survives mainly in isolated areas of Iran and in India, especially around Bombay. Zoroastrian embroidery is, not surprisingly, similar to some Kutch work, with double cross stitch, darning stitch, herringbone stitch, ladder stitch, interlacing and laid and couched work executed in silk threads on a cotton ground fabric. Devices of peacocks and other birds, cones and floral shapes embellish women's dresses, shawls and trousers.

Some parts of Iran, notably Azerbaijan, Isfahan and Kerman, have specific embroidery styles. In the main, however, embroidery is not now widely worked except by some minority groups, substantially encouraged by government organizations. For commercial reasons, entrepreneurs concentrate on handmade knotted rugs and other textile forms but old examples of Iranian embroidery may still occasionally be found for sale in the bazaars of Tehran.

Azerbaijan

Particularly during the late 18th and early 19th centuries the Iranian district of Azerbaijan, in the north-west of the country, was famous for overlaid and inlaid appliqué, with pieces of felt or woven wool or cotton fabric applied to or set into a felt, woven wool or cotton ground. Especially in the city of Rasht, applied motifs, held in place with parallel lines of tamboured chain stitch, might be embellished with local seed

Rasht is famous for its appliqué work. This 19th-century portrait 'drawn' with silk on wool patchwork is further decorated with magic chain stitch.

pearls sewn on as beads or with gold and silver thread laid and couched with silk.

Appliqué, worked by both men and women, featured floral designs, although occasionally portraits of monarchs and other notables were worked. It was generally used for wall hangings and many of the best surviving examples are now in museums in western Europe.

Azerbaijan embroidery today is usually worked with brightly coloured floss-silk satin stitching on a ground of black cotton. Each block of stitching is separated from its neighbour by a long straight stitch or a laid and couched thread. A few caps and other costume items are produced for sale.

Delicate Isfahani whitework mat showing pulled-thread techniques.

Isfahan

The Isfahan area, in central Iran, is famous for whitework embroidery, with fine tamboured cotton chain stitch worked on a cotton ground. Devices such as cones with added scrolls almost in arabesque form are outlined with chain stitch and infilled with russian drawn ground and other pulled-thread fillings. In the past, Isfahan whitework, executed on tablecloths and other domestic items, was made for sale to travellers to Iran.

The women of Isfahan were particularly skilled embroiderers. Especially during the 19th century they produced some of the finest decoration on enormous wall hangings for weddings and other special occasions, and also on everyday items such as women's trouser cuffs. They also worked tree of life and cone devices, and a particular Isfahani motif, a circular face known as 'mother sun', on circular mats usually measuring about 25 cm (10 in) in diameter.

Kerman

Kerman stitch.

Colourful border from Kerman, decorated with leaves and strange bird-like shapes in kerman stitch and stem stitch.

Kerman, a city to the south-east of Isfahan, has given its name to a versatile filling stitch which can be worked with stitches close together or separated from each other.

Kerman embroidery, worked by women for their own use or for sale, is traditionally executed with brightly coloured fine wool thread on a soft fine-weave woollen ground, often scarlet. Motifs such as concentric circles with reserves filled with cone and other typical Iranian devices, or with the ground fabric completely covered with floral themes, are often outlined with stem stitch and infilled with closed or open kerman stitch.

Particularly during the late 19th and early 20th centuries, Kerman embroidery backed with black wool was used on tea-cosies or in small wall hangings about 90 cm (36 in) square. Embroidered items were given as presents by dignitaries or sold to travellers.

Afghanistan

Many Afghan women still wear the *chadri*, a long, plain-coloured cotton veil with self-coloured embroidery in chain, herringbone, ladder and satin stitches and with a pulled-thread facial 'visor'.

Except for local and imported cotton, Afghanistan's embroidery resources come from sheep, which are raised throughout the country, particularly in the north-east, on the northern slopes of the Hindu Kush, and in Kandahar in the south.

Afghanistan is peopled by many groups, such as the Baluchi in the south-west and the Turkmen and Uzbeks in the north-west, whose embroidery styles are not peculiar to Afghanistan. Other groups with their own embroidery styles include the Hazara, descendants of Mongols who settled in the country in the 13th and 14th centuries and now live mostly in the central mountainous region of Hazarajat, and the Pathans, living mainly in the south and east, especially in Paktya and Kandahar.

Afghan embroidery, worked by men and women with silk or cotton thread on ground fabrics of cotton or sheepskin, is executed mostly in satin stitch and tent stitch although many other stitches are employed. Embroidery designs are generally geometric, but some prayer mats show mosques or praying hands. Embroidery is worked also on Koran covers, cushion covers and other secular items and on clothing.

Many Afghan women still wear the *chadri*, a full-length plain-coloured cotton veil, with a hexagonal facial grille to allow air and vision. The grille is worked in silk thread the same colour as the veil, with russian drawn ground and other pulled-thread stitches. Around the 'visor' surface embroidery is executed in chain stitch or parallel satin stitch in repeating triangular and other geometric devices and cones. A similar complex design is worked in surface embroidery on the central chest 'flap', a conical pocket with opening at the base.

In the past many *chadris* were executed as whitework. Today, for practicality, most of them are worked with a self-coloured thread on an orange, purple, grey or another coloured cotton ground. A wide spectrum of different-coloured robes, with surface embroidery generally worked on a Cornely machine, can be seen for sale in shops and markets.

Particularly in the south and east of Afghanistan, women wear a simple head veil, often of plain black cotton, over

Hazara woman's prayer mat.

Mat worked with mosque motif.

an ankle-length dress, which is sometimes of brightly coloured printed cotton with elaborately embroidered yokes and sleeve panels. Women throughout the country wear loose full-length trousers, some of which are made of white cotton fabric with narrow borders of drawn-thread work on the cuffs.

Men of Afghanistan do not normally have embroidered clothing although in winter some of them wear sheepskin coats with decoration worked in brightly coloured silk chain stitch or satin stitch. These 'Afghan coats' have become increasingly popular in the west in recent years.

Afghan skull caps, worn by men and some women and young boys, are usually made of cotton fabric in one of four main styles. All have narrow straight-cut brims but the crowns may be cut to produce conical, toque or mitre shapes. They are embroidered by men, traditionally working buttonhole stitch, chain stitch, cross stitch, satin stitch and pattern darning by hand, although now some machine chain stitching is used. The crown is often divided, with embroidered chain-stitch radii forming four or more wedge-shaped segments subsequently in-filled with a cone, heart or other device which may be characteristic of the region. The brim is embroidered in a complementary style.

Embroidery continues to be worked in most areas of Afghanistan. Many people still wear traditional dress, and women's robes have become increasingly popular with foreign visitors to Afghanistan. Cushion covers are other domestic items that are also produced today and intended primarily for sale.

Strawberry-shaped spot motifs
in chain stitch decorating an
antique Afghan dress.

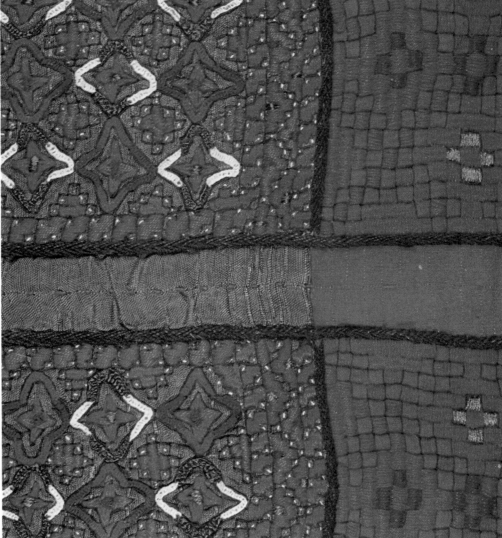

A splendid cover for a noble steed.
The velvet is embroidered with
satin stitch, sometimes padded,
with chain stitch and straight
stitch. It shows different couching
techniques in gold and silk
threads, and glistens with tiny
pieces of mirror.

Kerman stitch, ladder stitch, stem
stitch and straight stitch, worked
in silk or cotton, are among the
techniques used to embroider
Afghan costume and religious
items.

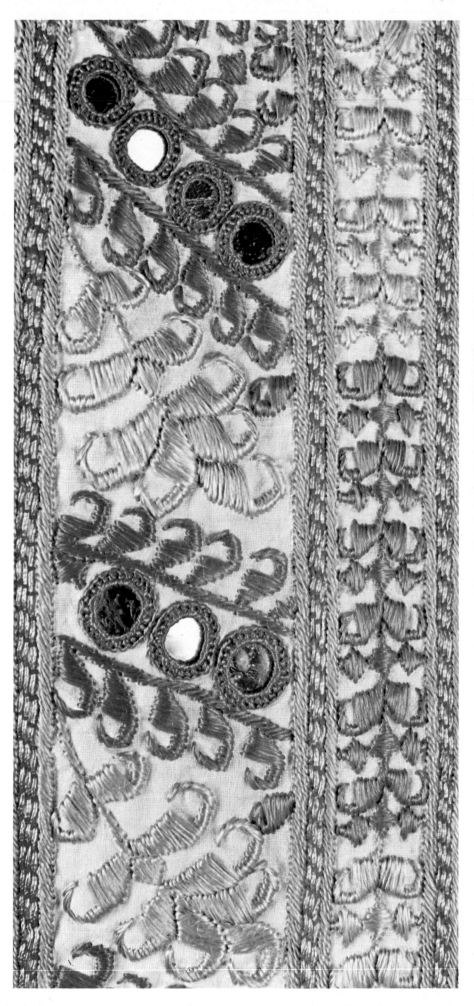

Tiny mirrors glinting in the midst of dense embroidery stitches are special features of Kandahar work.

Paktya embroidery (below) is often further embellished with applied *guls* (roses) of stitched beadwork.

Mazar-i-Sharif

The embroiderers of the city of Mazar-i-Sharif and the surrounding region of northern Afghanistan are particularly versatile, employing many different stitch forms. They work, for instance, monochrome needle chain stitch, with deep plum-coloured stitching in carefully designed symmetrical scrolls on a white cotton ground, decorating cushion covers, sleeve panels and other items of domestic use or personal wear.

In this region skull caps are generally not divided by radial lines of embroidery. Instead, a black cotton crown may be decorated with many circular motifs, with exterior radiating lines, spotted over the main ground. Colouring of embroidery thread for this design, usually worn by men, is often bright, and worked in back stitch and ringed back stitch.

Appliqué is sometimes practised in Mazar-i-Sharif. A mitre-crowned cap, worn by both men and women, may be decorated with yellow cone-shaped cotton pieces hemmed to an orange cotton crown and subsequently embroidered with satin stitching, sometimes with silver thread.

Skull caps are embroidered for every-

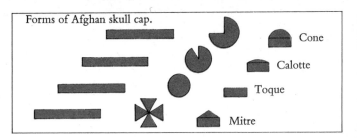

Unusual prayer mat embroidered with symbolic 'hands' each side of a central, stylized tree design, the whole worked in chain stitch, stem stitch, satin stitch and closed kerman stitch.

Brightly coloured Kandahar skull cap worked with close rows of buttonhole stitch.

Another Kandahar skull-cap design has a crown embroidered in laid and couched gold thread and spangles held in place with french knots.

In some areas of Afghanistan brides wear skull caps embroidered with gold and silver threads.

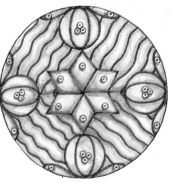

day use and for special occasions. Brides and newly married girls wear calotte caps decorated with gold and silver thread laid and couched with silk thread. A hexagonal star is worked in the centre of the crown and around it are placed four motifs shaped like pomegranates. These are highlighted with spangles and held in place by french knots.

Hazarajat

The Hazara, in the central region of Afghanistan, have equally distinctive embroidery styles, often worked on white cotton prayer mats.

Women embroider and design the prayer mats, generally about 40 cm (16 in) square, for themselves. Using a wide assortment of brightly coloured silk threads, they execute back stitch, chain stitch, cross stitch and satin stitch in geometric or highly stylized pictorial designs of mosques, shrines, arches, arrows and hands. The hands, some with red nails, are usually placed where the embroiderer's hands might go when the rug is used for prayer. The designs are surrounded by an outer border of repeating geometric devices, sometimes with lettering worked in back stitch or satin stitch.

Paktya

Women of the Paktya region, in the east of Afghanistan, prefer to embroider for costume use. They decorate the yokes and upper sleeves of their cotton dresses with back stitch, cross stitch, tent stitch and pattern darning worked in mosque shapes, eight-pointed stars, diamonds and other geometric shapes. Embellishment is provided by mirror work, like that of neighbouring parts of Pakistan, or with *guls* (roses). These are flat cotton circular discs covered with concentric rows of stitched beadwork.

Paktya embroiderers also decorate purses with gold thread or golden silk cord laid and couched with silk retaining stitches and surrounded with eyelet-stitch and satin-stitch embroidery, all worked in symmetrical designs.

Kandahar

In the Kandahar region, in the central southern part of Afghanistan, colourful mirror work on dress panels, cushion covers and other domestic items is still produced in large quantities, both for sale in the markets of Kandahar itself and for export.

Other Kandahar techniques include buttonhole stitch, stem stitch, straight stitch, laid and couched work and machine embroidery.

Costume embroidery is chiefly worked on skull caps, sometimes made of velvet backed with card. One popular calotte crown design has four petalled shapes of a different-coloured velvet material hemmed to the main ground and subsequently embellished with metal spangles, pieces of glass sewn on as spangles, and gold thread laid and couched. Another Kandahar skull-cap decoration consists of parallel lines of brightly coloured buttonhole stitch worked so close together that none of the ground fabric shows through.

223

Afghan Dress

This pretty peasant-style dress with its flattering neckline has a counted-thread design on the bodice reminiscent of the rich stitchery of Afghanistan.

You will need:

4 m (4⅜ yd) red lawn fabric 90 cm (36 in) wide

0.5 m (⅝ yd) coarse linen 90 cm (36 in) wide, approx. 10 threads to 2.5 cm (1 in) to match lawn

0.2 m (¼ yd) non-woven interfacing 90 cm (36 in) wide

five skeins coton à broder in four colours:

red 2 skeins
orange 1 skein
dark green 1 skein
light green 1 skein
1 reel sewing cotton to match the lawn
crewel needle
embroidery hoop (optional)

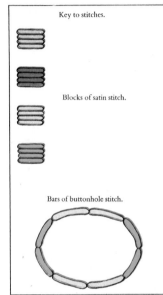

Key to stitches.

Blocks of satin stitch.

Bars of buttonhole stitch.

Stitch chart.
Each line of the grid represents one thread of the linen.

Size: to fit bust 81 cm (32 in). See page 272 for enlarging patterns.

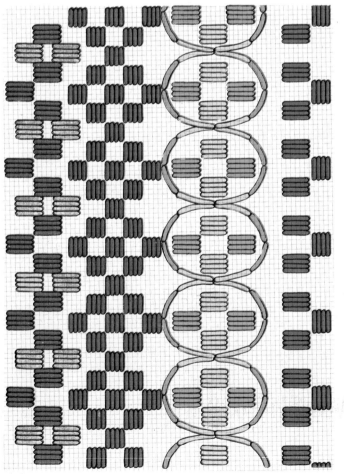

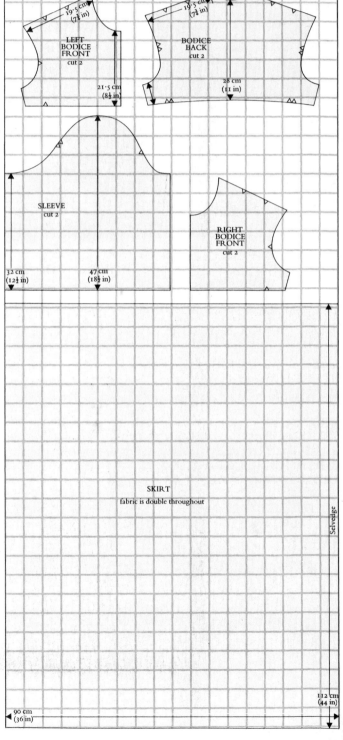

INTERFACING

FRONT   FRONT

BACK

1 sq = 5 cm

19·5 cm (7¾ in)

LEFT BODICE FRONT cut 2

21·5 cm (8¼ in)

19·5 cm (7¾ in)

BODICE BACK cut 2

28 cm (11 in)

SLEEVE cut 2

RIGHT BODICE FRONT cut 2

32 cm (12½ in)

47 cm (18½ in)

SKIRT
fabric is double throughout

Selvedge

90 cm (36 in)

112 cm (44 in)

Preparing the Fabric

Scale up the pattern pieces (see page 272) so that each square on the grid is enlarged to 5 cm (2 in). Cut out the lawn following the pattern layout. (The second set of bodice pieces will act as linings.) Cut two bodice fronts and one bodice back in linen, taking care to set the straight centre-front edges of the bodice on the straight grain of the fabric. Scale up and cut out the interfacing.

Baste each of the linen bodice pieces onto a corresponding piece of lawn. Mark the centre-front seam lines, allowing a 1.5 cm (⅝ in) seam.

Embroidery

Starting at the centre fronts, work the counted-thread embroidery using the chart as a guide to colours. Using the embroidery thread double, work the blocks of four satin stitches over four or six linen threads as shown. Work the oval shapes in buttonhole stitch using a single embroidery thread.

Making the Dress

Use a 1.5 cm (⅝ in) seam allowance throughout and press each seam as it is stitched.

Baste the interfacings to the wrong side of the bodice pieces. Stitch the shoulder and side seams of the bodice and of the bodice linings. Right sides together, baste and stitch the lining to the bodice round the neck and the front edges; leave these open 1.5 cm (⅝ in) at the bottom.

Trim the interfacings close to the stitching. Trim and clip the seams and turn the lining to the inside.

Stitch the skirt side seams. Run two lines of gathering threads round the top edge inside the seam allowance. Pull up the gathers to fit the bodice, concentrating the fullness between the notches. Stitch, leaving the lining free.

Stitch the sleeve seams and turn up a 2 cm (¾ in) hem along the bottom edge of each. Run two lines of gathering threads inside the seam allowance between the notches at the top edge. Right sides together, and leaving the lining free, pin the sleeves into the armholes. Match the notches and seams and pull up the gathers to fit. Baste and stitch.

Press all bodice and armhole seams towards the centre. Turn raw edges of the bodice lining under 1.5 cm (⅝ in). Pin, baste and hem them to the seams.

Turn up the hem. Remove all basting threads and press the finished garment, omitting the embroidery.

India

The Indian sub-continent comprises the predominantly Hindu republic of India bordered by the Moslem republics of Pakistan and Bangladesh on the west and east. The religious boundaries are by no means rigid, however, with Hindus living in the Moslem areas and Moslems forming a large minority in India.

The main embroidery regions of Baluchistan, Swat, Kashmir, the Punjab, Chamba, Sind and Kutch are concentrated in the north-west. Also important are Goa, on the west coast of India, and Bengal in the north-east.

Outside influences have been few. Contact with western and central Asia has been hampered by the mountain ranges that extend from the Hindu Kush to the Himalayas. The deserts of Iran and Afghanistan form a boundary to the west and the hills and low mountains of Burma to the east.

Embroidery is practised by both men and women throughout the sub-continent and is used for decorating clothing as well as for creating wall hangings, rugs and accessories. But while the items embroidered may be similar, the people of each region produce unique patterns remarkably dissimilar in appearance. This is true even of the neighbouring Baluchi and the Sindi, both of whom produce *shishadur*, or mirror work.

Embroidery and appliqué seem to have been worked in India since the dawn of history. Archaeological finds at Mohenjo-Daro, centre of a major civilization known as the Indus Valley culture, indicate that by 2000 B.C. cotton was cultivated and its fibres spun into thread and woven into cloth. Dyeing with mordants was also practised. Among the fragments of cloth recovered by archaeologists are some decorated with embroidery and appliqué.

Until the invention of synthetic fibres, most garments and other items were made of locally produced cotton. Wealthy people often wore silk, which was grown throughout the eastern part of the sub-continent and is still farmed on a small scale in the northern Deccan Plateau and around Madras and Bangalore. Some of the silk is made into embroidery thread.

Silk thread is often used in Indian embroidery, and so is cotton. Although many of the finest cotton threads were spun with hand spindles made from a slim bamboo rod with a pellet of clay at its base, the spinning wheel is thought to have been invented in India. Spinning was usually a domestic craft, which has been largely superseded by manufactured yarns.

Wool is not much used for embroidery except in Kashmir, and although the Baluchi raise sheep, they sell the wool or make carpets and wall hangings from it. Neither jute string nor twine is used for embroidery at all, despite the fact that the Ganges delta is the world's foremost jute-growing area.

Locally available natural dyes account for the traditional colourings of fabrics and threads. Among them are common madder, the cochineal insect *coccus cacti*, kermes and logwood (reds); indigo (blues and purples); carthamus and saffron (orange and yellow); and iron filings (black). More recently, green dye has been achieved by boiling baizes and broadcloths imported from England. The main mordant was alizarin, from madder root.

Many embroideries have a ground of black, indigo or white cotton. Most of them are stylized, especially among the people

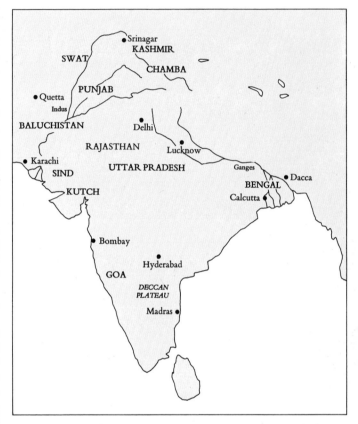

of Baluchistan, Swat and Sind. Other areas, such as Kashmir, the Punjab, Chamba and Kutch, produce more representational work, showing people, flowers, trees and human activities. No matter what the design, the most popular forms of embroidery are satin stitch and *shishadur*, which are most frequently worked on articles of clothing.

Religion plays a marked role in embroidery design. In some Hindu areas, for instance, the god Vishnu is manifest in the forms of Agni (fire), Indra (rain, thunder and lightning) and Surya (sun). This representation has been particularly revered by the Vaishnava sects of the north-east, although the tripartite device is found in many different forms throughout the sub-continent. Moslems reject the representation of the human form, using stylized figures and symbols instead.

Not only the design but also the colouring of embroidery is connected with Hindu religious belief. Red and yellow, the colours associated with joy and merriment, are often used for Indian bridal outfits.

The earliest garments were made from simple lengths of fabric that were wrapped around the person rather than sewn. Women wore the sari, and men had loin cloths, turbans and shawls. The first stitched garments were introduced by invading Moslems in the 8th century.

Today most embroidery is found on the tunics, which Moslem women wear over baggy, full-length trousers, and also on their veils, shawls and hats. Decorative embroidery is used to brighten up the home and wall hangings, quilts, cloths and Koran covers are traditional in many areas.

Baluchistan

The Baluchi are a nomadic people living on the steppes of western Pakistan and neighbouring parts of southern Afghanistan and eastern Iran. They are primarily a pastoral people, whose economy is based on the raising of sheep and goats. They export considerable quantities of high-quality wool as well as weaving carpets and wall hangings. Little cultivation takes place, since water is generally scarce, but some cotton is grown in the northern part of the region and is used locally to make cloth.

The Baluchi are Sunni Moslems whose main festivals are connected with

Elaborate dress yokes involving a good deal of work are sometimes first embroidered on a flat piece of fabric. They are subsequently applied to the garment or incorporated when it is made up.

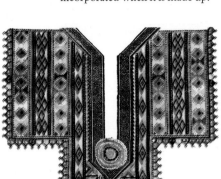

Couching, the tying down of one thread with another, is common in Baluchi embroidery. The thread to be couched is laid flat and is then oversewn with a contrasting colour.

marriages, fairs, horse races and wrestling matches. They claim descent from Nimrod, King of Babylon, described in Genesis as 'the first man on earth to be a mighty man'.

Baluchi embroidery has always been used to embellish practical garments.

The women dress in black cotton, which is often richly embroidered with cotton or silk threads in orange, rust, dark green, black and white and sometimes red. Some of the most beautiful work adorns the *kus*, a knee-length or full-length robe with a front yoke panel and a remarkable central stomach pocket,

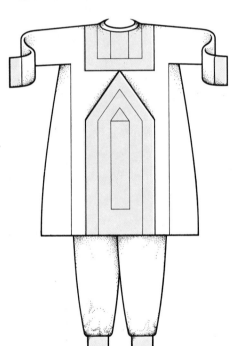

Baluchi women traditionally wear the *kus*, which is usually embroidered round the cuffs, on the front and back yokes and on a large central pocket. This garment may be full or knee-length, in which case it is worn over baggy trousers whose cuffs may be embroidered.

This Baluchi dress has a heavily embroidered yoke, front pocket and sleeves. Its rich colour combination is characteristic of the area.

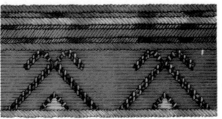

Geometric motifs couched on a straight-stitch background are often found in Baluchistan. They can easily be simplified and adapted for use today as these examples of border designs show.

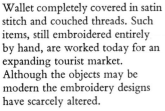

covered by a triangular flap open along its two uppermost sides. The Hausa costume (see chapter 8) has a similar front pocket which is placed not in the centre but over the left breast. The front yoke, the cuffs and the hem of the *kus* and also the legs of the *shalwar*, or trousers, are embroidered.

The designs are geometric and worked in bands, with emphasis on diagonal lines. Main bands of horizontal satin stitches are bordered by narrow dividing bands of diagonal satin stitches. These divisions of the main bands are outlined with black thread laid and couched with a brightly coloured thread stitched diagonally across it. Sometimes two parallel black threads are laid, and the couching spaced so that it forms an attractive spiral pattern.

Although most of the old Baluchi dresses were made from local cotton, some were fashioned from imported silk. Colour combinations on such out-of-the-ordinary robes frequently included orange, black and white silk embroidery worked on a ground of fuchsia-coloured silk. These colour combinations were especially favoured by the Brahvi tribe in the Chagai district of northern Baluchistan.

Fragments and even complete pieces of old Baluchi embroidery are still readily available throughout the world for anyone who wants and asks for it. Produced from natural dyes, their colouring is subtle and muted compared with modern work. Chemical dyes are now generally favoured, and the embroidery is likely to be more garish in colouring as a result. Commercially produced wallets, bags and coats decorated with embroidery can be found in the markets throughout Baluchistan.

Wallet completely covered in satin stitch and couched threads. Such items, still embroidered entirely by hand, are worked today for an expanding tourist market. Although the objects may be modern the embroidery designs have scarcely altered.

A large central pocket rising to a triangular flap with openings either side is a striking feature of the *kus*. Reduced in size, it could be adapted by the embroiderer to make an attractive and practical pocket on a modern blouse or top.

Baluchi women still wear beautifully worked garments as everyday dress; in many parts of Baluchistan the natural dyes which produce such subtle colours continue to be used in preference to synthetic dyes.

Shisha Blouse

As a safety precaution, first wash the cotton fabric in hot soapy water to remove excess dye.

After cutting out, press the centre fold lengthwise on both tunic and sleeves with a hot iron. This will act as guides for positioning your embroidery design.

Match centre of motif A design tracing to centre fold, approximately 9 cm (3½ in) from bottom of tunic and 14 cm (5½ in) from bottom of sleeve. Working outwards in both directions, add motif B. Repeat motifs to front edge.

You will need:
1.75 m (2 yd) black cotton
  fabric 122 cm (48 in) wide
105 shisha mirror glasses
48 cm (½ yd) narrow elastic
stranded embroidery cottons
  in ten strong colours:
scarlet 5 skeins
yellow 4 skeins
white 2 skeins
wine red 1 skein
magenta 1 skein
azure blue 1 skein
olive green 1 skein
spring green 1 skein
purple 1 skein
orange 1 skein

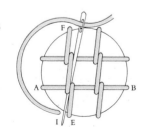

1

Tie small knot in thread. Bring needle out at A while holding down shisha glass with left thumb. Take a small stitch over shisha glass inserting needle into fabric close to lower edge at B. Bring needle out at C.

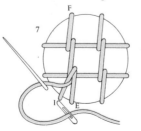

2

Return to top edge, entering fabric at D and coming out at E.

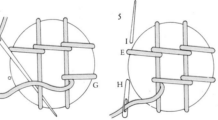

3   4   5

Begin by working a stem stitch over the vertical line AB. Slide needle under AB from the lower right side to the upper left. Pull thread through and hold in place with left thumb. Repeat stitch over line DC keeping threads taut. Enter fabric at F, coming out at G.

For the second bar come up at G, and work the stem stitches from right to left.

Insert needle at H, taking it under the background fabric and bringing it out at I, slightly away from the edge of the shisha glass.

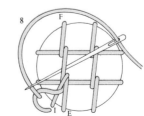

6   7   8   9

Turn the work so that it is at the lower left. Slide needle from above behind the intersection of the line AB and the stem stitch EF and pull through carefully.

Working in a clockwise direction take a tiny stitch into the background fabric, beginning at I. Place working thread under needle. Pull through to make a chain stitch.

Work a second cretan stitch on the line EF, close to the first. For the second chain stitch insert needle into fabric through the same chain from which you came

up. Take a small stitch and pull through over the working thread. Repeat steps 7-9 so that when finished, the shisha glass is encircled with embroidery.

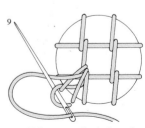

Diagram (right side):

14 cm (5½ in)   11 cm (4⅜ in)   shoulder seam

6 cm (2⅜ in)

armhole

26 cm (10¼ in)   21 cm (8¼ in)

centre back   TUNIC cut 2   front

73 cm (28¾ in)   9 cm (3½ in)

55 cm (21⅝ in)

gathering line   51 cm (20 in)

SLEEVE cut 2

66 cm (26 in)   1 sq = 5 cm

Embroidery

Motif A

Beginning at the centre, attach shisha glass with three strands of embroidery cotton (see diagrams).

Work outwards using three strands of cotton in single circles of chain stitch in two different colours.

Outline the star with two lines of chain stitch.

Fill in the points of the star with cretan stitch (see chapter 7) beginning with the top point and working clockwise. Make each point a different colour.

Centre shisha glasses between the points of the star and sew them down with three strands of cotton. Outline them with two strands of cotton in single satin stitches.

Outline the scalloped edge of the motif with a double line of chain stitch using two strands of cotton.

Fill in the small areas between these lines with open chain stitch using two strands of cotton in many different colours.

Fill in the tiny lozenge-shaped area with satin stitch using two strands of cotton.

Outline the six 'fingers' with chain stitch using two strands of cotton.

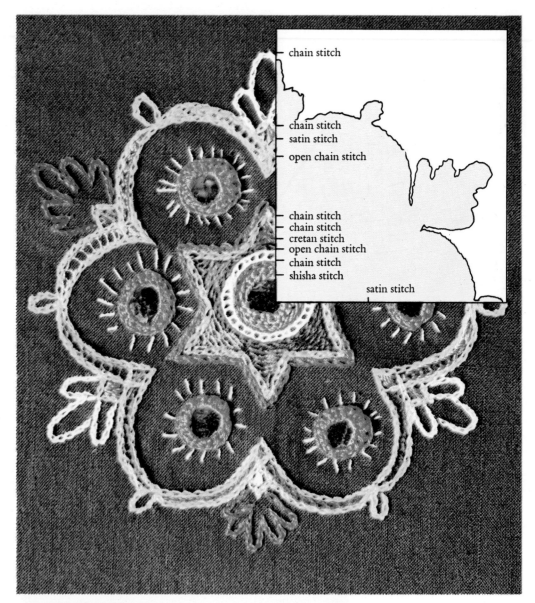

chain stitch

chain stitch
satin stitch
open chain stitch

chain stitch
chain stitch
cretan stitch
open chain stitch
chain stitch
shisha stitch

satin stitch

Motif B

Attach the centre shisha glass with three strands of cotton.

Encircle it with one line of chain stitch using two strands of cotton.

Outline the star with chain stitch using two strands of cotton.

Fill in the points of the star with cretan stitch using two strands of cotton.

Progressing clockwise from the top of the star attach shisha glass with two strands of cotton. Outline it with one circle of chain stitch in a different colour.

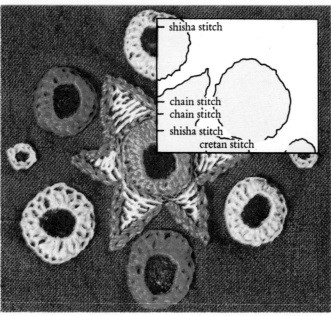

shisha stitch

chain stitch
chain stitch
shisha stitch
cretan stitch

Making the Blouse

Join the shoulder seams.

Turn up a 1 cm (½ in) hem around the sides and bottom of the blouse.

Stitch the sleeve seams.

Gather the top of the sleeves and sew the sleeves into the armholes.

Turn in and hem the neck opening allowing sufficient space for the drawstring.

Turn in and stitch the sleeve hems, inserting elastic to fit the wrist.

Make the drawstring (see page 126).

Hangings incorporating mirror
work are often given at marriage.
Red and yellow, being associated
with joy, are used for bridal outfits.

This traditional mirror work shows
mirrors used in a restrained way
to complement rather than to
dominate the design.

Mirror Work

The Baluchi also produce *shishadur*,
or mirror work. Quetta, in Pakistani
Baluchistan, is particularly famous for
this kind of embroidery which is used
for both clothing and decorative items.

Shishadur is created by attaching
minute pieces of silvered glass or mica to
the ground fabric by a retaining network
of stitching round their circumference.
This web is then further secured with
blanket or buttonhole or any other
similar binding stitch. 'Shisha stitch',
named for this type of embroidery and
popular in America today, is a descrip-
tive name for any of the stitches used for
sewing down shisha glass.

The silvered glass used in the past for
mirror work was produced by blowing
glass into spheres, silvering the insides of
the spheres, and then breaking them into
pieces of the required size. This slightly
convex glass was thought to frighten
away evil spirits, who were terrified by
the sight of their own image.

In older pieces of mirror embroidery,
the silvered glass was often as large as
3 cm (1¼ in) in diameter. The overall
effect was, however, more artistic and
controlled than much of the modern
work, which tends to marry numerous
tiny pieces of mirror with as little
surrounding embroidery as possible.

Sometimes the shisha 'wheels' are
surrounded by flowers, generally worked
in satin stitch, or by cones defined with
back stitch. Then small dividers of
straight black stitches are worked between the motifs, dividing the design
into small panels. These are then filled
with satin stitches, covering the ground
completely and resulting in a stained-
glass effect. The direction of stitching is
uniform throughout each panel, but
adjacent panels can face different ways.

Modern, chemically produced yarn
colours have led to a complete change in
the character of mirror work. Recent
shisha embroidery often combines such
colours as shocking pink and bright
citron. Older pieces of mirror work used
more restrained and sympathetic ethnic
colour schemes based on rust, moss green
and indigo.

Mirror work today is generally carried
out on a ground of heavy cotton. The
finished embroidery is made up into
cushion covers, yokes, collars and cuffs
of shirts or dresses, bags, belts and
similar accessories.

Shisha embroidery motifs are very
often worked in satin stitch with
back-stitch outlines as this example
shows. To simplify the motif you
could omit one of the satin-stitch
colours, leaving the ground
showing.

Swat

Located in the mountainous north of Pakistan, Swat lies on the border with Afghanistan. The Yusufzai Pathans, who are related to the Afghans and live in the lower valleys, are the main practitioners of embroidery.

The economy of the area is based on agriculture, and fruits and honey are the main exports. The main cottage industries are the manufacture of curtains and woollen blankets, which are seldom embroidered. Most of the embroidery is carried out on Moslem prayer mats and clothing.

Yusufzai designs owe their controlled lines and curves to the Moghul rulers of India, who introduced Asian styles and techniques during the zenith of their power from the 16th to the 18th century.

Detail of costume embroidered with coins and tree of life motifs.

Geometric motif taken from a pillowcase; it could be used alone or as a repeat on a cushion cover.

Swat pillowcase.

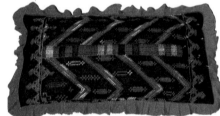

Moghul influence is seen in the curvilinear free-form *mihrab* arch designs found on some embroidered prayer mats. The cotton mats, which are sometimes quilted with silk thread, have chain-stitched flowers and leaves surrounding the embroidered arch shape on a rectangular ground.

Trees feature in many Yusufzai embroideries. They are associated with rites of sexuality and fertility and the belief in rebirth, and many villages have a sacred tree revered by the entire community. Trees and other natural forms are found in both the embroidered prayer mats and the more geometric costume embroidery.

The women of Swat wear knee-length tunics over full-length baggy pants and they cover their heads with knee-length veils. The garments are made of black or deep indigo cotton, and show no Moghul influence. The seams, hem, neck panel and sleeves of the tunics are embroidered with various shades of bright pink and purple silks with some outlining in black, white and yellow. The most frequently used filling stitch is satin stitch and outlining is worked in either satin stitch or running stitch.

Much costume embroidery consists of simple repeating patterns. In one sequence, long-necked earth mothers are shown wearing floor-length skirts, which is particularly interesting since the wearers of the tunics are trousered.

Kashmir

Situated in the mountains to the east of Swat, Kashmir is divided into the Indian states of Jammu and Kashmir and Pakistani Azad Kashmir. The people are Moslems, Hindus and Buddhists. Embroidery in Kashmir is usually associated with shawls, which are worn over the shoulders and one arm by both men and women. The traditional Kashmir shawls were white and embellished with woven decoration. In 1803 an Armenian, Khwaja Yusuf, introduced embroidered decoration to the Kashmir shawl, and they

Detail of intricately embroidered Kashmir shawl, worked on the traditional ground of white wool. The flowing border pattern, which is worked all round the shawl, used in the past to be in subtle colours such as these but is to be found in much brighter colours today.

became cheaper to manufacture. Since then the *amli*, or embroidered shawl, has grown in popularity, and at times has been a popular fashion in Europe.

Shawls are made either from fine, locally produced wool or from imported yarn of the soft inner fleece of Himalayan goats and their production is very much a man's work. The designer, who may also be the embroiderer, is the most skilled of all the craftsmen involved. He is paid substantially more than the weaver.

Detail of the famous Srinagar map, a vast embroidery of the capital of Kashmir executed in the middle of the 19th century. Here life on the Jhelum river is depicted in careful detail. The embroidery is worked in multi-coloured wools in darning, satin and stem stitch, creating the effect of a woven design.

Motif filled with open herringbone.   Motif outlined in stem stitch and filled with satin stitch.

Kashmiri embroiderers work at lightning speed. They produce minute stem stitches as if by machine, with no outline on the ground fabric to aid the alignment of each device. They frequently pull the thread away from them, rather than bringing it towards them as embroiderers generally do.

Embroidery is ordered, quite literally, by the stitch. The greater the volume of embroidery, the more costly the finished item will be. Customers choose from the many designs shown on a carefully worked sampler which the embroiderer keeps by him. Most of the traditional shawl themes are floral, and often a cone in one form or another is included.

The outlines of the designs are worked in dark thread, often indigo or black, and the infilling can be either monochrome or in a wide range of colours. Stem stitch, cretan stitch and satin stitch are the most commonly used.

Shawls are either square or rectangular. The *doshalla*, or rectangular shawl, is often worked in pairs, so that two shawls can be sewn together to make one thicker reversible item—a fashion attributed to the greatest of all Moghul emperors, Akbar, who wore two woven shawls sewn back to back.

Another form of Kashmiri embroidery is the *numdah* or decorative rug. It is traditionally worked on a ground of matted felt, but today a few designs are executed on sacking made from Bengali jute. The pattern is worked in either wool or cotton with a heavy rug hook which produces an outsize continuous tamboured chain stitch. Even today colours remain traditionally muted and earthy, the small natural dye-lots causing a noticeable variety of shades in any one block of colour.

Numdah designs can be geometric, with eight-pointed star or similar motifs, or pictorial. Many *numdah* themes depict delightfully stylized visions of real and imaginary life in Kashmir. Wedding themes are popular. A recurring scene shows the bride on the night before her wedding wearing a Kashmir shawl and flowers in her hair. She sits on a special wedding podium surrounded by lady escorts, some of whom play drums or trumpets. A companion *numdah* may depict her groom coming to her house with his retinue. Sometimes a third will show the feast, and the couple leaving together.

Another type of story-telling embroidery is worked not with a hook but with a needle. A famous example is the Srinagar map, created in the middle of the 19th century. It shows the meandering Jhelum River spanned by seven wooden bridges. The river and its connecting canals are full of minute *shikaras*, the floating gondolas and houseboats that still provide exciting water-borne holiday homes for visitors to Kashmir. Srinagar is the summer capital of Kashmir and, appropriately enough, its Shalimar Gardens and other green areas are intricately embroidered on the map.

Embroidered Kashmir shawls have been popular since the 15th century. Today you pay for the embroidery by length and by design, choosing from an embroiderer's sampler.

Numdah designs are very often geometric. They are worked on wool with a rug hook which produces a thick chain stitch.

Punjab

The Punjab lies in the plains area south of Kashmir. Divided between Pakistan and India, it stretches from the Indus valley in the west to the foothills bordering Tibet on the east. The population embraces most of the religions of the sub-continent and includes Hindus, Moslems and Sikhs.

The most common of the Punjabi embroideries is the flat, geometric decoration of *phulkari*, or flower art, work which is thought to have originated with the Indo-Aryan Jat tribe of the south-eastern Punjab. *Phulkaris* consist of large areas of cotton ground covered with floss-silk embroidery worked in parallel blocks of satin stitch. They are used for covers and various items of clothing.

Since many Punjabi women are still veiled, they cover their heads and faces with large shawls and veils, similar in shape to Iranian veils. Both shawls and veils are often embroidered.

Each length of embroidery yarn is used to maximum effect. Stitching is superficial with only the smallest of retaining stitches taking the yarn to the reverse of the fabric. Colouring is simple consisting, perhaps, of beige silk thread on a deep rust cotton ground. Generally only one or two colours are used.

Phulkari designs may consist simply of border decoration or may cover the ground completely. In the latter case the item may be known as a *bagh*, or garden. Many of the best *baghs* come from the Pakistani Hazara districts of the northern Punjab. Most are used for table, bed and food covers, but they are sometimes found on clothing.

Phulkari flower art sometimes shows repeating patterns of simple water-lilies,

similar to the rhombic design of the male form but with a stalk beneath. Another flower head consists of a lozenge shape with diagonal lines of satin stitch radiating from the calyx. The stitching is of the same diagonal nature as many other of the embroideries of the sub-continent.

Not all *phulkari* embroidery consists of repeating patterns. Separate motifs appear on hangings, featuring delightful figures of men, animals and birds placed at random on a dark, usually indigo-coloured, cotton ground. The devices are infilled with neat lines of parallel satin stitch and outlined in white. They

are worked in floss silk, often using a colour scheme of red, orange and yellow.

One Punjabi wall hanging shows at one end a lady with water pot on her head holding a child by one hand. The child and another small person carry a fourth person in an explorer's sling on a shoulder hoist. At the other end, the cloth shows two rather large people greeting a third, who holds two buckets suspended on a shoulder yoke. Along one edge of the hanging is a train with a single passenger sitting in each of the dome-roofed carriages, and the guard waving his flag at the rear.

Floral *phulkari* design worked with diagonal dividing bands.

Variation on the plain *phulkari* diamond with traditional border.

Phulkari embroidery is not always completely regular in design.

Intricate diamond *phulkari* pattern worked in floss silk.

Phulkari Evening Bag

The zigzag design on this evening bag is derived from Punjabi *phulkari* embroidery. It is worked in diagonal satin stitch and the regular pattern is achieved by counting threads.

You will need:
0.25 m (⅜ yd) medium-weight evenweave linen with 28 threads to 2.5 cm (1 in)
0.25 m (⅜ yd) fine white cotton fabric for lining
pearl cotton in three colours:
ivory 2 skeins
pink 6 skeins
red 5 skeins
sewing cotton in white
stiff white card
fabric adhesive

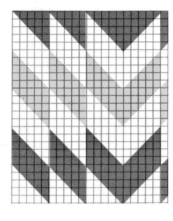

Alternative patterns.

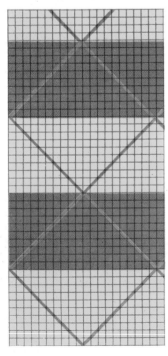

Zigzag pattern for the bag.
Reverse the pattern alternately
to complete the effect.

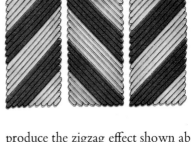

Positions of the card panels which
stiffen the bag. Check the
measurements against your own.

Preparing the Fabric

Mark the area of embroidery on the linen, leaving an equal margin all round. The embroidery area should measure exactly 32.4 x 20 cm (12⅜ x 8 in).

Embroidery

Leaving 3 cm (1¼ in) at the bottom edge and starting at the left-hand edge, work the panels of stitches as shown. Stagger the lengths of the stitches at the corners to make the blocks into rectangles.

Leaving one woven thread between each one, repeat the panels across the bag. Reverse the design on alternate panels to

Alternative pattern.

produce the zigzag effect shown above.

Work 10 more rows of panels, reversing the design on alternate rows. Leave a woven thread between each row.

Begin the next row in the same way but after the second pink stripe work 10 stitches in ivory and 5 in pink alternately to the top of the area. Do not miss any horizontal woven threads.

To complete the opposite end of the bag, turn the fabric so that the unworked area is at the top. Start the panels as before and work two stripes in each colour, taking the stitches over the full width of the panel.

Change to ivory and work five full-width stitches. Work seven more stitches in ivory, reducing in size to fit the corners. This edge will form the bottom of the flap.

Making the Bag

Pin the work out flat, stretching it to size. Press with a damp cloth.

Trim the edges of the linen leaving a 2 cm (¾ in) margin round the embroidery.

Divide the length of the embroidery by three and cut two pieces of card to this measurement by the width of the embroidery. Cut a third piece of card to the same width but 2.4 cm (⅞ in) shorter.

Place the embroidery face down with the flap edge at the top. Lay the card on the embroidery, leaving gaps between the pieces as shown. Turn the fabric margin onto the cards and glue down.

Cut a piece of lining fabric 37 x 25 cm (14½ x 9½ in). Turn in the edges to make it exactly the same size as the bag. Press the turnings and pin the lining, right side up, to the wrong side of the bag.

Cut two pieces of lining fabric 23 x 11 cm (9 x 4½ in) and fold them in half widthwise. Turn in the raw edges on the side opposite the fold and oversew to make them equal to the bag's depth.

Insert one raw edge of each gusset between the lining and the bag in line with one of the larger pieces of card at each side. Pin in place. Fold over the gussets and insert the opposite edge between the lining and bag in line with the second piece of card. Slip hem the lining to the bag all round, catching in the gussets. Slipstitch the bottom edges of each gusset and push them inside the bag. Add a button and loop fastening.

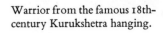

Chamba

Rumal depicting dancing couples embroidered in back stitch and satin stitch on a cotton ground.

The Chamba district in Himachal Pradesh lies between Kashmir and the Punjab in north-west India. Its economy is based on agriculture, although cloth is woven at two factories in Chamba Town.

Chamba is the home of the *rumal*, a square or rectangular saga embroidery depicting scenes full of movement and action. Figures are worked in back stitch and satin stitch using brightly coloured silks on a ground usually of cream or off-white cotton. The human figures are generally more realistically represented than the animals which sometimes seem rather wooden.

Themes can be war-like, domestic or festive. An 18th-century *rumal*, for instance, shows a circle of five doe-eyed ladies and their gentlemen dancing round a central couple. The ladies wear full-length striped skirts and the men are resplendent in flowing fringed shawls.

The most famous *rumal* is the 18th-century Kurukshetra hanging, which once graced the palace of the Raja of Chamba. The hanging, which measures 76 cm x 9.9 m (30 in x 32 ft 6 in), tells the story of the battle of Kurukshetra, as set down in the Sanskrit Mahabharata, a vast compilation of some 100,000 couplets and almost eight times the length of the Iliad and the Odyssey combined.

The story focuses on two sets of cousins, the five Pandavas and the Kauravas, who aspired to the throne of Kurukshetra. The Pandavas, with their one shared wife, Draupadi, were banished for thirteen years. When they returned home their cousins refused to give up their share of the land and a great battle ensued. Only six, among them the five Pandava brothers, survived on the winning side.

Snake charmer's quilt. Cotton appliqué forms a quilted pattern simulating snakeskin.

Sind

Traditional peacock and flower designs worked in chain stitch, ladder stitch, sind stitch and cretan stitch.

One of the regions of Pakistan, Sind lies in the hot, dry lowlands east of the lower Indus valley. The area, and especially the eastern part, has been somewhat isolated from outside influences, owing to the mountain ranges of Baluchistan to the west, the Arabian Sea to the south and the Thar Desert to the east. At the time of partition in 1947, a major exchange of populations took place, reducing the number of Hindus from twenty-five to about ten per cent.

Much of the best Sind embroidery comes from the eastern area of the province around Umarkot and Chor. Embroidery in silk and cotton thread is usually worked on a ground of local cotton fabric, generally dyed indigo.

Hurmitch, also known as armenian interlacing (see chapter 6), and ladder stitch are used for borders and single devices. Filling is worked in a special sind stitch with a finished appearance not unlike that of romanian couching.

Flowers and wheel forms are worked in sind stitch, producing wheel shapes with a double twist round the edge. Mirror work is popular, and seams are often hidden beneath interlacing stitches.

It is the Sindi women who do the embroidery and use it to decorate clothing, quilts, covers and hangings. Koran covers, which are embroidered all over, are made from large squares of cloth with all the corners folded to the centre to form an envelope.

Sindi Moslem women wear knee-length tunics over full-length trousers. Their dark indigo cotton tunics are embroidered with geometric designs stitched in vertically worked satin stitch. The devices are outlined with black cord which is sometimes laid and couched with beige thread.

The tree of life is a frequent motif and so is that of the double-rhombus male form. The female motif is sometimes used, appearing as an elongated

Repeating design for modern Sind shisha work with chain stitch, sind stitch and romanian stitch.

Sind top richly worked with bands of floss-silk embroidery incorporating a floral design.

Sind stitch.

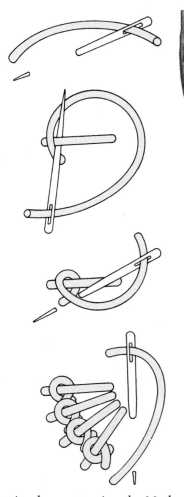

triangle, representing the Moslem tunic, with trousered feet underneath.

The Hindu women wear *paros*, skirts of voluminous proportions, made from two horizontal hoops of fabric, the lower one with a depth of 50 cm (19½ in) and an overall length of 5.5 m (6 yds).

The *paro* is made of heavy, rust-coloured cotton, often resist-dyed with an indigo, free-form, repeating pattern. The embroidery, which is also free-form and repeating, is not related to the printed design underneath. Flower and bird motifs are often used and the peacock is particularly popular. Designs are worked in ladder stitch, sind wheels and buttonhole stitch. Considerable mirror work is used, often with unusually shaped pieces of glass incorporated in the design.

Dresses, shirts and tunics frequently have black edging round the neck. This is not only for the practical purpose of obscuring any dirt, but also for warding off the evil eye.

Three-pointed motifs worked in sind stitch and ladder stitch recur frequently.

Sind border can be worked in ladder stitch with wheels of sind stitch forming the central circles.

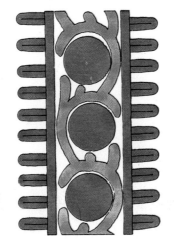

241

Until recently travelling Sindi embroideresses would visit Karachi, Hyderabad and other cities to offer their services for custom-embroidery, producing dress yoke panels and other items to order. The standard of embroidery of the panels was high, with brightly coloured satin-stitch devices outlined with black cord couched with cream thread. Further embellishment would be added in the form of rosettes known as *guls* and silk tassels, sometimes made of the same thread as the special silk ground of the yoke panels.

Another speciality in Sind is the *rilli* quilt, made with the cut-paper method similar to that found in Hawaii. Squares of cotton fabric are folded and cut so that, when opened out, they make circular patterns of cut-out holes like large doilies. They are then applied to a plain ground and quilted, often producing an effect of great intricacy.

More conventional quilting is also undertaken, some of it highly symbolic in design. A snake-charmer's quilt has jagged border patterns worked in four-sided stitch, the finished stitching strikingly resembling snakeskin in both appearance and touch.

Tree of life designs which could be copied today in surface satin stitch.

Corner design, the outline black thread couched with green silk.

Boy wearing traditional dress with shisha embroidery.

Kutch

Cotton, including the plain Gujarat calico known as *baftas*, is produced in Kutch, which lies inside the Indian border to the south of Sind.

Embroidery, some of which is quite outstanding, is worked on a ground of deep indigo or rust cotton. The most commonly used stitches are herringbone, interlacing, darning, satin, ladder and double cross. Mirror embroidery is also found. One of the characteristics of the region is the laid and couched thread used to outline each device.

Kutch embroidery patterns are more curvilinear than those of Sind. Peacocks are popular for designs, but they are more stylized than their Sindi counterparts. Another popular device is the swastika, a religious symbol believed to be a token of long life, good wishes and good fortune.

Most of the embroidery appears as costume decoration. The women house builders of Kutch have their own uniform, the *choli*, which is a short-sleeved backless bodice with a long front panel that tucks into the skirt. *Cholis* can be beautifully worked with interlacing, ladder and romanian stitch and mirror work.

Other women wear tunics with embroidery round the hem and on the yoke. Young girls wear the *ungia*, a bodice with embroidery down both sleeves and all over the front of the yoke, and boys wear an embroidered cap with a long back flap to shield them from the summer sun.

Curvilinear designs worked mainly in chain stitch are often found on wall hangings from Kutch.

Kutch women are still engaged today in producing fine embroidery.

Sind Dress

You will need:
4.5 m (4⅞ yd) fine cotton mixture fabric 90 cm (36 in) wide
16 m (17¼ yd) braid approx. 3 cm (1¼ in) wide to match fabric and with a woven pattern in gold

2 reels sewing cotton to match fabric
1 skein non-stranded embroidery cotton
2 spools washable metallic thread in gold
1 or 2 little buttons embroidery ring

Making the Dress

Make a full scale pattern from the diagram (see page 272), noting the position of the notches and the straight grain of the fabric. Turnings of 16 mm (⅝ in) have been allowed on all seams and 2.5 cm (1 in) on the bottom and sleeve hems.

Pin the pattern to the fabric and cut it out, adjusting the length if necessary.

Mark the centres of the front, back and sleeves. Baste and then sew a length of braid down each line. Add the other vertical lines of braid (see diagram). Finish them about 5 cm (2 in) from the hem where the horizontal braid will cover the ends.

Stitch the shoulder seams of the facings and kaftan and press them open. Overcast the unnotched edge of the facing.

Right sides together, pin the facings to the neck edge, matching centres and seams. Baste then stitch the neck edge. Sew a second line of stitching over the first as reinforcement.

Stitch the centre front opening. Trim the seam and corners, clip curves. Press the facing to the inside and catch stitch to the kaftan on the shoulder seams.

Pin the sleeves into the armholes, right sides together. Stitch and clip the curves and trim the seams. Press the seams away from the sleeve.

Embroidery

Mark the outlines of the embroidered designs on the fabric. Work the outlines in stem stitch using the matching cotton thread. Fill them with herringbone worked in gold. Use a large-eyed needle for the gold thread. Hold the work in an embroidery ring and avoid pulling the stitches too tightly.

Press the embroidery on the wrong side.

Finishing

Sew the side and sleeve seams all in one. Press them well.

Sew short lengths of braid in position over the bottom of the side seams.

Turn up the hems. Baste braid round the hems making sure it reaches the very edges of the garment, then stitch it. Press it well.

Sew one or two tiny buttons at the neck edge and fasten them with embroidered loops.

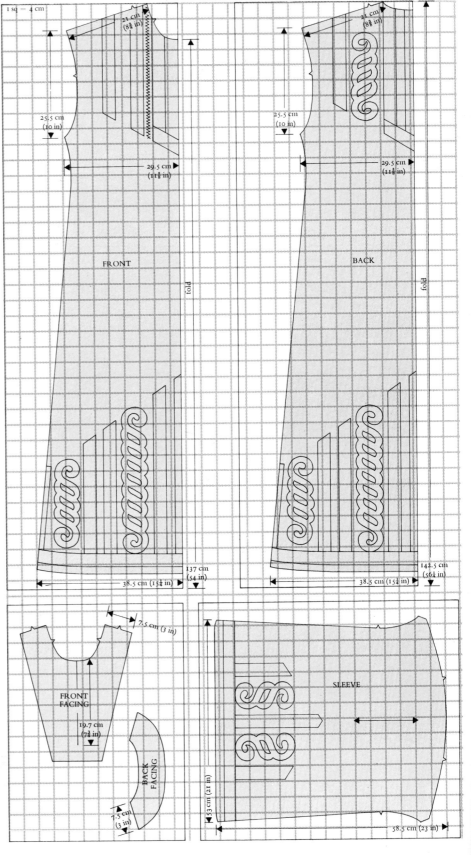

A glittering kaftan guaranteed to add sparkle to that extra special evening out. The design, inspired by the richly decorated Sind top on page 241, uses strips of metallic braid in place of embroidered bands together with gold thread embroidery worked in herringbone stitch.

Repeating design for the embroidery. Enlarge it to scale (see page 272) and make two tracings, once omitting the top curve and once omitting the bottom curve. Overlap the tracings to form the required number of segments for each embroidery position.

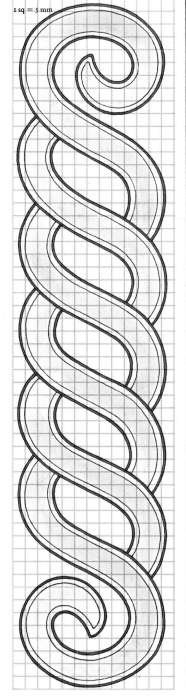

1 sq = 5 mm

Bengal

Motif with three flowers originally worked on natural linen with stitches radiating from the centre.

The old region of Bengal comprised the lowland areas drained by the Ganges and Brahmaputra rivers. It was bounded on the west by Bihar and on the east by Assam and Burma, and stretched almost as far as Bhutan in the north. Today it is divided between India (West Bengal) and Bangladesh, and has become one of the most densely populated regions in the world.

Bengal is noted for two types of embroidery, *tussur* silk quilts and *kantha*. *Tussur*-quilt making was apparently centred in the area north of Calcutta. Its heyday, at least for export, seems to have been from 1570 to 1677. Designs were pictorial though stylized and were worked with yellow monochrome silk in chain stitch and back-stitch quilting, some of them incorporating appliqué. The ground was coarse cotton or jute.

Bengal has long been known for its *tussur* silk fabric and thread, which is produced by the wild silkworm *Antheraea paphia*. *Tussur* is characteristically yellow in colour, although it is not as bright as *muga* silk from the worm *Antheraea assama*. In cocoon stage both species of worm hang from their host trees, and European merchants once thought that the silks were produced by plants and not worms.

The silk was used for both ground fabric and embroidery thread and embroidered pieces used to be made up into quilts, hangings, covers and tablecloths, worked with satin stitch and back stitch. Today, however, little or no work seems to be carried out with these materials.

Frugality has always played a major part in the everyday life of Bengal, and any scraps of cotton cloth are carefully saved to make *kanthas*, or rag embroideries.

The scraps, which are frequently salvaged from old cotton saris, are pieced together to achieve the proper size, and then embroidered. Even the embroidery thread is sometimes culled from the worn-out garments. The finished *kanthas* are then made up into quilts, wall hangings and clothing.

Kantha embroidery is designed and worked by women. Motifs are steeped in local traditions and symbolism. Triple shapes such as three flowers on one stalk and three prongs on a trident are used repeatedly, together with such motifs as the eight-petalled lotus flower, the tree of life, undulating lines, zigzags, vortices,

circles, squares and triangles.

The designs, which are outlined in dark blue thread, bear no relation to the pieced materials on which they are worked. They are filled in with either the same or a contrasting colour. Continuous lines are worked in back stitch, and an overall dotted effect, close parallel lines and geometric shapes are all produced with running stitch.

Early-19th-century marriage top with profuse shisha embroidery. Such a garment is a prized possession and handed down for generations.

Kantha embroidery with characteristic lines of running stitch and back stitch.

Goa

Indo-Portuguese bed quilt worked in golden silk in double running stitch and chain stitch which was probably tamboured.

The land settlements of Goa and Daman and the island of Diu, all on the west coast of India, were Portuguese colonies until 1962, when they became part of India. Embroidery had been a well-developed art even before the Portuguese arrived. It is said that when Affonso d'Albuquerque captured Goa in 1511, he was so impressed with the standard of embroidery that he sent some of the best embroiderers to Portugal as a gift for his queen. The ship, alas, capsized en route, with the loss of all on board.

Since then Goan embroidery has been greatly influenced by Christianity and by Portuguese work. Indeed, much of what is said about Portuguese embroidery in chapter 4 applies to Goan embroidery too.

Goan embroidery is generally associated with quilts of bleached white cotton decorated with tamboured chain stitch in yellow floss silk. There are marvellous hunting scenes, with men mounted on horses or elephants pursuing deer, birds or other game. The motifs are worked in outline embroidery only. Designs are freely interpreted and pictorial, and their execution usually skilful and intricate, resulting in work rather more complex than other floss-silk designs produced in the sub-continent.

Beetles' wings were used as spangles contrasting with laid and couched gold cord.

Detail of beetle-wing embroidery incorporating the traditional cone shape in a floral design.

Overseas Markets

The Indian sub-continent had already begun to export some embroidery before the 17th century, and in 1650 the East India Company began sending regular bulk shipments of embroideries to Europe. In many cases the work seems to have been based on European designs, which were carried out in the local style.

Tussur silk quilts were one of the early export favourites and in 1603 one was listed in the household inventory of Bess of Hardwick, an English gentlewoman and celebrated needlewoman, whose home gave a vivid interpretation of Elizabethan taste. In Napoleonic times Kashmir shawls became the rage in western Europe and then, towards the end of the 19th century, European vogue turned to innovation and extremes. In response, embroiderers in Madras and Hyderabad began to use the iridescent green wings of beetles, each about 2 cm ($\frac{3}{4}$ in) long, as spangles, piercing the wings with a retaining thread. Beetle-wing embroidery was used for table linen and a variety of covers, and also became popular as extraordinary fashion wear. Demand, albeit limited, continued for many years and as recently as 1928 Liberty's of London offered for sale a dress with beetle-wing decoration.

Indian ethnic embroidery is particularly popular today. Exports apparently come from all parts of the sub-continent, for the styles are diverse. Some of the embroidery is of high quality, but on the whole it has been rapidly produced and lacks the finish of the embroideries worn by local people.

China

The rich tradition of China's embroidery, which has influenced the art in many parts of the world, reflects the cultural importance of the Imperial court of Peking rather than the geographical divisions of this enormous country. The most famous and characteristic types of Chinese embroidery were worked in the court of the Imperial City before the Revolution of 1911. Between 1911 and 1949, during the Nationalist Republic, war with Japan and civil war, less embroidery was done in China, but today it is again being officially encouraged. This chapter considers the symbolism of Chinese embroidery, costume decoration, the embroidery of modern China, and Tibet, with its unique embroidery characteristics.

The Chinese were the first to discover how to spin and weave cloth from silk. Today China still produces nearly a quarter of the world's raw silk. Cotton is also farmed, but although cotton thread and fabric are sometimes employed, especially for folk embroideries, the embroidery of China generally consists of silk and metal thread stitching on a silk ground, sometimes in the form of a very fine gauze.

The Chinese had dye workshops as early as 3000 B.C. The five dominant colours traditionally used are blue, yellow, red, white and black, all produced from natural dyes. Safflower, used elsewhere to produce a soluble yellow dye, was generally used by Chinese dyers to achieve a red, in many cases a pinkish shade similar to legal 'red tape' binding.

Satin stitch is that most frequently used. Sometimes two embroiderers work together on a vertical frame to produce double-sided satin stitch in which exquisite pictures are worked without a 'reverse side'. Peking or chinese stitch is a form of interlaced back stitch, and a knot known as peking, chinese or

Worked in chain stitch on a silk ground fabric, this partridge was found in a tomb dating from the 5th century B.C.

Five-clawed *lung* dragon and sun motif in satin stitch, stem stitch and laid and couched thread, from an 18th-century emperor's robe.

the 'forbidden' knot is used for infilling motifs (see page 256).

'Voiding' between satin-stitch blocks is a characteristic technique of traditional Chinese embroiderers. Few western embroiderers, even in 18th-century France, ever attained the perfection of Chinese voiding, which is, however, rarely practised in China today. Another distinctive technique is to infill entire motifs with two parallel threads, usually gold, laid in coils and couched with bright red silk thread.

Appliqué was used for costume items such as collars worn by mandarins or officials at court. Patchwork, incorporated into some court embroideries, may still be used for domestic items. A type of Madeira work using pale blue thread on a white cotton ground decorates handkerchiefs and costume accessories exported to the West. Monochrome stitching may be done but China has no indigenous blackwork. Mirror work, sometimes padded, has been used to highlight silk embroidery on curtains and hangings.

Needlepoint is another popular Chinese technique. In the past silk and metal-thread tent stitches were worked in bird designs or in geometric patterns on a fine single-mesh silk canvas to decorate costume items and accessories.

Sampler embroidery was prevalent only at the beginning of the 20th century in the rural areas of Shensi and Szechwan and in Yunnan. Women worked with indigo-coloured cotton thread on a white cotton ground in cross-stitch motifs such as birds, butterflies and fish that may later have been used on aprons and children's clothing.

In the past, court embroideries—costume decoration, hangings and cushions—were generally worked by highly skilled men or women. In rural areas women embroidered. Some professional embroiderers worked specifically for the export market and panels of embroidered cloth would sometimes for example be made up into shoes in Italy. 'Export embroidery' may be distinguished by western features on the faces in the design, which was usually executed in silk and metal thread on a silk ground.

Detail of a mandarin's square: the golden pheasant, impresa of the first or second rank of civil official, embroidered in satin stitch, stem stitch and laid and couched work.

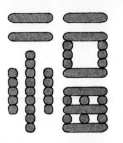

Symbolism

Most Chinese embroidery motifs are important for their symbolic significance. A white crane, symbol of the highest-ranking officials, might be shown looking towards a sun representing the emperor, to emphasize an official's loyalty to his ruler.

Many designs, especially those around the hems of court robes, have a natural composition of water, land and sky. Water is often represented by diagonal lines with scrolled waves above. Occasionally, rounded waves are shown. The 'sky' part of the design may be filled with a sacred mountain, various shapes of cloud, and with many symbolic devices.

Dragons may be shown with a water and sky backdrop or by themselves, usually with a front view on the front of a robe and seen from the side or from behind on the back. Despite their often ferocious appearance, with wisps of flame emphasizing their supernatural character, dragons are benevolent in oriental lore. They are often shown with an adjacent 'flaming jewel' motif.

Supreme in the dragon hierarchy is the five-clawed *lung* dragon. It is said to have been reserved for imperial use, but people outside the emperor's immediate family did sometimes wear robes embroidered with *lung* dragons. At least two Manchu emperors decreed that only they and their families could wear embroidered *lung* dragons and some lesser men had literally to unstitch one claw of the motif.

The four-clawed *mang* dragon could be worn by people outside the immediate royal family. Other dragon species included the *ying-lung*, a five-clawed dragon with giant bat-like wings particularly popular during the Ming dynasty (1368-1644), and the *tou-niu*, with down-sweeping horns and generally without an adjacent 'flaming jewel' motif. The *ch'ih* dragon, found decorating some children's robes, has only one horn and paw-like feet.

Other mythical beasts are also portrayed. The *ch'i-lin* has two horns on a dragon's head, the body of a stag covered with scales, cloven hoofs and a lion's tail. The *pai-tse*, another legendary beast, has a dragon's head with two horns, a lion's body and tail, and claws. Tigers, leopards and bears also feature in many Chinese embroideries, particularly on officials' robes.

Butterfly motifs symbolize conjugal felicity. Pink bats, also representing happiness, may occur in groups of five, symbolic of the five states of long life, wealth, tranquillity, love of virtue and a happy death.

Some birds significant in Chinese lore include the cock (like the sun, a symbol of masculinity), crane (symbol of long life and a messenger of the gods), dove (standing for long life as well as dullness and orderliness), duck (felicity, beauty and conjugal fidelity), falcon (authority and courage), goose (faithfulness), parrot (fidelity and brilliance), peacock (beauty and dignity), phoenix (generally reserved for the empress's personal use, a symbol of beauty and good fortune) and the swallow (speed and daring).

Among the many floral motifs found in Chinese embroideries are the almond, aster, azalea, camellia, cherry, gardenia, iris, jasmine, oleander, poppy and peony, all symbolizing feminine charms such as beauty, grace, good health and youth. The chrysanthemum sometimes stands for joviality and ease. There are two 'marriage' flowers, the convolvulus and the peach, which also stands for youth and immortality. The pomegranate hopes for fertility while the lotus combines fruitfulness with purity. The narcissus wishes good fortune, the pear symbolizes purity and justice and the rose stands for fragrance and prosperity.

There are also groups of related symbols such as the so-called twelve symbols first described in the ancient *Shu-ching* (Book of History). They are shown either alone or together, sometimes with the first six painted on a robe and the rest embroidered, usually on the skirt. The first ten symbols, namely the sun and moon, the constellations (which

The 'double felicity' character of calligraphy, here executed in close parallel satin stitches, is symbolic of conjugal happiness.

Detail from a 19th-century chair cover showing the *ch'i-lin*, a mythical animal of good omen, above a border of turbulent water.

White crane, symbol of the first-ranking civil official, facing the sun, which was one of the emperor's devices. Silk tent stitch on a silk ground.

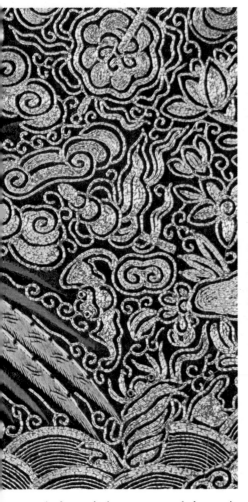

stand for enlightenment and heaven), mountains (protection and the earth), a dragon and pheasant (literary refinement), a pair of bronze sacrificial cups (filial piety), water-weed (purity), grain (the ability to feed the people) and fire (brilliance), were associated with various forms of court dress. The last two symbols, an axe (standing for the power to punish) and the *fu* device of prosperity and the power to judge, could be worn only by the emperor himself.

The four seasons are represented by the peony for spring, the lotus for summer, the chrysanthemum for autumn and the prunus or poppy for winter.

Other groups represent religious beliefs such as the eight Taoist genii (fans, bamboo flutes, swords, pairs of castanets, swords and crutches, drums, baskets and lotuses) and Buddhist lore (canopies, conch shells, fishes, lotuses, umbrellas, vases, wheels and knots).

The butterfly, symbolizing conjugal felicity, is one of a variety of airborne devices popular in Chinese embroidery. Here the design is worked in satin stitch with voiding, straight stitch and laid and couched thread.

Dragon pursuing the flaming jewel, with pink bats of happiness, cloud motifs and a border of diagonal lines which represent *li shui*, 'deep' or 'strong' water. Executed in satin stitch and laid and couched thread.

Design worked in indigo cross stitch on cotton. This was inspired by the legend of the carp which turned into a dragon after leaping through the Dragon Gate barring the gorge of the Hwang Ho, or Yellow River.

In two-sided satin stitch both threads pass through the same hole in the ground fabric, take a small stitch and return to the first side for a longer stitch.

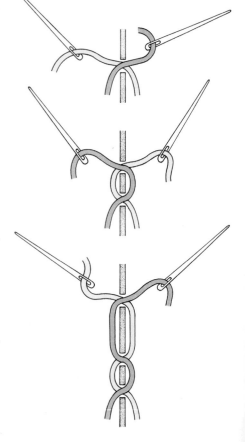

Calligraphy may be used symbolically in embroidery—an example is the double felicity character. Geometric devices like the swastika, symbolic of long life, are occasionally worked.

Human scenes portrayed often do not have any symbolism. Hunting and warring scenes are popular, sometimes with opposing factions' faces worked with differently coloured silk thread, and other themes include people in boats or feeding animals. Other Chinese designs recall legends such as that of the carp which leapt through the Dragon Gate

and was transformed into a dragon. When this motif is worked next to one of a small boy standing in a pavilion, it signifies the successful career of the boy.

In rural areas in western China, embroidery is often used as a substitute for more costly materials. Embroidered 'locket' designs on the upper front yokes of children's clothing take the place of silver lockets worn by more affluent children. Traditionally given by an elderly female relative, these supposedly contain the family's goodwill towards a child.

Costume

Dragon robe.

Court robe with *jen*.

Lady's court robe

'Mandarin's collar' with characteristic arabesque shapes.

Since the time of the Tang dynasty at least, ceremonial dresses of successive Chinese emperors and their retinues have been lavishly embroidered.

One of the emperor's various prerogatives was the wearing of yellow robes. His wardrobe included such items as short shirts made of yellow satin with embroidered medallions showing the *lung* dragon pursuing the flaming jewel.

The styles and decoration of the dress of other members of the court were rigidly controlled. In 1759 the Emperor Chi-ien formulated *Huang Ch'ao li Ch'i t'u shih* (The Illustrated Catalogue of Ritual Paraphernalia), which set out at least one hundred and fifty different costumes. The two best-known styles of men's court dress, worn by emperors and also by mandarins and other dignitaries, were the dragon and court robes, both made of heavy satin or other silk, although in summer a lightweight silk gauze might be preferred.

A dragon robe usually had these motifs embroidered on the front and back yokes, right across the central vertical seams of a made-up garment, and had other dragons set into a deep wave and sky border round the hem. It

was a full-length garment with a rounded neck opening extending diagonally from the front of the neck across the right chest. The upper sleeves, cut in one with the main body of the garment, were attached to lower sleeves of another fabric, which in turn were attached to cuffs with a rounded hemline.

A court robe had the same rounded shape transposed to front and back yoke panels. Side bodice panels cut in one with the sleeves were sewn, as before, to tight-fitting cuffs with rounded hemlines. The neck opening was the same as that of a dragon robe, and the whole upper 'tunic', attached to a wide waist belt, was worn with a pleated skirt which may or may not have been detachable. A distinguishing *jen*, a small flap of material attached below the side front of the belt, was a vestige of earlier versions of the court robe when the flap covered skirt fastenings underneath.

Both the dragon and court robes were liberally embroidered with silk and metal threads. Borders were usually worked round the edges of the diagonal neck opening, on the sleeves and cuffs and in a deep 'wave and cloud' or other design round the main hem. Medallions

or spot motifs decorated the main body of the robe, particularly on the central front and back yokes. The emperor's robe, with its exclusive yellow or navy ground fabric, often included the twelve symbols among its designs. Officials might wear motifs denoting their rank.

The first-ranking civil official was entitled to wear an embroidered crane or golden pheasant, the second a golden pheasant, the third either a peacock or a wild goose, the fourth a wild goose, the fifth a silver pheasant, the sixth an egret, the seventh a mandarin duck, the eighth a quail and the ninth and subsequent unclassified ranks a paradise flycatcher. In the military hierarchy, the first-ranking official could choose between a lion or a unicorn, his immediate inferior was represented by a lion, the third-rank official by a leopard, the fourth by a tiger, the fifth by a bear, the sixth by a panther, the seventh by a tiger cat, the eighth by a seal and the ninth by a rhinoceros.

With the main court dress a variety of other embroidered clothing was worn, including waistcoats and over-collars. Sleeveless hip-length waistcoats were front-opening, with high rounded necks

and deep fringing round the hem. Embroidery was worked either direct on both front and back yokes of the garment or, especially since the Ming dynasty, on *p'u-tzu*, square or round panels, often known as 'mandarins' squares'. Pairs of panels were worked with the same design. One was hemmed to the back of the waistcoat and the other, divided into two before being embroidered, was attached on either side of the front opening.

Officials also wore over-collars, unattached to any other item of clothing, formed from diamond shapes of silk about 56 cm (22 in) square. The four corners were cut in distinctive arabesque outline and the whole ground was decorated with a smaller applied piece of fabric of similar shape. A round neck hole was cut, and a front opening bisected one of the corners of the collar. As well as the main applied panel, braid was sewn on, and embroidery worked in polychrome silks in satin stitch and tent stitch in floral or picturesque devices before the whole was finally surrounded by deep silk fringing.

Women's main court robes were similar to those of the men. The empress,

who had a personal motif of a phoenix, wore the most sumptuously decorated costume. Women at court sometimes wore a robe cut like a man's except that the front diagonal opening was somewhat modified and the upper sleeves extended direct from the side of the upper part of the dress. Over her dress a woman could wear a front-opening sleeveless coat similar to a man's, and also decorated front and back with officials' panels denoting the rank of her husband. Women also wore full-length trousers with tight cuffs, sometimes embroidered with small water and cloud motifs, and a variety of shoes, including silk slippers embroidered all over with motifs infilled with peking knots, or platform slippers raised on high wooden soles. Hemmed to the main front ground of the silk uppers of these were applied pieces of black silk, embroidered with gold thread laid and couched in symmetrical motifs.

Accessories such as men's tobacco pouches, bags and fans, used both by men and women, were sometimes embroidered, usually with peking knots, satin stitch and laid and couched work forming floral or other typical devices.

Detail of a marriage robe in the Imperial yellow, embroidered with the five-clawed *lung* dragon and other motifs including clouds, fans and pink bats of happiness. 'Double felicity' characters appear, as well as geometric devices, among them the swastika.

Mandarin's square or *p'u-tzu* showing a mythological beast surrounded by symbolic devices. Blocks of satin stitch are separated by voiding and the beast's mane and tail are of laid and couched gold thread.

The white crane on this mandarin's square symbolizes long life and the messenger of the gods as well as being the emblem of the first-ranking civil official.

The *p'u-tzu* or mandarin's square was often circular in shape.

Sumptuous coats are sometimes made from pieces of different-coloured brocades and other silks before being richly embroidered.

Sleeve band of yellow silk, said to have belonged to the Empress Dowager Tz'u-hsi, embroidered with a crested pheasant.

Children at the court wore clothing similar to that of their elders. A prince's dragon robe, for instance, was simply a smaller-scale version of a man's costume, sometimes embroidered with the distinctive *ch'ih* dragon.

Outside the court, priests sometimes wore silk shoulder-length hoods embroidered with typical Chinese satin-stitch motifs such as dragons and flowers, and their main robes were either decorated with appliqué or embroidered with laid and couched silk and gold cord.

Particularly in the 18th and 19th centuries, Chinese theatrical costume was often embroidered. Some robes were cut as simple versions of court costume, rather like a man's loose dressing gown with a characteristic Chinese diagonal front opening. Embroidery was subsequently worked in a water pattern around the hem and in spot motifs over

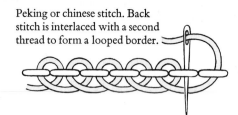

Peking or chinese stitch. Back stitch is interlaced with a second thread to form a looped border.

Peking knot. Hold the thread down gently at A and pull the needle through for the next stitch at B.

Peking knots worked as infilling to a design outlined in laid and couched white cord.

Voiding. A hair's breadth of fabric shows between adjacent blocks of satin stitch.

Flowing design worked on a silk sleeve band in tamboured chain stitch.

the main ground. For special roles, actors wore unique embroidered outfits suitable to the part they were playing.

Traditional dress throughout rural China was often not embroidered. A basic Chinese costume, established about the 6th century B.C. and worn by both sexes, consisted of a long belted tunic with a coat on top. From this stemmed regional costume such as that of Peking, where men and women both used to wear hip-length tunics over loose full-length trousers. Women's tunics, with distinctive diagonal front openings, were sometimes embroidered in silk with satin-stitch designs on the front yokes and around the main hems.

In Fukien, in the south-east of the country, women traditionally wore full-length trousers under knee-length front diagonal-opening tunics with wide sleeves attached to cuffs about 9 cm (3½ in) wide. Some of these were embroidered in silks and gold threads with flowers and butterflies in satin stitch and

laid and couched work.

To the far north, in Manchuria, which was subject to Japanese occupation during the 19th and early 20th centuries, some forms of traditional dress, including women's tall winged hats and front diagonal-opening full-length coats with wide sleeves, are similar to Korean and Japanese designs. Cuffs as well as borders round the neck, down the front opening and round the main hem are decorated with applied bands of embroidery.

Apart from theatrical costume, embroidered dress has not been worked in China since 1911. Fortunately many exquisite items have survived in private and museum collections, especially in western Europe and North America. Old court and dragon robes are still occasionally to be found in auction houses and exclusive boutiques. Embroidered bands of silk fabric intended for sleeve cuffs or border edging for robes, and sometimes having been used as such, are frequently on sale.

Details of voiding and (foot of page) split stitch and laid and couched work.

Embroidery Today

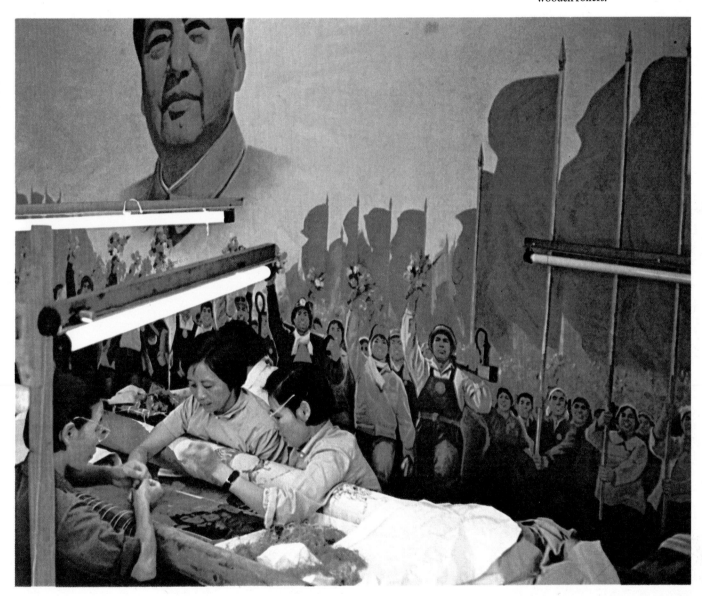

Dragons or other symbolic Chinese emblems were in the past worked on court and domestic items such as cushions, banners, particularly for weddings, and wall hangings as well as on costume. Some decorative embroidery is still being worked today, usually in government factories, and it is generally women who embroider. Wearing white aprons and protective arm bands, they work in well-appointed surroundings.

Some embroiderers work beautiful two-sided satin-stitch pictures which are then framed, glazed on both sides and exported, often to Australia. Alternatively, using single-needle satin stitch and working from one face only, women execute gigantic and sometimes complex patterns of animals, flowers and geographical scenes with polychrome silks on a plain silk ground fabric. The required design is drawn on to the material before embroidery commences, and the embroiderer works on a horizontal frame, sometimes with a mirror so angled that she can see the reverse of the ground fabric. As with two-needle satin-stitch embroideries, these single-face pictures are usually intended for export, as are such costume items as women's white or cream silk blouses decorated with self-coloured silk satin stitch in floral motifs with stem-stitch foliage. Other pieces worked primarily for export include handkerchiefs and tablecloths decorated with Madeira work, reticella or another cutwork technique.

Needlepoint is still executed, particularly in the Hung Shin Needlepoint Factory in Shanghai and the Yingtai Tapestry Centre in Shantung. Men and women embroiderers usually work two to an item, one seated at either end of a waist-high horizontal frame. They work from colour photographs directly onto the canvas, executing cross stitch and tent stitch in woollen yarns, and may use 700 different shades on a design. Hangings with themes such as 'the Great Wall of China' are popular, as are portraits of tigers and other animals, and trees.

Dragon Robe

This heavy oriental-style robe with its richly embroidered dragon is ideal for formal dinner parties. The design may be worked by hand or machine.

You will need:
3.5 m (3⅞ yd) heavy cotton fabric 90 cm (36 in) wide
3 m (3¼ yd) lightweight calico 90 cm (36 in) wide for the backing
3.5 m (3⅞ yd) satin lining 90 cm (36 in) wide
sewing cotton to match
44 skeins stranded cotton hand embroidery) or
28 reels mercerized sewing cotton (machine embroidery) in 8 colours:
red 5 skeins/3 reels
yellow 6 skeins/4 reels
orange 8 skeins/6 reels
light blue 7 skeins/5 reels
dark blue 6 skeins/4 reels
silver grey 4 skeins/2 reels
brown 4 skeins/2 reels
black 4 skeins/2 reels
bias seam binding (optional)
4 hooks and eyes
embroidery hoop

Preparing the Fabric

Make a full-size copy of the pattern pieces (see page 272), following the appropriate outline for the required size.

Pin the pieces to the cotton fabric and baste round all the outlines but the front. Cut out the piece for the front but do not cut out the other pieces yet (this allows for damp stretching after the embroidery has been worked).

Cut out a piece of backing for the front and baste the fabrics together round the edge. Baste the remaining backing to the wrong side of the other sections, using vertical and horizontal lines of stitches 5 cm (2 in) apart. Cut out the lining.

Scale up the dragon using grid lines 3 cm (1¼ in) apart and transfer the design to the fabric using basting stitches of a different colour from those holding the backing. Transfer the embroidery design to the neck and cross-over bands, repeating it as necessary to fill the area.

Embroidery

By hand. Mount the fabric in a hoop. Using two strands of cotton, work the motif from the top down, using vertical long-and-short stitch in the colours indicated.

By machine. Mount the fabric in a hoop by placing it over the larger ring and

Full-size motifs for the neckband. Trace and repeat as many times as necessary, adjusting heights of motifs as desired, for the length of the band.

inserting the smaller ring from the right side (this is the reverse of hand embroidery).

Prepare the machine by removing the presser foot, lowering the feed dog and setting to swing-needle stitching. Adjust the tension so that the bobbin thread is tighter than the upper thread.

Using mercerized cotton in the colours indicated, work one area of the design at a time. There is no need to change the bobbin thread each time you change the top colour because the adjusted tension ensures an evenness of colour on the right side.

Making the Robe

Damp stretch the embroidery (see page 272) using a large table, smooth door, piece of chip board or bare floorboards as a base. Wait until the embroidery is perfectly dry before unpinning (this could take up to three days).

Pin the paper pattern pieces to the embroidered fabric, making sure the dragon is placed centrally on the back and 12 cm (5 in) down from the nape of the neck. Cut out.

Use 1.5 cm ($\frac{5}{8}$ in) seams throughout and press them well at every stage.

Join one of the back neck pieces and one of each of the cross-over bands at the shoulders. Repeat this with the other pieces, which will act as facings. Baste the two sets of pieces together, right sides facing, and stitch along the neck edge and along each short side.

Join the shoulder and side seams of the robe, leaving the left side open at the bottom for the split.

With right sides together, baste and stitch the neck pieces to the top of the garment. Set in the sleeves.

Assemble the lining. Turn the garment inside out and pin the lining to it. Check that the garment hangs properly before turning in the raw top edge of the lining and sewing it to the neck facing.

Neaten the side slit by turning the extra seam allowance to the inside over the lining and hemming it down.

Turn up the hems of both sleeves and robe, using binding if you wish.

Sew on the neck fastenings.

Remove all the pins and basting threads and give the garment a final pressing.

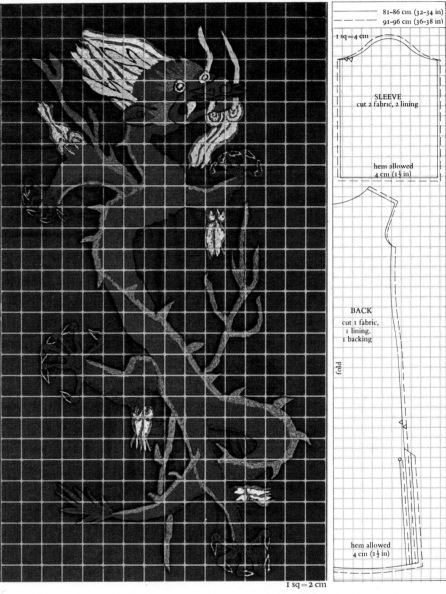

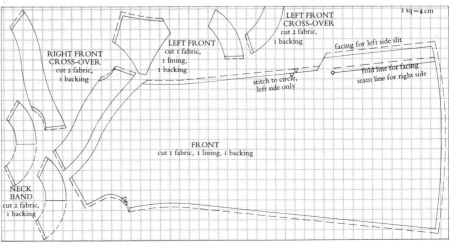

Tibet

Religious wall hangings known as *tankas* are a famous feature of the autonomous region of Tibet. Some are worked in silk and gold threads on plain or printed silk ground fabrics. Sizes range from 61 × 51 cm (24 × 20 in) to 203 × 102 cm (80 × 40 in). Although women spin and weave, men embroider, either hemming motifs to the ground fabric or working long-and-short stitch or satin stitch directly on that fabric.

Until the Chinese intervention of 1951 and the departure eight years later of the Dalai Lama, an estimated one quarter of the adult populace was involved in religious orders of Tibetan Buddhism. Aspects of Tibetan Buddhist beliefs are shown in the designs of some of the embroidered wall hangings, most of which feature at least one *bodhisattva* ('celestial Buddha to be'), invariably haloed and bejewelled and sometimes with more than one pair of hands. The Great Buddha of the West, known variously as Amitabha ('boundless light') or Amitayus ('boundless life'), is one popular theme, generally with the figure sitting cross-legged on a throne backed by clouds, trees or mountains.

Some terrestrial beings are portrayed on *tankas*, although it is difficult for the uninitiated to distinguish between a true god and a guru such as Padmasam-Bhava, who introduced Tantric doctrines into Tibetan Buddhism in the 18th century. Alternatively, the main embroidered motif may be one of the many forms of Buddhist wheel of life, with five or six segments representing components of life such as material qualities, feelings, perception and consciousness, or with buddhas representing the universe and compass points.

On festivals such as the Tibetan New Year (February or March of the Gregorian calendar) or the fifteen-day-long Smom-lam prayer festival which begins three days later, special religious hangings as large as 4.5 m (5 yd) in height, were displayed at lamaseries throughout Tibet.

Organized religion is now outlawed in Tibet but many of the best examples of *tankas* have been preserved in collections elsewhere, particularly in places with current or former trading links with this part of Asia, such as India and Nepal.

As well as religious hangings, appliqué

Tanka embroidered on brocaded ground fabric. The haloed god and four-clawed *mang* dragon are worked in satin stitch, stem stitch and laid and couched thread.

Brocaded Tibetan costumes are worn with hats and full-length back scarves, both of them decorated with beadwork.

has traditionally been used for secular purposes in Tibet. Sometimes combined with patchwork of different-coloured triangles and squares of fabric hemmed one to the other, applied motifs are used to decorate the tents and animal trappings of some of the nomadic peoples scattered throughout this mountainous country. Dragons and god-like devices, rough arabesques and fret designs cut from pieces of woollen and cotton fabric are either hemmed by hand or machine stitched to a ground of thick cotton.

Tibetan Motif

The flower motifs worked on the ties of this blouse have been adapted from a traditional national costume of Tibet and the colours have been kept as close as possible to the originals. Use the motifs to decorate any part of a dress or blouse. Alternatively, work them on a bag or belt.

You will need:
stranded embroidery cotton,
   1 skein in each of six colours:
yellow
blue
green
pale pink
dark pink
pale mauve

Preparing the Fabric
Unpick the seams of the garment as necessary so that the embroidery may be worked through one thickness of the fabric only. If the decoration is to go on a pocket, unpick the stitching completely.

Trace the motifs, or make them larger or smaller as necessary (see page 272) and transfer them to the fabric.

Embroidery
Use two strands of cotton throughout.

Large motif
Work all the outlines in stem stitch using dark pink for the outer petals and central diamond, blue for the inner petals and pale pink for the shape holding the diamond. Fill the shapes with satin stitch using the chart as a guide to colours. To avoid forming long, loose stitches, work them in the shortest direction across each segment of the motifs. Check that the stitches in corresponding segments on each side of the motifs lie in the same direction.

Small motif
Work all outlines in blue stem stitch and fill them with satin stitch as before.

Finishing
Press the embroidered area with a damp cloth and medium-hot iron. Re-sew any seams. If the motifs have been worked on blouse ties, slipstitch the unpicked edges together.

East and South-East Asia

The strongest embroidery traditions in the area which stretches eastwards from Burma to Hawaii, skirting China and reaching north to include Japan, are found in the Korean peninsula, the Japanese islands, south-east Asia with Burma and Thailand, Indonesia, the Philippines and in other Pacific islands. Other parts of the area, including Australia and New Zealand, practise embroidery extensively and skilfully but have no indigenous ethnic style.

Appliqué is an almost universal form in this vast area. Stitches that are widely used include buttonhole stitch, especially in Burma, chain stitch and cross stitch, particularly in Indonesia, and satin stitch, especially in Korea, Japan and Indonesia. Laid and couched work and metal-thread embroidery are also associated with Korea, Japan and Indonesia. Padded embroidery is a Japanese speciality and needlepoint is also popular there. Whitework embroidery is practised in the Philippines, some of it in drawn-thread and pulled-thread techniques. Hawaii is famous for quilting.

Throughout the region most embroidery is worked with silk or metal threads on a ground of silk or cotton. Silk is still extensively farmed on the west coast of Korea, in Japan and in Thailand. Cotton is grown in Burma, northern Thailand and the Philippines. Sometimes the ground fabric is an ikat, made by a process in which yarn, before being woven, is dyed by the tie-dyeing method to correspond with the desired pattern.

Silk and cotton are among many materials found in embroidery in these areas. Pineapple fibre is used in the Philippines; the Ainu of Hokkaido used bark and leather; cowrie shells are worked as spangles by the Shan of eastern Burma and in Indonesia; and stitched feathers are found in work from some Pacific islands.

Natural dyes that have been used include safflower for red and yellow, heart wood of *Caesalpinia sappan Leguminosae* for another red, and indigo or *Polygonum aviculare* for blues.

Embroideries of many parts of eastern Asia betray foreign influences and have in turn lent their styles to embroiderers elsewhere. In Vietnam, for instance, artists have adapted many Chinese designs for silk embroidery worked in long-and-short stitch and laid and couched work. Techniques of Chinese embroidery were also transmitted via the Korean peninsula to Japan as early as the 5th century A.D. European embroidery techniques were introduced into Indonesia from the Netherlands, particularly during the 19th century. Drawn-thread and pulled-thread embroideries reminiscent of some western European styles are found in the Philippines, and quilting was introduced to Hawaii in the early 19th century by American women. In contrast, Japanese styles became popular in western Europe at the end of the 19th century.

Every major world religion is represented in these widely scattered countries, and several of them have influenced embroidery designs, although no theme is common to the entire area. Buddhism is prevalent in the Korean peninsula, in Burma and Thailand, and is important in Japan. Islam is dominant in Indonesia and is important in the southern Philippines. Christianity has influenced traditional embroidery in the mainly Catholic Philippines. Secular motifs employed widely include

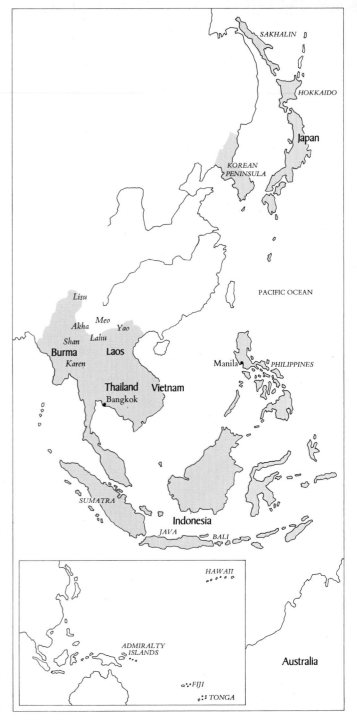

18th-century Japanese *fukusa*,-silk and gilt thread on satin.

flowers, animals and birds, and triangles and other geometric devices.

In the past embroidery was used in Korea and Japan for men's and women's robes. It is still used for costumes worn by Shan women in eastern Burma, by Ainu men and women in Hokkaido, by some of the hill tribes in Thailand, and by women in Indonesia. Wall hangings and curtains are embroidered in Korea, Japan, Burma and Thailand; cushion covers and table linens are worked in Indonesia and the Philippines, and quilted bedcovers are a Hawaiian speciality. In Australia and New Zealand women practise universal forms of embroidery with some of the highest standards in the world.In Japan, Burma, Thailand, the Philippines and Hawaii, local techniques continue to be popular.

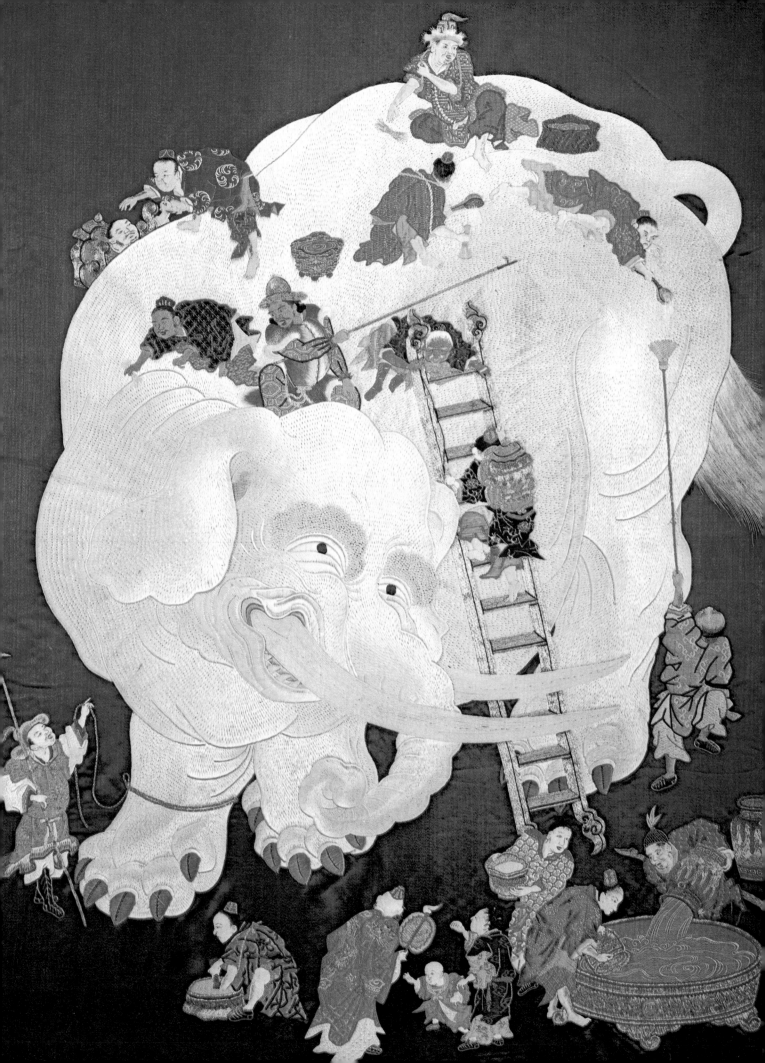

Japan

Most of the fabric and thread used in traditional embroideries is provided by the country's own extensive silk industry. Popular techniques include long-and-short stitch, peking knots, satin stitch—often with voiding—and straight stitch. Laid and couched work is widely practised, either outlining a device or as infilling, and sometimes in 'diaper' formation (diagonal couching). Another popular form is pattern darning, sometimes known as *kogin* work.

Buddhism has had more influence than other religions on Japanese embroidery designs, particularly on priests' robes, pictures and religious hangings as well as everyday items. Secular embroidery includes many flower, fruit, bird, cloud and fan devices, often bordered by a curved band of close parallel satin stitches. Secular embroidery in Japan, unlike China, has generally been worked by skilled women, either professionally or for themselves.

Japanese Imperial court dress derived its styles from those of the court in Peking. Women wore multi-layered outfits, the outermost garment beautifully decorated with brushwork painting, tie-dyeing and embroidery in silk and metal thread.

In about the 16th century the *kosode*, a garment worn by men or women under full court dress, was elevated to outer wear. Two lengths of silk or occasionally of linen fabric were folded horizontally at the shoulders and partly joined together to form back and side vertical seams. Short sleeves were set into the main body of the garment. In later examples, longer pieces of fabric were used for the sleeves, and the kimono developed. Various forms of kimono are still worn by Japanese women. Embroidery may be worked over most of the ground fabric, in a wide yoke panel or with motifs spotted throughout. The obi, a wide sash tied under the bust, may also be embroidered.

The Japanese theatre, like that in China, has made use of embroidered decoration —particularly in the highly stylized Noh dramas, with masked actors in symbolic costume.

Sets of large silk wall hangings, embroidered in silks and in metal thread, depicting natural or traditional themes

Motifs worked in satin stitch may be subsequently embroidered with long straight stitches regardless of the alignment of the satin-stitch base.

Performers in *Manzai Raku*, solemn court music, wear long embroidered robes with trains.

worked in surface stitching and with some motifs padded to give a three-dimensional effect, were sometimes presented to important visitors by members of the Imperial court. On a more modest level were *fukusas*, covers of silk about 46-61 cm (18-24 in) square, used to wrap presents, but later returned to the donor. They were made either individually or in sets of related designs.

Rozashi, needlepoint, was traditionally used to decorate bags and household items. Today it is generally worked on double-weave canvas over a small horizontal frame. Motifs such as flowers, butterflies and fans are worked in vertical blocks of horizontal satin stitches and perhaps outlined with a laid and couched thread. The canvas is then turned through 90° so that the effect is of upright gobelin stitch.

The Ainu, living on Hokkaido and on the more northerly Russian island of Sakhalin, traditionally wear ankle-length

Fukusa dating from the 18th century. Silk ground fabric embroidered with satin stitch and laid and couched work in silk and gold thread.

coats, sometimes of bark or skin, decorated with motifs such as crescent shapes similar to those used by Siberian embroiderers, and symmetrical devices resembling mazes. Ainu women work embroidery on fronts, backs and sleeves of coats and on matching skull caps.

18th-century bride's dress (detail).

Korea

Until the Treaty of Shimonoseki (1895) and the end of Chinese rule in Korea, high-ranking court officials wore embroidered dress in the Chinese style (see chapter 12). For special occasions people wore sumptuous silk brocaded coats embroidered with polychrome silks and gold thread, often in satin stitch.

Characteristic of traditional Korean embroidery is the use of a number of gold or silk threads laid and couched in close parallel formation, following the contour of a design. Korean motifs, adapted from Chinese symbols or from devices of Buddhism or Taoism, included vases, baskets and lotuses and were formalized into more rigid, almost geometric shapes. Even the typical Chinese water and cloud design was further stylized, Korean waves being executed with tight concentric circles of laid and couched threads. Nowadays, however, embroidery is less widely practised in the Korean peninsula than in other parts of south-east Asia.

Thailand

Appliqué is practised in Thailand as in neighbouring Burma but although Buddhist symbols sometimes appear, the motifs are principally secular.

Thai women work wall hangings, generally about 96 x 56 cm (38 x 22 in), either for their own homes or, increasingly today, for sale in stores in Bangkok. They hem motifs of dragons, lions and other animals cut from printed or plain fabric to a plain-coloured locally produced cotton ground, often red or green, and add ric-rac or straight braid or ribbon held to the ground with long straight stitches. Buttons or narrow oval seeds are sewn on as beads and buttonhole stitch and other stitches are worked direct to the ground fabric.

These wall hangings are worked mainly in the Bangkok area; Thailand's other principal region of embroidery interest is in the northern hills. Here women spin local cotton and weave it on upright looms. They then use the fabric to make costume items for their family.

Although most of the hill tribes of this area wear clothes of black or indigo cotton, various decorative techniques are employed. The Lahu and the opium-cultivating Meo, many of whom crossed into Thailand from northern Laos in recent times, practise buttonhole stitch, cross stitch and appliqué with bright-coloured cotton motifs, often pink, machine stitched or hemmed by hand to the ground fabric. The Karen, another hill group, living also in neighbouring Burma, generally embroider directly on a ground fabric; the Akha work in both appliqué and direct embroidery; the Lisu concentrate on appliqué and the Yao prefer appliqué and cross-stitch embroidery.

Traditional dress, still in general use, varies from tribe to tribe, but in many instances men wear loose cotton jackets with applied neckbands hemmed to the main ground, sometimes with wide cummerbunds and small frontal aprons decorated with applied cotton strips, and below-the-knee loose cotton trousers. Most women wear simple blouses and *sarongs*, knee-length skirts made of single long pieces of cotton fabric wrapped around the body.

Meo women favour hip-length long-sleeved cotton tunics with waist-deep

front neck openings bordered with brightly coloured cotton appliqué, below-the-knee full skirts with deep bands of appliqué parallel to the hem, and full-length tight-fitting trousers, usually undecorated. Applied motifs such as horseshoe shapes, triangles or other geometric devices are usually worked in repeating form and are machine stitched or hemmed by hand to the ground fabric.

As well as on everyday dress, embroidery appears on some of the hill tribes' special flirtation costumes worn during courting ceremonies which may last many days. Meo girls, for instance, make up their faces with red paint on their cheeks and with other cosmetics. They wear many silver neckbands and other items of jewellery and over their everyday dress they wear bright turquoise ankle-length front waist aprons, about 38 cm (15 in) wide, with horizontal bands of differently coloured cotton

Eight-pointed star motif worked in cross stitch, with characteristic Yao use of colour.

Although the Lisu most frequently work appliqué, they also do some embroidery using pattern darning, stem stitch and cross stitch, usually on a black or indigo background.

The 'double eye' pattern of the Black Lahu is worked as a border on women's tunics. Applied motifs are hemmed to a cotton ground fabric and decorated with laid and couched cords.

Detail of cotton appliqué from the Bangkok area. Outlined in chain stitch, the motif is decorated with stem stitch, running stitch, straight stitch and with sewn-on buttons.

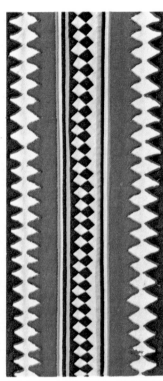

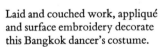

Laid and couched work, appliqué and surface embroidery decorate this Bangkok dancer's costume.

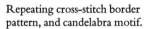

Repeating cross-stitch border pattern, and candelabra motif.

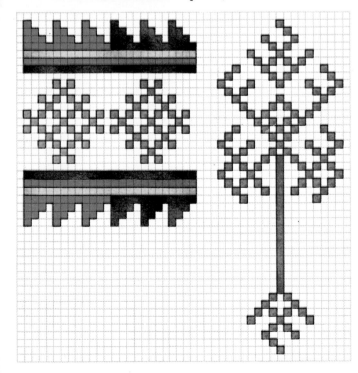

267

Thai actresses, like dancers,
wear costumes richly embroidered
with metal thread and spangles.

fabric sections hemmed to the ground material.

Courting costume is also a speciality of neighbouring Yao embroiderers. Girls of marriageable age wear full-length trousers with cuffs embroidered in special designs known as 'big flower tail', 'tiger's ear' and so on. The Yao are scattered throughout northern Thailand as well as parts of Vietnam, Laos and China. The Thai Yao women work polychrome silk threads, with many shades of the popular Thai pink dominating, in vertical and diagonal cross stitch and single straight stitch, executing repeating diamond, horseshoe or step shapes or complicated individual swastika or candelabra motifs.

Yao women are enthusiastic embroiderers and can be seen in their villages sitting on low stools embroidering in groups. Girls learn the art when they are five or six years old and, unusually for eastern Asia, they sometimes execute designs on trouser cuffs as samplers.

Burma

Detail from a Shan embroidered border. The designs are infilled with buttonhole stitch and outlined with split stitch.

This *kalanga*, with hemmed appliqué and laid and couched work, is of non-religious origin and once hung in a tobacco shop.

More than three-quarters of the people of Burma profess Buddhism and their religion inspires many *kalangas*, appliqué hangings decorated with pictorial themes, stories of Buddha's incarnation or of the cults of spirits and divinities. They can be seen in temples and in private homes on festival and special occasions. Working with scraps of local cotton fabric, Burmese women cut out motifs and hem the raw edges to a ground fabric of cotton or velvet. Ric-rac braid, spangles and laid and couched metal thread or silk straight stitches are then added.

In the high Shan plateau in the east of the country, women wear loose hip-length or knee-length short-sleeved jackets and ankle-length skirts formed either from one length of cotton fabric usually imported from China, or from a joined tube of fabric. In both cases, parallel tucks are made along the warp threads near one selvedge, which later forms the hem of the garment. Silk buttonhole stitch and running and double running stitch, sometimes highlighted with cowrie shells, are worked on the sleeves, front yoke and lower body of the jacket or tunic, and in a deep band above the skirt tucks, in repeating patterns which include zigzags and buttonholed 'wheels'.

Indonesia

Detail of a jacket from the west coast of Sumatra worked in chain stitch, straight stitch, satin stitch and pattern darning.

Skirts formed of lengths of cloth sewn into tubes are occasionally embroidered. This design comes from southern Sumatra.

The Indonesian archipelago is most famous in textile terms for batik, ikat and printed decoration. The embroidery worked today still displays a Dutch heritage in such techniques as cross stitch, satin stitch and pattern darning. Men and women embroider, using imported thread and fabrics. As well as plain-coloured silk and cotton, velvet is a popular ground fabric, especially for women's ceremonial headdresses.

Embroiderers practise a variety of different techniques including appliqué and needle or tamboured chain stitch, sometimes in parallel lines of alternating colours. Laid and couched work is popular, with gold threads couched with silk, singly or in pairs, with infilling in diamond formation or with flat gold strips laid in zigzags and couched at each bend with long straight stitches. Alternatively, gold or silver thread is laid in zigzag form over a card template and similarly couched at each

bend. Pattern darning, a speciality of the western island of Sumatra, is worked with long straight vertical stitches forming pot-shaped motifs, their outlines subsequently emphasized by a single gold thread laid and couched with silk. Cowrie shells and small pieces of coloured glass are sometimes incorporated.

The majority of Indonesians profess the Sunni form of Islam and embroidery designs are therefore often abstract, although some bird motifs are employed. Devices such as intertwined circles reminiscent of streamers or ribbons suggest Japanese influence. Floral designs are popular, sometimes built up with small petal- and leaf-shaped cotton motifs hemmed to a ground fabric and connected with stems consisting of a single laid and couched thread. Other floral designs are worked entirely with satin stitch or with parallel lines of laid and couched gold thread. Geometric devices are also worked, with basic

eight-pointed stars stylized to look rather like calligraphy.

Embroidery is used especially for decorating women's costume and for household items. Women wear satin *kebayas*, waist-length blouses with inset below-the-elbow sleeves and front neck openings, sometimes tied at the waist. Some *kebayas* have embroidery around the neck and cuffs, with repeating floral designs worked in satin stitch. With their *kebayas*, women wear the ubiquitous south-east Asian *sarong*, sometimes embroidered with repeating cross-shaped motifs formed from double lines of gold thread laid and couched with silk, or with bird-like figures outlined with pairs of laid and couched gold threads and infilled with diamond-couched gold thread and pieces of coloured glass attached in mirror-work style.

As well as costume decoration, embroidery embellishes square or round silk scatter cushions and large tablecloths.

Sumatran Cushion

You will need:
cushion pad 0.9 m (3 ft) square
2 pieces of hessian (burlap)
    0.95 m (38 in) square, 16
    threads to 2.5 cm (1 in)
knitting yarn in two colours:
light colour 1 ball
dark colour 1 ball
sewing cotton to match hessian

This striking floor cushion incorporates chain-stitch motifs as well as pattern darning based on Sumatran designs. The simple stitches worked in wool on a coarsely woven fabric are quick to embroider and make a practical and cheerful item for the home.

Preparing the Fabric

Overcast the edges of the hessian (burlap) squares by hand or with zigzag machine stitch to prevent fraying. Fold one of the squares in half vertically and then horizontally and baste along the crease lines.

Embroidery

Using the chart as a guide to both the colours and the stitches, start at the centre with a single eyelet stitch.

Work outwards from the centre until you reach the band of chain-stitch motifs. At this point it may be helpful to make a tracing of the full-size motifs, and transfer it to the fabric (see page 272). Enlarge the tracings so that the depth of the corner motif is 16.5 cm (6½ in) and that of the other motifs is 14 cm (5½ in). Alternatively, draw the motifs onto the hessian freehand, using a felt-tipped pen.

Continue the embroidery, working inwards from the border to the chain-stitch motifs and leaving 5 cm (2 in) between the edges of the fabric and the detached chain stitches.

Making the Cushion

Press the work face down on a thick towel taking care not to flatten the embroidery.

With right sides facing, baste the two squares together round three edges taking 2.5 cm (1 in) turnings. Stitch, press and turn the cover right side out.

Insert the cushion pad. Turn in 2.5 cm (1 in) on the open edges and slipstitch the folds together.

centre   star stitch   brick stitch   running stitch

chain stitch

chain stitch

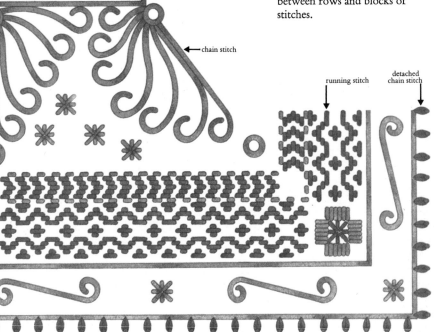

running stitch

detached chain stitch

This diagram shows an eighth of the design plus part of the adjoining segment to indicate how the corners are worked. Complete this second segment in mirror image of the first and then draw in the remaining three-quarters in the same way.

Work each eyelet star stitch over six threads in each direction from its centre and all the other stitches over four or eight threads of fabric. Leave two threads between rows and blocks of stitches.

Philippines

Catholicism was introduced to the Philippines when the islands were a Spanish colony and today Filipino girls are still taught to embroider in convents and schools. They work fine embroidery with white silk thread on a ground fabric of fine white cotton. Most cotton and silk is imported, but the Philippines do possess indigenous fibre-producing plants. One of these is the pineapple, whose leaves are sometimes scraped to produce fibres from which *piña* cloth is woven. Traditionally this is embroidered with buttonhole stitch, satin stitch and various pulled-thread techniques such as russian drawn ground filling; however, similar techniques are more often worked today on a ground of imported cotton than on authentic *piña* fabric. Men's shirts, women's blouses, tablecloths and other household items are produced, generally for export to North America or for sale.

Corner motif from a *piña*-cloth design worked in buttonhole stitch with pulled-thread infilling.

Pacific Islands

Embroidery is by no means a universal art in the Pacific islands. In places little clothing is worn and costume is not embroidered, although in Tonga and some other islands men's traditional outfits include helmets, masks for ceremonial occasions, skirts, arm and leg bands and shields decorated with stitched feathers. In other areas such as the Admiralty Islands, seeds and shells are attached to ground fabrics of cotton with long, dark brown straight stitches. In some Pacific islands lines of shells pierced and sewn in close formation with one straight stitch to each shell decorate bags, pouches and other ceremonial items. Apart from the decorative wall hangings being worked in Fiji and the quilts produced in Hawaii, little embroidery is being practised today.

Hawaiian quilted bedcovers, usually about 210 x 190 cm (83 x 75 in), are typified by large cotton motifs, usually in one colour, hemmed to another plain-coloured cotton ground fabric, padded and lined. The 'sandwich' is subsequently quilted with running stitches in diagonal trellis formation or in wave or contour quilting following the outline of the applied motifs.

Most Hawaiian quilt designs have simple or complex curvilinear shapes such as the breadfruit pattern, with four corner motifs and a coordinating central design all cut from bright yellow cotton and hemmed to a ground of deep red cotton. Other popular themes include lilies of the valley, pineapples, prickly pears and *leis* or garlands, and designs are sometimes adapted from legendary items such as a fan belonging to a former Hawaiian queen, Kapiolani.

The art of quilting was introduced to the islands by American women in the early 19th century. Unlike their teachers, who had small pieces of leftover material with which to 'piece' quilts, Hawaiian women had no scraps ready to hand and had, instead, to decorate their quilts with motifs cut from new lengths of fabric. Thus evolved the typical two-coloured quilt.

Hawaiian quilt. Lines of stitching follow the contours of the curvilinear applied motif.

Quilting is currently enjoying a revival in Hawaii, just as it is in areas of mainland America. People are both making and appreciating these items, and Hawaiian quilts in traditional styles are worked both for the embroiderers' homes and for sale.

Basic Embroidery Information

Equipment
Dressmaker's pins; tape measure; thimble.

Needles
It is important to use the correct needle for your work. Needles are graded from fine to coarse, the higher numbers being finer sizes. As a general rule the finer the needle the better the embroidery (provided the eye of the needle is large enough to take the thread easily). Blunt or bent needles will produce poor stitches.

Type	Use
Crewel	surface stitchery
Sharps	general sewing
Betweens	quilting
Tapestry	counted-thread work
Chenille	all thick threads
Bodkin	cord, ribbon, elastic
Straw and beading	beadwork

Scissors
Have three pairs in different sizes.

Type	Use
Small, sharp	threads
Medium	paper and card
Dressmaker's	fabric

Frames
A frame is essential for even tension in quilting, canvas and counted-thread work and for stitches made in two or more movements. (Other stitches, such as needle chain stitch, are more easily worked with the fabric held in the hand.)

There are two types of frame. Both types may be bought with a table or floor stand, which leaves your hands free for the embroidery.

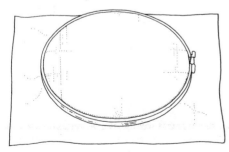

Ring, hoop, or tambour frame. This consists of an inner and an outer ring with a screw for adjusting tension. It can be used for light- or medium-weight fabrics—choose the most suitable size for the design you are working.

To mount the fabric:
1 Separate the rings. Bind the inner ring with bandage or tape to prevent the fabric from slipping or marking.
2 Lay the fabric over the inner ring and press the outer ring over it.
3 Tighten the tension screw and check that the weave of the fabric is square.
Rectangular or slate frame. Use for canvas and for large areas of fabric, such as quilts or wall hangings. To use this type of frame for an irregularly shaped piece of embroidery, mark the shape on a rectangle of the fabric and mount this onto the frame.

Frames consist of four lengths of wood: two rollers or runners which form the top and bottom and have a length of webbing attached, and two stretchers which form the sides of the frame and have a series of holes at each end so that the frame can be adjusted in size.

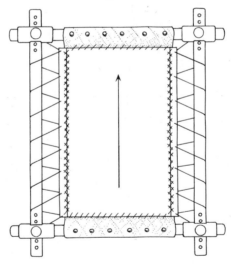

Sizes of frame, which are measured by the length of webbing on the rollers, range from about 26 cm (10 in) upwards. The length of webbing also determines the width of fabric which may be mounted on the frame.

To mount the fabric:
1 Measure and make a permanent mark halfway along each strip of webbing and on the fabric to be mounted.
2 Turn a 1 cm (½ in) single hem at the top and bottom of the fabric. Place lengths of tape over the side edges of the fabric so that the outer edges are level and attach with herringbone stitch.
3 Lay the top edge of the fabric onto the webbing so that it overlaps by 1.5 cm (½ in) and the centre points match. Starting from the centre and working outwards, oversew or herringbone the two together firmly. Repeat along the bottom edge.
4 Insert the rollers into the stretchers following the manufacturers' instructions. Wind any excess length of fabric round one of the rollers. Adjust the frame so that the fabric is stretched between the rollers.
5 Attach a strong length of carpet thread, fine string or twine to the top of each stretcher and lace it through the tape on the side of the fabric and round the stretcher for the length of the exposed fabric. Knot the threads round the bottoms of the stretchers.

Fabrics and Threads
One of the attractions of original examples of ethnic embroidery is the strong affinity of fabric, thread and dye. The use of natural fibres and vegetable or mineral dyes causes the materials to mellow with time.

For this reason, as well as their time-tested qualities of durability and ease of working, natural rather than synthetic materials were chosen for the projects. Although cost is an important consideration, it is false economy to buy inferior materials when many hours will be spent on the embroidery.

Before embarking on any project, it is advisable to carry out a quick washing test on the proposed fabrics and threads to avoid any disastrous dye-run or shrinkage problems. Cut a 7.5 cm (3 in) square of fabric and a selection of short lengths of threads. Wash them in soapy water, rinse well and then dry. Examine for shrinkage and loss of colour.

Fabrics suitable for embroidery grounds are cotton, cotton/wool mixtures, linen, silk and wool. Linen is especially suitable for napery and counted-thread work, and cotton and cotton/wool mixtures are good for garments which are to be washed frequently. Silk and wool, although expensive, are a pleasure to embroider on and are suitable for garments which may be dry cleaned.

Canvas with single threads is less confusing for the beginner than double thread, which is used for petit point. The more expensive linen, rather than cotton, canvas is recommended for better wearing qualities. Most people will find that canvas with 14–16 threads to 2.5 cm (1 in) is easy to work on.

Hessian (burlap) may be bought in a wide range of colours and is quite hardwearing although unsuitable for complete garments. It is not washable and tends to fade. It may be used for bold embroidery and pulled-thread work on bags, cushions and wall hangings.

Scrim, a loosely woven natural-coloured fabric made from jute or linen, may also be used for pulled-thread work.

Threads of a wide variety are available in natural fibres and in metal.

Dyes

Although commercially available chemical dyes are consistent and easy to use, true ethnic colours are obtained from vegetable and mineral dyes.

Most substances need the addition of a mordant to improve the colour and fastness of the dye. One suitable substance is iron (ferrous sulphate) which is obtainable from pharmacies.

A considerable amount of plant material is needed to extract dyes and the amount varies with each plant, but 450 g (1 lb) of plant material to 110 g (4 oz) fabric or yarn is a useful guideline. For the same amount of fabric or yarn you will need about 4 g ($\frac{1}{8}$ oz) iron mordant. Always experiment on a small piece of material before dyeing a large amount.

To extract the dye from the plant material, simmer it in a large container of soft water for up to three hours. Strain the liquid and cool it to hand

Many dyes can be obtained from ingredients in your kitchen while others can be obtained from the garden. These are a few examples.

Yellow: golden-rod tops and flowers (*Solidago* species) and onion skins (*Allium cepa*).
Blue: indigo (*Indigofera tinctoria*) and Mahonia berries (*Mahonia aquifolium*).
Brown: black walnut hulls (*Juglans nigra* or *J. regia*) and larch needles (*Larix* species).
Red and orange: dahlia flowers (*Dahlia* species) and madder roots (*Rubia tinctorum*).
Rose, pink, purple: black currant fruits (*Ribes nigrum*) and sloe fruits (*Prunus spinosa*).
Green: bracken (*Pteridium aquilinum*) and nettle leaves and tops (*Urtica dioica*).
Black or grey: blackberry tips (*Rubus* species) and roots of yellow flag iris (*Iris pseudacorus*).

heat. Wet the fabric or yarn, add it to the dye bath, raise the temperature again and simmer gently until the required colour is reached (it will appear darker when wet).

To add the mordant, lift out the fabric during the last 20 minutes of dyeing, stir in the mordant, replace the fabric and simmer for the remaining time.

When the colour is deep enough, lift out the fabric, allow it to drip over the dye bath for a minute and then squeeze it lightly. Rinse it well in clean, warm, soft water to remove all surplus dye.

Altering Patterns

Most of the garments shown in projects are size 86 cm (34 in) unless otherwise stated. Loose-fitting garments will also fit sizes 81 cm (32 in) and 91 cm (36 in) without more alteration than slight adjustment to the seam allowances when fitting the garment during making up.

For other sizes, the pattern may usually be altered by adding to or subtracting from the pattern pieces.

To check the exact amount required, divide the stated size by the constituent number of pattern pieces (a), and then by the required size (b).

Subtract figure (a) from the actual size of each piece to give the amount allowed for ease and seam allowances (c).

Add together figures (b) and (c) to give the dimension of the new piece.

Check the new dimensions against the fabric cutting chart and make any necessary adjustment. If you find that the pieces will no longer fit the width, you will have to allow extra length and re-arrange the pieces to fit.

Thread	Use	Thread	Use
Six-stranded cotton (floss)	Twisted, separable, shiny thread, suitable for surface stitchery, counted-, pulled- and drawn-thread work, hardanger.	Tapestry wool	Thicker, four-ply wool. Use as for crewel wool plus pattern darning.
Pearl cotton	Twisted, shiny thread, available in two thicknesses. Use as for stranded cotton where you require a heavier effect, plus blackwork, smocking, cutwork.	Rug wool	Two- or six-ply, sometimes available cheaply as thrums (broken lengths). Suitable for coarse canvas.
		Twisted silk	Fine twisted thread for surface embroidery.
Soft cotton	Matt, fairly thick, twisted thread. Use for surface stitchery, couching, hardanger, pattern darning.	Filo floss silk	Six-stranded silk, suitable for couching and laid work.
Coton à broder	Fine, shiny twisted cotton. Use as for stranded cotton, plus cutwork and smocking.	Passing gold	Soft, smooth gold thread, suitable for surface stitchery or couching.
		Japanese gold	Gold thread coiled over silk core. Suitable for couching but difficult to use.
Linen	Strong, twisted, shiny thread, suitable for cutwork, drawn- and pulled-thread work, smocking and blackwork.	Maltese silk	Gold-coloured silk suitable for couching metal threads.
		Pearl/check/ smooth/ rough/purl	Different threads of spiral metal thread, suitable for couching.
Crewel wool	Fine, two-ply wool which can be used in one or more strands as required. Suitable for surface stitchery, couching, canvas.	Lurex	Synthetic/metal fibre, suitable for surface stitchery and couching.

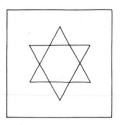

Enlarging Designs

This method may be used for enlarging or reducing a design from photographs or artwork.

1 Trace the original design onto paper and enclose with a rectangle or square, depending on the shape of the design.

2 Divide the rectangle or square into squares of equal size to form a grid.

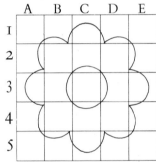

3 Draw a second rectangle or square to the required size of the design and divide it into the same number of squares as the original. Number the squares for easy identification.

4 Carefully copy the design square by square. If you have to copy a flowing curved line across several squares, mark the points at which it crosses the lines of the grid and then join them up in one smooth movement.

5 If you are enlarging a garment pattern from a graph, check that the edges to be joined are the same length and shape (e.g. neck curves and facings, side edges of the front and back of a dress).

Compare the main measurements of the pattern with your own (using a garment of similar shape as a guide) and make any adjustments before cutting out.

Transferring Designs

There are six main methods of transferring designs to ground fabric, and each is suitable for particular fabrics.

Dressmaker's carbon paper (A)

This is a general method of transferring designs and suitable for most fabrics

except heavy woollens, velvet or hessian (burlap) which will not register carbon paper. Carbon paper may be bought in a variety of colours. You will also need tracing paper and a medium (HB) pencil.

1 Trace the design onto the tracing paper.

2 Iron the ground fabric. Pin the tracing in position on the right side of the fabric with the carbon paper, shiny side down, sandwiched between the two.

3 Trace the design firmly and evenly.

4 If working a border design, move the tracing along, then repeat the process.

Tracing and basting (B)

This method is particularly suitable for heavy woollen, velvet or hessian (burlap) fabrics which will not register

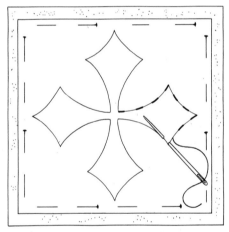

carbon paper. You will need tissue paper, needle, basting thread in contrasting colour to ground fabric, round-pointed tweezers.

1 Trace the design onto tissue paper.

2 Position the paper on the right side of the ground fabric and secure with pins.

3 Baste along the lines of the design through the paper, using small stitches on the right side of the fabric to allow for easy removal of the paper.

4 Carefully tear tissue away from the fabric, using tweezers to pull off any tissue caught under the stitches.

5 Remove any visible basting when the embroidery is complete.

Offset tracing (C)

Use this method on light-coloured fabrics as an alternative to carbon paper. You will need tracing paper and soft (2B) and medium (HB) pencils.

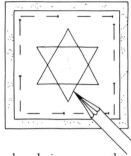

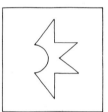

1 Trace the design onto the tracing paper with the soft pencil.

2 If the design is symmetrical, pin the tracing, pencilled side down, in position on the right side of the fabric. Trace over the lines of the design with the medium pencil, using firm, even pressure. This offsets the first pencilled outline onto the fabric.

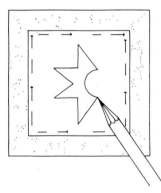

3 If the design is asymmetric, turn the tracing over and outline it again from the wrong side with the soft pencil. Place the tracing in position on the fabric with the second pencilled outline facing down. Trace over the lines of the design with the medium pencil, using firm, even pressure.

Direct tracing (D)

Use for canvas and semi-transparent fabrics such as silk and fine cotton. You will need a fine black felt-tipped pen, a hard pencil (for cotton and silk) and tracing paper.

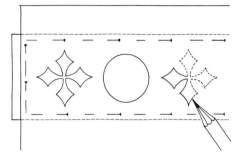

1 Using the felt-tipped pen, outline the design on paper.

2 Pin the fabric over the design and trace it onto the fabric, using the felt-tipped pen for canvas or pencil for cotton and silk

Templates (E)

Use this method for repeating shapes. You will need lightweight card, pencil, tailor's chalk or basting thread and needle.

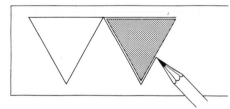

1 Accurately measure, draw and cut out the required shapes from the card.

2 Register the template on the ground fabric and either baste or draw round.

Charts (F)

Use for intricate counted-thread or needlepoint designs. Most charts are based on squares which indicate one stitch and the number of threads over which it should be worked and the colours to be used. Motifs may be enlarged or reduced either by working the stitches over a different number of threads than specified or by using fabric or canvas with a different thread count. Most charts can be used in alternative ways from that specified in the original design. For example, a cross-stitch motif originally shown on linen can be translated into tent stitch on canvas.

To work from a chart, refer to it as you would to a knitting pattern, beginning at one end and embroidering the design and background in rows or motifs.

These methods of transferring designs are recommended for the following projects.

Molas (A, C)
Huipil Blouse (A, C)
Peruvian Eagle Bag (A, C)

Beadwork Belt (E)
'Stained Glass' Quilt (E)
Indian Needlepoint Bag (D)

Pulled-work Mats (F)
Telemark Bolero (A, C, B)
Suede Appliqué Bag (A, E)
Finnish Pouch Bag (A, C, B)

Dutch Sampler Designs (A, C, F)
Breton Skirt (A, C)
Bargello Cushion (F)
Bavarian Blouse (A, C)

Yugoslavian Blouse (A, D)
Romanian Apron (A)

Armenian Skirt (B)
Uzbek Cap (B)

Greek Shawl (A, C)
Greek Island Dress (F)
Palestinian Smock (F)

Hausa Motif (A, C)
Hausa Smock (A, C)
Fon Appliqué Hanging (E, B)

Moroccan Sundress (A, C)
Egyptian Kaftan (A, C, F)

Marsh Arab Rug (B)
Afghan Dress (F)

Shisha Blouse (A, C)
Phulkari Evening Bag (F)
Sind Dress (A, D, E)

Dragon Robe (A, D, B)
Tibetan Motif (A, D)

Sumatran Cushion (A, D, F)

Wall Hangings

There are three ways of mounting embroidery to make a wall hanging or panel.

1 A mola, rug or design with a strong border pattern can be made into a scroll, hanging from a pole or batten.

2 Embroidery to be framed or pieces which tend to pucker can be stretched over hardboard and laced at the back.

3 Light- and medium-weight fabrics can be stretched over a wooden stretcher (a rectangular frame) and secured with staples or tacks. This method is suitable for unframed hangings.

Scroll

1 Cut a piece of heavy, non-woven interfacing or canvas to fit within the hem lines of the embroidery.

2 Lay the embroidery flat, face down, and pin the interfacing in position on the

---

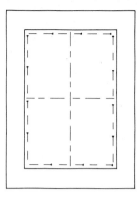

reverse side. Baste central, vertical and horizontal lines through the two layers.

3 Turn, press and pin the surplus fabric over the edges of the interfacing. Baste and stitch down with open herringbone stitch.

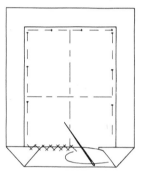

4 Cut a lining to the same size as the interfacing. Turn under 5 mm (¼ in) all round and pin in position on the reverse side of the embroidery. Slipstitch the lining to the turnings of the embroidery. Remove the basting.

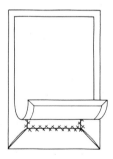

5 Sew curtain rings or tabs of matching fabric to the top edge of the embroidery. Insert a length of dowel, a wooden batten or a brass rod through these to hang the embroidery.

6 Attach a cord to the rod for hanging.

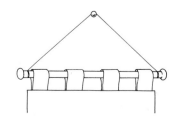

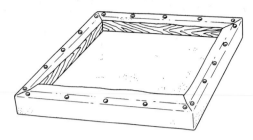

Hardboard

Use a piece of hardboard of the same size as the finished embroidery. Allow at least 7.5 cm (3 in) extra fabric all round for turnings.

1 Oversew the edges, or stitch on tape, to prevent the edges from fraying and disintegrating during lacing.

2 Lay the embroidery flat, face down, and place the hardboard centrally on the reverse side.

3 To mitre the corners, fold each corner diagonally onto the hardboard and press firmly with your fingers. Secure with small pieces of adhesive tape.

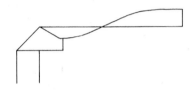

4 Fold the top and bottom edges onto the hardboard. Thread a chenille or darning needle with a long length of twine, carpet thread or thin string. Knot the end to the centre of the top edge, take a stitch on the centre of the bottom edge. Make a second stitch on the top edge, 1.5 cm (½ in) further on and repeat on the bottom edge. Continue lacing in this way to the corners and repeat on the opposite side. Join on more thread where necessary, with a non-slipping knot. Occasionally turn the board over to check that the design is straight and tighten the thread so that there is an even pull on the fabric. Fasten off securely.

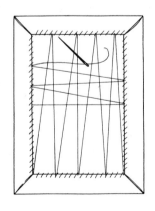

5 Repeat the process for the remaining sides.

6 Finish the back as for scrolls.

Stretcher method

Use a stretcher which is the same size as the finished embroidery and allow at least 10 cm (4 in) extra fabric all round for turnings. The stretcher can be constructed from wood measuring 5 x 2.5 cm (2 x 1 in) x the appropriate length, or you could buy a canvas stretcher of the right size from an art shop.

1 Lay the embroidery flat, face down, and place the stretcher in position on the reverse side.

2 Stretch the fabric smoothly and tautly over to the back of the frame and secure with drawing pins (thumbtacks), spaced about 2.5 cm (1 in) apart. Mitre the corners neatly.

3 Replace each pin, one at a time, with a staple or tin tack.

4 Finish the raw edges by covering with self-colour binding or ribbon, stuck in place with adhesive.

Washing Embroidery

Embroidery on cotton, linen and some silk grounds can be washed by the following method.

1 Dissolve soap flakes in very hot water.

2 When the water is hand hot, immerse the fabric and gently squeeze it in the lather. Transfer to clear water of the same temperature and squeeze again.

3 Rinse in clear water.

4 Spread the fabric on an absorbent towel, smooth it out and cover with another towel to remove excess moisture. Leave until nearly dry (see below).

Pressing Embroidery

Press cotton, linen and mixtures while still damp. Press silk when just dry.

Never leave the embroidery damp or rolled up for future pressing.

Place the fabric face downwards on a towel or blanket folded into four layers and cover with a piece of dry muslin. Press gently, treating any shisha glass, metal threads, spangles etc. with care.

Dry Cleaning

Embroidery on wool and some silk should be dry cleaned, rather than washed, as should embroidery worked with a mixture of fabrics, threads and beads, to prevent uneven shrinkage.

Damp Stretching

Sometimes it is necessary to stretch embroidery before making up to remove puckers. To do this, dampen the wrong side with a sponge, then place, right side up, on a soft board. Smooth it and pin out to shape. Leave it stretched until dry. *Canvas and wall hangings.* Cover a drawing board or piece of fibre board (which is larger than the full size of the embroidery) with a slightly dampened towel or three sheets of damp newspaper with a top layer of blotting paper.

Place the embroidery on the pad with the right side up. Stretch the longest edge parallel with the edge of the board and pin each corner with a drawing pin (thumbtack). Place further pins in between at 4 cm (1½ in) intervals. Stretch and pin the opposite edge in the same way.

Pin the remaining edges, ensuring that the edges are straight and the angles square. Dampen the work well with water from a sponge.

Leave until bone dry—at least 24 hours or longer.

Useful Tips

1 Sit on a chair which properly supports your back and always work where there is a good source of light. In artificial light, an angled desk lamp shining over the opposite shoulder from your working hand is invaluable.

2 A small, shallow basket, containing only the materials necessary for the work in progress, will help you to be orderly.

3 Do not thread your needle with too long a strand of thread or it will become rough and unmanageable.

4 Try to avoid knotting the end of your thread to begin and finish off. Instead, make a few running stitches on the wrong side of the fabric where the embroidery will cover them. Finish off by running the thread under a few stitches on the back of the embroidery.

5 Work samples of new stitches and techniques before starting a project.

Bibliography

General

Clabburn, Pamela. *The Needleworker's Dictionary*, Macmillan, London; Morrow, New York, 1976.

Dillmont, Thérèse de. *Encyclopedia of Needle-Work*, Th. de Dillmont, Mulhouse, 1886.

Enthoven, Jacqueline. *The Stitches of Creative Embroidery*, Van Nostrand Reinhold, New York, 1964.

Gostelow, Mary. *A World of Embroidery*, Mills & Boon, London; Scribner's, New York, 1975.

Schuette, Marie (with Sigrid Müller-Christensen). *The Art of Embroidery*, Thames & Hudson, London, 1964.

Snook, Barbara. *Embroidery Stitches*, Batsford, London, 1963.

Thomas, Mary. *Mary Thomas's Dictionary of Embroidery Stitches*, Hodder & Stoughton, London, 1934.

Wilson, Erica. *Erica Wilson's Embroidery Book*, Scribner's, New York, 1973; Faber, London, 1975.

Latin America

Hahn-Hissink, Dr Karin. *Volkskunst aus Guatemala*. Museum für Völkerkunde, Frankfurt, 1971.

—*Volkskunst in Mexico*, Museum für Völkerkunde, Frankfurt, 1968.

Harcourt, Raoul d'. *Textiles of Ancient Peru and their Techniques* (ed. Grace G. Denny and Caroline M. Osborne, trans. Sadie Brown), University of Washington Press, Seattle, 1962.

Jessen, Ellen. *Ancient Peruvian Textile Design in Modern Stitchery*, Van Nostrand Reinhold, New York, 1972.

Kapp, Kit S. *Mola Art from the San Blas Islands*, Kapp Publications, Cincinnati, 1972.

King, Mary Elizabeth. *Ancient Peruvian Textiles from the Collection of the Textile Museum, Washington DC*, New York Graphic Society, New York, 1965.

Means, Philip Ainsworth. 'Pre-Columbian Art and Culture in the Andean Area', *Bulletin of the Rhode Island School of Design*, Providence, XXVIII: 3 (December 1940).

von Hagen, Victor W. *The Ancient Sun Kingdoms of the Americas*, Thames & Hudson, London, 1962.

Altamerikanische Kunst Mexico-Peru, Staatliches Museum für Völkerkunde, Munich, 1968.

Brasiliens Indianer, Museum für Völkerkunde, Vienna, n.d.

Chilean Tapestries from Isla Negra, I.C.A., London, 1972.

Indianer in Südamerika, Museum für Völkerkunde, Vienna, 1973.

Molas: Art of the Cuna Indians, Textile Museum, Washington DC, 1973.

Ornamental Costumes from the John Wise Collection of Ancient Peruvian Textiles, Los Angeles County Museum of Art, 1972.

North America

Bolton, Ethel Stanwood (with Eva Johnston Coe). *American Samplers*, National Society of the Colonial Dames of America, Massachusetts, 1921; Dover, New York, 1973.

Brett, K. B. *Women's Costume in Early Ontario*, Royal Ontario Museum, Toronto, 1966.

Cammann, Nora. *Needlepoint Designs from American Indian Art*, Scribner's, New York, 1973.

Garrett, Elisabeth Donaghy. 'American Samplers and Needlework Pictures in the D.A.R. Museum', *Antiques*, New York, CV:2 (February 1974) and CVII:4 (April 1975).

Ginsburg, Cora. 'Textiles in the Connecticut Historical Society', *ibid.*, CVII:4 (April 1975).

Harbeson, Georgiana Brown. *American Needlework*, Coward-McCann, New York, 1938.

Hedlund, Catherine. *A Primer of New England Crewel Embroidery*, Old Sturbridge Village, Mass., 5th edition 1973.

Hornor, Marianna Merritt. *The Story of Samplers*, Philadelphia Museum of Art, 1971.

Howe, Margery B. 'Deerfield Blue and White Needlework', *Bulletin of the Needle and Bobbin Club*, New York, 47:1-2 (1963).

—*Deerfield Embroidery*, Scribner's, New York, 1975.

Landon, Mary Taylor and Susan Burrows Swan. *American Crewelwork*, Collier Macmillan, London; Macmillan, New York, 1970.

Lane, Rose Wilder. *Woman's Day Book of American Needlework*, Batsford, London; Simon & Schuster, New York, 1963.

McClellan, Elisabeth. *History of American Costume 1607-1870*, Tudor, New York, 1937.

Mera, H. P. *Pueblo Indian Embroidery*, William Gannon, Santa Fé, 1975.

Ring, Betty. 'The Balch School in Providence, Rhode Island', *Antiques*, New York, CVII:4 (April 1975).

Safford, Carleton L. (with Robert Bishop). *America's Quilts and Coverlets*, Dutton, New York; Studio Vista, London, 1972.

Schiffer, Margaret B. *Historical Needlework of Pennsylvania*, Scribner's, New York, 1968.

Swain, Margaret. 'Moose-hair Embroidery on Birch Bark', *Antiques*, New York, CVII: 4 (April 1975).

Turner, Geoffrey. *Hair Embroidery in Siberia and North America*, O.U.P., 1955.

Indianer Nordamerikas, Museum für Völkerkunde, Vienna, 1968 and 1972.

Scandinavia

D.M.C. *Drawn Thread Work*.

D.M.C. *Hardanger Embroideries* (1st series).

Fisher, Eivor (ed.). *Swedish Embroidery*, Batsford, London, 1953.

Gudjónsson, Elsa E. *Icelandic Embroidery*, (private copyright), Reykjavik, 1973.

—'National Costume of Women in Iceland', *Iceland Review*, Reykjavik, 3 (1967).

—'Traditional Icelandic Embroidery', *Bulletin of the Needle and Bobbin Club*, New York, 47:1-2 (1963).

Melén, Lisa. *Drawn Threadwork* (ed. Lynette de Denne, trans. Joan Bulman), Van Nostrand Reinhold, New York, 1972.

Ollila, Aino. *Etupistokirjonta Eli 'Luotuksittain Kirjuttaminen'*, Porvoo, Helsinki, 1951.

Petersen, Grete (with Elsie Svennås). *Handbook of Stitches* (trans. Anne Wilkins), Høst & Sons Forlag, Copenhagen; Batsford, London, 1970.

Sterner, Maj. *Homecrafts in Sweden* (trans. Alice Staël von Holstein), Lindbergs Tryckeriaktiebolag, Stockholm; F. Lewis, Leigh-on-Sea, 1939.

Western Europe

Anthony, Ilid E. 'Quilting and Patchwork in Wales', *Bulletin of the National Museum of Wales*, Cardiff, 12 (Winter 1972).

Boyle, Josephine Elizabeth. *The Irish Flowerers*, Holywood: Ulster Folk Museum and Institute of Irish Studies, Queen's University, Belfast, 1971.

Brett, Katharine B. *English Embroidery, 16th to 18th century . . . collections of the Royal Ontario Museum*, Toronto, 1972.

Cavalieri, Alina. 'The Embroideries of Italy', *The Embroideress*, London, I (1923).

Cave, Oenone. *English Folk Embroidery*, Mills & Boon, London, 1965.

—*Linen Cut-work*, Vista Books, London, 1963.

—'Old English Smocks and Smocking', *Embroidery*, London, XII:4 (Winter 1961).

Christie, Mrs A. G. I. *English Mediaeval Embroidery*, Clarendon Press, Oxford, 1938.

Davis, Mildred J. *The Dowell-Simpson Sampler*, Valentine Museum, Richmond, Virginia, 1975.

Digby, George Frederick Wingfield. *Elizabethan Embroidery*, Faber, London, 1963.

D.M.C. *Assisi Embroideries*.

Dobson, J. 'Smocking', *Embroidery*, London, IV:4 (Winter 1953).

Dreesmann, Cécile. 'Dutch Costumes and their Embroideries', *ibid.*, VII:2 (Summer 1956).

—'Notes on the History of Embroidery in Switzerland', *ibid.*, VII:1 (Spring 1975).

Edwards, Joan. *Crewel Embroidery in England*, Batsford, London; Van Nostrand Reinhold, New York, 1975.

Evans, Ruby. *Embroidery from Traditional English Patterns*, Batsford, London, 1971.

Gostelow, Mary. *Blackwork*, Batsford, London, 1976.

Hackenbroch, Yvonne. *English and Other Needlework Tapestries and Textiles in the Irwin Untermyer Collection*, Harvard University Press, Cambridge, Mass., 1960.

Hake, Elizabeth. *English Quilting Old and New*, Batsford, London, 1937.

Hughes, Therle. *English Domestic Needlework 1660–1860*, Lutterworth Press, London, 1961.

Irwin, John. 'Indo-Portuguese Embroideries of Bengal', *Indian Art and Letters*, London, XXVI:2 (1952).

—'Reflections on Indo-Portuguese Art', *Burlington Magazine*, London, 97 (1955).

Jones, Mary Eirwen. *British Samplers*, Pen-in-Hand Publishing, Oxford, 1948.

—*English Crewel Designs*, Macdonald, London; William Morrow, New York, 1974.

—*History of Western Embroidery*, Studio Vista, London, 1969.

Jourdain, Margaret. *The History of English Secular Embroidery*, Kegan Paul, London, 1910.

Kendrick, A. F. *English Embroidery*, Newnes, London, 1905.

—*English Needlework*, Black, London, 1933.

Kiewe, H. E. 'Florentine', *Embroidery*, London, II:3 (Autumn 1951).

Levey, Santina. *Discovering Embroidery of the Nineteenth Century*, Shire Publications, Princes Risborough, England, 1971.

Maclagan, Eric. *The Bayeux Tapestry*, Penguin, London and New York, 1943.

Meulenbelt-Nieuwburg, Alberta. *Embroidery Motifs from Dutch Samplers* (trans. Patricia Wardle and Gillian Downing), H. J. Bechts Uitgeversmaatschappij b.v., Amsterdam, 1974; Batsford, London, 1974.

Minto, Isobel. 'Embroidery in Italy', *Embroidery*, London, II:1 (Spring 1951).

Moore, Muriel. 'Coggeshall Tambour Work', *ibid*, VII:2 (Summer 1956).

Morris, Barbara. *Victorian Embroidery*, Jenkins, London, 1962.

Nevinson, J. L. *Catalogue of English Domestic Embroidery*, Victoria and Albert Museum, London, 1938.

Pass, Olivia. *Dorset Feather Stitchery*, Mills & Boon, London, 1957.

Pesel, Louisa F. *Historical Designs for Embroidery*, Batsford, London, 1956.

Proctor, Molly G. *Victorian Canvas Work: Berlin Wool Work*, Batsford, London, 1972.

Remington, Preston. *English Domestic Needlework of the XVI, XVII and XVIII Centuries*, Metropolitan Museum of Art, New York, 1945.

Ricci, Elisa. 'The Revival of Needlework in Italy', *Studio*, London, 61 (15 April 1914).

Ridjuejo, Maria Antonia. 'Traditional Spanish Embroidery', *Embroidery*, London, XIV:4 (Winter 1963).

Snook, Barbara. *The Craft of Florentine Embroidery*, Mills & Boon, London, 1974; Scribner's, New York, 1971.

—*English Embroidery*, Batsford, London, 1960; Transatlantic, New York, 1975.

Stapley, Mildred. *Popular Weaving and Embroidery in Spain*, Batsford, London, 1924.

Swain, Margaret H. 'The Floo'erin'', *The Scots Magazine*, Dundee, 96:1 (October 1971).

—*The Flowerers*, Chambers, London and Edinburgh, 1955.

—*Historical Needlework: A Study of Influences in Scotland and Northern England*, Barrie & Jenkins, London, 1970.

—'Tamboured Muslin in Scotland', *Embroidery*, London, XIV:1 (Spring 1963).

Townsend, Gertrude. 'Notes on Embroidery in England during the Tudor and Stuart Periods', *Bulletin of the Needle and Bobbin Club*, New York, 45:1-2 (1961).

van Hemert, Maria. *De Handwerken op het Eiland Marken*, Rijksmuseum voor Volkskunde, Arnhem, 1967.

Wace, A. J. B. *English Embroidery Belonging to Sir John Carew Pole, Bart.*, Walpole Society, London, 1933.

Williams, Elsa S. *Bargello. Florentine Canvas Work*, Van Nostrand Reinhold, New York, 1967.

Eastern Europe

Bazielich, Barbara. *Ludowe Wyszycia Technika Krzyzykowa na Slasku*, Bytom, 1966.

—'Slavonic Folk Embroidery', *Art Populaire Slovaque*, XXXI (1953).

—*Zlote Harty w Tradycyjnej Odziezy na Slasku*, Bytom, 1973.

—*Zabytki Ludowej Kultury na Slasku i w Czestochowskiem*, Bytom, 1975.

Fél, Edit. *Hungarian Peasant Embroidery* (trans. Annie Barát and Lily Halápy), Batsford, London, 1961.

Harkness, Dorothy Norris. *Romanian Embroidery: a Dying Folk-Art*, Iuliu Maniu Foundation, New York, 1960.

Johnstone, Pauline. 'Embroidery in Yugoslavia', *Embroidery*, London, III:2 (Summer 1952).

Jones, Nora. 'Albanian Costume', *ibid.*, XIX:2 (Summer 1968).

Mulkiewicz, Olga. 'Gorce "Parzenice"', *Embroidery*, London, X:2 (Summer 1959).

Ribaric, Jelka. *Folk Costumes of Croatia*, Spektar, Zagreb, 1975.

—*Yugoslavian/Croatian Folk Embroidery*, Van Nostrand Reinhold, New York, 1976.

Start, Laura E. *The Durham Collection of Garments and Embroideries from Albania and Yugoslavia*, Bankfield Museum Notes, Halifax, England, Series 3:4 (1939).

Szaad, Maria. 'Embroidery in Poland', *Embroidery*, London, XII:4 (Winter 1961).

Tschukanova, Rossitza. *Bulgarische Volksstickerei*, Sofia, 1957.

Varju-Ember, Maria. *Hungarian Peasant Embroidery*, Corvina Press, Budapest; Batsford, London, 1961.

Village Arts of Romania, British Museum, London, 1971.

Soviet Union

Allgrove, Joan. 'Turcoman Embroideries', *Embroidery*, London, XXIV:2 (Summer 1973).

Andrews, Mügül and Peter. *Türkmen Needlework*, Central Asian Research Centre, London, 1976.

Bazaar Coop. Association. *Ukrainian Embroideries*, Series 1:3, Philadelphia, n.d.

Gostelow, Mary. 'Three Embroidered Icons in Private Collections in Moscow', *Embroidery*, London, XXVI:3 (Autumn 1975).

Kaplan, N. *In the Land of the Reindeer: Applied Art in the North of the Soviet Union*, Aurora, Leningrad, 1974.

Manucharova, N. *Ukrainian Folk Embroidery*, Mistetstvo, Kiev, 1959.

Mayasova, N. A. *Old Russian Embroidery*, Iskusstvo, Moscow, 1969.

Okuneva, Irene. 'Russian Embroidery', *Embroidery*, London, IV:2 (March 1936).

Pronin, Alexander and Barbara. *Russian Folk Art*, Barnes, New Jersey, 1975.

Smith, Winifred. 'Russian Peasant Embroidery', *Embroidery* IV:2 (March 1936).

Start, Laura E. 'Embroideries, Old and New: XV and XVI, Russian Peasant Embroideries', *The Needlewoman*, London, 15 (1922) and 16 (1932).

Turner, Geoffrey. *Hair Embroidery in Siberia and North America*, O.U.P., 1955.

Russian Art: Icons and Decorative Arts from the Origin to the 20th Century, Walters Art Gallery, Baltimore, 1959.

Textilkunst des Steppen und Bergvölker Zentralasiens, Gewerbemuseum, Basel, 1974.

Eastern Mediterranean

Benaki Museum. *Crete, Dodecanese, Cyclades: Embroideries*, Athens, 1966.

—*Epirus and Ionian Islands Embroideries*, Athens, 1965.

—*Skyros Embroideries*, Athens, 1965.

Berry, B. Y. 'Turkish Embroidery', *Embroidery*, London, IV:3 (June 1936).

Crowfoot, G. M. 'Embroidery of Bethlehem', *ibid.*, V:1 (December 1936).

—(with Phyllis M. Sutton). 'Ramallah Embroidery: Introduction to the Study of Palestinian Embroidery', *ibid.*, III:2 (March 1935).

D.M.C. *Turkish Embroideries.*

Johnstone, Pauline. *A Guide to Greek Island Embroidery*, H.M.S.O., London, 1972.

MacMillan, Susan L. *Greek Islands Embroideries*, Museum of Fine Arts, Boston, 1973.

National Bank of Greece. *Greek Handicrafts* (ed. S. A. Papadopoulos), Athens, 1969.

Pesel, Louisa F. *Stitches from Eastern Embroideries*, Portfolio No. 2, Batsford, London, 1916.

Ramazanoglu, Gulseren. *Turkish Embroidery*, Van Nostrand Reinhold, New York, 1976.

von Palotay, G. 'Turkish Embroideries', *C.I.B.A. Review*, Basel, 102 (1954).

Wace, A. J. B. *Mediterranean Embroideries*, Liverpool Public Museum, 1956.

Weir, Shelagh. *The Bedouin*, World of Islam Festival Publishing, London, 1976.

—*Palestinian Embroidery: A Village Arab Craft*, British Museum, London, 1970.

—'The Traditional Costumes of the Arab Women of Palestine', *Costume* (Journal of the Costume Society), London, 3 (1969).

Sub-Saharan Africa

de Villiers, Marianna. *Creative Wool on Canvas*, Janssonius & Heyns, Honeydew, Transvaal, 1973.

Gostelow, Mary. *Embroidery of South Africa*, Mills & Boon, London, 1976.

Heathcote, David. *The Arts of the Hausa*, World of Islam Publishing, London, 1976.

—'Hausa Embroidery Stitches', *Nigerian Field*, XXXIX:4 (December 1974).

—'Insight into a Creative Process: a Rare Collection of Embroidery Drawings from Kano', *Savanna*, Zaria, 1:2 (December 1972).

Lamb, Venice. *West African Weaving*, Duckworth, London, 1975.

Trowell, Margaret. *African Design*, Faber, London, 1960.

van Wyk, Hetsie. *Borduur Só*, Afrikaanse Pers–Boekhandel, Johannesburg, 1969.

Dahomey: Traditions du Peuple Fon, Musée d'Ethnographie, Geneva, 1975.

North Africa

Beckwith, John. 'Coptic Textiles', *C.I.B.A. Review*, Basel, 12:133 (1959).

Benaki Museum. *Coptic Textiles*, Athens, 1971.

D.M.C. *Moroccan Embroideries*, 1969.

Gerspach, M. *Coptic Textile Designs*, Dover, New York, 1975.

Kendrick, A. F. *Catalogue of Textiles from Burying-Grounds in Egypt*, H.M.S.O., London, 1920–22.

Orbis Pictus. *Tissus Coptes*, Office du Livre, Fribourg, n.d.

Pfister, R. *Tissus Coptes du Musée du Louvre*, Ernst Henri, Paris, 1932.

Seagrott, Margaret. 'The Coptic Textile Collection', *Liverpool Libraries, Museums & Arts Committee Bulletin*, 10 (1961–62).

Simpson, B. Octavia. 'Embroidery in Egypt', *The Embroideress*, London, IV:29 (1929).

Start, Laura E. *Coptic Cloths*, Bankfield Museum Notes, Halifax, England, 1914.

Thompson, Deborah. *Coptic Textiles in the Brooklyn Museum*, New York, 1971.

Western Asia

Allgrove, Joan, 'Turcoman Embroideries', *Embroidery*, London, XXIV:2 (Summer 1973).

Andrews, Mügül and Peter. *op. cit.*

Ashworth, Norma. 'Ancient Dignity Unchanged in a Modern Jacket' (article on Oman), *The Times*, London, 18 November 1975.

Ballian, Anna. *Islamic Textiles*, Benaki Museum, Athens, 1974.

Johnstone, Pauline. 'Persian Dress and Western Embroidery', *Embroidery*, London, X:4 (Winter 1959).

Krishna, Mary. 'Zoroastrian Bridal Dress', *ibid.*, XV:4 (Winter 1964).

Kühnel, Ernst (with L. Bellinger). *Catalogue of Dated Tiraz Fabrics*, Textile Museum, Washington DC, 1952.

Wace, A. J. B. 'Persian Embroidery', *The Embroideress*, London, V:37 (1931).

Wulff, Hans. *Traditional Crafts of Persia*, Leipzig, 1939, M.I.T. Press, Cambridge, Mass. and London, 1966.

Textilkunst der Steppen- und Bergvölker Zentralasiens, Gewerbemuseum, Basel, 1974.

India

Dhamija, Jasleen. 'The Kanthas of Bengal', *Times of India Annual*, 1972.

Gupte, B. A. 'Embroidery', *Journal of Indian Art*, London, II:18 (April 1888).

Irwin, John. 'Indo-Portuguese Embroideries of Bengal', *Indian Art and Letters*, XXVI:2 (1952).

—*The Kashmir Shawl*, H.M.S.O., London, 1973.

—'Reflections on Indo-Portuguese Art', *Burlington Magazine*, London, 97 (December 1955).

Olson, Eleanor. *The Textiles and Costumes of India*, Newark Museum, New Jersey, 1965.

Pauly, Sarah Buie. *The Kashmir Shawl*, Yale University Art Gallery, New Haven, 1975.

China

Byron, Robert. 'Tibetan Appliqué-work', *Burlington Magazine*, 58 (June 1931).

Cammann, Schuyler, *China's Dragon Robes*, Ronald Press, New York, 1952.

—'Chinese Mandarin Squares: Brief Catalogue of the Letcher Collection', *Bulletin of the University of Pennsylvania Museum*, Philadelphia, 17:3 (June 1953).

Capon, Edmund. *Chinese Court Robes in the Victoria & Albert Museum*, H.M.S.O., London, 1970.

Digby, George Wingfield. 'Chinese Costume in the Light of an Illustrated Manuscript Catalogue from the Summer Palace', *Gazette des Beaux Arts*, XLI (1953).

—'Chinese Court and Dragon Robes', *Connoisseur*, CXXVI (1950).

Ernst, Henri. *Broderies chinoises*, Paris, 1930s.

Olson, Eleanor. *Catalogue of the Tibetan Collection and other Lamaist Articles in the Newark Museum*, IV, Newark Museum, New Jersey, 1961.

—'Tibetan Appliqué Work', *Bulletin of the Needle and Bobbin Club*, New York, 34:1–2 (1950).

Priest, Alan (with P. Simmons). *Chinese Textiles*, Metropolitan Museum of Art, New York, 1931.

Schuster, Carl. 'Some Peasant Embroideries from Western China', *Embroidery*, London, III:4 (September 1935).

Van der Wee, L. P. 'Tibetan Appliqué Hangings in European Collections', *Bulletin of the Needle and Bobbin Club*, New York, 58:1–2 (1975).

Whymant, Neville. 'Traditional Chinese Embroidery', *Embroidery*, London, III:4 (September 1935).

East and South-East Asia

Cammann, Schuyler. 'Chinese Mandarin Squares: Brief Catalogue of the Letcher Collection', *Bulletin of the University of Pennsylvania Museum*, Philadelphia, 17:3 (June 1953).

Crewdson, Wilson. 'Japanese Art and Artists of To-day: III. Textiles and Embroidery', *Studio*, 51 (15 October 1910).

Innes, R. A. *Costumes of Upper Burma and the Shan States*, Bankfield Museum, Halifax, England, 1957.

Jones, Stella M. *The Hawaiian Quilt*, Honolulu Academy of Arts, 1930.

Krishna, Mary. 'Burmese Appliqué Hangings', *Embroidery*, London, XIII:2 (Summer 1962).

—'Designs from Burmese Kalangas', *ibid.*, XIV:3 (Autumn 1963).

Moschner, Irmgard. *Ozeanien Australien*, Museum für Völkerkunde, Vienna, 1957.

Noma, Seiroku. *Japanese Costume and Textile Arts*, Phaidon, London and New York, 1974.

Okada, Yuzuru. *Japanese Handicrafts*, Japan Travel Bureau, Tokyo, 1956.

Photograph Credits

Introduction

1, 2-3, 4-5: Ulster Museum, Belfast. 6 L: Myndion; Thjódminjasafn, Reykjavik. 6 T1: Ianthe Ruthven; Macondo, London. 6 T2: Ianthe Ruthven; The Embroiderers' Guild, London. 6 T3: Ianthe Ruthven; Lilian Temple. 6 B3: Ianthe Ruthven; Angela Swan. 7 T4: Ianthe Ruthven; Jenny Cropper. 7 B1: Ianthe Ruthven; Trustees of the British Museum; Museum of Mankind, London. 7 B2: Ianthe Ruthven. 7 B4: Martin Gostelow. 8-9: Ulster Museum, Belfast.

Latin America

10: Vautier-Decool. 11 T: Kay Lawson; Rapho. 11 B: Los Angeles County Museum of Art. 12 T: Martin Gostelow; The University Museum of Archaeology and Ethnology, Cambridge, England. 12 C: Ianthe Ruthven; La Cucaracha Galleries, London. 12 B: Robert Harding Associates. 13 T: Ianthe Ruthven; Forbidden Fruit, London. 13 BL: Werner Forman Archive; Museo Nacional de Antropologia, Mexico City. 13 BR: Marc and Evelyne Bernheim; Rapho. 14: Ianthe Ruthven. 15 TL: Robert Harding Associates. 15 TR and B: Constance Howard. 16: Ianthe Ruthven; Anne Swain. 17: Ianthe Ruthven; Anne Swain. 18 T: Ianthe Ruthven; Anne Swain. 18 B: Angelo Hornak; Trustees of the British Museum; Museum of Mankind, London. 19 T: Michael Freeman; Bruce Coleman. 19 B: Angelo Hornak; Trustees of the British Museum; Museum of Mankind, London. 20: Ianthe Ruthven. 21: Roger Charity. 22 T: Hans Hinz; Museum für Völkerkunde, Basel. 22 B: Vautier-Decool. 23: Tony Morrison. 24: Museum of the American Indian, New York. 25: Michael Holford; Museum Staatliches für Völkerkunde, Munich. 26 L: Werner Forman Archive; Museum of Fine Arts, Dallas. 26 R: Vautier-Decool. 27 T: H. W. Silvester; Rapho. 27 B: Vautier-Decool. 28: Michael Holford; Trustees of the British Museum; Museum of Mankind, London. 29: John T. Underwood Memorial Fund, The Brooklyn Museum. 30 L: N. Aufan; AAA Photo. 30 R: Roger Charity. 31: Ianthe Ruthven; Macondo, London. 32 T: Ianthe Ruthven; Anne Swain. 32 B: Martin Gostelow. 33: Martin Gostelow.

North America

34 TL: Museum of the American Indian, New York. 34 TR: Minnesota Historical Society. 34 B: Abby Aldrich Rockefeller Folk Art Collection. 36 L: Adam Woolfitt; Susan Griggs Agency. 36 R: Field Museum of Natural History, Chicago. 37 T: Ernst Haas; Magnum. 37 B: Museum of the American Indian, New York. 38 T and B: Museum of the American Indian, New York. 39: Mark W. Sexton; Peabody Museum of Salem. 40 T: Museum of the American Indian, New York. 40 BL and BR: Angelo Hornak; Trustees of the British Museum; Museum of Mankind, London. 41 B: Museum of the American Indian, New York. 42: The Brooklyn Museum. 43 T, C and BL: Angelo Hornak; Trustees of the British Museum; Museum of Mankind, London. 43 BR: Museum of the American Indian, New York. 45: Roger Charity. 46 TL, BL and R: Museum of the American Indian, New York. 48: Cooper-Bridgeman. 49: Walter Parrish International; Victoria and Albert Museum, London. 50: From *Deerfield Embroidery* Copyright © 1976, Margery Burnham Howe, reprinted by permission of Charles Scribner's Sons. 51: America Hurrah Antiques. 52 L: Victoria and Albert Museum, London. 52 R: Martin Gostelow; American Museum in Britain, Bath. 53: Steve Bicknell. 54: John Wood. 55: American Museum in Britain, Bath. 56: Ianthe Ruthven. 57: Roger Charity.

Scandinavia

58-59: Martin Gostelow. 59 T: Photoresources. 59 B: Myndion; Thjódminjasafn, Reykjavik. 60 T: Icelandic Photo and Press Service. 60 B: Myndion; Thjódminjasafn, Reykjavik. 61: Martin Gostelow. 62 L: Martin Gostelow. 62 R: Martin Gostelow; Thjódminjasafn, Reykjavik. 63: Kunstindustrimuseet, Copenhagen. 64 T: David Kelly; Poula Hamilton Fairley. 64 B: Martin Gostelow. 64-65: Dansk Folkemuseum, Copenhagen. 66: Dansk Folkemuseum, Copenhagen. 67: Martin Gostelow; Danish Handicraft Guild. 69: Michael Boys. 70: Martin Gostelow. 71 T: Norsk Folkmuseum, Oslo. 71 B: Martin Gostelow. 73: Roger Charity. 74: University of Trondheim. 75 T: Photoresources. 75 B: Nordiska Museet, Stockholm. 76: Ianthe Ruthven; The Embroiderers' Guild, London. 77: Ianthe Ruthven. 78: Steve Bicknell. 80: Ianthe Ruthven; The Embroiderers' Guild, London. 81 T: Bryan Alexander. 81 B: Angelo Hornak. 82 T: Suomen Kansallismuseo, Helsinki. 82 BL: Finnish Embassy, London. 82 BR: Suomen Kansallismuseo, Helsinki. 83: Michael Boys.

Western Europe

84 T: Phaidon Press. 84 B: David Kelly; Phillips, Son and Neale. 84-85 B: Scala. 85: Martin Gostelow. 86 T: Michael Holford; Victoria and Albert Museum, London. 86 BL: Victoria and Albert Museum, London. 86 BR: Ronald Sheridan; Victoria and Albert Museum, London. 87 T and B: National Trust, London. 88: Royal Scottish Museum, Edinburgh. 89 T: David Kelly; Phillips, Son and Neale. 89 B: National Museum of Ireland, Dublin. 90 T: Michael Holford; Victoria and Albert Museum, London. 90 B: Ianthe Ruthven; Mrs Mary Moore. 91 T: Museum of English Rural Life, Reading. 91 B: Ianthe Ruthven; The Embroiderers' Guild, London. 92 T and B: Martin Gostelow; Victoria and Albert Museum, London. 93: Martin Gostelow; Victoria and Albert Museum, London. 94 T: Martin Gostelow. 94 B: George Wright. 95 T: Roger Charity. 95 B: George Wright. 96: Martin Gostelow. 97 T: Christine Osborne; Bruce Coleman. 97 B: Martin Gostelow. 98: Martin Gostelow; Victoria and Albert Museum, London. 99: Roger Charity. 100 T: Martin Gostelow. 100 B: Mas. 101 T: John Freeman; Phillips, Son and Neale. 101 B: Michael Holford; Victoria and Albert Museum, London. 102: Reflejo; Susan Griggs Agency. 103 T and BL: Martin Gostelow. 103 BR: Ianthe Ruthven. 104 T: Angelo Hornak. 104 B: Michael Holford; Victoria and Albert Museum, London. 105 T: Ianthe Ruthven; The Embroiderers' Guild, London. 105 B: David Kelly; Phillips, Son and Neale. 106 T: Martin Gostelow. 106 B: Victoria and Albert Museum, London. 107: Steve Bicknell. 108 T: Paolo Koch. 108 B: Ianthe Ruthven; Tania Smith. 109 L: Martin Gostelow. 109 R: Paolo Koch. 110 L: Paolo Koch. 110 R: Adam Woolfitt; Susan Griggs Agency. 111 L: Michael Holford; Victoria and Albert Museum, London. 111 TR and BR: Martin Gostelow. 112 T: Bavaria Verlag. 112 B: Martin Gostelow. 113 T, BL and BR: Martin Gostelow. 115: Michael Boys.

Eastern Europe and the Balkans

116-117: Martin Gostelow. 117: Ianthe Ruthven; British Hungarian Friendship Society. 118: Starfoto; Zefa. 119: Ianthe Ruthven; Mazowsze State Folk Song and Dance Ensemble. 121: Martin Gostelow. 122 T: Ianthe Ruthven; Ursula McLean. 122 B: Ianthe Ruthven; British Hungarian Friendship Society. 123 T: Ianthe Ruthven; Lilian Temple. 123 B: Ianthe Ruthven; British Hungarian Friendship Society. 124 TL and TR: Ianthe Ruthven; Lilian Temple. 124 B: Photoresources. 125 T and B: Ianthe Ruthven; Lilian Temple. 126: Ianthe Ruthven. 127: Roger Charity. 128: Ianthe Ruthven; Lilian Temple. 129 T: Kurt Scholz; Zefa. 129 B: Martin Gostelow. 130 T, BL and BR: Courtesy of Aberdeen University Anthropological Museum; Hasluck Collection. 131 L: Cruwell; *Elle*. 131 R: Ianthe Ruthven; Fay Maisner. 133: Roger Charity.

Soviet Union

135: Ianthe Ruthven. 136: Suomen Kansallismuseo, Helsinki. 137 T: Martin Gostelow. 137 BL: Ianthe Ruthven; Tamara Holbøll. 137 BR: Bankfield Museum, Halifax, England. 138 TL, TR and B: Malcolm Aird; Mrs Zenta Leeks. 139 T and BL: Ianthe Ruthven; Mrs K. Gorgodian. 139 BR: Martin Gostelow. 140: Ianthe Ruthven. 141: Michael Boys. 142 T and B: Ianthe

Ruthven. 143 T: Ianthe Ruthven. 143 B: Martin Gostelow; Victoria and Albert Museum, London. 144 T: Angelo Hornak. 144 B: Martin Gostelow; Cultural History Museum, Cape Town. 145 T: Martin Gostelow; Cultural History Museum, Cape Town. 145 C: David Kelly; Phillips, Son and Neale. 145 B: R. Todd-White; Jema Graman. 146: Steve Bicknell. 147: Suomen Kansallismuseo, Helsinki. 148: Suomen Kansallismuseo, Helsinki. 149 T and B: Suomen Kansallismuseo, Helsinki.

Eastern Mediterranean

151: Colin Watmough. 152: Colin Watmough. 153 T: Constantine Manos; Magnum. 153 B: Martin Gostelow. 154 T: Michael Boys. 154 B: Ianthe Ruthven. 155 T and B: Colin Watmough. 156: Colin Watmough. 157: Colin Watmough. 158 L: Colin Watmough. 158 R: Angelo Hornak. 159 T and C: Angelo Hornak. 159 B: Colin Watmough. 160: George Wright. 162 T and C: Colin Watmough. 162 B: F. H. C. Birch; Sonia Halliday. 163: Angelo Hornak. 164: Angelo Hornak. 165 T: Ianthe Ruthven; Fay Maisner. 165 B: Martin Gostelow; Victoria and Albert Museum, London. 166 T: Ianthe Ruthven. 166 BL and BR: Angelo Hornak. 167: Ianthe Ruthven; Fay Maisner. 168: Ronald Sheridan; Israel Museum, Jerusalem. 169 T: David Kelly; Betty van Gelder, Bazaar Shops, London. 169 B: Trustees of the British Museum; Museum of Mankind, London. 171: Roger Charity.

Sub-Saharan Africa

173 TL: Ianthe Ruthven; Trustees of the British Museum; Museum of Mankind, London. 173 BL: Alan Hutchison. 173 TR: Mirella Ricciardi; Bruce Coleman. 173 BR: John Bulmer. 174-175: Brian Seed; John Hillelson Agency. 174 B: Martin Gostelow. 175: Robert Harding Associates. 176 TL and BL: Angelo Hornak; Annette Brown. 176 TR: Margaret Murray. 176 BR: Angelo Hornak; Trustees of the British Museum; Museum of Mankind, London. 177: Ianthe Ruthven; Trustees of the British Museum; Museum of Mankind, London. 178 T: Angelo Hornak; Trustees of the British Museum; Museum of Mankind, London. 178 B: Ianthe Ruthven; Trustees of the British Museum; Museum of Mankind, London. 179 L: Ianthe Ruthven; Trustees of the British Museum; Museum of Mankind, London. 179 R: Field Museum of Natural History, Chicago. 180 TL, TR and B: Ianthe Ruthven; Trustees of the British Museum; Museum of Mankind, London. 181 T and B: Martin Gostelow. 182 T, C and B: Martin Gostelow. 183: Bill Carter. 185: Roger Charity. 185 Insert: Ianthe Ruthven. 186 T: Alan Hutchison. 186 B: The Brooklyn

Museum. 187: Museum voor Land- en Volkenkunde, Rotterdam. 188: Ken Randall. 189 T: Steve Bicknell. 189 BL and BR: Angelo Hornak; Trustees of the British Museum; Museum of Mankind, London.

North Africa

191: David Kelly; Trustees of the British Museum; Museum of Mankind, London. 192 T: Klaus Hackenberg; Zefa. 192 B: J. L. S. Dubois; Explorer. 193 T: Martin Gostelow; The Embroiderers' Guild, London. 193 B: Martin Gostelow. 194: David Kelly; Trustees of the British Museum; Museum of Mankind, London. 195 TL: David Kelly; Trustees of the British Museum; Museum of Mankind, London. 195 TR: Angelo Hornak. 195 B: Martin Gostelow. 197: Bill Carter. 198: David Kelly; Trustees of the British Museum; Museum of Mankind, London. 199 T: Duchemin; AAA Photo. 199 B: Klaus Hackenberg; Zefa. 200 T: Charles Edwin Wilbour Fund, The Brooklyn Museum. 200 B: Photoresources; Museo Archeologico, Florence. 201: Ianthe Ruthven; Jeannine Athas-Williams. 202 T and B: Ianthe Ruthven. 203: George Wright.

Western Asia

204: Eve Arnold; Magnum. 205: David Kelly; Phillips, Son and Neale. 206 L and 206-207: Angelo Hornak; Trustees of the British Museum; Museum of Mankind, London. 208: P. Weisbecker; Explorer. 209: Martin Gostelow; Israel Museum, Jerusalem. 210 L: Angelo Hornak. 210 R: Daryl B. Hill-Harrison. 211: Daryl B. Hill-Harrison. 212 L, TR and BR: Martin Gostelow. 213 T: George Wright. 213 B: Ken Randall. 214 T and B: Angelo Hornak; Trustees of the British Museum; Museum of Mankind, London. 215: Victoria and Albert Museum, London. 216-217: Victoria and Albert Museum, London. 217 R: Victoria and Albert Museum, London. 218 T and B: Martin Gostelow. 219 T: Paolo Koch. 219 BL and BR: Martin Gostelow. 220-221: D. Desjardins; Explorer. 221 T: David Kelly; Betty van Gelder, Bazaar Shops, London. 221 B: Ianthe Ruthven. 222 L: David Kelly; Betty van Gelder, Bazaar Shops, London. 222 R: Martin Gostelow. 223 L: Martin Gostelow. 223 R: Martin Gostelow; Israel Museum, Jerusalem. 225: George Wright.

India

227: Rex Features. 228 T: Martin Gostelow. 228 B: Ianthe Ruthven; Victoria and Albert Museum, London. 229 T: Martin Gostelow. 229 BL: Ianthe Ruthven; Victoria and Albert Museum, London. 229 BR: Tom Stacey; Robert Harding Associates. 231: Mike Busselle. 232 T and B: Mike Busselle. 233 L and R: Raghav Kaneria; John Hillelson Agency. 234 T: Martin Gostelow. 234 C: Ianthe Ruthven; Victoria and Albert Museum,

London. 234 B: Bury Peerless. 235: Ianthe Ruthven; Victoria and Albert Museum, London. 236: Martin Gostelow. 237 T, L, CL, CR and R: Martin Gostelow. 238: Michael Boys. 240 T and B: Ianthe Ruthven; Victoria and Albert Museum, London. 240 C: Martin Gostelow. 241 T and B: Ianthe Ruthven; Victoria and Albert Museum, London. 242 T and C: Martin Gostelow. 242 B: George Shelley; Rapho. 243: Ianthe Ruthven; Victoria and Albert Museum, London. 243 Insert: George Shelley; Rapho. 245: George Wright. 246 L: Ianthe Ruthven; Kathleen Smith. 247 T, BL and BR: Martin Gostelow.

China

248: Photoresources. 249: Michael Holford; Victoria and Albert Museum, London. 250-251: Victoria and Albert Museum, London. 251: Michael Holford; Victoria and Albert Museum, London. 252 T and B: Martin Gostelow. 253: Victoria and Albert Museum, London. 254: Michael Holford; Victoria and Albert Museum, London. 255 TL: Victoria and Albert Museum, London. 255 TR, C and BR: Werner Forman Archive. 255 BL: John Webb; Victoria and Albert Museum, London. 256 TL, TR, C and B: Martin Gostelow. 257: Bruno Barbey; Magnum. 258: Michael Boys. 260 T: Martin Gostelow. 260 B: The MacQuitty International Collection. 261: Bill Carter.

East and South-East Asia

263: Victoria and Albert Museum, London. 264-265: Almasy; Bildagentur Mauritius. 265 T and B: Victoria and Albert Museum, London. 266-267: Arthur Chesterman. 266 B: Martin Gostelow. 267 C and TR: Martin Gostelow. 267 B: Vautier-Decool. 268 T: A. Moineau; Explorer. 268 BL: Bankfield Museum, Halifax, England. 268 BR: Angelo Hornak. 269 L and R: Tropenmuseum, Amsterdam. 270: George Wright. 271 T: Martin Gostelow; Honiton and Allhallows Museum, Honiton. 271 B: American Museum in Britain, Bath.

The publishers would like to thank the following for their assistance:
Laura Ashley; Chelsea Girl;
Craftsmen Potters Shop; Dickens & Jones;
Fenwick; Habitat; Hard Rock Café;
Jane Norman; Sacha; Top Shop.

Index

Italic page numbers refer to practical diagrams.